ESSEX HERITAGE

Sir William Addison, Kt., J.P., D.L., F.S.A.

ESSEX HERITAGE

Essays presented to
SIR WILLIAM ADDISON
as a tribute to his life and work for
Essex history and literature

Edited by
Kenneth Neale

LEOPARD'S HEAD PRESS
1992

First published in 1992 by
Leopard's Head Press Limited
2a Polstead Road, Oxford OX2 6TN

© Kenneth Neale 1992

ISBN 0 904920 23 2

Illustration on title-page:
Gold stater of Cunobelin (A.D.10 – c. A.D.40)
inscribed CVNO(belin) and, on the reverse,
CAMV(lodunum) the tribal capital that preceded
the Roman Colonia and modern Colchester.

Typeset by Denham House, Yapton, West Sussex

Printed in Great Britain by
Nuffield Press, Oxford

CONTENTS

LIST OF ILLUSTRATIONS AND MAPS

LIST OF SUBSCRIBERS

Acres, Dr., D. I., C.B.E., J.P., D.L., Thundersley Lodge, Runnymede
    Chase, Thundersley, Benfleet, Essex.
Acton, Mrs. D. M., 26 Holmwood Avenue, Shenfield, Brentwood,
    Essex.
Adams, P. R., 52 Kings Avenue, Woodford Green, Essex.
Adcock, Miss B. U., 210 Ingrave Road, Brentwood, Essex.
Amor, A. R., 15 Foxholes Road, Great Baddow, Chelmsford, Essex.
Amy., C. A., 47 Paternoster Hill, Waltham Abbey, Essex.
Appleby, J. S., F.R.Hist.S., Little Pitchbury, Brick Kiln Lane,
    Great Horkesley, Colchester, Essex.
Argent, Mrs. D. M., Redcot, Loughton Lane, Theydon Bois, Epping,
    Essex.
Astor, Mrs. T. M., 8 Banyard Way, Rochford, Essex.

Bagnall, Mrs. R. W., 1 Foxley Drive, Bishops Stortford,
    Hertfordshire.
Bailey, Mrs. M. J., 2 Head Street, Goldhanger, Maldon, Essex.
Ballard, E. J., 135 Ainslie Wood Road, Chingford, London E4.
Barham, V. D., 44 Roding Road, Loughton, Essex.
Barker, Ms. A. E., 50 Shott Lane, Letchworth, Hertfordshire.
Barking and Dagenham, London Borough of, Central Library,
    Barking, Essex.
Bascombe, Dr. K. N., M.A., D.Phil., 25 Monkswood Avenue,
    Waltham Abbey, Essex.
Baxendale, A. S., 164 Tolmers Road, Cuffley, Hertfordshire.
Beale, Mr. and Mrs. J. E. M., The Laurels, The Street,
    Great Waltham, Chelmsford, Essex.
Beardsley, Mrs. J. R., Elm Tree Farm, Round Bush Road, Mundon,
    Maldon, Essex.
Bellis, M. J., Beck Farm Coach House, The Street, Kelling, Holt,
    Norfolk.
Belverstone, A. W. G., 61 Malford Grove, South Woodford,
    London E18.
Benham, Miss M. E. M., Tayspills, 6 Church Street, Goldhanger,
    Maldon, Essex.
Bettley, J., The Old Vicarage, Great Totham, Maldon, Essex.
Bircher, D. E., 52 St. Andrews Road, Boreham, Chelmsford, Essex.
Blowers, Mrs. J. C., 22 Priory Street, Colchester, Essex.
Bond, R. H., 88 Sandford Road, Chelmsford, Essex.
Booty, S. C. H., 83 Northfield Road, Peterborough.

Bossy, Miss M. M., 8 Brodie Road, Chingford, London E4.
Boutflour, R. W., Carbonells, Wix, Manningtree, Essex.
Boyes, J. H., A.R.Hist.S., 129 Endlebury Road, Chingford,
    London E4.
Brewer, Miss J. A., 50 Dorville Road, Lee, London SE12.
Broadhead, R. E. J., 13 Marston House, High Street,
    Grays Thurrock, Essex.
Brown, Mrs. M. N., 57 Romeland, Waltham Abbey, Essex.
Bryning, J., River Green House, Church Path, Great Sampford,
    Saffron Walden, Essex.
Buchan, Mrs. I. V. R.
Buggey, R. F. W., 28 Broomhill Road, Woodford Green, Essex.
Burnell, J. F., 49 Avondale Road, Benfleet, Essex.
Burrows, J. H., 253 Herries Street, Toowoomba, Queensland 4350,
    Australia.
Burton, J. T. A., 5 Quendon Drive, Waltham Abbey, Essex.
Burton, P. A., Goulds Farmhouse, Duck End Green, Rayne,
    Braintree, Essex.
Butler, P. M., Little Silvers, 7 Mendoza Close, Hornchurch, Essex.
Buxton, P. W. J., Castle House, Chipping Ongar, Essex.

Cambridgeshire Record Office, Shire Hall, Castle Street, Cambridge.
Cassidy, R. J., B.A., L.R.A.M., A.R.C.M., L.T.C.L., A.C.P., Fernside,
    Copthall Green, Upshire, Waltham Abbey, Essex.
Chalmers, Mr. and Mrs. J. R., 4 Janmead, Hutton, Brentwood,
    Essex.
Chelmer, Lord E., Peacocks, Margaretting, Essex.
Chelmsford and Essex Museum, Chelmsford Museums Service,
    Oaklands Park, Moulsham Street, Chelmsford, Essex.
Chelmsford Cathedral Library, c/o The Cathedral Office,
    Guy Harlings, New Street, Chelmsford, Essex.
Chissell, P. J., Oaktree House, 96 Candlemas Lane, Beaconsfield,
    Buckinghamshire.
Chown, C., F.C.A., Uplands, Upminster Common, Essex.
Clark, Dr. M., M.P., Rochford Hall, Hall Road, Rochford, Essex.
Clayton, B. T. B., 59 Priests Lane, Shenfield, Brentwood, Essex.
Clements, G. J., A.C.I.S., F.S.A., Dripping Pan Cottage,
    20 Second Avenue, Chelmsford, Essex.
Clough, Mr. and Mrs. D. I., 12 Wellstead Gardens. Westcliff-on-Sea,
    Essex.
Coales, J., F.S.A., The Mount, Parsonage Hill, Somerton, Somerset.
Colchester Archaeological Group, c/o A. J. Fawn, 2 Silvanus Close,
    Colchester, Essex.
Cole, Mrs. J., Watkins Lodge, Green Lane, Burnham-on-Crouch,
    Essex.
Collins, G. R., 51 Southview Drive, South Woodford, London E18.

Corder-Birch, A., F.Inst.L.Ex., M.I.C.M., The Maltings,
  North End Road, Little Yeldham, Halstead, Essex.
Correia, Mrs. M. J., 22 Hillcroft Crescent, Ealing, London W5.
Coverley, P. R. J., M.A., Pine Court, 105 High Street, Wivenhoe,
  Colchester, Essex.
Craddock, C., M.Inst., S.M.M., 37 Tamar Square, Woodford Green,
  Essex.
Cranefield, P. D., 4 Ashbridge Road, Leytonstone, London E11.
Crease, Mrs. C. A., 28 Harold Road, Chingford, London E4.
Crellin, M. S., Elm House, Rookery Road, Monewden,
  Woodbridge,Suffolk.
Cross, M. R., Monks Cottage, Great Sampford, Saffron Walden,
  Essex.
Crowe, K. L., B.Ed., A.M.A., 24 Alton Gardens, Southend-on-Sea,
  Essex.
Cuthbert, Mrs. B. M., 25 Kendal Avenue, Epping, Essex.

Dare, E. H., 21 Ibbetson Path, Loughton, Essex.
Davies, G. M. R., M.A., F.M.A., 29 Castle Road, Colchester, Essex.
Dean, Miss D. E. P., 316 Roundhills, Waltham Abbey, Essex.
Devonish, L. A., 118 Dugdale Hill Lane, Potters Bar, Hertfordshire.
Dickinson, H. O., 25a Lindsey Street, Epping, Essex.
Dodwell, E. J., 196 Benfleet Road, Hadleigh, Essex.
Doe, Mrs. J. L., Woodham Mortimer Hall, Maldon Road,
  Woodham Mortimer, Maldon, Essex.
Doncaster, A. B., Abberton Cottage, Layer-de-la-Haye, Colchester,
  Essex.
Driver, Mrs. H., 87 Brownlow Street, Clitheroe, Lancashire.
Duffin, Dr. G. F., Harrington House, High Easter, Chelmsford,
  Essex.
Dunell, W. M., 4 Orchard Road, Haslingfield, Cambridge.
Durgan, Mrs. S., 52 Humber Road, Chelmsford, Essex.
Durham, Mrs. S., 15 Queens Road, Loughton, Essex.
Dymond, D. P., 4 Honey Hill, Bury St. Edmunds, Suffolk.

Ellis, Mr. and Mrs. P. E., 132 Heath Row, Bishops Stortford,
  Hertfordshire.
Elphick, D. J., 12 Glanmead, Shenfield, Brentwood, Essex.
Elrington, C. R., Institute of Historical Research, University of
  London, Senate House, London WC1.
Emery, D. J., Colvenor, Mundesley Road, Knapton, North Walsham,
  Norfolk.
Emery, W. H., 4 John's Croft, Hampton Park Road, Hereford.
Enticknap, Dr. J. B., Tinkers, Wesley End, Stambourne, Halstead,
  Essex.
Essex County Council, Colchester Area Library, Trinity Square,
  Colchester, Essex.

Essex County Council, Greenstead Library, Hawthorn Avenue, Colchester, Essex.
Essex County Council, Planning Department, County Hall, Chelmsford, Essex.
Essex County Council, Tendring Area Library, Station Road, Clacton-on-Sea, Essex.
Essex County Council, Witham Area Library, 18 Newland Street, Witham, Essex.
Essex, University of, The Library, P.O. Box 24, Colchester, Essex.
Evans, Mr. and Mrs. I., Maple Lodge, 28 St. Anne's Gardens, Llanrhos, Llandudno, Gwynedd.
Evans, Mrs. K. A., 43 Yorick Road, West Mersea, Colchester, Essex.
Everitt, Mr. and Mrs. B. J., 20 Aubrey Close, Broomfield, Chelmsford, Essex.

Fairhurst, M. D., 46 Gaysham Avenue, Gants Hill, Ilford, Essex.
Fairman, R. J., Portree, Summer Hill, Althorne, Chelmsford, Essex.
Fairweather, Mr. and Mrs. B. C., 10 Jubilee Court, Dunmow, Essex.
Fawcett, Mrs. V. D., 127 Howard Road, Walthamstow, London E17.
Finch, P. F., 3 Ridge Green, South Nutfield, Redhill, Surrey.
Forbes, D. L., C.B.E., J.P., F.C.A., Lonach, 1 Woodland Close, Woodford Green, Essex.
Fox, Dr. A. W., 45 Cranham Gardens, Cranham, Upminster, Essex.
Francis, L. A. W., 81 Warren Road, Wanstead, London E11.
Frost, K. A., 3 Balmoral Road, Romford, Essex.
Fulcher, E. A., B.A., 35 Fullers Road, South Woodford, London E18.
Fuller, R. H., Tewes Farm, Little Sampford, Saffron Walden, Essex.
Fuller, R. H., 12 Field Road, Aveley, South Ockendon, Essex.
Fuller, R. W., Windrush, Coggeshall Road, Feering, Colchester, Essex.

Gadd, Miss L. I., 16 Willow Close, Buckhurst Hill, Essex.
Galbraith, Mrs. M. E., 34 Rainsford Avenue, Chelmsford, Essex.
Game, Mrs. M. L., 149 New Road, Chingford, London E4.
Garnham, Mrs. S. E., 13 Station Crescent, Cold Norton, Chelmsford, Essex.
George, Mr. and Mrs. B. F. H., 9 Knighton Lane, Buckhurst Hill, Essex.
Gepp, T. C., T.D., D.L., M.A., Margaret Roding House, Great Dunmow, Essex.
Gibson, Miss R., 126 Willingale Road, Loughton, Essex.
Gobel, Miss B. M., 7a Bosgrove, Chingford, London E4.
Going, C. H., Shepherds, Stebbing, Dunmow, Essex.
Gomm, Miss S. I., 112 Redbridge Lane East, Ilford, Essex.
Gonsa, Dr. H., Troststrasse 98/3/20, A-1100 Vienna, Austria.
Goodwin, Mr. and Mrs. D. H., Corner Cottage, School Road, Great Barton, Bury St. Edmunds, Suffolk.

Gray, R. C., 61a Monkswood Avenue, Waltham Abbey, Essex.

Green, Miss A., Tintern Cottage, Halstead Road, Aldham,
    Colchester, Essex.

Green, Mrs. G., 39 Smeaton Road, Woodford Green, Essex.

Greenman, S., 19 Giles House, 158–160 Westbourne Grove,
    London W11.

Grieve, Miss H. E. P., 153 New London Road, Chelmsford, Essex.

Griggs, C. L., 22 The Close, Clayton, Doncaster, South Yorkshire.

Grosvenor, W. J., Serendipity, Brent Mill Drive, Brent Eleigh,
    Suffolk.

Groves, Mrs. P. E., 30 Cumberland Crescent, Chelmsford, Essex.

Guy, S. G. G., 5 Burgess Court, Burland Road, Brentwood, Essex.

Hale, H. K., 13 Furrow Close, Stanway, Colchester, Essex.

Hales, Miss R., 2 The Lindens, Great Austins, Farnham, Surrey.

Hammond, W. J., Avocet, 64 Fobbing Road, Corringham, Essex.

Hands, R. J., 23 Sebright Road, Boxmoor, Hemel Hempstead,
    Hertfordshire.

Hardwick, G. P., 1 Munnings Drive, Clacton-on-Sea, Essex.

Harlow Museum, Passmores House, Third Avenue, Harlow, Essex.

Harrington, S., Flat 8, 1 Eldon Road, Reading, Berkshire.

Harris, Mrs. I. F., 43 High View Road, South Woodford, London E18.

Harrold, C., M.A., C.Chem., F.R.S.C., 6 Bradleigh Avenue,
    Grays Thurrock, Essex.

Harvey, Mrs. D., 8 Parkside, Grays Thurrock, Essex.

Harvey, G. W., 22 Meadowfield, Bradford-on-Avon, Wiltshire.

Hawkes, H. G., 55 Durban Road, Tottenham, London N17.

Haywood, Mrs., L. S., 39 Acaster Lane, Bishopsthorpe, York.

Helm, Mr. and Mrs. D. T., 8 Heybridge Drive, Barkingside, Ilford,
    Essex.

Hennessey, I. J., 12 Dorking Crescent, Clacton-on-Sea, Essex.

Henrys, R. E., 56 The Paddocks, Ingatestone, Essex.

Hewitt, Revd. Canon G. H. G., 8 Rainsford Avenue, Chelmsford,
    Essex.

Hewitt, Major and Mrs. W. A., Oak Cottage, 51 Crossways,
    Gidea Park, Romford, Essex.

Hilliar, Miss K. M., 42a Moulsham Drive, Chelmsford, Essex.

Hilliard, Mrs. R., 2 Carnarthen Street, Cambourne, Cornwall.

Holyoake, C. J., 28 Elmhurst Drive, Hornchurch, Essex.

Homer, Mr. and Mrs. J. W., Southview Cottage, 28 Stony Path,
    Loughton, Essex.

Hook, J. S., 29 York Road, Rayleigh, Essex.

Howell, Mrs. A. C., Jaylocks, Coleridge Lane, Chillington,
    Kingsbridge, South Devon.

Howes, J. W., F.L.A., 97 Staples Road, Loughton, Essex.

Howett, Mr. and Mrs. R. P. G., Lannarth Farm, Manaccan,
    Helston, Cornwall.

Howson, J., 10 Raphael Avenue, Romford, Essex.
Hoy, Mr. and Mrs. D. L., 7 Park Crescent, Enfield, Middlesex.
Hughes, A. S., 44 Hillcrest Road, Upper Walthamstow, London E17.
Hunter, D., 16 Hall Rise, Sudbury, Suffolk.
Hurrell, D. J., 241 Main Road, Broomfield, Chelmsford, Essex.
Hyland, H. S., Cage Cottage, Great Bardfield, Braintree, Essex.
Hyslop, E. P., 30 Kenilworth Avenue, Walthamstow, London E17.

Ingram, G. W., 53 Selborne Gardens, Hendon, London NW4.

Jacklin, Miss J. E., 8 Chichester Court, Lexden Road, Colchester,
    Essex.
Jackson, Mr. and Mrs. J. R., 7 Bournemouth Park Road,
    Southend-on-Sea, Essex.
Jarratt, Sir A. A., C.B., Barn Mead, Fryerning, Essex.
Jarvis, L. D., J.P., A.R.Hist.Soc., Middlesex Cottage, Mill Road,
    Stock, Ingatestone, Essex.
Jarvis, R. L., 29 Grantley Close, Shalford, Surrey.
Jeff, Mr. and Mrs. F. A., Brick House Farm, South Fambridge,
    Rochford, Essex.
Jellis, Mrs. J., 12 Nelson Road, Clacton-on-Sea, Essex.
Jemmett, R., 9 High Street, Saffron Walden, Essex.
Johnson, Mr. and Mrs. J. I., Trimpley, Coach Road, Great Horkesley,
    Colchester, Essex.
Johnson, Miss W. M., 284 The Ridgeway, St. Albans, Hertfordshire.
Jones, Revd. A. D., The Vicarage, Finchingfield, Braintree, Essex.
Jones, Mrs. J., Weir Bank Lodge, Monkey Island Lane, Bray,
    Maidenhead, Berkshire.
Jones, Mrs. M. F., 4 Scott Drive, Lexden, Colchester, Essex.
Joyce, Mrs. J. M., Flat 1, 58 Heathfield Road, Keston, Kent.

Kear, Miss E. M. H., 8 Queen's Road, Brentwood, Essex.
Killick, A. R., 19a Hazlemere Gardens, Worcester Park, Surrey.

Lacey, Mrs. M., 12 Graham Close, Perry Street, Billericay, Essex.
Lake, P. M. J., 1 Yeoman Way, Hainault, Ilford, Essex.
Lamb, Mrs. E., 3 Garwoods, Norton Mandeville, Ingatestone, Essex.
Langford, K. F., 33 Tor Bryan, Ingatestone, Essex.
Langstone, Miss M. R., Peace, Church Green, Terling, Chelmsford,
    Essex.
Law, A. D., A.M.A., Clydfan, Tegryn, Llanfyrnach, Dyfed.
Lawrence, P., 273 St. Barnabas Road, Woodford Green, Essex.
Lawrence, P. J., Hawkes Cottage, Stambourne Road,
    Little Sampford, Saffron Walden, Essex.
Leslie, D. A., 57 Washington Road, Maldon, Essex.
Levey, Ms. A., St. John's Cottage, 51 Chapel Hill, Stansted, Essex.

Lipscombe, Mrs. R. J., 8 Borradale Court, Steeple Bumpstead, Essex.

Lloyd, R. J., 1 Eastacre, Chater's Hill, Saffron Walden, Essex.

Lockwood, Mr. and Mrs. H. H., 10 Alloa Road, Goodmayes, Ilford, Essex.

London, Corporation of, Bibliographical Services Section, City of London Libraries, Guildhall Library, London EC2.

Lovell, Mrs. O., 64 Forest Approach, Woodford Green, Essex.

Ludgate, Miss E. M., Shovellers, Clavering, Essex.

Lyons, T. C. H., Hole Farm, Stansted, Essex.

McIntosh, Dr. M. K., Department of History, University of Colorado, Boulder, Colorado 80309, U.S.A.

McLaren, D. J., Hill Farm, Great Sampford, Saffron Walden, Essex.

Mallinson, T. S., 28 Albion Street, London W2.

Manning-Press, Lt. Col. C. B., 14 The Avenue, Colchester, Essex.

Marson, G. L., M.A., F.R.G.S., Dip.Ed., 31 Westmorland Avenue, Hornchurch, Essex.

Mason, Dr. A. S., M.D., Pelham, 61a Main Road, Gidea Park, Essex.

Matthews, Dr. R. M. S., M.B., A.R.Hist.S., 2 Repton Avenue, Gidea Park, Essex.

Mendelsson, W., 57 Leeside Crescent, London NW11.

Millidge, Miss M. P., 27 Feering Hill, Feering Colchester, Essex.

Monk, Mrs. P. M., Eleys Farm, Roxwell, Chelmsford, Essex.

Moore, B. L., 55 Leighwood Avenue, Leigh-on-Sea, Essex.

Moore, P. J., The Old Granary, Justice Wood, Polstead, Suffolk.

Moore, Dr. R. A., 11 Eccleston Gardens, Billericay, Essex.

Moran, D. J., 32 Parkview Court, 54 Brancaster Road, Newbury Park, Ilford, Essex.

Mundby, L. M., 16 Carisbrooke Road, Cambridge.

Mynott, S. E., 13a Rosslyn Road, Billericay, Essex.

Nash, Revd. D., 9 Boscundle Avenue, Golden Bank, Falmouth, Cornwall.

Neale, Mr. and Mrs. K. J., Honeysuckle Cottage, Great Sampford, Saffron Walden, Essex.

Newell, Mr. and Mrs. G. J., Phipps Farm, Lower Road, Layer Breton, Colchester, Essex.

Newell, Mr. and Mrs. T. A., East View Farm, Moss Lane, Little Hoole, Preston, Lancashire.

Newens, A. S., M.E.P., The Leys, 18 Park Hill, Harlow, Essex.

Newland, Mrs. J. F., 30 St. Vincents Road, Westcliff-on-Sea, Essex.

Newman, R. J., 46 Great Cob, Chelmsford, Essex.

Nicholls Palmer, Dr. K. W., O.B.E., E.R.D., T.D., Siver Birches, 17 Briarwood Road, Woodbridge, Suffolk.

Nichols, D. J., 64 Bedford Road, Walthamstow, London E17.

Nuttall, Mrs. H., 23 Madeira Avenue, Worthing, West Sussex.

Oliver, A. G., 23 Beresford Road, Chingford, London E4.

Palmer, Mrs. D. E. L., 40 Park Court, Grosvenor Park Road,
    Walthamstow, London E17.
Palmer, R. M., 11 Elm Grove, Thorpe Bay, Southend-on-Sea, Essex.
Patterson, M., Little Wick, 38 High Street, Wivenhoe, Essex.
Paul, W. N., 32 Watermans, Junction Road, Romford, Essex.
Peel, Miss M., 20 Ruskin Drive, Kirkby Lonsdale, via Carnforth,
    Lancashire.
Perry, Mrs. M. G., B.A., 87 Inglehurst Gardens, Redbridge, Ilford,
    Essex.
Petre, The Rt. Hon. Lord, Writtle Park, Highwood, Chelmsford,
    Essex.
Pewsey, S., 18 Beryl Avenue, Beckton, London E6.
Porter, K. F., Howzat, 54 Welbeck Drive, Langdon Hills, Basildon,
    Essex.
Potter, S. P., Lower Barn Farm, Purleigh, Mundon, Maldon, Essex.
Potts, Mrs. P. E., 12 Keene Way, Galleywood, Chelmsford, Essex.
Puttock, Mr. and Mrs. F. W., 57 Hobleythick Lane, Westcliff-on-Sea,
    Essex.

Qvist, A., Chestnut Cottage, Old Heathfield, Sussex.

Ramsay, Mrs. M., Flea Hall, Little Sampford, Saffron Walden, Essex.
Rawlingson, K. A., 18 Twyford Avenue, Great Wakering,
    Southend-on-Sea, Essex.
Redbridge Libraries, London Borough of,
Reed, Major J. L., North Farm, Theydon Mount, Epping, Essex.
Robbins, Mrs. M. I., 108 Redbridge Lane East, Ilford, Essex.
Rochford Hundred Historical Society, Rochford, Essex.
Rodwell, Dr. W. J., The Old Vicarage, Stockhill Road, Downside,
    Chilcompton, Somerset.
Roffey, Miss J. A., 21 Priory Road, Loughton, Essex.
Romford and District Historical Society, Romford, Essex.
Rust, B., The Hutch, Newcourt Road, Chelmsford, Essex.

Sadler, W., Flat 34, London Road, Stanford-le-Hope, Essex.
Sainsbury, F., B.E.M., A.L.A., A.R.Hist.S., 16 Crownfield Avenue,
    Newbury Park, Ilford, Essex.
Sanders, P. B., 5 Bentfield End Causeway, Stansted Mountfitchet,
    Essex.
Sanders-Hewett, Mr. and Mrs. G. S., 16 Alwyne Avenue, Shenfield,
    Brentwood, Essex.
Scarborough, Mrs. S. J., 12 Springfield Place, Springfield Green,
    Chelmsford, Essex.
Searle, R. N., 118 Meldreth Road, Whaddon, Bassingbourne,
    Cambridgeshire.

Sheppard, P. R., 20 Bawtree Way, Colchester, Essex.

Sibley, W. J., 49 Gaywood Road, Walthamstow, London E17.

Simons, P. D., Mallards, South Green Lane, Fingrinhoe, Colchester, Essex.

Sims, Mrs. J., 8 The Orchards, Epping, Essex.

Sippitt, R. W., 157 Coppins Road, Clacton-on-Sea, Essex.

Smale, J. R., D.M.S., F.C.I.O.B., Millers Croft, Little Orchard Lane, Broomfield, Chelmsford, Essex.

Smith, H. G., 137 Endlebury Road, Chingford, London E4.

Smith, Miss J. T., c/o Essex Record Office, County Hall, Chelmsford, Essex.

Smith, Revd. W. J. T., 7 Trelawn, Church Road, Boreham, Chelmsford, Essex.

Spinner, Miss M. E., 152 Moulsham Drive, Chelmsford, Essex.

Starr, C. R., M.I.P.M., F.R.G.S., A.R.Hist.S., 63 Abbey Gardens, London W8.

Stevens, W. C., 202 Wembley Drive, Sudbury, Ontario, Canada.

Stone, M. W., 23 Samson Street, Plaistow, London E13.

Stuchfield, H. M., Lowe Hill House, Stratford St. Mary, Suffolk.

Sturmer, R. C., 49 Tor Bryan, Ingatestone, Essex.

Sunnocks, J. H. G., East Mersea Hall, Colchester, Essex.

Swain, V. A. J., F.R.C.S., 45 The Bowls, Vicarage Lane Chigwell, Essex.

Terry, R. D., 2 Hillside Close, Woodford Green, Essex.

Thomas, Dr. E. G., 12 Drake Park, Felpham, Bognor Regis, West Sussex.

Tiernan, M. J., M.A., 2 Caroon Drive, Sarratt, Rickmansworth, Hertfordshire.

Tingey, F. J., 1 Lyndhurst Gardens, Barking, Essex.

Toms, M. M. S., 17 St. James Gate, 105 Palmerston Road, Buckhurst Hill, Essex.

Turner, M. J., Highways, 1 Priory Road, Bicknacre, Chelmsford, Essex.

Vicary, Mr. and Mrs. P. G., 22 Crows Road, Epping, Essex.

Wager, R. J., Reddens, Doddinghurst Road, Canterbury Tye, Brentwood, Essex.

Waite, C., Capricorn, Victoria Gardens, Saffron Walden, Essex.

Wall, Miss R. M., 19a Lindsey Street, Epping, Essex.

Wallis, M. G., The Spinney, Bletsoe, Bedfordshire.

Want, Mr. and Mrs. R. H., 12 Roundmead Avenue, Loughton, Essex.

Ward, Mrs. E., 42 Rosehill Court, Liverpool.

Warner, Sir Henry, Bt., M.A.(Oxon.), The Grove, Southend Road, Chelmsford, Essex.

Warren, Mrs. J. C., Southdene, Arundel Road, Worthing,
West Sussex.

Waters, J., 62 at Courtlands, Patching Hall Lane, Chelmsford, Essex.

Watsham, Mrs. A. R., Red House Farm, Bildeston, Ipswich, Suffolk.

Wawn, Mrs. P. V., Ventnor Lodge, Quendon, Saffron Walden, Essex.

Webb, J. B., C.Eng., M.I.C.E., 10 Woodview, Grays Thurrock, Essex.

Webb, L. D., 31 Quebec Avenue, Southend-on-Sea, Essex.

Wells, Dr. M. K., D.Sc., C.Eng., F.I.M.M., F.G.S., Hillside,
15 Russell Road, Buckhurst Hill, Essex.

West, A. R., Hoggets, Easthorpe, Colchester, Essex.

Whitcher, Miss J., 6 Valance Avenue, Chingford, London E4.

Wilby, A. R., Brynffynnon, Llanfabon Road, Nelson, Treharris,
Mid Glamorgan.

Wilce, Miss R. M., B.Sc., 2 Hastingwood Court, Pembroke Road,
Walthamstow, London E17.

Wilford, W., 6 Brook Road, Brentwood, Essex.

Wilkinson, D., 25 Broomfield Avenue, Loughton, Essex.

Wilkinson, Miss P. M., 18 Forest Drive East, Leytonstone,
London E11.

Willesden, R., 3 Grey Towers Avenue, Hornchurch, Essex.

Williams, T. J., The Croft, North Fambridge, Chelmsford, Essex.

Wilson, Miss R. J., Hartcroft, 14 Pear Tree Close,
Chipping Campden, Gloucestershire.

Wolfe, Mrs. M. E., 43 Bouverie Road, Chelmsford, Essex.

Wood, J. S., 144 Vicarage Road, Chelmsford, Essex.

Woodward, Mr. and Mrs. S. W., Hares Form, Sparepenny Lane,
Great Sampford, Saffron Walden, Essex.

Woolford, Miss I. E., 43 Vicarage Road, Chelmsford, Essex.

Wort, Mrs. J., 3 Oatlands, Elmstead Market, Colchester, Essex.

Wright, P. J., 174 Aldborough Road South, Seven Kings, Ilford,
Essex.

Writtle, Baroness Platt of, C.B.E., F.Eng., D.L., 46 The Green,
Writtle, Chelmsford, Essex.

LIST OF FINANCIAL CONTRIBUTORS

Financial support towards the cost of this publication has been gratefully received from:

Dr. Douglas I. Acres, C.B.E., J.P., D.L.

Chigwell and Loughton History Society

Augustine Courtauld Trust

Essex Archaeological and Historical Congress

The Essex Heritage Trust

Essex Society for Family History

Essex University

Marc Fitch Fund

The Friends of Essex Churches

The Friends of Epping Forest

The Friends of Historic Essex

Intercity Print (Financial) Limited

The Magistrates' Association

Romford and District Historical Society

Waltham Abbey Historical Society

Walthamstow Historical Society

EDITORIAL NOTE

IT WAS WITH pleasure and a sense of gratitude that the Essex Archaeological and Historical Congress decided to promote a volume of essays devoted to the heritage of Essex in honour of Sir William Addison.

A particularly happy coincidence, in the year of publication, is that it marks also the centenary of the birth of the *Essex Review*. The *Essex Journal*, itself launched in 1966 by the Congress, is its commendable successor, and, like the *Essex Review*, deeply concerned with heritage topics. On the title page of the first issue of the *Essex Review* in 1892 there was printed a quotation attributed to the German historian, Barthold Niebuhr:

> 'He who recalls into existence that which has vanished, enjoys a bliss like that of creating.'

That is highly pertinent for those who value the Essex heritage. For, although I cannot vouch for the bliss, certainly nothing has been lacking in creativity in William Addison's work or in the endeavours of the essayists who have contributed to this book which, I hope, reflects the spirit and purpose of Niebuhr's remark.

The duties of an editor extend beyond the familiar requirements of content, relevance and house-style which are owed to the project and the readership. The editor must also promote a fruitful liaison with the contributors and devote time and energy to their needs. That in this case those efforts may be described as positive and rewarding rather than onerous, is due to the excellence of the work of these scholars, their friendship and the alacrity with which they complied with the editorial disciplines and criteria of the Project Group.

There is a sad note. John Rayment died in 1991 shortly after he had completed his essay. His sincerity and enthusiasm for his subject was a beacon for genealogy in Essex which prospered under his leadership. We were saddened too, to learn of the death of Gus Edwards early in 1992. He will be remembered with affection for the qualities of scholarship, good sense and humour that characterised all he did.

More happily, I am glad, in offering my thanks to the essayists, to acknowledge also the help of others whose support has been invaluable. The Project Group, John Webb its Chairman, Martin Stuchfield the Business Manager and Dorothy Lockwood our Secretary whose commitment and various skills made the editorial tasks manageable and enjoyable. The preparation of the index, so important to works of record and reference, is owed to the expertise and industry of Wyndham Woodward. I am very grateful to them all.

It is fitting too, that I should acknowledge with gratitude, on behalf of the Congress, the financial contributions received from the people and organisations listed in the book, especially the major support received from the Marc Fitch Fund, The Friends of Historic Essex, The Essex Heritage Trust and the Augustine Courtauld Trust.

Finally, as in other enterprises of value to Essex historiography, we have consistently received from Roy Stephens the benefit of his considerable experience and professional knowledge in preparing and publishing specialist texts. All this has been given with purpose and good grace. We owe him a special debt of gratitude.

My own devotion to Essex and friendship with William Addison were rewarded with the privilege of being asked to edit this work and the satisfaction of seeing it all come to fruition in this volume. That could not have been done without the help of those I have mentioned.

Kenneth Neale

Great Sampford, 1992

BIOGRAPHICAL NOTES

Nancy Briggs, M.A., F.S.A.

Came to Essex in 1953 after reading history at Oxford and training as an archivist at the Bodleian Library. She worked at the Essex Record Office until 1987, latterly as Supervisor of the Search Room. Her publications include *Georgian Essex* (1989) and *John Johnson: Georgian Architect and County Surveyor of Essex* (1991). She married A. C. Edwards (*q.v.*) in 1978.

Arthur Brown, B.A., D.U.

Chairman, Essex Federation, Workers Educational Association; Senior Fellow, Department of History, University of Essex; Vice-President, Essex Society for Archaeology and History; Co-Director, Local History Centre, University of Essex. Publications include *Chartism in Essex and Suffolk* (1982) and *Meagre Harvest* (1990).

Janet Cooper, M.A., Ph.D., F.S.A., F.R.Hist.S.

Became Editor of the Victoria History of the County of Essex in 1986 after many years as Assistant Editor of the Victoria History of Oxfordshire. She contributed to four volumes of the Oxfordshire V.C.H. (including the volume on the City of Oxford), and is now working on the history of Colchester. She has published articles on Oxfordshire and Essex history, and a calendar of *The Oxfordshire Eyre of 1241* for the Oxfordshire Record Society.

A. C. Edwards, M.A.

Born 1905, the Addison vintage year. Read history at Bristol, and taught at Arnold School, Blackpool and Maldon Grammar School. In 1949, he joined the education staff at Chelmsford as history adviser and lecturer at the Essex Record Office. He retired at Christmas, 1968. His writings include *John Petre, The Account Books of Benjamin*

Mildmay, Earl Fitzwalter, A History of Essex, Pleasant Abode and a number of Essex Record Office booklets. He died on 16 February, 1992.

F. G. Emmison, M.B.E., D.U.(Essex), F.S.A., F.R.Hist.S.

County Archivist of Essex, 1938–69; Past President, Essex Societies for Archaeology and History and for Family History; Past Deputy President, Historical Association and Medlicott Medallist; Vice-President, British Records Association, British Record Society, Society of Archivists, and Essex Victoria History; compiler or editor of numerous H.A., B.R.S. and E.R.O. publications; author, *Tudor Secretary: Sir William Petre at Court and Home* (1961), *Archives and Local History* (1966), *Elizabethan Life* (5 vols., 1970–76), *Essex Wills, 1558-1603* (7 vols., 1982–91); editor, *Feet of Fines for Essex, 1547-80* (1991).

Victor Gray, M.A.

Became County Archivist of Essex in 1978 after nine years working in county record offices in Devon and Suffolk. He is a past Chairman of both the Association of County Archivists and the Society of Archivists. His interest in the Countess of Warwick's 'circle' springs both from a literary historical background (he read English at King's, Cambridge) and a growing interest in the social ideals and improvements of the late Victorians and Edwardians, on which he has lectured widely in Essex.

Bill and Sue Liddell

Have lived in Billericay, Essex, throughout their married life; teach for the Centre for Extra-Mural Studies, Birkbeck College, University of London; until recently were Chairman and Secretary respectively of the Essex History Fair Group; she still runs the Billericay Literary Society; he is Hon. Secretary of V.C.H., Essex.

Herbert Hope Lockwood, B.A.(Hons.)., A.K.C.

University of London, King's College; former Lecturer in History and Social Studies at Tottenham College of Technology; Vice-Chairman, Essex Archaeological and Historical Congress, 1987–92, President, 1992; contributor to *V.C.H., Essex V* (1966); author, *Sources and Development of Local*

Historical Studies in Barking and Ilford (1969),*Where was the First Barking Abbey* (1986), contributor, *An Essex Tribute* (1987), author, *Barking 100 Years Ago* (1990), editor and co-author, *Long Ago and Not So Far Away* (1991).

Geoffrey Martin, C.B.E., M.A., D.Phil., D.Univ., F.S.A., F.R.Hist.S.

Research Professor of History, University of Essex, and Fellow of Merton College, Oxford since 1990; born in Colchester and educated at Colchester Royal Grammar School, Merton College, Oxford and the University of Manchester. From 1952 he lectured in history at the University of Leicester where he was Professor of History, 1972–82 and Pro-Vice Chancellor, 1979–82. Keeper of Public Records, 1982–88. He is the author of several studies of urban history, including a history of Colchester published in 1959, and a Vice-President of the Essex Society for Archaeology and History (formerly the Essex Archaeological Society).

Robert Mitchell, O.B.E., M.A.

Educated at St. John's College, Cambridge and served in the Royal Air Force, 1939–46. He has enjoyed a varied career in business and in politics, including being a member of the Greater London Council, 1964–86 and Chairman of the Council, 1971-2. He is the holder of several foreign decorations. He represented England and Great Britain at swimming and water polo, 1933–48, including the 1936 and 1948 Olympic Games. Trustee London Ecology Centre, 1984–89. Served as a Verderer of Epping Forest since 1976 and is a Freeman of the City of London. Author of *Bob Mitchell's Epping Forest Companion* (1991); he describes his recreation as 'planting trees then sitting watching them grow'.

Kenneth Neale, O.B.E., F.S.A.

Author, lecturer, consultant (international penology) to Council of Europe and Open University; served in Royal Navy, Civil Service, Colonial Service and Diplomatic Service. Chairman, Essex Archaeological and Historical Congress, 1984–87, President, 1987–90; Chairman, Friends of Historic Essex since 1986. Published books include, *Discovering Essex in London* (1969), *Victorian Horsham*

(1975), *Essex in History* (1977), *Her Majesty's Commissioners 1878–1978* (1978); editor, *An Essex Tribute* (1987). He has also published studies and articles on local history, natural history and penology.

W. Raymond Powell, M.A., M.Litt., F.S.A., F.R.Hist.S.

Past President of the Essex Archaeological and Historical Congress and also of Essex Society for Archaeology and History. He was Editor of the *Victoria County History of Essex* from 1951 to 1986, and is a Fellow of the Royal Historical Society and of the Society of Antiquaries. Among his publications is *Essex in Domesday Book* (Essex Record Office, 1991). He is now preparing a book on the historian John Horace Round.

Oliver Rackham, M.A., Ph.D.

Fellow of Corpus Christi College, Cambridge. Botanist. Introduced to Essex woods by Colin Ranson from 1969 onwards. Has used much Essex material in his books and articles on the history of woodland and of the countryside. Author of two books about Essex: *Ancient Woodland of England: the Woods of South-East Essex* (1986) and *The Last Forest: the story of Hatfield Forest* (1989).

John Rayment, F.S.G.

After leaving technical school he worked for a gas company, May and Baker, and water authorities. Served with the R.A.O.C. from 1942–47. Retired in 1968. He joined the Society of Genealogists in 1963; served on several committees and was a member of its Executive. In 1985 he was elected Fellow of the Society of Genealogists. He virtually founded the Essex Society for Family History in 1974; was its Chairman for the first ten years and its President from 1984. He was also involved in helping to found the five Greater London family history societies. He was the author of the standard *Notes on the Recording of Monumental Inscriptions* and inventor of a hand-held micro-film viewer. He died on 10 October, 1991.

Ian G. Robertson, M.A., F.M.A.

Read Modern History at The Queen's College, Oxford; Museums Diploma with Archaeology Option; Assistant

Curator, Chelmsford and Essex Museum, 1965–67; Curator, Passmore Edwards Museum, 1967–88; President of the Society for Post-Medieval Archaeology, 1982–85; member of the Statutory Ancient Monuments Advisory Committee of English Heritage, 1984–90; President, Museums Association, 1986–88; Director, National Army Museum, 1988 to date.

Frank Sainsbury, B.E.M., A.L.A., A.R.Hist.S.

Born in 1915 at Canning Town, West Ham. Educated at Russell Central School, Custom House and West Ham Municipal College. West Ham and Newham Public Libraries Service, 1930–76; Borough Librarian, West Ham, 1956–65 and Deputy Borough Librarian, Newham, 1965–76. Chairman, Victoria History of the County of Essex since 1989. Author of *West Ham 800 Years*; *Six Men from Tolpuddle*; *The Church and Parish of St. John, Seven Kings* and other articles on local history.

Jennifer C. Ward, M.A., Ph.D., F.R.Hist.S.

Lecturer in History at Goldsmiths' College, University of London. She has published articles on the Clare baronial family and on Essex history, has edited *The Medieval Essex Community — The Lay Subsidy of 1327* for the Essex Record Office series, *Essex Historical Documents*, and is author of *The Essex Gentry and the County Community in the Fourteenth Century* for the series, *Studies in Essex History*, published by the Essex Record Office in collaboration with the Local History Centre, University of Essex. Her book on *English Noblewomen in the Later Middle Ages* will be published late in 1992.

FOREWORD
by
Admiral Sir Andrew Lewis

WILLIAM ADDISON'S BOOKS are widely enjoyed by all those who cherish the Essex Heritage. It is fitting, therefore, that a book compiled in his honour should bear this title. Although a north-countryman by birth he came to love Essex and has served the county with distinction for over half a century. He has been rewarded, as he would himself gratefully acknowledge, with the respect and affection of numerous people in all areas of Essex life.

The production of this book has, I know, been a labour of love by all concerned. The excellence of the contributions from Essex historians and naturalists reflects both the devotion of his friends and the high standards of scholarship and industry on which he has always insisted in his own work. The county will be grateful to him and to them.

This work comes at a time when concern for the Essex heritage is a high priority. I have myself been glad to be closely involved in the work of The Essex Heritage Trust whose resources and efforts are now engaged in the important task of preserving this precious legacy. As is evident, the county organisations, such as The Friends of Historic Essex and the Essex Archaeological and Historical Congress have played their parts in this for many years and they continue to do so. It is my hope that this new book will mark not only the county's debt to one of its most eminent personalities but also encourage interest in the Essex Heritage. There could be no more appropriate tribute to William Addison.

Lord Lieutenant of Essex

July 1992

William Addison: Essex Worthy

'Of all the things which man can do or make here below, by far the most momentous, wonderful, and worthy are the things we call books.'

Thomas Carlyle

KENNETH NEALE

I WAS ONE of those fortunate young people whose appetite for Essex history and literature was nourished and delighted by William Addison's brilliant topographical and biographical studies of county interest. Alongside that, although I had been introduced to London's great architectural and historical heritage by my parents and a grandfather who valued books and education, it was the fine Norman fane at Waltham Abbey that most excited my earliest historical instincts and imagination. It was natural, therefore, that his cultured study of *Worthy Dr. Fuller*[1] should have been, and remains, a literary favourite. Many years later he published *Essex Worthies*[2] which, obviously, omitted himself, although by any lexicographer's criteria he was amply qualified for inclusion. A 'worthy' is commonly defined as a distinguished or eminent person. The dictionaries also place among the attributes of the word, whether used adjectively or as a noun, the qualities of excellence, value, distinction and entitlement to honour and respect. These are all words that come readily to mind in contemplating the life, work and personal traits of William Addison.

It is tempting and somewhat self-indulgent, therefore, of his Essex friends to think of William, now Sir William, as essentially a man of Essex. He is, but we may not neglect the importance of his north-country birth and ancestry the resonances of which have continuously enriched his life. Tennyson, born in Lincolnshire though not devoid of Essex associations albeit somewhat rueful, opined

'That bright and fierce and fickle is the South,
And dark and true and tender is the North.'

1 W. Addison, *Worthy Dr. Fuller*, Dent, 1951.

2 W. Addison, *Essex Worthies*, Phillimore, 1973.

Northerners at least would not dispute that. And I, with my own Anglo-Scottish ancestry, would certainly not wish to quarrel with the affectionate and admiring sentiments that William has expressed to me when musing about his northern roots. Indeed, it will be a pleasant necessity, in this biographical essay, to dwell a little upon that aspect of this remarkable man even though it will be a primarily Essex perspective on which I shall seek to rely in outlining his career and contribution to society. He is, manifestly, a versatile and energetic man whose sagacity, poise and manner have inspired his roles in all the fields in which he has worked. Pre-eminent among them have been those devoted to literature, the magistracy, Epping Forest and local history. Although the latter is not without important wider values he has himself consistently emphasised the local character of his interests and work. In his first book[3] he opposed the title-page with a quotation from G. K. Chesterton 'to make a thing real, you must make it local' and he still insists on the validity of this approach. Certainly, if Essex history is local, in the sense that Marc Bloch intended when he averred that all history is local history, then William Addison has sustained the integrity of his theme with sincerity and tenacity. His endeavours, as we shall see, have also made their mark upon the national scene. Thus he has become known and respected in many areas of public life. It is, however, perhaps through his books that he has entered into a kindly and wider relationship with countless appreciative readers. Books, those he reads, as well as those he has written, have been an essential element of his being. However, before embarking in greater depth on those facets of his career it is appropriate to set down his personal background and the broad biographical aspects of an industrious and rewarding life.

'More than a fair share'

William Addison was born on 4 April, 1905 at Mitton in the Ribble valley, near the point in the Hodder valley where, at Dunsop Bridge, the road plunges into a gorge called the Trough-of-Bowland leading through Abbeystead to Lancaster and the Lake District. It is a beautiful area for which he retains an affection rooted in a sense of belonging that has compelled him to return as frequently as opportunity has allowed. There he has relished

3 W. Addison, *Epping Forest: Its Literary and Historical Associations*, Dent, 1945.

the riverside villages of Slaidburn, Newton and Whitewell and particularly those parishes like King's Meaburn, Crosby Ravensworth, Appleby and Crossrigg which have been home to the Westmorland Addisons over the centuries. The robust and melodic character of such place-names that identify and decorate the north-country must surely help to explain William's own fascination with the subject and his labours in this field. We must, however, dwell first upon the life and background of this remarkable man the richness of whose life is, as is generally the case, obscured by the prosaic style and concision of the entries in *Who's Who*.

The Addisons of King's Meaburn, William's direct ancestors, are one of the oldest families of Westmorland. They first appear in official records of the Barony of Kendal as three brothers, Thomas Addison of Grasmere, John Addison of Applethwaite and Robert Addison of Bowness, Windermere, all customary tenants of the major fisheries along the east bank of the lake from Grasmere to Bowness from the beginning of the fourteenth century. They were closely associated with the Lowthers, also an established Westmorland family, whose homelands extended throughout the Forest of Bowland to the north bank of the River Ribble. In the south, these territories were administered from the castle in the ancient borough of Clitheroe by members of two generations of the Addison family who served as Recorders. They lived in the district and were generous benefactors to local charities, especially two grammar schools, in one of which William was educated, and in supporting the restoration of two parish churches, those of Mitton and Chipping. In these neighbouring parishes, the Addison coat-of-arms is displayed in stained glass in both churches, most proudly when one member of the family, Thomas, in recognition of distinguished services, was appointed Constable of Lancaster Castle.

The local activities of the Lowthers and Addisons were most closely linked in their long family connection by a bequest in the will of the widow of Hugh de Lowther. In this was bequeathed sufficient land for the building and endowment of an abbey on Shap Fell for the use of an order of Friars who had been evicted by the Scots from the monastic establishment which they had enjoyed by the favour of the Countess of Dorset, Pembroke and Montgomery, the owner.

The design and building of the abbey on Shap Fell was entrusted to Robert Addison, ecclesiastical architect and sculptor of King's Meaburn, William's direct ancestor. He was then head of a family pioneering the adaptation of Norman castles for the use of religious orders, in contrast to the Scots who had no such pious intentions! The fifteen monks of the Premonstratensian Order who welcomed their newly found home had second thoughts when the winter gales arrived and they discovered that residence in such exposed and remote quarters was only tolerable to families bred to endure such conditions. Thus, when the wealthy living of the parish of Kirkby Thorpe was offered by the patrons, the Lowther family, the abbot consented to become an absentee abbot. He was joined at Kirkby Thorpe by Edward Addison, the son of the builder of Shap Abbey and friend since boyhood, who had been invited to build a dignified modern house in a distinctive style for John Lowther, who was the first of the family to be made a member of the baronetcy. Clearly both families were prospering, the Lowthers as administrators, the Addisons as architects of what was to become a distinctive style in Cumbria.

Shortly after these events, which followed in quick succession, the new Sir John received a letter from his cousin, the countess. In this she complained that at fifty years of age, she was weary of life in the south, bored with her husband and longing for the north where she had four castles, Appleby, Brough, Brougham and Pendragon, all of which were more or less in ruins. Sir John replied describing his scheme for educating the young by combining the role of schoolmaster with that of parish priest. The scheme was an educational success, church buildings were restored or rebuilt and local leadership had placed Westmorland second to none in the provision of grammar schools.

It was into this stimulating family background and evocative landscape that William was born and in which he was nurtured. The recollection of this and the sense of belonging to this eminent family he has cherished ever since. In 1929 a new and rewarding chapter of his life opened when he married Phoebe, daughter of Robert Dean of Rimington in the West Riding of Yorkshire, who had been a family friend since girlhood. But life in the north was changing. Both were country lovers and the thought of the places they loved being blackened by the smoke from factory chimneys creeping closer to the beautiful Ribble valley was too much. So they bought a small sports car and a caravan in which to search England for a place where they could live their own natural lives. They asked for nothing more and the choice was East Anglia and especially Suffolk to which they gave their hearts. To their great joy a couple they had met there wrote inviting them to spend a few days at a place called Buckhurst Hill in Epping Forest, which included the prospect of a day in Suffolk where they were fascinated by small towns which exuded the aura of history and unique qualities of gentle beauty that both found irresistible. 'In aspect and character it is softer and kinder than Norfolk . . . it is a county to settle down with' William was to write later in his contribution to the *County Books*[4] series in 1950. But it was Essex, enjoying its proximity to East Anglia, that eventually captivated William's heart and mind.

The stay at Buckhurst Hill was to establish the pattern of the rest of their lives. The north may have been the mould in which he was cast. The preliminary flirtation with East Anglia probably eased the break with the family background. It was to be Essex in which the achievements and satisfactions of his life were to mature. The young Addisons enjoyed their introduction to Epping Forest and, sensibly, found their way to a bookshop which, by happy chance, happened to be for sale. William reflects 'We bought it and our lives were transformed. For the next twenty years, weather permitting, I wandered in the Forest every morning before breakfast and lived a simple but good life . . . Essex was my sort of county.' In what sense was that? Surely in the beauty and tranquillity of Epping Forest, the wealth of medieval churches in which he delights and the vigour of local history studies in a county that was so rich in them, lying as it did between London and the continent.

The bookshop in Loughton was the base from which he embarked upon a remarkable range of cultural activity and public service. During those early years he wrote the first of his three books on Epping Forest, served as a Verderer for over twenty years and even longer as a student of its history. He presided over a number of historical organisations in the county including the Family History Society and chaired the inaugural meeting in 1964 at which the Essex Archaeological and Historical Congress was planned. It is to those aspects of his life, in all their diversity and quality, to which the remainder of this essay is devoted. 'Altogether', he told me, 'I am profoundly conscious of having had more than a fair share of interesting jobs in my life and I can fairly assure you that I have been grateful for it'.

Man of Affairs

William Addison's intellectual ability, breadth of view and balance were given ample scope in the work which he undertook

4 W. Addison, *Suffolk*, Hale, 1950.

over a period of more than twenty-five years in the criminal justice system. There have never been sufficient people of the necessary calibre available to fulfil the demanding tasks that need to be done to ensure the levels of justice, humanity and full effectiveness of the courts, the penal system and those social agencies concerned with people sentenced to non-custodial penalties that are compatible with a modern civilised society. It was a fortunate day for the Bench when William Addison became a Justice of the Peace in 1949. By 1955 he was Chairman of the Epping Petty Sessions and from 1968 to 1976 of the Epping and Ongar Petty Sessions. His deep interest and commitment to the magistracy led to a place on the Council of the Magistrates' Association in 1959. Subsequently he was elected to the prestigious office of Chairman of the Council of the Association for England and Wales, a post in which he served with distinction from 1970 to 1976. William Addison also devised the motto *Ratione et Consilio* (by reason and sound judgement), that was adopted by the Association for its coat-of-arms, as epitomising the philosophy and social responsibilities of the lay magistracy. He thus earned the admiration not only of the magistrates in England and Wales, but of those officials in the Home Office with whom he necessarily dealt and of other organisations active in the same field. It had long been one of the essential duties of magistrates to serve as Visiting Justices who thus bore responsibily for the general oversight of the prisons with a right of direct access to the Home Secretary. Certain disciplinary and advisory roles were also carried out by the magistrates appointed to those posts. A shrewd and responsible attitude was needed if the magistrates and their lay colleagues on the Boards were to enjoy the respect and confidence of the prison governors, staff and prisoners of the institutions to which they were appointed. These duties could be onerous as well as rewarding in the best sense. William Addison served in this capacity as a member of the Boards of Visitors at Hill Hall, the women's open prison located in that beautiful sixteenth century transitional building at Theydon Mount, at the traditional Chelmsford prison and the modern Bullwood Hall, a girls' borstal near Rayleigh, all in Essex, during the years from 1955 to 1970. His stature on the criminal justice scene and his wide knowledge of its basic structure, mechanisms and the many difficult political and philosophical issues with which it is beset, meant that William Addison's expertise was frequently engaged on a number of advisory bodies concerned with these important social problems. In terms of our contemporary penality his was a voice of progressive and humane moderation.

The other sphere in which he etched his credentials was that of local history especially in Essex to which we shall come. But he was engaged too in a number of other areas of public service. His long and devoted love affair with Epping Forest was symbolised by his term from 1957 to 1984 as a Verderer of the Forest, an appointment of considerable antiquity. In their earliest roles the Verderers are known to have carried out various judicial functions within the Forest jurisdiction. These legal duties were gradually developed to include more general responsibilities for the maintenance and administration of the Forest which was, of course, considerably more extensive than the Epping remnant of today. Records show that Verderers were appointed by the Forest Courts from the time of Cnut and some are known by name from as early as 1250.[5] William Addison's appointment stemmed from the Epping Forest Act of 1878 under which the Corporation of the City of London was designated as Conservators of the Forest. The Verderers, who are elected by the Commoners, serve on the Epping Forest Committee which is nominated by the Court of Common Council of the Corporation. Doubtless William Addison's sensitivity to history and circumstance will have inspired his own feelings of affinity with the local Verderers in Fisher's fascinating list.

His constant interest in ecclesiology found an agreeable personal outlet when he became a founder member of the Friends of Essex Churches, served on its Council for over forty years and, eventually, accepted the Presidency. He was also a Vice-President of the Association of Genealogists and Record Agents from 1985 to 1988 and was called upon to preside at meetings in the absence of Garter Principal King of Arms, the President. This and his Vice-Presidency of the Council for the Protection of Rural England (Essex) from 1984 were roles reflecting his fascination with genealogy and his belief in conservation. In 1973 he was appointed one of the Deputy Lieutenants of Essex. In its original concept the office of Deputy Lieutenant was essentially that of support for the Lord Lieutenant's military responsibilities. Nowadays, the Deputy Lieutenants, whose appointments are approved by Her Majesty the Queen, are expected to assist the Lord Lieutenant in his more general duties when called upon to do so. The burdens of these public offices would tax the time and energy of the most able and industrious of public-spirited people. But that is not all.

5 W. R. Fisher, *The Forest of Essex*, Butterworth, 1887.

Essex local history, especially in its administrative and organisational aspects owes William Addison an especial debt for he has combined his academic and literary contributions in this field with the less conspicuous but important roles of promotion and consolidation. The Essex Archaeological and Historical Congress was set up in 1964 and William Addison, then President of the Chigwell Local History Society, was one of those founders who devised its first constitution and set out the guidelines for its work.[6] Along with the ebullient John O'Leary[7] and the other pioneers his inspirational presence and continuing support for its roles and ambitions have been greatly valued by the Congress. It is the only forum for local history and archaeology to embrace the whole historic county of Essex and its local societies. He served as President of the county's senior society, the Essex Archaeological Society (now the Essex Society for Archaeology and History) from 1963 to 1966, an honour which he has enjoyed along with other distinguished Essex historiographers and archaeologists. From 1960 to 1963 The Friends of Historic Essex, then in its early years but having already established its valuable role in supporting the Essex Record Office and Essex history,[8] benefited from William Addison's able and vigorous chairmanship. He was also President of the Essex Society for Family History from 1977–84 and helped to ensure its great success. All Essex historians are indebted to the academic excellence of the *Victoria County History of Essex* not least William Addison. It is a debt which in his case was generously repaid through twenty-five years service as its Chairman and friend.

Nearer to his home the Waltham Abbey Historical Society had the privilege of William Addison's Presidency for almost as long, twenty-three years. He has always been an ardent supporter of local societies in Essex to which he has been ready to respond with encouragement and wise counsel for more than half a century. On the national scene his professional qualifications were recognised by his Fellowships of the Society of Antiquaries and the Royal Historical Society in 1965. It is apt that in her brilliant history of London's learned Society of Antiquaries, Joan Evans should have quoted,[9] in reference to scholarly antiquarian books and research, William Addison's famous ancestor Joseph who in *The Spectator* of 1711/12 wrote:

6 J. B. Boyes, *A Footprint in Time*, E.A.H.C., 1989.

7 K. Neale, 'J. G. O'Leary 1900–1985', *Essex Journal*, vol. 21, no. 2, 1986.

8 *The Friends of Historic Essex: The First Twenty-five Years*, 1979.

9 Joan Evans, *A History of the Society of Antiquaries*, 1956.

'I have heard one of the greatest Geniuses this age has produced, who had been trained up in all the polite Studies of antiquity, assure me, upon his being obliged to search into several rolls and records, that not-withstanding such an employment was, at first very dry and irksome to him, he at last took an incredible pleasure in it . . .'

William would certainly approve of that and enjoy its pertinent sentiments.

Man of Letters

'It is a good thing to read books and it need not be a bad thing to write them, but it is a pious thing to preserve those that have been written.'

With characteristic Scottish sagacity and moderation so wrote George Walker in his delightfully serious study[10] of the handsome grey northern city of Britain in its literary and social aspects. In Aberdeen 'Books, even rare and precious were abundant' and when in all England there was but Oxford and Cambridge, the granite city could itself boast of two universities, he reminds us! William Addison would have been content at Brown's bookshop among the well-worn volumes and bookish browsers. Carlyle, quoted at the head of this essay, also struck an harmonious note. Of all that William has done, so much as we have seen, it will be his books that will out-live the immediate recollection of his other work. As his contemporaries depart the worldly scene, who can doubt that William's rich mix of erudition and aesthetic style will continue to delight and inform succeeding generations of Essex historians, topographers and devotees of literature? His books will be sought, no longer unhappily in Brown's, but in David's and Galloway and Porter's in Cambridge, the Castle Bookshop in Colchester, hopefully in small bookshops for the discerning reader like Margaret Pole's at Thaxted, for as long as good literature with an historical flavour excites the minds and the imagination of bibliophiles.

William has, as his friends and colleagues know well, been an original and regular contributor to the Essex historical and archaeological journals and the author of an excellent guidebook for Queen Elizabeth's Hunting Lodge at Chingford. Here we shall concentrate on a representative selection of the twenty books he

10 G. Walker, *Aberdeen Awa'*, Brown and Menzies, 1897.

has published in almost fifty years of literary endeavour. It is convenient to do so in three broad areas, the Epping Forest trilogy, books on Essex topics and those concerned with general topography or aspects of local history.

Epping Forest has been one of the abiding passions of his life. He knows the Forest with the caring intimacy that all of its champions from Buxton to Leutscher and himself have lavished upon it. In his first book *Epping Forest: its Literary and Historical Associations* he portrayed the Forest in all its variety and richness. We enjoy the Forest that Essex shares with London and which, as a result of its proximity to the capital and its attractive environmental qualities, became the object of royal patronage and privilege, of literary inspiration and popular recreation. In this book we meet the Tudor monarchs and their courtiers, the giants of English drama, poetry and literature such as Jonson, Donne, Clare, Pepys and Dickens. Legend is blended with history and narrative with skilful integrity. In *Portrait of Epping Forest*[11] the theme is concerned with the historical development of the Forest from the preserve of royal interest to the People's Forest as it was declared to be by Queen Victoria in 1882 and its preservation and administration by the Corporation of the City of London. In what William has called a companion volume to the others, *Epping Forest: Figures in a Landscape*[12] he has offered a further interpretation of the legends, personalities and topography of the Forest and the surrounding areas. These three books afford the best and most enjoyable introduction to the Forest and would themselves have been enough to establish the author's credentials and his devotion to local themes. There is so much more.

His other Essex books are more restricted in their foci. The broadest literary brushwork was reserved for *Essex Heyday*,[13] a colourful account of various aspects of social life in the county during the seventeenth century. William's devoted readership will endorse the view that it contains some of his finest prose writing. It is characterised by the panache with which he deploys the language to enliven his anecdotal references and the deftness of touch in interpreting events and the interplay of personalities. In it we view Essex life in this turbulent century through the activities of the rich and influential and the more muted experience of humbler folk. The lives and times of kings and

11 W. Addison, *Portrait of Epping Forest*, Hale, 1977.

12 W. Addison, *Epping Forest: Figures in a Landscape*, Hale, 1991.

13 W. Addison, *Essex Heyday*, Dent, 1949.

queens, the nobility, the squirearchy, the clergy, farmers and villagers are depicted with a Chaucerian flavour and Pepysian perception. His choice of title for this book shews how clearly he has grasped the essential character of a difficult period in county history and with what thoughtful care he chooses words. In sharper focus *Audley End*[14] gave William the opportunity to indulge himself, and vicariously his readers, in further research in the archives of the seventeenth century with which he is so obviously fascinated. This is a book in which he finds full scope for his scholarship and the fruits of painstaking research that, when combined with his felicitous literary style, has produced an Essex classic. One of the great houses of Essex, indeed in its original conception of England, the story of Audley End and its great families the Howards and the Nevilles was ripe, in 1953, for rehearsal by a modern author of literary distinction and technical expertise. William Addison was admirably equipped for this and his fine study, handsomely produced by Dent the publishers, was the happy result.

I have already alluded to *Worthy Dr. Fuller* the subject of William Addison's excellent biography of the genial and scholarly Cavalier parson who found contentment and intellectual refreshment at Waltham Abbey. It is another example of how much at home William Addison is with the personalities and subtleties of the seventeenth century. A further contribution to the biographical dimensions of Essex history is *Essex Worthies*, a book of reference and utility to all who delve into the county's past. In it are summarised the lives and work of the many personalities whose presence or activities have left their marks on Essex topics and Essex history. It is a kind of Who's Who of Essex history and literature; but, written by William Addison, it is also pleasantly readable.

The range of William Addison's interests and knowledge of local history and topography found its most prolific expression in a series of books that he has written about vernacular architecture, parish churches, place-names, fairs and markets. This he has usefully extended in books about Suffolk, the Thames Estuary, the English spa towns and in a charming and entertaining book *In the Steps of Charles Dickens.*[15] Few authors in these fields have compiled such a comprehensive tally of reference in studies that local historians need to clothe their work, with specialist

14 W. Addison, *Audley End*, Dent, 1953.

15 W. Addison, *In the Steps of Charles Dickens*, Rich and Cowan, 1955.

information on particular topics. They are books of utility and immense interest written to the high standards that characterise all of William Addison's literary work. Here I can offer only brief thoughts on but a few that I have found of special value and have enjoyed. After the definitive series of books on the life and character of the English clergy, their wives, clerks, curates and parishioners written by Dr. Tindal Hart one would not have thought that there was anything left to read on this subject. William Addison's *The English Country Parson*[16] which preceded Hart's fine studies is an exception. It has not been superseded by that series,is a joy to read and replete with colourful characters and authentic historical and social scenery. *English Fairs and Markets*,[17] published by Batsford in 1953 and vigorously illustrated by Barbara Jones in bold coloured brushwork, is another fine genre book that catches the atmosphere of its topic in splendid style and fine detail.

It is in his contribution to the County Books on *Suffolk* that William Addison's love of his subject surfaces with manifest sincerity. His enjoyment of this tranquil eastern county emerges on every page. The furtive charm and gentle character of Suffolk has captivated the author as it has so many of the greatest English artists and, naturally, William Addison's readers. He relishes the lovely villages and elegant little towns along the Suffolk–Essex borderlands. He lingers easily with the broad landscapes and the literary and artistic associations that have idealised our images of the East Anglian scene. William Addison has paid his homage gladly to Suffolk in this book as Henry Warren of Finchingfield did for Essex in the same series and Esther Meynell for Sussex in the first of the County Books to be published. One could hardly ask for more and William has earned a secure place in this select company of authors.

As a reader who enjoys poetry and fine prose I have long been addicted to the exquisitely crafted essays of Richard Church who lived for a while at Cole End close by Saffron Walden in the nineteen-thirties. William Addison has achieved what Church apparently could not as far as Essex and East Anglia are concerned. Although one of the most talented and sensitive of writers, Church never seems to have grasped this part of England and was, eventually, happier in Kent. To him, Essex was 'a lot of temperament and time, still more time'; and 'East Anglia is all of a piece.

16 W. Addison, *The English Country Parson*, Dent, 1947.

17 W. Addison, *English Fairs and Markets*, Batsford, 1953.

Its nature is that of the oyster . . . Sometimes I have half-prised it open, and fancied I was peering at the pearl within. But that was only in moments of illusion . . .'[18] William Addison's interpretation of Essex and East Anglia certainly recognises these hidden features of the landscape and the reticent charms of the eastern counties. He, as have other authors, has sensed the elusive character of much that is beautiful and tranquil in the rural and estuarine reaches of Essex and beneath the high, mobile skies of Suffolk and Norfolk. Yet he clearly comprehends and is comfortable with them. His sensitive and elegant prose, mingled with his scholarly standards and personal dedication to the county have made him one of the most authoritative interpreters of Essex history and the Essex scene.

The Essex Worthy

Few in this generation have been more closely in harmony and associated with the Essex Heritage in its various aspects than William Addison. In this cursory review of his life and work it is evident that in its historical, literary and topographical facets William has been a major contributor. He has been deeply involved too, as we have seen, in a number of administrative and judicial functions in county life. In such he has endowed all of the offices he has held, often for lengthy and arduous periods, with a unique personal idiom. His competence and style as an experienced chairman have been of lasting benefit to those organisations privileged to enjoy his leadership. As a master of language his services as a speaker on every kind of occasion, from the formal lecture to the spontaneous words of thanks and kindness at social gatherings, have always been in great demand. His presence has always graced the occasion and delighted the participants.

How has he found the time and energy for all this? His rugged health until very recently and the clarity of a capacious mind, brimming with knowledge and enthusiasm have been essential ingredients in his lifestyle. I have always remembered too a conversation we had, many years ago, when we were involved together in a penological conference and had both just published books. He remarked 'It is only busy people like you and me who can find time to do all these things'. His time was not only well spent but well organised. Little of this precious commodity has

18 R. Church, *Calling for a Spade*, Dent, 1939.

been wasted in William's fruitful life and Essex and his numerous friends and readers have been the fortunate recipients of its wonderful harvest of achievements. Apparent has been the deep sense of his belonging to the northern counties of his birth and youthful experience. Subsequently his long involvement with and the depth of his devotion to Essex have symbolised this Essex worthy as a significant man of his time. Scholar, author, bibliophile, administrator, magistrate, these, and other such appellations are germane to the colourful pageant of this remarkable life. We know him too as a sensitive student of history and landscape with a facility for expressing his perceived images in vivid and memorable prose.

We read in Geoffrey Chaucer's *Prologue to the Canterbury Tales*:[19]

> 'A knyght ther was and that a worthy man
> That fro the tyme that he first bigan
> To riden out, he loved chivalrie,
> Trouthe and honour, fredom and curtesie.
> Full worthy was he . . .'

An apt note on which to close this account of an Essex knight, for in 1974 William in truth the 'verray parfit, gentil knyght' received the royal accolade. His friends and numerous admirers of his work rejoiced that his immense endeavours in public life and in the world of literature should have been so recognised. It is, traditionally, the way in which exceptionally distinguished service and personal merit is honoured in Britain. Now William's scholarly friends and colleagues have worked together, under the auspices of the Essex Archaeological and Historical Congress, to compile this book of essays as the county's tribute to the man it is proud to call an Essex worthy.

---

19 *The Works of Geoffrey Chaucer*, Globe Edition, MacMillan, 1898.

The Victoria County History

JANET COOPER

THE WRITING OF county history can be traced back for over three
hundred years, to William Dugdale's *Antiquities of Warwickshire*, published in 1656. That and Robert Thoroton's *Antiquities
of Nottinghamshire* which followed it in 1677 set a high standard
of historical writing, including the provision of references. Essex
had to wait another century for its first complete history, Philip
Morant's *History of Essex* published between 1763 and 1768,
although the work had been begun almost a century before when
Thomas Jekyll of Bocking had started to collect material for a
history of the county, and Nathanael Salmon had published the
history of fourteen of the nineteen Essex hundreds between 1740
and his death in 1742. Despite the publication of other histories,
some of them largely copied from it, Morant's *History* remained
until the start of work on the Victoria County History, and for
many parts of Essex remains, the standard scholarly history of the
county.[1] By the middle of the nineteenth century most English
counties had their histories. Most were collections of short parish
histories, dealing with a restricted range of subjects, notably the
descent of the manor or manors, a description of the manor house
or houses and of the tombs in the church, with some account of the
church itself. Many antiquaries wrote for noble patrons; others
were members of county families or incumbents of livings in the
county. Their interests reflected those of their patrons, and
potential subscribers. Other subjects were considered unsuitable
for treatment in parish histories, but John Hutchins in his *History
of Dorset* (1774) provided an introduction in which he dealt with
antiquities, ecclesiastical and natural history, fairs, markets, and
roads, and with the text of Domesday Book. Morant included in
his footnotes and appendices the text of many documents,

---

1 G. Martin, Introduction to Facsimile edition of Morant, *History of Essex*;
   Christine E. Cobbold, 'The Writing of Essex County History, *c*.1600—1768',
   Essex Journal, viii, 2.

including the whole of Essex Domesday. His parish histories also contain some details of agricultural practices and of domestic architecture, and he was particularly interested in earthworks and antiquities.

The aims of the early county historians varied. Some would no doubt have agreed with Robert Plot, who told the reader of his *Natural History of Oxfordshire* (1677) that he had undertaken the work for his own pleasure, the subject being 'so pleasant and of such great variety'. Others seem to have felt the need to explain or justify their work. Dugdale prefaced his *Antiquities of Warwickshire* with a quotation from Sir Walter Raleigh, 'It is history that hath given us life in our understanding since the world itself had life and beginning', and added that history 'increases knowledge, far more than could otherwise be acquired in a single life'. The physician Thoroton explained that the aim of his *Antiquities of Nottinghamshire* (1677) was 'to practise upon the dead, intending thereby to keep all which is or can be left of them, to wit the shadow of their names, to preserve their memory as long as may be in the world'. A century later William Borlass argued a more didactic purpose for his *Antiquities of Cornwall* (1769),

> 'There is no study more instructive and entertaining than that of ancient and modern history, and though the latter may be more interesting and easy and pleasant, yet the former is also a most necessary part of knowledge, as it enlarges our prospects, furnishes us with a great variety of examples both of Virtue and Vice, produces frequent instances of Science and Error, discovers the manner in which great actions have been conducted, and great attempts have miscarried.'

George Lipscomb in the introduction to his *History of Buckinghamshire* (1847) introduced an element of apology for writing county rather than national history,

> 'Impressed with the conviction that Buckinghamshire possessed local features and artificial embellishments united with objects highly interesting to the Antiquary and the Scholar. . . that its connexion with events of national importance, together with the fame and distinction of many eminent characters identified with it in ancient and modern days as heroes, patriots, statesmen, orators, and poets, dignifying and adorning the spheres in which they moved, must be the author's apology for having undertaken so laborious a task.'

The Victoria County Histories grew out of the tradition of the earlier county histories, specifically out of a plan by the publisher Arthur Doubleday to compile a history of Hampshire. He asked the assistance of the folklorist and antiquary George Laurence (later Sir Laurence) Gomme, who persuaded him to undertake the much more ambitious project of a series of uniform histories of all the English counties.[2] The new *History* was to be a history of each county as a whole rather than simply a collection of parish histories, and was to cover topics which had been largely ignored by earlier county historians. Its originators hoped that such county history would contribute to national as well as local history, and, perhaps with this in mind, sought Queen Victoria's patronage. The description of the planned series sent to the Queen, stated that the work partook of a National Character,[3] and J. H. Round, the distinguished Essex-born historian, writing to Doubleday in 1900 about the Hampshire political history article, commented, 'it has been your fundamental idea that (1) the history of the county as a whole should be written for the first time, (2) that it should be written as a part of national history.'[4]

The V.C.H. articles which perhaps reflect most clearly the desire to include national history are those on the political history of a county, including as they do an account of the battles, political struggles, and other national events, which have taken place in the county, but those political history articles are also an important part in the county component of the Victoria County Histories. The development of the *History* since the Second World War has to a large extent obscured the 'county' element in the series as the histories of individual parishes have loomed ever larger in it, but the original plan was that each county set should comprise about four volumes (six were allowed for Yorkshire), two of which were to be 'general' volumes, containing articles covering the county as a whole.[5] The arrangement was at once new and archaic. On the one hand the general articles dealt with the county as a whole, and dealt with such matters as natural history (including geology), social and economic history, endowed schools, ecclesiastical history, and the history of industries and sport, which had not been covered at all in the earlier county histories. On the other

2 London University, Institute of Historical Research, V.C.H. Muniments (hereafter V.C.H. Mun.), Box A 30.

3 *Ibid.*

4 *Ibid.*, Box A 45.

5 *V.C.H. General Introduction*, 3.

hand, the coverage of these subjects in the general articles left the parish histories in the topographical volumes to cover much the same ground as those in earlier histories; the only major additions were an introduction which dealt with the appearance of and a brief history of the settlement, and the history of endowed charities for the poor.

Queen Victoria agreed early in 1899 to accept the dedication of the new *History*, and thus to give it its name, but she declined to become its patron on the grounds that that might make her appear to be its sponsor.[6] Meanwhile work was progressing on the *History*, the first volume of which, *Hampshire I*, was published in 1900. The general volumes proved easier to write than the topographical ones. Some of the work, notably on Domesday Book and on antiquities, was done by major scholars; J. H. Round himself wrote the introductions to and translations of Domesday Book for twelve counties and supervised the work on a further twelve.[7] Other Domesday articles were written by James Tait, and by F. M. (later Sir Frank) Stenton. Even with such eminent scholars the work was not always trouble free. The two founders of the V.C.H., Doubleday and Gomme, appear to have fallen out over the writing of the article on the prehistory of Hampshire, Gomme complaining that he felt Doubleday was no longer taking his advice, and finally saying in March 1900, 'It was never part of my agreed practise to devil for Professor Boyd Dawkins or any other author'.[8] Dr. J. C. Cox, writing the ecclesiastical history of Northamptonshire in 1899, obviously resented the imposition of Doubleday's views, but admitted, 'Probably you are right — a percentage of fools would not care to hear of the things that explain the shape and construction and details of their parish churches and would be alarmed at this in the prospectus!'.[9] Another of Cox's ecclesiastical history drafts, however, caused Round to comment, 'It is wonderful how interesting and readable he can make a somewhat dull subject'.[10]

The topogaphical volumes of parish histories, which required detailed local knowledge, were more difficult to write than the general volumes, and there were problems in finding

---

6 V.C.H. Mun., Box A 30.

7 W. R. Powell, 'J. Horace Round, the County Historian', *Essex Archaeology and History*, xii, 1980, 28.

8 V.C.H. Mun., Box A 30.

9 *Ibid.*, Box A 52.

10 *Ibid.*, Box A 45.

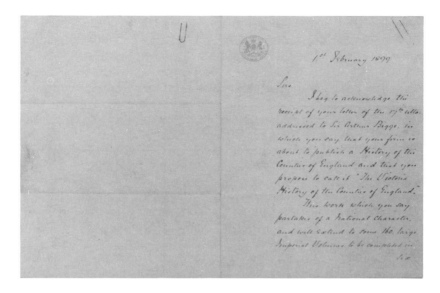

*Figures 1 and 2. Letter from Buckingham Palace, 1 February, 1899,
conveying to the publishers Queen Victoria's acceptance of the Dedication
of the* History.   (Victoria County History)

acceptable authors, and editors. Cox resigned all connection with the Nottinghamshire and Derbyshire topographical volumes on learning that 'young Mr. Stenton' (later Sir Frank Stenton), a newcomer to the county, was to be in charge of the Nottinghamshire volumes.[11] In the event, the topographical volumes for Nottinghamshire were not completed, presumably being casualties of the financial crisis which temporarily stopped work on the V.C.H. in 1908–9.[12] The original intention seems to have been to get local men, particularly clergymen, to write the parish histories, but this proved difficult if not impossible. Round commented of Essex in 1899, 'As is usually the case there are probably not half a dozen really qualified workers in the county'.[13] By c. 1903 the problem had to a great extent been solved by the employment of about a dozen women assistants, most of whom had qualified for Oxford or Cambridge degrees. They systematically searched the indexes to many printed and manuscript sources, making notes of all topographical references for all counties,[14] and some also wrote parish histories.

Almost more serious than the question of authors was the question of content of the parish histories, which comprised an introduction and sections on Manors, Churches, and Charities. They were to be kept short: in 1899 one contributor, submitting to Doubleday a specimen history (of a fictitious parish), commented, 'I really do not see how *any* locality can be done much shorter than the 700 words it contains'.[15] Such brief articles would hardly have been histories at all, and in fact published parish histories were all longer, at least 2,000 words. Their content also caused controversey. Round wrote to Doubleday in March 1899 after seeing a notice in the *Morning Post*, 'It speaks of an "elaborate history" of every county, dealing with its art, minerals, resources, agriculture, sport, and distinguished men. These are all suitable subjects for a *Survey* of England, but they do not constitute, as the paragraph implies, county history. And it was for county histories that I agreed to join in the work.'[16] Four months later he reported that Maxwell Lyte, like others, was still unhappy about 'the topographical department' and had emphasised the importance

11 *Ibid.*, Box 52.

12 *V.C.H. General Introduction*, 7.

13 V.C.H. Mun., Box A 45.

14 *V.C.H. General Introduction*, 7.

15 V.C.H. Mun., Box A 30.

16 *Ibid.*, Box A 45.

of searching *Feudal Aids*, which was then in progress.[17] Presumably there was at that date some doubt as to how fully even printed works could be searched for the parish histories. The problem was to some extent, as it has remained, one of combining thorough research with speedy production of parish histories. Round wrote again to Doubleday in September 1900,

> 'Thinking over our conversation of yesterday, I feel even more strongly the necessity of at once defining and limiting our sphere in the "topography". From the first it seemed doubtful to me whether we should trouble to go much into original record research, and I often hinted as much. If you can now form an idea of the normal number of pages available for a parish and then try to apportion them, allowing for the strong "survey" element and description of the church, there will be precious little room for the sort of stuff we should get from records . . . Another item that will trench on topographical space is a description, however brief, of present residents and residences, which people will of course expect.'

Round concluded by suggesting it would be necessary to reduce the amount of space occupied by manorial history and pedigrees,[18] a sentiment which was to be shared by many later twentieth century reviewers!

In fact the early topographical volumes contained parish histories which were brief, and, by modern standards, limited in scope. Nevertheless, they do contain a description of the parish, including remarks on geology and land use. Some Manors articles include details, such as the short histories of mills and of markets and fairs, which would now be covered in Economic History, and in their manorial descents they make use of many manuscript sources, particularly those in the Public Record Office. There were full descriptions of many buildings, particularly churches and manor houses. With all their limitations, these parish histories are histories, not simple surveys.

Not surprisingly, Round early tried to start work on an Essex V.C.H. By April 1899 he had contacted the secretary of the Essex Archaeological Society, and on 20 April he addressed the Society about the project. He reported to Doubleday, 'I addressed the meeting at Colchester today on the scheme, distributed prospectuses and asked the press to ventilate the subject. Interest was

17 *Ibid.*   18 *Ibid.*

shown in the scheme, and approval expressed'.[19] The Society had already in 1896 shown its interest in local history by recommending the publication of the *Feet of Fines for Essex*,[20] the first volume of which was published in 1899, the second in 1900. Another historical scheme, mooted in 1896, the publication of Holman's church notes,[21] seems to have come to nothing, probably because it proved impossible to borrow the manuscript from Colchester borough council rather than because of lack of enthusiasm for the work. Many members of the Society served on the first Essex V.C.H. committee. Round made regular reports to the Society on the progress of the *History*, and in 1906 the Society lent a set of their *Transactions* for the use of the Essex V.C.H.[22]

An Essex Victoria County History committee, chaired by the Lord Lieutenant, the Earl of Warwick, was formed in 1901. It included Sir Walter Gilbey, wine merchant and writer on sport, horse-breeding and agriculture, of whom Round had commented in 1899 that he was 'one of the few really wealthy men now in the county',[23] as well as the Colchester newspaper proprietor and historian William Gurney Benham, the architect and amateur archaeologist Frederic Chancellor (a founder member of the Archaeological Society), the Essex historian and naturalist Miller Christy, the zoologist and local historian E. A. Fitch (a founder member of the Essex Field Club), the archaeologist Henry Laver, the musicologist and past president of the Archaeological Society F. W. Galpin, and J. H. Round himself.[24] A prospectus was issued advertising a history of the county in four volumes which 'As the history of each county is part of the history of the whole country', would not only deal with local matters relating to the history of the county, but would 'show what part it played in the larger History of the Empire'. (Round may still have been hoping to tap overseas, particularly American, money!) The articles were to be written by 'specialists whose aim it will be to make the work not only interesting to the general reader but of value to the student and to the antiquary'.[25]

19 *Ibid.*
20 *Trans. Essex Arch. Soc.*, new series, vi, 287.
21 *Ibid.*, vii, 112.
22 Essex Arch. Soc. Min. Bk. 1894–1910, council meetings of 19 April, 1906 and 30 April, 1907.
23 V.C.H. Mun., Box A 45.
24 *V.C.H. Essex*, i, xiii; W. Addison, *Essex Worthies*, 23, 40, 43, 85.
25 Photocopy of prospectus in Essex V.C.H. office.

*Figure 3.   William Page, General Editor of the Victoria History of the
Counties of England, 1902–1934.*
(Victoria County History)

The first volume of the Essex *History* was published in 1903 under the editorship of Doubleday and William Page, a professional record agent who had joined the V.C.H. that year. They acknowledged in their preface 'their great indebtedness to Mr. J. Horace Round, not only for the infinite pains he has expended under adverse circumstances of health on the Domesday section, which in the case of Essex is one of peculiar difficulty, but also for the valuable help he has given to others in the preparation and revision of their articles'. The volume contained articles on Natural History (including geology, botany, and zoology), Early Man, Ancient Earthworks, Anglo-Saxon Remains, and Domesday Book; the last, Round's contribution, occupied nearly 250 pages. Volume Two, edited by Page, who had succeeded Doubleday as General Editor in 1902, and Round, appeared in 1907. It included articles on Ecclesiastical History, Religious Houses, Political History, Maritime History, Social and Economic History, Industries, Schools, Sport, and Forestry. The preface notes that the additions made by Round to the articles on Ecclesiastical and Political History, originally written by Dr. J. C. Cox and Miss Ethel Stokes, had been so substantial that his name had been added as joint author. The views of Cox and Stokes on Round's alterations to their work do not appear to have survived, but Miss Nora MacMunn, author of the article on Social and Economic History, wrote to Page in 1906, 'I fully recognise the value of his [Round's] suggestions, and if I had had them earlier could have incorporated them with great advantage', but felt that to add extra detail at a late stage would obscure her argument. She suggested putting Round's material into footnotes, an arrangement which was not acceptable to Page.[26] Nevertheless the published article does contain several long footnotes which may well be the work of Round. They include the note on the sixteenth-century conversion of arable to pasture, 'An instance of the reverse process occurs in the Pipe Roll 1 John, where the abbot of Waltham is entered as paying £15 for the cultivation of 100 acres of his pasture',[27] and the similar note to the statement that the navigable rivers of Essex have been improved by engineering, 'A remarkable early instance of this is found in the writ of Longchamp in or about 1190 to the sheriff of Essex announcing that he had given leave to the abbot of Waltham Holy Cross to divert the course of the Lee there "ad commodum navigii" '.[28] The long note on the medieval Colchester Jewry[29] may also be Round's. Miss Fell Smith, who wrote the

26 V.C.H. Mun., Box A 30.   28 *Ibid*., 334n.
27 *V.C.H. Essex*, ii, 322n.   29 *Ibid*., 329n.

article on Schools and for whom Round seems to have had a particular dislike, wrote when she returned the proofs of her article, 'Mr. Round's remarks would be more articulate if they were less denunciatory. If he would point out what he considers the correct reading as well as fasten on what (to him) seem errors, his comments would be salutary.'[30]

Work had started on Volume Three, which was to have contained some general articles, including that on Roman Remains, and some parish histories, when the Victoria County History ran into serious, although temporary, financial difficulties, and the volume was abandoned. It had not got off to a good start. Round, when shown some of the parish histories, had exploded, 'these are really achievements of ineptitude . . . I cannot possibly associate myself with topography of this character . . . this stuff might have been written in Berlin with the aid of a map, and it practically ignores all modern times and existing things'.[31] Perhaps because of Round's failing health and preoccupation with other work, the Essex *History* was not revived when the Victoria County History resumed in 1910 with the support of W. F. D. Smith of W. H. Smith and Sons. Work on some counties, however, continued until the First World War brought an end to research and publishing. In 1920 the County History Syndicate, which had owned the V.C.H. since its foundation, went into liquidation. William Page, still General Editor, tried for two years to rescue it, but local history was neither a popular nor a commercially viable subject. In May 1922 the Oxford University Press refused to accept the V.C.H. as a gift, and Page commented resignedly to one of the delegates, 'No doubt you are right: local history is perhaps of little importance in itself, but it is the foundation of all branches of national history'.[32] The *History* was saved by W. F. D. Smith, by then Viscount Hambledon, who bought it from the liquidator and authorised Page to continue the work as best he could, making him an allowance to help him to do so. Between then and 1932 Page brought out sixteen volumes, almost single handed, working from a hut in his Sussex garden.[33] Those volumes, inevitably, followed the form of and covered the same range of subjects as those written before the First World War; indeed much of the research on which they were based had been done then. In 1932 Viscount Hambledon was forced to discontinue his support, and conveyed

30 V.C.H. Mun., Box A 30.
31 *Ibid.*, Box A 47.
32 *Ibid.*, Box A 31; *V.C.H. General Introduction*, 12.
33 *V.C.H. General Introduction*, 7–10.

the *History* to Page who gave it in the same year to the Institute of Historical Research in the University of London.[34]

That year a group of historians in Oxford met to discuss the continuation of the Oxfordshire History, and when the transfer of the *History* to the Institute was completed in 1933 a local Oxfordshire committee was formed which, with funds supplied mainly by the Oxford colleges and the City of Oxford, began work on a volume on the city and university of Oxford, appointing a local editor and assistant.[35] The acquisition of local authority funding was to prove a significant step in the future of the V.C.H.; so too was the decision to devote a whole volume to a single city, albeit an important university one. Page died in 1934, and in 1935 Dr. L. F. Salzman was appointed general editor. By then work had been resumed on Warwickshire and Cambridgeshire, including the volume on the city and university of Cambridge. In 1938 the 100th volume of the *History* was published, but the celebrations did not attract the large benefaction for which London University had hoped, and when war broke out in 1939 the future of the *History* looked far from secure.[36]

In 1944 the university commissioned a report into the *History*, describing it as 'an historical encyclopaedia of the English counties rather than an ordinary "county history" '. The report's authors were enthusiastic, calling the series 'a mine of information, compiled at first hand and not, like so many of the older histories, extracted from older publications'. While acknowledging that a concentration on manorial descents would have limited interest, would lack colour and personal detail, and 'would not enter . . . into the economic questions which are now engaging the primary attention of students of agrarian history', the Committee felt that there could be no doubt as to the scientific value of the *History* in its current, that is essentially early twentieth century, form. It suggested that 'space might be allowed for the treatment of commercial and industrial developments in districts where these are of pre-eminent importance', and that the revolutionary changes which had taken place in agriculture in the last thirty years might also be dealt with. Such work, however, should always be 'subsidiary to the main purpose of the *History* — the accurate registration of the manorial descents which form the central thread of English social history'. It was a somewhat old-

34 *Ibid.*, 12–13.

35 *V.C.H. Oxon.*, iii, xv.

36 *V.C.H. General Introduction*, 13–15.

*Figure 4.   Professor R. B. Pugh, General Editor of the Victoria History of the
Counties of England, 1949–1977.*   (Victoria County History)

fashioned definition of local history and of the part of the V.C.H. in
it, but the Committee did conclude with a strong recommendation
that the *History* should be continued.[37]

   After the War the *History* was revived on a much more secure
basis than formerly. In 1945 Swindon corporation expressed an
interest in local history, and was encouraged by R. B. Pugh, a
Wiltshire man later to become General Editor, to consider funding
the V.C.H. In 1947, after two years of discussions, a local V.C.H.
committee was established in Wiltshire, funded by local
authorities and in partnership with the Institute of Historical
Research.[38] The Wiltshire committee has served as the model for
all post-War V.C.H. county committees. The Essex *History* was
revived in 1951, largely as a result of a visit by the General Editor,

37 'Report of the Committee on the Victoria County History appointed by the
    Academic Council, 30 October, 1944': copy in Institute of Historical
    Research.

38 C. R. Elrington, 'R. B. Pugh: an Appreciation', *Wilts. Coroners' Bills* (Wilts.
    Rec. Soc. xxxvi), xiv–xv.

R. B. Pugh, to the Essex Record Office in March 1950. He talked informally to F. G. Emmison, then County Archivist, about the possibility of restarting the Essex V.C.H., and Emmison gave the project his enthusiastic support, recommending it to the Essex committee of the National Register of Archives at its meeting later that month. In April the N.R.A. committee agreed to offer its services to London University to continue the work of the Essex V.C.H., and on 25 May it resolved itself into a provisional V.C.H. Committee. Conferences with the Local Authorities were held in Ilford on 5 October and in Chelmsford on 12 October, 1950, at which Pugh pointed out that few Essex boroughs or districts had a modern local history based on sound historical research, and argued that the publication of such histories would supply a real demand, 'and will serve the needs of local authorities as well as the student and general reader'. At a further conference at Ilford on 7 December, 1950, a total of twenty-four authorities, including Essex County Council, agreed to support the venture, and an Essex Victoria County History Committee was set up. As well as representatives of the subscribing authorities, the urban and rural districts, and the Institute of Historical Research, it included 'persons closely identified with the history of Essex', specifically William Addison and F. G. Emmison; its secretary was John O'Leary, borough librarian of Dagenham.[39] A County Editor, W. R. Powell, was appointed in June 1951. Since then eight volumes have been published: two volumes of Bibliography, one general volume on Roman Essex, and five volumes of topography, covering the south-west of the historic county, including the area now within the London boroughs of Barking and Dagenham, Havering, Newham, Redbridge, and Waltham Forest.

Not only the method of financing the V.C.H. changed in the late 1940s and 1950s. Its writing of history changed too, although not as fast as some reviewers would have liked! In 1950 the standard scheme for parish histories was enlarged by the addition of three new sections, Roman Catholicism and Protestant Non-conformity, 'the inclosure of the common fields', and village schools, to the existing General Introduction, Manors, Churches, and Charities. (Earlier volumes had ignored Roman Catholicism and Protestant Nonconformity altogether; schools and agriculture were considered to have been adequately dealt with in the general volumes.) Soon afterwards Economic History and Local Govern-

39 Correspondence in V.C.H. files, 1949–54, Essex folder, at Institute of Historical Research.

ment were added; the Essex volumes have been particularly strong on the last subject.

The Victoria County History still aims to produce histories of parishes and towns containing as many and as accurate facts as possible. As interest in local history generally has widened, so the scope of the volumes, and their length, have increased. Readership too has changed since the early years of the century when the volumes were aimed at the country gentry and a few specialist scholars and antiquarians. Modern readers want to know about far more than the manor and its occupants. They also want, and the editors and their staff want to produce, more than a collection of facts. Since the revival of the *History* in the 1950s more interpretation has crept into V.C.H. volumes; we are writing history, not a survey — the distinction Round drew in 1899 is still important. The growth of local record offices and the progress both there and in the Public Record Office in indexing and listing documents has meant that many more original sources than were available to the early workers on the *History* can now be used. Indeed, modern parish histories make use of a wide range of documentary sources, and of archaeological and architectural evidence for ordinary as well as major buildings. The result is a much more complete history than that produced in the early years of the century. More complete in the sense that it covers all aspects of a town or parish history, in that it uses all readily accessible sources, and in that it covers all periods from the prehistoric to the present day. The V.C.H. histories are not absolutely complete; no history could be that, but they do provide a solid foundation on which others can build. The increase in length of the parish histories is to be welcomed, but it has altered the balance between the 'county' and the 'parish' element in the V.C.H. which as it enters its second century comes in plan to resemble the earlier county histories in its concentration on town and parish history. The parish, or even the town, is not necessarily the best unit for the study of some aspects, particularly of economic history, and this is beginning to be reflected in the expansion of the originally brief Hundred article with which most V.C.H. volumes begin. As some local historians look to the region or the 'pays' rather than to the parish will the pendulum swing back towards a more truly 'county' history?

Medieval Essex Gilds

GEOFFREY MARTIN

GILDS FLOURISHED EVERYWHERE in medieval Europe, and in many different guises; they were a vital institution, and a powerful agent of social development over several centuries. Their origins lay in the pre-Christian past, so deeply rooted in society as to make their use seem instinctive, and the Church itself came to find them indispensable. They have left many traces behind them, and they have some tenuous descendants today, but their nature has not always been well understood, and the abundant evidence of their activities has often been misinterpreted.

Essex in the Middle Ages was a reasonably populous and prosperous member of the kingdom of England, and its gilds were widespread and variously busy. We have records of some eighty of them, and there were undoubtedly many more. Their story, or what we know of it at present, is not unique, but their multifarious purposes are instructive, and as counties have been remarkably long-lived communities it is always worth considering what has gone on inside their boundaries.

Essex belongs to the select company of English counties which were formerly tribal kingdoms, and took its shape from the earliest period of the Anglo-Saxon settlements. The Stour marked it off from the Angles to the north, and the marshland settlements of Fobbing and Mucking, and Vange, the *ge* or *gau* of the fenmen, gave the East Saxons a grip on the Thames and the approach to London. The status and definition of the Middle Saxons is uncertain, but Middlesex emerged late as a county, and it is most likely that in the eyes of the Angles and of other Saxons, Middle and East were for some time one. At its greatest extent the territory of the East Saxons seems to have included not only Middlesex but even Surrey.[1]

The early kingdom certainly embraced London, which for some time was its principal town and perhaps even its capital. Those are not terms which would have occurred naturally to an

---

1 D. Dumville, 'Essex, Middle Anglia, and the expansion of Mercia', *Origins of Anglo-Saxon Kingdoms*, ed. S. Bassett, London, 1989, 123–40.

East Saxon who fell to considering such matters, but they express a reality which had some important consequences. The East Saxon kings had control of London, and kept some hirsute state within its walls, not improbably about the site of the present Guildhall Yard, where the Roman amphitheatre once stood.[2]

When at the end of the sixth century Pope Gregory the Great sent Augustine to convert the English to Christianity, he instructed him to establish two archbishoprics, at London and York, each with twelve suffragans. On his arrival in Kent in 597 Augustine succeeded in converting King Æthelbert, who already had a Christian wife, but it was an important advance when he also secured the conversion of Seberht, king of the East Saxons, who was a client of Æthelbert's. The long history of St. Paul's cathedral begins c.604 with the installation of Mellitus, one of Augustine's followers, as the first bishop of London. Some twelve years later, however, disaster followed Seberht's death. His sons had remained pagans, and encouraged their traditional cult, which included the worship of idols, amongst their followers. When Mellitus excluded them from the Mass, a ritual feast to which they demanded admission as their father's heirs, they indignantly drove him from the kingdom. The reconversion of the East Saxons had to wait upon St. Cedd's mission in the middle years of the century.[3]

The loss of London ensured that Canterbury remained the principal base of the Roman mission, and eventually, with Augustine canonised, emerged as the primatial see. Another effect of the otherwise unedifying episode on Ludgate Hill was that it gives us a brief glimpse of a pagan society which had developed over some centuries in northern Europe, and was then substantially, though not entirely, overlaid by the triumph of Christianity.

We know little of the pagan religion beyond the denunciations and bans of the Church, but it was naturally much concerned with the seasons, with sympathetic magic, and with the rhythms both of the pastoral and of the agrarian farming year. It had rituals based upon the family and household, but with sacred groves and enclosures for other rites and assemblies. It involved animal sacrifices, which came to be commuted into commemor-

2 R. Merrifield, 'Roman London', 19, and M. Biddle, 'A city in transition', 21–23, *The City of London from pre-historic times to c.1500*, ed. M. D. Lobel, The British Atlas of Historic Towns, 3, Oxford, 1989.

3 *Bede's ecclesiastical history*, eds. B. Colgrave and R. A. B. Mynors, Oxford, 1969, 152–53. 380–84.

ative feasting. The sacred drink was ale, brewed for the occasion by the women of the family. The gild, which at heart was a solemn drinking, became the central ritual of the cult, and certainly proved to be the most adaptable and longest surviving feature of its ceremonies and institutions.[4]

The return of the East Saxons to their ancestral cult for a substantial part of the seventh century probably accounts for a relatively strong survival of heathen elements, widely distributed, amongst the place-names of Essex. They include an enclosure or grove for an idol preserved in the name of Weeley (*weoh-leah*), and a badger shrine commemorated at Broxted, a name which still speaks for itself. Such incidental references are only the remnants of a system that would have matched the whole pattern of settlement in the county, and which no doubt persisted for a long time after the re-establishment, or in the remoter parts the introduction, of Christianity from the 650s onwards.[5] With time the old sacred sites were displaced and abandoned, though it is not improbable that some of them were actually adapted to the new religion. One of their rites most certainly was.

For some time gilds were proscribed by the Church together with other specific pagan practices, but by the ninth century they were comfortably assimilated to Christian rites. The emergence of clerical gilds was a clear sign that attitudes had changed, but the ready proliferation of gilds of all kinds from that time onwards suggests that the Church had adapted itself to a social institution which it could not suppress rather than sanctified it upon its own terms. Whatever the process may have been, however, the social consequences were immense.

The appeal of the gild was elemental; eating and drinking in common has its own symbolic force, and the ritual of the gild, with its overtones of sacrifice and the explicit invocation of mystic brotherhood, gave it great strength. Its sanctions were reinforced by an oath, and the conventions prescribing harmony and moderate speech during the gild's sessions suited it to almost any ends. What was essentially a domestic ceremony could readily be turned to assimilate strangers to the comfort and reassurance of both parties. The gild was an association to which the men and

---

4 The best account of the ritual of the gild and its significance is in M. Cahen, *Etudes sur vocabulaire religieux de Vieux-Scandinave: la libation*, Société de Linguistique de Paris, 1921. There are some notably sensible observations upon pagan practices and survivals in E. K. Chambers, *The medieval stage*, 1, Oxford, 1903, 89–115.

5 P. H. Reaney, *The place-names of Essex*, English Place-Name Society, 12, Cambridge, 1935, xxi.

women of the time turned naturally, almost instinctively, to accomplish any purpose that needed the co-operation of others, who were not of their own kin. The familiar and universally-accepted rules of the committee in our own world offer an enlightening analogy.

Records of pre-Conquest gilds are comparatively rare, and there are none from Essex. There are however some traces of activities for which gilds were responsible, and which provide a link with still earlier times. The network of parishes which we rightly associate with the medieval church was of comparatively slow growth, and conceals a protracted communal effort.

In the first stages of the Christian mission religious houses were central both to the evangelical and the pastoral role of the Church, and the name of minster, from *monasterium*, for a central or district church preserved that tradition. The ancient endowment of St. Paul's was spread through the county, with a strategic coastal estate at *Ædulfsnasa*, the Naze, and the bishops and canons presumably made some provision for pastoral care on their own estates at an early date. The interesting post-Conquest churches on the bishop's manors of Copford and Great Clacton, which are unlikely to have been the first buildings on their sites, are comparatively late reminders of the resources which such a patron could command. The aisled and richly-decorated church of St. Nicholas, below the de Veres' castle at Hedingham, is another.[6]

However, the provision of local places of worship fell generally to lesser lords of the soil, who provided an endowment, the glebe, for a priest, and so retained the right to present his successor. When the priest wanted a shelter for the altar, as he not unreasonably might, he built a chancel, the upkeep of which thereafter remained his own responsibility. It was then, as it still remains, the business of the parishioners as a whole to supply and maintain the fabric of the rest of the church. The recruitment of materials, labour, and funds called naturally for a gild, which was in effect the first embodiment of the parish, and the meeting-place of which was not infrequently the church itself.[7]

6 For the tally of parishes, see W. R. Powell, 'The making of Essex parishes', and 'Essex parishes, 1300–1450', *Essex Review*, 62, 1953, 6–17, 32–41; and M. D. Owen, 'Chapelries and rural settlements', *Medieval settlement: continuity and change*, ed. P. H. Sawyer, London, 1976, 66–71.

7 On gilds and church-building, see further J. Campbell, 'Norwich', *The atlas of historic towns: 2, Bristol, Cambridge, Coventry, Norwich*, ed. M. D. Lobel, London, 1975, 22, n.87; G. Rosser, 'The Anglo-Saxon gilds', *Minsters and parish Churches*, ed. J. Blair, Oxford, 1988, 31–34.

Throughout the Middle Ages that primal assembly was periodically reconstituted by the church-ale, an institution distinct from the many devotional and other gilds which appeared in the churches, though often enough displaced or absorbed by one of them. It is not extravagant to assert that in that sense every parish church, whether its original form was a timber-framed hall, somewhere between the simplicity of Greensted by Ongar and the great belfries of Blackmore and Stock, or a stone church like Inworth, presupposes a gild.

As gilds and people were inseparable most gilds were rural, but there were also gilds in towns. Domesday Book refers incidentally to a thegns' gild in Cambridge, which must have been a club of substantial social and political importance, and to townsmen's gilds at Canterbury and Dover. Before the appearance of Charles Gross's *The gild merchant* in 1893 it was widely believed that merchant gilds played an essential part in securing and defining municipal liberties in England. Gross dismissed the notion, demonstrating that the doctrine of *liber burgus* could be perfectly well established in towns like Colchester, with no trace of a merchant gild amongst its liberties, but his learned and cogently-argued thesis served to encourage the classification of gilds by their functions, and to emphasise the differences between them rather than their fundamental kinship.[8]

In fact the negotiations to secure charters from the king, or from the lords of seignorial boroughs, must regularly have entailed the convocation of a gild amongst the townsmen: formal, of a kind to feature in the eventual grant of liberties, or informal, assembled for the particular purpose and then abandoned, or absorbed into some other sodality. Colchester and Maldon were prescriptive boroughs, which is to say that their early gilds were unobtrusive. The name of the Guildhall at Harwich is a reminder of the general usefulness of a gild in a town in which the range of municipal liberties was restricted.

Early efforts to organise and protect crafts would similarly have involved more assemblies and oaths and libations than the handful of gilds of which we know. Those which have left some mark on the royal records in the twelfth century did so either because, like the weavers of London, they won royal approval, or because the king moved to suppress them. Once again, Essex has no examples of its own, but one of the earliest craft gilds in

8 On urban gilds see F. W. Maitland, *Domesday Book and beyond*, Cambridge, 1897, 191, 201. On 'The gild merchant', see Tait, *The medieval English borough*, Manchester, 1936, 22–34.

London, the saddlers', had some Essex connections. From a later period, however, the Cutlers' guildhall at Thaxted is one of the county's most famous monuments.[9]

The first formal account of gilds in Essex dates from the late fourteenth century, in the returns made to an inquiry by the crown into the numbers and constitution of gilds and fraternities in 1388–89. Behind the investigation there lie two centuries of economic and social change, accompanied, reflected, and sometimes led by developments in the liturgy and devotional practices of the Church. The concentration of wealth, power, and intellectual resources in the great religious houses of the eleventh and twelfth centuries had been followed by a dissemination of their accomplishments throughout society. Not only had the secular state gained strength from the administrative skills of the clergy, but the diffusion of wealth greatly increased the range and scope of patronage. The laity were more actively concerned with the church than ever before, and especially with the rebuilding and adornment of parish churches, and with the elaboration of their services.

Under that stimulus, gilds were established to maintain, enlarge, and furnish churches and the chapels, to support parish and gild chaplains, and to pay for particular prayers and other services. Most gilds, probably all, provided lights for altars and shrines, and kept vigils to maintain them. One strand in the beginning of the secular drama of later centuries can be traced to the elaboration of the liturgy at Easter, and the revelation of the empty sepulchre. The cult of the Eucharist itself, the feast of Corpus Christi, spread widely after the first quarter of the fourteenth century, and from 1349 onwards the visitations of the bubonic plague were a terrible stimulus to propitiatory and commemorative acts of piety.

Beyond those developments, which had their own power, the elaboration of society had multiplied the number of gilds with social and economic ends. However prosaic their objects they were provided with pious invocations and rituals, but the fact remained that the gild was as well suited to conspiracy and subversion as to social amenity and good works. In the anxious years of Richard II's minority the cumulative strains of the French

---

9 On the London saddlers, see G. H. Martin, 'The early history of the London saddlers' guild', *Bulletin of the John Rylands University Library of Manchester*, 72, no. 3, Autumn, 1990, 145–54. On Thaxted and its gild, see K. C. Newton, *Thaxted in the fourteenth century*, E.R.O. Publications, 33, Chelmsford, 1960.

*Figure 1.   Thaxted: The Gild or Motehall of the Borough, situate in the Market-Place (*Morant*).*

*Figure 2.   Steeple Bumpstead: A School-house was built here by the Inhabitants of Bumstead, before Queen Elizabeth's reign (*Morant*).*

wars and the dislocation caused by the plague produced an explosion of popular discontent in the rebellion of 1381, in which the men of Essex played a forward part, though the swiftness and confidence of their movements probably owed as much to recent military experience as to covert political debate. It was a time, nevertheless, for seeking scapegoats.[10]

Whilst most gilds with public functions were at pains to emphasise their cultivation of piety, the virtuous and loving peace which was enjoined amongst the fraternity was reinforced by oath, which even in the wholly pious gild of All Saints at Moreton extended to protecting the confidentiality of the gild's proceedings.[11] There was a manifest risk that bodies so constituted might be turned to seditious purposes, but the most respectable of gilds were also open to temptations of another kind. They were well known to hold property, and there was some suspicion that, like other members of the propertied classes, they had found means of avoiding the provisions of the Statute of Mortmain, under which the king sought to license all alienations in perpetuity, whether to churches or to trustees, in order to reduce his losses as overlord. The suspicion was not altogether ill-founded, though most gilds appear either to have had no endowment, or to have commanded only modest means.[12]

The government in 1388 was not the administration which had been confronted with the dangers of the revolt in 1381. It was the product of an aristocratic faction which in 1386 had used the unpopularity of the king's ministers to destroy them, and was now looking, not very successfully, for convincingly popular policies of its own. Beset by rising expenditure and the threat of further political disorder it was therefore moved to ask after the purposes, resources, and rules of gilds throughout the kingdom, and the

10 On the inquest into gilds, see H. F. Westlake, *The parish gilds of medieval England*, London, 1919. For the cult of Corpus Christi, see M. Rubin, *Corpus Christi: the Eucharist in the later Middle Ages*, Cambridge, 1991. On the revolt in Essex, see W. H. Liddell and R. G. Wood, *Essex and the great revolt of 1381*, E.R.O. Publications, 84, Chelmsford, 1982; and N. Brooks, 'The organization and achievements of the peasants of Kent and Essex in 1381', *Studies in medieval history presented to R. H. C. Davies*, eds. H. Mayr-Harting and R. I. Moore, London, 1985, 247–70.

11 For the statutes of the Moreton gild, which date from 1473, and a prayer, see T. H. Curling, 'The gild of All Saints, Moreton', *Transactions of the Essex Archaeological Society*, N.S. 11, 1911, 223–29.

12 S. Raban, *Mortmain legislation and the English Church, 1279–1500*, Cambridge, 1982, 171–73; J. L. Barton, 'The medieval use', *Law Quarterly Review*, 81, 1965, 562–67.

answers which survive, all irreproachably reassuring in tone, give us a detailed account of eight Essex gilds amongst the rest.

The inquiry was a solemn one, and the officers of the gilds were generally called upon to testify before the king's officials in Chancery in making their returns. They were asked for an account of the foundation, management, and resources of their gilds, together with a copy of their statutes and ordinances, and in many places it is clear that they conferred with their neighbours before committing themselves. Not all the statutes have survived, but it is clear that many returns have been lost altogether.

The certificates are drawn up variously in Latin, French, and English. Those in English were edited separately by Joshua Toulmin Smith for the Early English Texts Society in 1870, and the whole corpus was calendared by F. H. Westlake in 1919. At the same time the surviving certificates from Essex were published in full by R. C. Fowler in volume twelve of the Archaeological Society's *Transactions*. [13]

Three of the eight Essex gilds were at Walden, and two at Maldon, in All Saints' and St. Peter's churches. The others were at Chelmsford, Hatfield Broad Oak, and Rayleigh. All the returns are in Latin except that from Hatfield, which is in French. All the gilds dated were of fairly recent foundation: the officers at Chelmsford and Rayleigh used the same phrase, saying that they had been founded 'twenty years ago'; Hatfield gild began with a partnership to maintain a light, in 1362, which was expanded into a fraternity; the Maldon gilds dated from 1377 and 1379, and the Corpus Christi gild at Walden from 1377–78. No date is given for the other gilds at Walden. Of their dedications or invocations, four were in honour of the Holy Trinity, at Chelmsford, All Saints', Maldon, Rayleigh, and Walden, one of the Assumption (St. Peter's, Maldon), one of Corpus Christi and one of All Saints' (both at Walden). Only at Hatfield, where the parish used the nave of an Augustinian priory church, was the patronal saint explicitly invoked.

All the gilds collected dues from their members, which in the Trinity gild at Walden were specifically (and in the others perhaps silently) apportioned to their means. The gild at Hatfield and those at Maldon also benefited from property in the hands of trustees; only Hatfield admitted to owning chattels, in the form of

13 R. C. Fowler, 'The religious gilds of Essex', *Transactions of the Essex Archaeological Society*, N.S. 12, 1913, 280–90, prints the Essex certificates in full, with notes on thirty other gilds. Further notes follow in vols. 15, 1921, 98, 101; and 16, 1923, 59.

an unspecified vestment, though as we shall see a good deal of such property was probably taken for granted. The fullest reply came from the gild of the Assumption in St. Peter's, Maldon, which gave details of the services and collects which it supported, and also spoke of rolls of living members, and of the register or calendar in which the deaths of brethren (more precisely of gild-brothers and sisters, for all had women members) were noted for future commemoration.

The benefits of prayer, especially for the dead, were universally assumed, which was a measure of the extent to which the gild, though still a charismatic act in itself, had been assimilated to Christian thought. All the gilds provided lights for altars and images, and supported services of various kinds, which meant that all found fees for priests, whilst Hatfield and the Maldon gilds spoke of chaplains in terms which implied that they retained them for regular rather than for annual commemorative services. They also cultivated other good works, however. Beyond the common benefits of prayer and masses for members, living and dead, Hatfield undertook the repair of roads and the relief of the poor, and the Corpus Christi gild at Walden provided for the churching of poor women, the burial of poor strangers, the relief of women in childbirth, and other distributions of alms.

At Hatfield the certificate describes the way in which the gild began, and appointed two masters to collect and spend its dues, but gives no account of its annual routine. The aldermen of All Saints' and Trinity gilds at Walden said that their only rule was that the officers should be chosen annually at the patronal festival, and all the others had provisions which specify or imply the participation of all members in annual elections. The gild of the Assumption at Maldon, besides its other prescriptions, expected the chaplain to keep annual accounts of the dues, and provided for the removal of the names of brethren who were obstreperous, or tardy in paying. There was also a Michaelmas audit, held before all the fraternity.In the Maldon Trinity gild and at Chelmsford the elections were held at an annual feast, and the members wore livery hoods. Only the Walden gilds refer to their chief officer as the alderman, though that was the commonest usage, and one that derived from the earliest times in England.

If those were our only indications we might, even making allowance for the loss of some returns, have supposed that gilds in Essex were pious, useful, but far from common. They were in fact much more numerous, and although the evidence of their existence comes largely from the sixteenth century it greatly expands what we have from medieval sources.

When the monasteries were dissolved in the 1530s collegiate churches, chantries, and parochial endowments of all kinds were left undisturbed. By the end of Henry VIII's reign, however, they were marked for confiscation by the Statute 37 Hen. VIII c.4, and two commissions, one of 1546, and the second issued in Edward VI's name, in 1548, collected details of their functions and property. Chantries, which were endowed to secure the celebration of masses and other commemorative services, either in perpetuity or for terms of years, were both numerous and comparatively prominent. Gilds, on the other hand, although some were notably well endowed, were often more informal, and might subsist entirely upon the dues of their members. They were consequently more carelessly treated by the commissioners, who were primarily intent on real property. Nevertheless the returns add another twenty gilds to the list of 1388.[14]

Besides three additional gilds at Chelmsford and two at Maldon, the new gilds, which were all dissolved and disendowed, were at Ashdon, Belchamp Walter, Chigwell, Coggeshall, Danbury, Dovercourt, Feering, Finchingfield, Great Horkesley, Hornchurch, Prittlewell, Romford, Ulting, and two at Waltham Holy Cross. The priests of Corpus Christi, Chelmsford, and those of Finchingfield, Hornchurch, and Prittlewell, were charged with keeping a school. Most of the gilds were quite modestly endowed, and some are signalled only by the presence of a priest called the gild priest, whose presence implied some supporting endowment or stipend from a fraternity. Two are inferential: Danbury had a tenement called the Church House, the rent from which maintained the Paschal and other lights, and Horkesley had a small income from a croft given to support a drinking house for the poor.

In the absence of other evidence the last two endowments might be explained away as provisions peculiar to their parishes. The benefaction at Horkesley is by any standards certainly far removed from the spirit of the Poor Law Amendment Act of 1834, although it has post-Reformation echoes, long after the seizure and dispersal of gild lands, in the houses provided in some parishes to accommodate wedding-feasts for the poor. Both provisions have to be seen, however, in the context of the gild's central traditions: it was a congregation with religious overtones, and although in its origins it had been in conflict with the Christian

14 The gild and chantry certificates are in P.R.O. E301. For the assault on the chantries, see the introduction to C. J. Kitching, *London and Middlesex chantry certificates, 1548*, London Record Society, 16, 1980. On the Edwardian Reformation in Essex, see J. E. Oxley, *The Reformation in Essex*, Manchester, 1965, 150–78.

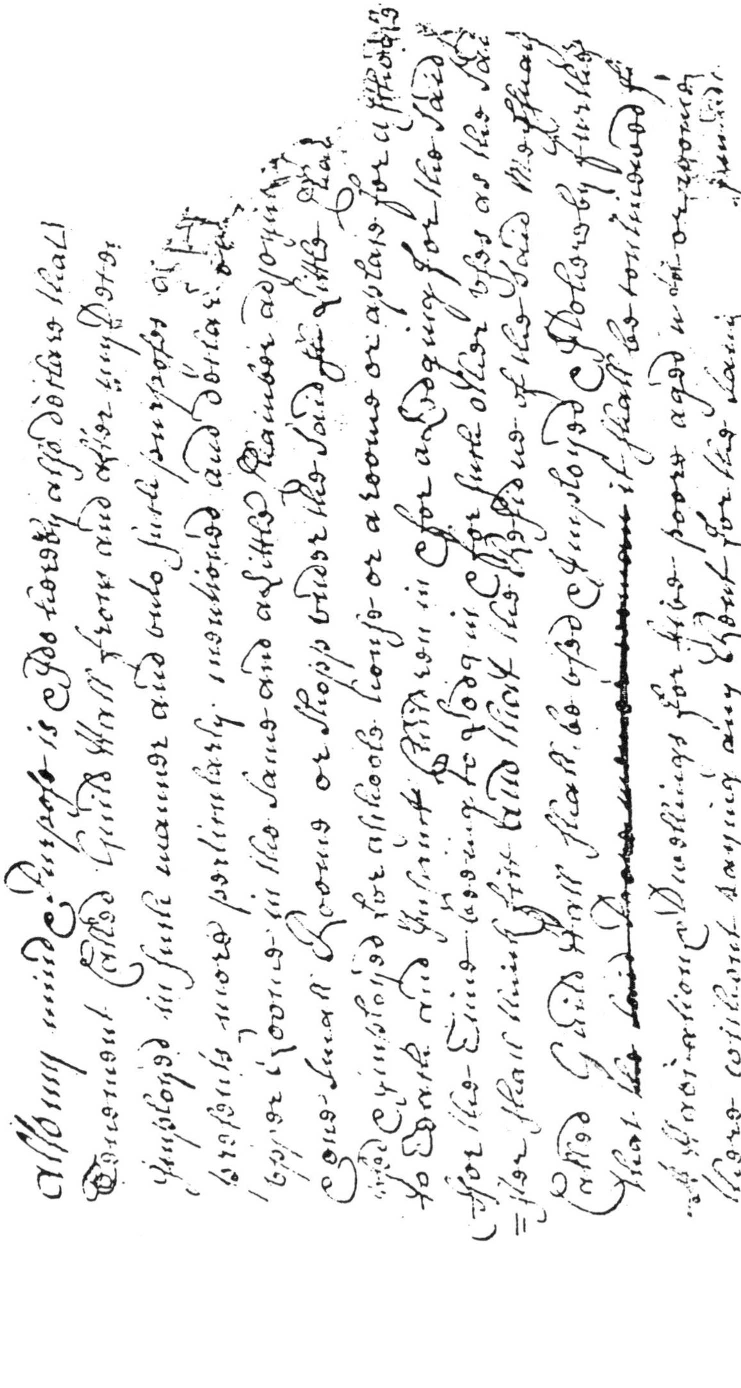

Figure 3.   *Finchingfield: Here was a gild called Trinity Gild* (Morant) (E.R.O., D/DRs Q3).

(Essex Record Office)

church, the great business of providing places of worship for every settlement, a legacy of the Middle Ages which continued to inform pastoral policy down to the twentieth century, had come to identify closely church, alehouse, and parish. There is abundant other evidence of such parochial drinking houses, which together with the church itself were constantly available for other kinds of business, and which ranged from the handsome tenement which still commands the entrance to the churchyard at Finchingfield to the merest shacks and cottages. That they survived and their use persisted alongside the more elaborately constituted gilds which characterise the late medieval parish is a measure of the indestructible vitality of the institution.[15]

Although the returns of the Tudor commissions swept both large and small gilds into the reformers' net (and the speculators' hands, for not all the zeal of the times was spent upon religion), there were evidently many more such bodies in late medieval Essex than appear in the schedules. Some undoubtedly escaped notice for want of means, and others were concealed for a longer or shorter time. As the law was directed against the application of endowments to superstitious practices, that is to say against prayers for the dead and the doctrine of Transubstantiation, it was technically possible for a craft-gild, for example, to continue to function, though extremely difficult for it to retain any endowment. Determined parishes could also rescue charitable funds: Canewdon, in the Crouch marshes, had two gilds, one of which was hunted down by the diligent seekers of concealed lands. The other, St. Anne's, had a fund to maintain lights in the church, and distributed any surplus to the poor in beans and herrings, in Lent. The parish still administered the dole in another form in Morant's day.[16]

Larger prizes called for greater exertions. At Saffron Walden, where the size of the church speaks for the late medieval textile trade, the burgesses had acquired some civic franchises, but not an untrammelled lordship over the soil of the town. The Holy

---

15 On the alehouses, see footnote 7 above. Morant has many notes of such church houses, and there may be others to be identified on the periphery of churchyards. The School House or Mote Hall of Steeple Bumpstead, is removed from the church, but has something of a gild house about it and is said to have been built by the parish 'before Elizabeth's reign': Morant, 2, 335.

16 H. H. Lockwood, 'Those greedy hunters after concealed lands', *An Essex Tribute: Essays presented to F. G. Emmison*, ed. K. J. Neale, London, 1987, 153–70.

Trinity gild, which appeared in 1388–89 as simply a religious brotherhood, embodied the leading citizens, and by joining them in the performance of pious works gave them the advantages of a political and social forum of the highest respectability. By 1514 they were in a position to negotiate for and purchase control of the town's market and mills, the last substantial perquisites of manorial lordship.

The town was now effectively autonomous, but in the 1540s the attack on gilds raised an obvious threat to the engine of its independence. The burgesses' solution was to obtain a royal charter in 1549 which effectively continued the gild in the irreproachable guise of a municipal corporation, with a senior brotherhood of twenty-four from whom the officers were chosen. A decade earlier the corporation of Colchester, a borough by prescription, and chartered since the late twelfth century, had rescued a valuable piece of patronage by dissolving two rich chantries, rather ahead of the field, to endow the town school. There had been a link between the two towns in the person of Thomas Audley, lord Audley of Walden, who was town clerk and an M.P. for Colchester before he became chancellor of the duchy of Lancaster, speaker, and Lord Chancellor. Audley was undoubtedly helpful to Colchester, and although he died in 1544 his daughter's marriage to Thomas Howard, duke of Norfolk, and more particularly his connection with the duchy of Lancaster, may have guided the Trinity gildsmen in their successful search for security.[17]

Colchester too had its civic social gild, refounded or reconstituted in 1407 in honour of God and St. Helen, in the church of the former house of the Crossed or Crouched Friars on the London road outside the Headgate. The friary had long since given place to a hospital, which the friars had probably first maintained, and which was now endowed to serve, after the manner of its time, simultaneously a religious, charitable, social, and political purpose. Fraternities for prayer and the maintenance of services needed no urging, neither did the relief of the poor and infirm; the enlargement of patronage was an end in itself, and so was the social life of a gild.

The cult of St. Helen, mother of Constantine, the first

17 For the Saffron Walden charter, see *Calendar of the Patent Rolls, 1548–9*, London, 1924, 211–12; for the gild lands, *ibid.*, 387–89. See further, Morant, 2, 545, 547–48, and G. H. Martin, *History of Colchester Royal Grammar School*, Colchester, 1947, and *The story of Colchester*, Colchester, 1959, 40, 45.

Christian emperor of Rome, and the discoverer of the True Cross, had its roots in the late Saxon town, and was revived in the early fifteenth century, when Helen was depicted with the Cross in the initial letter of Henry V's charter of 1413. The revival may have been a matter of conscious antiquarianism, evinced also in the borough's desire to bear arms, but the gild was a substantial body, with five chaplains, and provision for thirteen poor bedesmen to pray for the good estate of the gild and the town. It remained at the centre of the town's affairs, without constitutional functions, but a meeting ground for the successful and the ambitious, until the general demise of the sixteenth century.[18]

It did not stand alone in Colchester, although the town's gilds are not mentioned in the gild and chantry certificates. The leading burgesses and lesser men and women could apportion their time, means, and energies between more than a dozen gilds in the parish churches, chapels, and religious houses of the town. They included the Jesus Mass in St. Peter's, which maintained the water supply, a Corpus Christi gild in St. Nicholas's, a gild of the Virgin in the Greyfriars, and an interesting gild of St. James in the Old Hythe, or Old Heath, which may or may not have been a manifestation of an unnamed gild in St. Giles, the parish church of that superseded haven.[19]

A parishioner of St. James's referred in 1435 in his will to gilds of St. James, St. John, All Saints, and St. Francis, all apparently in St. James's, and all, some, or none of which may have been busy with the plays which were being staged there in 1490, to support building work in that large church, when a royal

---

18 For the gild of St. Helen, see W. G. Benham, ed., *The Oath Book or Red Parchment Book of Colchester*, Colchester, 1907, 24–25.

19 There are many notices of gilds in Colchester wills and the borough court rolls; I am grateful to Dr. Janet Cooper for notes of the following: All Saints (St. Barbara, 1507, E.R.O. D/ACR 1, f.127); Greyfriars (Our Lady, St. Anne, 1517, E.R.O. D/ACR 2, f.58); St. Giles's (1511, E.R.O. D/ACR 2, f.9v); St. James's (1435, Borough Court Roll 63, r.9); St. Leonard's (Our Lady, St. Helen, St. Leonard, 1486, P.R.O. PROB 11/8, f.317v; Jesus Mass, 1520, E.R.O. D/ACR 2, ff.109v, 140v); St. Nicholas, (Corpus Christi, 1448, Borough court roll 63, r.12; St. Nicholas, 1534, E.R.O. D/ACR 3, f.1); St. Peter's (St. John, 1443, Borough court roll 62, r.10; 1457, St. John and St. Barbara, P.R.O. PROB 11/4, f.149; Jesus Mass, 1488, P.R.O. PROB 11/8, f.136v). For the gild at Old Heath, E.R.O. D/ACR 1, f.101v. There was also a demimonde of what might be called involuntary gilds: an entry in the Oath Book denounces the town serjeants for holding *bedales* and fining people for not attending them. W. G. Benham, ed., *The Red Paper Book of Colchester*, Colchester, 1902, 14.

proclamation was read at the East Gate of the town. They cannot have been the only performances of their kind, but we know about them because the occasion of the proclamation was noted by the town clerk. Chelmsford had plays, the tradition of which was exceptionally renewed after the Reformation. The much smaller town of Braintree had plays in the 1520s on various days, and feasts and other celebrations amongst a range of gilds including a plough gild, a torch gild, a title which almost any church gild might use, a gild of SS. Crispin and Crispinian, which was probably for leather-workers, and a women's gild presided over by an alderwoman.[20]

Colchester was not an exceptionally pious town, and indeed had some early experience of Lollardy in the fifteenth century as well as being a centre of Protestantism in the sixteenth. The numbers and activities of its gilds, like those of Braintree, were a function of its civic life, a register of social purpose, in an age when religious forms, expressed in and furthered by formalised surrogate brotherhood, were the natural means of recruiting and directing communal energies.

So were the unnumbered gilds of the countryside, in village churches and chapels, and in their modest gildhalls, the traces of which are dispersed amongst individual testaments, the Edwardian parish inventories, and the proceedings in pursuit of concealed lands, to be purposefully gathered together first by Philip Morant in the eighteenth century, and then by the Victoria County History in our own day. Their records, vestments, furniture, brewing tubs, cups and flagons, have vanished from our sight, but not wholly from our knowledge, and some of their works live on.[21] They are monuments of an extraordinarily resilient and useful institution which sustained and advanced European society for almost a millenium, and which has been substantially underrated since it gave place to other, certainly more prosaic, and perhaps more sober, forms of association. Its role in medieval Essex was no minor part of the county's life.

Acknowledgement; I am grateful for the support of a Leverhulme Emeritus Fellowship in the preparation of this paper. – G.M.

20 For the proclamation, see W. G. Benham, ed., *The Red Paper Book of Colchester*, Colchester, 1902, 109. For Braintree, see Morant, *History and antiquities of Essex*, 1768, 2, 399–400. There was a gild at Manningtree with a feast that echoes in *Henry IV, part 1* (2.4), see Morant, 1, 463.

21 The Edwardian inventories of church goods are printed in *Transactions of the Essex Archaeological Society*, N.S. 1–3. They include the sale of gild and parish utensils, including brass pots and vessels at St. Osyth, 1, 23.

Elizabeth de Burgh and Great Bardfield in the fourteenth century

JENNIFER WARD

SEVERAL PLACES IN Essex have castles associated with the medieval nobility, such as Castle Hedingham, Pleshey and Saffron Walden, but relatively little is known as to the impact of noble residence on the surrounding community. Historians have suggested that the existence of the castle or great house and the presence of the lord from time to time encouraged local trade and attracted new inhabitants, and certainly markets and fairs often became established in such places in the twelfth and thirteenth centuries. Yet it is difficult to prove in any detail the sort of impact which the lord's household had, as manorial accounts and court rolls were primarily concerned with the manor and rights of lordship and only incidentally with the life of the lord or lady. Baronial household accounts however often throw light on patterns of residence and purchase as well as on the style of life enjoyed by the nobility, and therefore it is possible to gauge from them the importance of the local community to the lord, whether it was a question of securing provisions, finding servants and labourers, or making use of the parish church. The greatest survival of these accounts for the fourteenth century comes from the household of Elizabeth de Burgh, lady of Clare, who had one of her principal residences in Great Bardfield and spent a considerable part of her life there.

Elizabeth de Burgh was one of the wealthiest and most powerful noblewomen of the fourteenth century, and her interests extended far beyond Essex.[1] She was born in 1295, the youngest daughter of Gilbert de Clare, earl of Gloucester and Hertford, and his second wife, Joan of Acre, daughter of Edward I. Elizabeth and her two sisters were in the centre of the political turbulence of Edward II's reign after their brother, the last Gilbert de Clare, earl

---

1 Elizabeth de Burgh's life and activities are discussed more fully in Jennifer C. Ward, *English Noblewomen in the Later Middle Ages*, forthcoming.

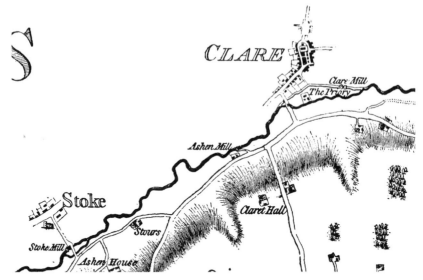

Figure 1. Clare, taken from the Chapman and André map of Essex, 1777. Clare and Claret Hall were both demesne manors of the honour of Clare and the Benedictine priory at Stoke had close ties with the honour. Elizabeth herself was a benefactor of the priory of Augustinian friars at Clare

(Essex County Record Office)

of Gloucester, was killed at the battle of Bannockburn in 1314, leaving no son to succeed him. The Clares can be described as the leaders of the baronage, and the division of their estates in England, Wales and Ireland among Gilbert's sisters and heiresses was not made until 1317. The delay was partly due to the king's desire to ensure that the heiresses' husbands were trusted and loyal. Elizabeth's first marriage to John de Burgh, the eldest son of the earl of Ulster, only lasted about five years, as he died in 1313. In 1316 she made a runaway match without the king's consent with Theobald de Verdun who may well have had his eye on her potential inheritance but who died a few months after the marriage. The following year she was married to the royal favourite Roger Damory and the inheritance was partitioned shortly afterwards, Elizabeth receiving as her one-third share lands in Dorset, the lordship of Usk in Gwent, and much of the honour of Clare in the eastern counties which was administered from Clare castle.[2] The years after 1317 saw her and her husband involved in rebellion because her brother-in-law and royal

2 P.R.O., C47/9/25, m.1.

favourite, Hugh le Despenser the younger, took over Usk; Roger died in 1322, but Elizabeth played an active part in backing Queen Isabella's invasion which led to the deposition of Edward II five years later. Elizabeth never remarried after 1322, but lived as a widow until her death in 1360. She was responsible for running her household and estates, and it is from this time that we know most about her way of life.

Great Bardfield had been one of the demesne manors of the honour of Clare since the late eleventh century, and had always been kept in the family's hands, supplying them with food and revenue. The size of the population before the Black Death of 1348–49 is not known, but the reference to forty customary (unfree) tenants in Earl Gilbert de Clare's inquisition *post mortem* in 1314 points to a fairly large community;[3] the number of freeholders who were numerous in this part of Essex was not specified. The assessments for taxation in 1327 and 1332 only gave the better-off members of the community, listing twenty-four men in 1327 and twenty-five five years later.[4] Only three men paid the minimum tax of sixpence in 1327, and it is likely that a large number of inhabitants were considered too poor to be taxed, having less than the minimum of ten shillings' worth of goods. The highest tax on both occasions was paid by Elizabeth de Burgh, but there were three men in 1327 and five in 1332 who paid tax of five shillings or more and therefore had moderate wealth.

The relationship between the lady and her tenants can be seen in the surviving manor court rolls for 1350–51.[5] The court was held on Thursday at three-weekly intervals. The tenants themselves brought their own pleas of trespass, debt and detinue against their neighbours which were determined by a jury of inquiry or by settlement out of court. These cases throw light on both agricultural and industrial pursuits, as when Robert Orgor was found guilty of trespass against John Crowe because Robert's wife had taken wheat from John's barn, or when John le Gardiner accused John de Poley of keeping fifteen ells of cloth which he had handed over to him for fulling.[6] The overwhelming impression

---

3 P.R.O., C134 file 42, m.3.

4 *The Medieval Essex Community: the Lay Subsidy of 1327*, ed., Jennifer C. Ward, Essex Historical Documents I, E.R.O., Publication no. 88, Chelmsford, 1983, 54. P.R.O., E179/107/17, m.24d.

5 P.R.O., SC2/171/16. No. 16 m.1 has a few items dating from 1318-19 when Roger Damory was lord, and some items from after Elizabeth's death.

6 P.R.O., SC2/171/16, m.3.

from the court rolls is however of the extent to which Elizabeth de Burgh was vigorously pursuing her rights as lady of the manor. Suitors who did not attend the court were fined, as were aletasters who did not carry out their office; John Raven and Richard atte Forde were fined threepence each for this at the court of 30 September, 1350.[7] Entry fines and reliefs were levied for the acquisition of or succession to land, and new tenants performed fealty at the court. Numerous trespasses on the lady's crops were punished, as when Geoffrey Wolston was fined because his pigs were found in the lady's wheat.[8] Dues were collected from unfree tenants, such as heriot, the payment of the best beast at the death of a villein; one foal was handed over as heriot from Alice Crowe who had held one messuage and thirty acres of land.[9]

There are a few pointers to the resentment over serfdom which was to snowball over the next thirty years. The number of labour services due from a whole and from a half virgate were ordered to be certified to the court.[10] A few holdings were leased out in return for a money rent, a sign that it was difficult to find holders for all vacant lands after the Black Death on the old terms; for instance, the lady gave Thomas Wymer a croft containing sixteen acres of land on a five year lease at a rent of ten shillings a year.[11] In a few cases tenants refused to perform labour-services; at the court of 7 April, 1351, John Russel was summoned to explain why he did not turn up to make faggots, and John Crowe and William Conyn were fined twopence each later in the year for not coming to hoe and weed.[12] There is no sign that Elizabeth de Burgh was making personal interventions in the court, but her officials ensured that her rights were maintained.

The wealth of the medieval nobility was derived primarily from land, and it was usual in the thirteenth and first half of the fourteenth century for estates to be farmed directly by their officials rather than leased out. It was essential for demesne manors to be run profitably and efficiently, and important manors were put under the control of a bailiff or serjeant and also of a reeve who was a local villein responsible for day to day farming operations. At Great Bardfield, as on other Clare manors, a policy of demesne expansion through the acquisition of smallholdings was pursued in the later thirteenth and early fourteenth century,

7 *Ibid.*, m.2.   10 *Ibid.*, m.5.

8 *Ibid.*   11 *Ibid.*, m.4.

9 *Ibid.*   12 *Ibid.*, m.4d, 7.

and Elizabeth continued this policy at Bardfield.[13] As a result, the lands she succeeded to in 1317 were much more extensive than they had been half a century before. When her grandfather, Richard de Clare, earl of Gloucester, died in 1262, Great Bardfield was valued at £59. 19s. 0d. and the demesne arable land amounted to 491 acres. By 1314 the arable had increased to 841 acres, and rents of freemen had risen from just under £10 to nearly £19. At the time of the 1317 partition the manor was said to be worth £124. 18s. 9d.[14]

The emphasis on all the Clare demesne manors in the eastern counties at this time was on grain production, notably wheat and oats. At Bardfield in 1314 there were only twenty-two acres of pasture and twenty-five acres of meadow. The grain went to supply the lord's household or was sold. The other main source of revenue was rents, and only small sums accrued from the market, windmill and manorial court. The park was more profitable, as, apart from providing venison and firewood for the lord, some wood could be sold and pasture rented out, bringing in £1 and £4 respectively in 1314.[15]

The valuation of 1317 marks the peak of Bardfield's farming prosperity, and with the fall in grain prices before the Black Death Elizabeth de Burgh and her officials had to adapt their agricultural policy on all her demesne manors. Four accounts for Great Bardfield survive for the years between 1337 and 1348 together with two valuations for all Elizabeth's estates for 1329–30 and 1338–39;[16] it is unfortunate that no accounts survive for the period after the Black Death. The drop in value is apparent in the valuation of 1329–30 when the borough and manor together were said to be worth £80. 15s. 10d. and there had been a loss of nearly £14 on the arable husbandry. There was some improvement by 1338–39 when borough and manor were valued at £89. 19s. 0d. The demesne acreage however fell to about 300 acres by the early 1340s. Wheat and oats remained the principal crops, 188¾ quarters of wheat and 230½ quarters of oats being harvested in

13 British Library, Additional MS. 6041, fos. 64v–66.

14 *Close Rolls, 1261–64*, 291. P.R.O., SC11, Roll 610; C132 file 27(5), m.27; C134 file 42, m.3; C47/9/25, m.1.

15 P.R.O., C134 file 42, m.3.

16 P.R.O., SC6/836/7, 8, 10, 12; the figures are tabulated in C. A. Holmes, *The Estates of the Higher Nobility in Fourteenth-Century England*, Cambridge, 1957, 155. P.R.O., SC11/799, m.7; SC11/801, m.4d; these figures are tabulated in Holmes, *op.cit.*, 143–47.

1338–39, but grain no longer had the overwhelming importance that it had had at the beginning of the century. Instead, Elizabeth had diversified into livestock, especially sheep, and Bardfield supported a flock of about 340 sheep in 1338–39. A similar policy was followed on all her demesne manors in the eastern counties. As a result her main sources of revenue from Bardfield came to be derived from both arable and animal husbandry as well as from rents which remained at about the same level as in 1314. Costs were kept low through the use of labour-services of the customary tenants.

In addition to the revenue from the demesne manors, the lady's household relied on them for its basic food supplies. Amounts varied from year to year as the household officials determined what was needed; any surplus left on the manor would be sold. The provisions were taken to wherever the lady was living; Bardfield did not only supply food when the lady was resident on the manor. Thus in 1336–37 the manor supplied nearly eighty-three quarters of wheat, five quarters of malt barley, sixty quarters of oats, two oxen, four cows, one boar and twenty pigs. In 1349–50, however, the officials needed nearly twelve quarters of wheat and sixteen quarters of barley, about ninety-eight quarters of oats and six quarters of peas, two boars and ninety-one pigs, 13,860 faggots, and one cartload of litter.[17] The household used wheat for bread and barley for ale, and the large quantities of oats are a reminder of the importance of horses for transport and travel.

All Elizabeth's demesne manors were run in this way, whether she was resident or not. Her officials were responsible for organising the farming, supplying the household, handing over money to the lady's receiver at Clare, and regulating relations with tenants through the manor-court, and, although the lady was ultimately responsible for the running of her estates, there was little call for her to intervene. Twice a year her auditors visited the manor, to take the view of account half way through the year, and to audit the full accounts after Michaelmas (29 September). Estate policy, such as the decision to develop sheep farming, was decided by the lady in consultation with her councillors who included her auditors and top officials, and was implemented by the bailiffs on the individual manors.

It made little difference to the day-to-day running of the manor whether the lady was there or not, but Elizabeth's lengthy

17 P.R.O., E101/92/4, m.1; 93/6, m.1.

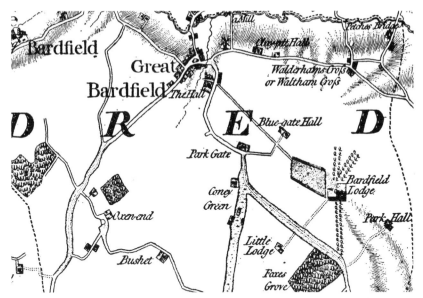

Figure 2. Great Bardfield, taken from the Chapman and André map of Essex, 1777. Place-names indicate the site of Elizabeth de Burgh's park. The present Hall dates from the sixteenth century.

(Essex Record Office)

stays at Bardfield may well have brought some business and employment to the village. By the early fourteenth century the English nobility was not travelling as frequently between residences but staying longer in each place. Elizabeth de Burgh maintained her castles at Clare and Usk, had residences at Anglesey in Cambridgeshire and at Bardfield Hall, and towards the end of her life in 1352 built a house in the outer precinct of the convent of the Minoresses outside Aldgate in London. She spent more time in Eastern England than at Usk, and once settled at a place she usually stayed several months, often paying short visits elsewhere during her stay. Between March and September 1334, for instance, she divided her time between Anglesey, Clare and Bardfield, being at Bardfield for much of the summer between the middle of June and early September, although she made visits to Saffron Walden and Pleshey. She was at Bardfield from the end of September 1339, until the beginning of February 1340, returning to Clare in mid-December for the funeral of her half-brother, Sir Edward de Monthermer. She spent at least eighteen months at Usk between 1348 and 1350, but once back at Clare in April 1350, she passed the summer at Clare and Bardfield. Once she had her

London house, she divided her time between London, Clare and
Bardfield; thus she was at Bardfield from the end of November
1357, until the beginning of May 1358.[18]

When moving from one residence to another, the medieval
nobility travelled with their households, and it is therefore
unlikely that Elizabeth's stays at Bardfield gave employment to
local people within the household. There was only a skeleton staff
at Bardfield when she was not there; the 1342—43 account
provided for the wages of John de Thrillowe the chaplain,
Laurence le Porter and a groom working in the court and the
garden.[19] Once it was decided to change residences, all household
departments had to pack up and be ready to move. The main
departments were the chapel, the hall where the lady presided
over dinner and supper, the chamber where she worked with her
ladies and slept, the stables, and the departments concerned with
food — the kitchen, larder, poultry, saucery, bakery and buttery.
All these were essential considering the amount of cooking,
processing and preserving food necessary in a large household
which frequently entertained visitors. The scullery was in charge
of dishes, many of them of silver and silver-gilt. The wardrobe was
responsible for purchases of spices, wax and parchment, and the
clerk of the wardrobe was in overall charge of household pro-
visioning and organisation. Each department had horses and carts
assigned to it when the household moved. In early August 1334,
two horses were needed to carry the kitchen pots, and one horse
carried the hall furnishings from Clare to Bardfield; presumably
the main item here was the hangings of worsted or tapestry which
were usually bright and colourful, like those of tawny worsted with
blue parrots and cockerels which Elizabeth left to her daughter in
her will.[20]

Although the whole household accompanied the lady to
Bardfield, it is likely that extra casual labour was needed from
time to time on building work and in the park. The 1334 account
shows that the buildings at Bardfield were inadequate for all the
household operations, and it is possible that the Clares had not
used Bardfield much as a residence before Elizabeth's time.
During her stay at Bardfield in 1334 the officials of the saucery
went over to Clare to see to the salting and mustard. William de

18 P.R.O., E101/92/2; 92/12; 93/4; 93/20.

19 P.R.O., SC6/1110/10, m.4d.

20 *Ibid.*, 92/2, m.6d, 8d. J. Nichols, *A Collection of All the Wills of the Kings
and Queens of England*, London, 1780, 34.

Stoke went back to Clare to see to the office of the larder. Four men stayed at Clare for fifty-seven days while the lady was at Bardfield to deal with the baking and brewing because, as the account says, of the lack of houses at Bardfield.[21] These deficiencies were remedied by new building in the early 1340s, and the resulting residence must have been extensive. The accounts refer to the great gate and outer court; probably the offices of the household were located in the outer court, while the hall and chambers were round an inner court. In addition to the lady's chamber, references are found to the king's chamber, the Ferrers chamber, presumably used by the lady's daughter Isabella and her husband, the Marshal chamber, and the chamber of the clerks.[22]

What is not clear is how much of the paid labour for this work came from Bardfield itself. When a new timber-framed building was erected in 1343–44, one of the two carpenters was named as John de Berdefeld, and 18,000 tiles were bought from tilers in Bardfield and Stebbing for £1. 16s. 0d.[23] Sawyers, tilers, daubers, carters and labourers were employed although usually only for short periods, like the two men who helped the carpenters for sixteen and a half days to raise the house and who received 1½d. a day each. These men were in all probability local. Labour was also required regularly in the park, and in 1351–52 certain Bardfield tenants petitioned for the payment of their wages for work in the park in the year of the plague.[24] Here obviously local labour had been used.

As well as generating some employment, Elizabeth's residence brought some extra business to the locality. Great Bardfield had had a market since the early thirteenth century, but it is likely to have been small as stallage and toll of the market were only valued at £1. 6s. 8d. in 1314.[25] The valor of 1329–30 recorded that the borough was worth £9. 10s. 10d, and it was worth approximately the same in the valor of 1338–39.[26] This figure however would include rents as well as market profits, but it may reflect

21 P.R.O., E101/92/2, m.1d, 4d, 11, 13d.

22 P.R.O., SC6/1110/10, m.4; 1110/25, m.3, 3d.

23 P.R.O., E101/458/4, m.1.

24 P.R.O., SC6/1110/25, m.1.

25 R. H. Britnell, 'Essex Markets before 1350', *Essex Archaeology and History*, XIII, 1981, 15. P.R.O., C134 file 42, m.3.

26 P.R.O., SC11/799, m.7; 801, m.4d.

some increased business as a result of the lady's residence. The size and type of purchases depended on the lady's needs and varied from year to year. Elizabeth was not dependent on local markets for her supplies of wine, cloth and furs which she usually bought in the larger towns, including London, or at the great fairs. Fish mostly came from the East Coast, Usk and the River Severn, and much of her meat from her Midland manors or the region round Usk. Yet if she were in residence in the eastern counties, she often needed more barley, oats and hay than her demesne manors could supply; normally little wheat had to be purchased. In these circumstances her officials made purchases within the region, making use of markets on the demesne manors and elsewhere. Thus in 1337–38 wheat and oats were bought in the markets at Bardfield and Clare, and extra purchases of oxen and pigs were made at Bardfield. The lady's officials were also buying supplies in other places including Dunmow, Stebbing, Birdbrook, Royston, Braintree and Bishop's Stortford.[27] The lady's residence probably encouraged some trade in basic commodities, but at Bardfield it was not a demand for very large quantities. In 1337–38, the household purchased about 600 quarters of oats, as compared with about 300 quarters supplied from the demesne manors. Of this only about four quarters came from Bardfield market, and the quantities bought in Stebbing, Birdbrook, Clare, Standon in Hertfordshire, and Wisbech in Cambridgeshire were far larger. In the same year, the household purchased six quarters of wheat, six cows, two oxen and ten pigs in Bardfield. The lady's connection with the village did not bring great business to the local market.

Apart from some use of local labour, a varying amount of local purchases and almsgiving to the poor, there was little contact between the lady and her household in residence at Bardfield Hall and the village community. Household and village had their own duties and work and their own routines. A possible point of contact was the parish church, but it has to be remembered that Elizabeth de Burgh had her own chapel and chaplains and only occasionally attended the parish church. One such occasion may well have been Palm Sunday, 1352, when 6s. 8d. was paid to an Augustinian friar who preached in Bardfield church. Requiem masses for her officials were sometimes said in parish churches, as for her councillor Thomas de Cheddeworth in February 1352 in Bardfield and Finchingfield churches, as well as

27 P.R.O., E101/92/7, m.1–3.

in the lady's chapel.[28] Elizabeth remembered the parish churches of her demesne manors in her will, leaving to Bardfield £3 and a cloth of gold.[29] Whether she had any part in the erection of the stone screens at Bardfield and Stebbing is not known. The Stebbing screen certainly dates from her lifetime, but the Bardfield one probably dates from after her death.

At Bardfield as at her other residences Elizabeth de Burgh followed a lifestyle which was utterly different from that of the local community. Wherever she was living she was occupied with the administration of her estates, litigation, and relations with the Crown and the government. Estate matters were discussed and decisions reached as when it was decided at Bardfield to lease the ironworks at Tudeley in Southfrith Chace near Tonbridge to Richard Colepeper in 1354.[30] Letters were sent to officials on other estates; Robert Wulwy was sent from Bardfield to Cranborne in Dorset in 1351 with letters to the receiver, the financial official of that bailiwick.[31] Councillors such as Sir John de Wauton of Wimbish and Sir Andrew de Bures of Acton in Suffolk journeyed to Bardfield for meetings with the lady and were sent off to carry out her orders. In addition to acting on business matters, they represented the lady on ceremonial occasions, as when three councillors went from Bardfield to Bury St. Edmunds for the funeral of Thomas de Brotherton, the Earl Marshal, in 1338.[32] After the funeral one of the councillors went on to Cambridge on the lady's business.

When Elizabeth de Burgh was at Bardfield, there was constant coming and going of officials and messengers. Food supplies arrived from other parts of the country, such as the 109 oxen purchased at Usk and driven to Bardfield in 1336.[33] Griffith Balon who brought lampreys and salmon from Usk to Bardfield in January 1352, was rewarded with 12d. by the lady, while John Odmel who brought herons from Usk received 3s. 4d.[34] Venison

28 *Ibid.*, 93/12, m.3, 4.

29 J. Nichols, *A Collection of all the Wills of the Kings and Queens of England*, London, 1780, 33.

30 M. S. Giuseppi, 'Some fourteenth-century accounts of ironworks at Tudeley, Kent', *Archaeologia*, lxiv, 1912–13, 149–50.

31 P.R.O., E101/93/8, m.10.

32 *Ibid.*, 92/9, m.11.

33 *Ibid.*, 92/3, m.3.

34 *Ibid.*, 93/12, m.2, 4d.

was regularly procured in the park at Bardfield, but in August and September 1338, Robert Mareschal was away on the Dorset and Welsh estates taking venison.[35] In October 1339, John de Claketon was sent into Cambridgeshire to take pheasants.[36] There was moreover a constant interchange of letters with members of the nobility and leading Churchmen. In October 1338, Nicholas Throm was sent from Bardfield to Newport in South Wales on the lady's business to her sister, Margaret Audley, countess of Gloucester, while Thomas Scales was sent off to find the earl; the reference in the accounts to his going to Nottinghamshire, Leicestershire and Northamptonshire indicates that he only had a rough idea where the earl was. The journey from Bardfield to the bishop of London at Southminster in 1356 was considerably easier.[37]

Although it was essential for Elizabeth de Burgh to be aware of what was happening on her estates and to run them efficiently, it would be a mistake to think of her only in connection with business. With an income of about £2,500 a year, she was wealthier than many barons and could afford to live lavishly. Her household accounts and her will show that she enjoyed rich furnishings and clothes, and dispensed hospitality on a grand scale. Through her entertaining she was in touch with the royal family and many of the leading members of the nobility throughout her life. A large number of these people were entertained at Bardfield, and the omissions, such as her especial friend, Marie de St. Pol, countess of Pembroke, may be the result of losses among the household accounts. The scale of her entertaining is well illustrated by the daily accounts for 1343–44 when she was at Bardfield from 9 October until 19 January. Visits were generally limited to two or three days, but in a period of just over three months Elizabeth entertained thirteen people, some of them more than once. In 1357–58, when she was at Bardfield from 28 November to 1 May, she entertained seven visitors, but the Black Prince visited her three times and William de Bohun, earl of Northampton twice.[38]

Elizabeth de Burgh enjoyed the company of her family and friends and she was related to the royal family and to many nobles. Her visitors can be divided into her immediate family, kinsmen,

35 *Ibid.*, 92/7, m.4.

36 *Ibid.*, 92/11, m.11.

37 *Ibid.*, 92/9, m.11; 93/19, m.11.

38 *Ibid.*, 92/24, m.2–10; 93/20, m.8–26; 23d–25d.

friends and neighbours, and business visitors, and examples of all these categories can be found at Bardfield. Her only son, William de Burgh, earl of Ulster, was killed in 1333, so her heiress was his daughter, Elizabeth, countess of Ulster, who married Edward III's second son, Lionel of Antwerp. Elizabeth made regular visits to her grandmother, as when at the age of twelve she was fetched from Bury St. Edmunds for a five day visit to Bardfield in December 1344, and taken back to Bury afterwards.[39] Elizabeth de Burgh had one daughter by her second marriage and one by her third, and both visited her at Bardfield. Isabella was the wife of Henry de Ferrers of Groby, and Elizabeth married Sir John Bardolf of Wormegay in Norfolk. Isabella was fetched from Groby to Bardfield immediately after the funeral of her husband in the autumn of 1343, and it is probable that her mother's officials saw to it that Isabella received her inheritance and dower. In early December Sir Bartholomew de Burghersh was recorded as visiting Bardfield; his wife and Isabella were two of the four daughters and co-heiresses of Theobald de Verdun, and it is likely that Bartholomew was making a business visit connected with the inheritance.[40]

Elizabeth de Burgh's friends and neighbours included the Bohun earls of Hereford and Essex and the de Vere earls of Oxford whom she often entertained and with whom she exchanged visits. Earl John de Vere and his wife Matilda sometimes came to Bardfield together but more often on their own, and usually only stayed for the day; this practice of husbands and wives making separate visits was widespread among the medieval nobility. The most frequent Bohun visitors were William de Bohun, earl of Northampton, and his wife who came for two or three days; William and Elizabeth de Burgh were cousins, their mothers both being daughters of Edward I. Elizabeth's guests at Bardfield also included Ralph de Stafford and his wife who was Elizabeth's niece and who inherited her mother's share of the Clare inheritance (her mother was Margaret Audley, countess of Gloucester). They had made a runaway marriage when Ralph abducted her from Thaxted.[41]

Elizabeth de Burgh was the cousin of Edward III, and

39 *Ibid.*, 92/28, m.1.

40 *Ibid.*, 92/24, m.4, 7. Isabella de Ferrers died in 1349; Elizabeth Bardolf was the only one of the children to outlive her mother.

41 *Ibid.*, 92/12, m.5; 92/24, m.4–10; 93/20, m.8–26; 23d–25d. *Calendar of Patent Rolls 1334–8*, 298. Ralph became earl of Stafford in 1351.

entertained the king, queen and their children on various
occasions. She seems to have been particularly close to the Black
Prince who visited her three times at Bardfield in 1357–58.[42] The
account of his entertainment between 5 March and 7 March 1358,
illustrates Elizabeth's splendid hospitality to her guests. He was
not the only visitor at the time, as John Paschal, bishop of
Llandaff, was also there that week. Noble visitors brought a
retinue with them, and the number of people and horses who had
to be fed increased considerably. This is reflected in the accounts
for the stables; whereas fifteen horses, seven hackneys and three
oxen had to be fed on Friday, 2 March, on the following Monday
when the prince arrived the numbers grew to thirty-four horses,
eight hackneys and three oxen. As it was Lent no meat was served
in the household, and the basic diet consisted of bread, ale and
herrings. On Tuesday, 6 March, the pantry issued 290 loaves, the
buttery 100 gallons of ale, and the kitchen 488 herrings. There was
however greater variety for the lady, her guests and the leading
members of the household. Six sesters of wine were handed out by
the buttery,[43] and a great variety of fish was served by the kitchen,
including ten stockfish, three cod, one and a half salmon, eight
pike, six lampreys, four pieces of sturgeon, eels, fifty whiting,
forty-two codling, three sole and a quarter of a porpoise. Shellfish
included one crayfish, 650 whelks, and 400 oysters. Hospitality on
such a scale was needed in view of the size of the household and
the number of guests. In this way Elizabeth de Burgh proclaimed
her rank and status to her visitors and to the neighbourhood.

   When Elizabeth de Burgh was at Great Bardfield she and her
household formed a distinct and largely separate community from
the village. From time to time she made use of local labour and
purchased certain necessities in the market; she gave alms to the
poor and occasionally she attended the parish church. Yet she had
her own lifestyle and social and business commitments just as the
manor had its own routines and organisation. Lady and manor
were tied by custom, by the lady's rights and her tenants'
obligations, but otherwise they rarely came into contact, and the
lady's residence made little difference to local people's lives. Yet it
must have created considerable stir in the village as members of
the royal family and great nobles came and went, and as Elizabeth
de Burgh's officials and messengers kept her in touch with the
court, London and the rest of the country.

42 P.R.O., E101/93/20, m.9, 16, 21.

43 The sester usually contained four gallons.

The Essex Country Parson, 1700–1815

ARTHUR BROWN

BY 1723 ESSEX had ceased to be 'a place of most life of religion in the land'.[1] A Diocesan questionnaire of that year elicited not a word of 'enthusiasm' from Essex clergymen while, with the coming of Toleration, Nonconformity's early vigour was also subsiding. Yet beneath the complacency of official religion there remained some popular hunger for Christian brotherhood and some willingness to respond to appeals to the spirit. In 1739–41 Whitfield and Charles Wesley struck a note long absent from Anglican services.[2] Whitfield preached to four hundred on Wimbish Green, a thousand at Thaxted and two thousand at Saffron Walden; after the last event he and his friends returned through the night to Wimbish, 'singing and praising God', a performance by then unfamiliar to Essex ears. His congregation on Felsted Common was estimated at twelve thousand. Nor had the capacity for spiritual elation abated when in 1760, at Langham, John Wesley preached to a deeply moved congregation in a January sleet storm.[3]

Anglican clergymen felt pride in their detachment from such exhibitions of enthusiasm, yet took few steps to evoke more measured responses. Those Essex villagers who frequented a parish church in the abiding hope of a satisfying experience were often disappointed. They longed for moving sermons or, it seems, for any sermon at all. Panfield and Pentlow people stayed away if there was no sermon. A second Sunday service consisting only of prayers sent Cold Norton parishioners to any neighbouring parish

Note — Except when otherwise stated, the sources for this essay are Essex clergymen's own replies to Diocesan enquiries issued at intervals between 1723 and 1810. These may be consulted at the Essex Record Office on microfilm (T/A 778, 1–31). They are arranged alphabetically by parish.

1 *Historical Manuscript Commission, 7th Report, Part 1*, 1879, 551, 1643 John Hampton to Sir John Barrington.

2 *George Whitfield's Journals*, Iain Murray, 1959, 290.

where there was to be a sermon. Instead of heart-warming or uplifting worship in communion with parson and neighbours, congregations had frequently to endure perfunctory performances by curates loth to offer any stronger commitment than that merited by their miserable stipends, so that services were often sparsely attended and sometimes completely deserted. At Ashingdon they took place once a fortnight because otherwise 'a congregation cannot be had'. At Aveley there was no second Sunday service 'for want of a congregation'. At Birch there might be a second service 'when any will attend, which is hardly to be obtained in the Summer, in the Winter not at all'. At Little Baddow, Pattiswick, Steeple, Wennington and White Notley catechising had ceased and in several places Communion services had either been discontinued or, if held, were conspicuous for the advanced age of the communicants; the poor, too, were rarely present, though in better-off Dedham and Danbury attendance remained high. Meanwhile, church buildings were sometimes left unrepaired or even derelict. In 1709 Tillingham church had to be re-erected.[4] The Rector of Great Holland, on his induction, had to reconstruct a 'ruinous' chancel[5] and at Rayne, in 1756, John Powell arrived to find the building in decay, the pews rotting, the pulpit dangerous, the churchyard gateless and hogs rooting up the graves.[6]

Church life seems to have been almost non-existent. If clergymen did seek active support in their parish, which evidently they rarely did, they turned to the affluent and the well-born, a few of whom did respond. 'A worthy person' at Ugley built a parsonage at the cost of £600, and a few parishioners gave from their own pockets to repair Rayne church. On the other hand at High Easter and Little Parndon rich residents were reported to be indifferent and the Rector of Great Parndon could not 'induce the modern gentleman farmer to set a good example respecting religion to their servants and dependants'. Even when support was forthcoming, it involved no voluntary participation in church work, as the term was understood in later times. There was, it seems, almost a complete absence of the warm fellowship in church activity often observable in contemporary Nonconformity

3 N. Curnock, ed., *The Journals of the Revd. John Wesley*, 1909, vol. iv, 363.

4 P. Morant, *History of Essex*, 1768, vol. 1, 372.

5 The Revd. T. Crompton, *An Exact Diary of My Life*, ms., 1731–53.

6 E.R.O., D/P 136/3/2.

and to be experienced with Anglicanism a century later. Another feature of nineteenth century co-operation between clergy and laity rarely witnessed in the eighteenth century was joint endeavour in the promotion of Anglican schools. There was a mechanism by which such education could have been promoted. The Society for the Promotion of Christian Knowledge was eager to give advice and technical assistance in the founding of Charity Schools and in the early years of the century it did meet a small response. The squire's wife at Rivenhall in 1723 was paying school fees for some poor children, as were other well-off people at Little Dunmow and Great Wakering. The establishments where these children were taught, however, were dame schools, not Charity Schools of the recommended kind, of which few were founded in rural Essex before 1800.[7]

Some clergymen served with devotion and there certainly were others whose devotion has gone unrecorded. W. C. Unwin, Rector of Stock, was commended for:

> 'his weekly religious meetings at his own house; his fervent exhortations to his people from the pulpit; his familiar catechitical lectures to their children; his affectionate visits to their families; his vigilant attention to their temporal interests; his liberal supply of their wants . . . his inflexible opposition to the oppression of the powerful.'[8]

Thomas Barnard, of Little Bardfield, was known for 'great benevolence to the poor whose wants he relieved with a generosity becoming his station and genteel fortune' and for his 'worthy example to his brethren, the clergy in particular, for his discharge of his religious, moral and social duty'.[9] A Rector of Little Leighs was 'father to the fatherless and a strenuous asserter of the poor man's cause'. A Southminster curate worked for the welfare of the dependents of the sailors who had died at Trafalgar.[10] Others claimed to be zealous in performance of parochial duties. 'My Lord', wrote the Rector of Wimbish, 'I know of no such country parish as Wimbish is, where there is preaching twice a day all the year, which I constantly perform'. The Vicar of Hatfield Broad

7 See Report of Commission on Charities (Essex), H.C. 216, *passim.*

8 The Revd. F. W. Austen, *Rectors of Two Essex Parishes,* 1943, 328.

9 *Chelmsford Chronicle,* 5 July, 1773.

10 *Chelmsford Chronicle,* 20 April, 1776; *Essex Review,* no. 228, 176.

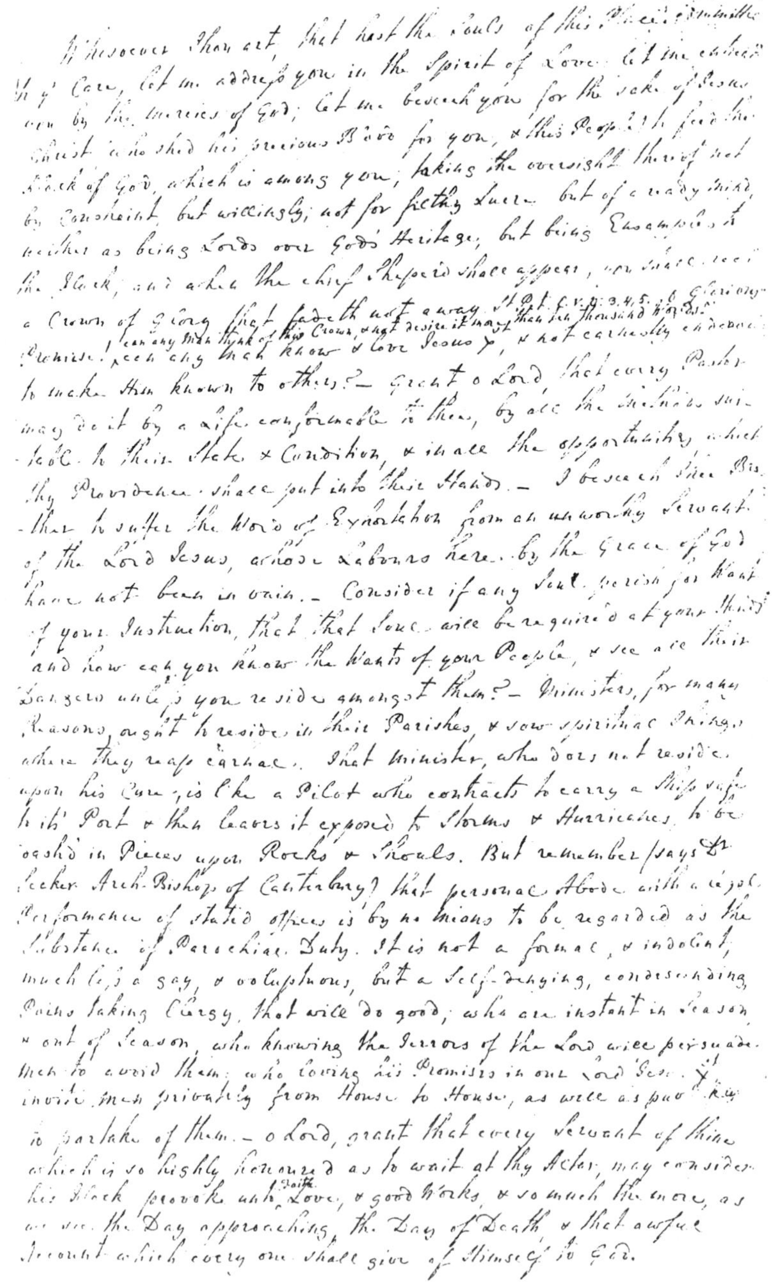

Figure 1. *Extract from the Vicar of Boxted's preface to the new Parish Register, c.1760.*

(Essex Record Office)

Oak took two services each Sunday, besides reading morning prayer during the week, 'when at home'. A Vicar of Boxted prefaced a new Parish Register with the words:

> 'That Minister, who does not reside upon his cure, is like a pilot who contracts to carry a ship safe to its port and then leaves it exposed to storms and hurricanes to be dashed in pieces upon rocks and shoals.'[11]

Others reminded their Bishop that they were not absentees, their vehemence implying that many were. 'I do live in my parsonage' wrote the Rector of Peldon, 'and have done so for thirty years and upwards, and nowhere else'. The Vicar of Clavering protested, as if denying an accusation, that 'I always do, and always have, resided personally upon my cure'. In 1738 the Rector of Little Baddow, after thirty-eight years in the parish, answered with some pride, 'I have one benefice and no more, and never would accept of any other cure, though earnestly invited to do so'. Some made an effort to visit the sick. In 1723 the Vicar of Great Bursted did so; the Rector of Cold Norton, though an absentee, claimed to do so; and the clergyman holding East Donyland and Layer Breton confessed to residing in neither but had 'a room already furnished in East Doniland where I often lye and go about to visit the sick'. The Ardleigh Vicar of 1736 performed this duty in his other parish, Great Wigborough, in the summer, and sometimes in the winter, too. The Rector of Widford admitted absenteeism but added that 'I keep up an acquaintance with some of the more substantial part of that parish and frequently relieve the wants of the poorer sort'. Philip Morant, who held Aldham along with a Colchester parish, would ride out to that village in his chariot when needed. He was also friendly with his one Quaker parishioner whom he described as 'of a most benevolent disposition and universally loved', a tribute to a Dissenter so rare as to merit recording; another was the statement of a Rector of Little Baddow that the local Congregationalists 'are a peaceable people . . . We live in harmony which I am unwilling to destroy'. The Colne Engaine curate wrote in 1723 that he held two services on Sundays and 'with particular care do catechise the youth every Lord's Day, looking upon this great duty . . . to be of the greatest service, especially in a country village of which, I bless God, I have had the most comfortable experience'.

The immediate cause of clerical neglect seems to have been the increasing pluralism and its accompanying absenteeism. Had

11 E.R.O., D/P 155/1/3.

parsons been minded to preach twice a Sunday or to open a school, they were too often not present to do so. A recent history of Stifford[12] discusses its five eighteenth century Rectors. The first failed to maintain the Registers for ten years. His two successors were absentees, keeping schools in Kent; the fourth, being Rector of Mucking, largely ignored Stifford; and the last, an active sportsman, employed curates there. Visitation questionnaires reveal that the first of these was a pluralist, who also held Rainham, and the last had the rich living of Sible Hedingham. How many villages enjoyed the undivided service of a parson with no other paid responsibility can be estimated from the replies of a majority of the Essex rural clergy to their Bishop between 1723 and 1778. The estimate is as follows:

1723–7	24%
1738–42	16%
1778	12%

The total situation may have been an even sorrier one, because some of those who failed to reply did so precisely because they were absentees. For devout, or would-be devout, Anglicans this was a time of discouragement, though there was another aspect; for Nonconformists or those resenting any religious doctrine being thrust upon them, clerical absenteeism could mean a greater degree of social freedom in the village.

Perhaps the most blatant pluralism occurred when London clergy were allowed an Essex parish to support their genteel style of living in the capital, a practice from which it was usually the Essex parish that was deprived of clerical services. A Vicar of Little Braxted took services at St. Sepulchre's, London, and as regards his Essex parishioners he wrote, 'my business in Town would not permit me to be with them above one Sunday each year'. A mere curacy in London deprived South Shoebury of its Rector's presence. A new Rector of West Tilbury started with the best intentions, only to succumb to the attraction of a London appointment, as his curate explained:

> 'Mr. Gough used to be at his parish twice or thrice a year and stay about a week . . . This last year he has not been down at all, which I believe is owing to the difficulties he labours under. I am informed that he is in London, where there I know not but am told he preaches for the Dean of Westminster at St. Martin's.'

12 Dean and Studd, *The Stifford Saga, 1180–1980*, 80, 116-9.

A Rector of Danbury was chaplain at the Royal Hospital, Greenwich, and admitted that 'my constant residence is in Greenwich'. The Rector of Dengie failed his Essex parishioners because,'I am daily employed in the parish of St. James, Westminster'; a Little Tey Rector, because he held the living of St. Mary de Bone; and the Vicar of Great Totham, because he was Vicar of St. Stephen's, Walbrook. The Rector of Great Stambridge did better, for his parishioners did see him for three months a year; however, he reserved six months for a small chapel at St. Martin's in the Field and the remaining three months for an unspecified activity.

An excuse for absenteeism, advanced by incumbents of Essex coastal parishes, was their dread of such unhealthy places. According to one of them, they preferred to live in Colchester where 'all the clergy of these parts live in hired houses'. Curates, too, shunned these parishes, one assuring the Bishop 'that your Lordship will not find another resident Minister . . . within several miles' of the coast. The reason, the incumbent of Southminster and Woodham Ferrers thought, was 'the unwholesomeness of the air'. One Rector feared 'fevers and agues', another 'the agueish air'. A Rector of North Ockendon was 'restless all the nights and faint all the days, when there'. The mud flats at South Shoebury were the explanation of why 'no Rector or Curate has been known to reside there without danger to his life'. The mere sight of Thorrington's mud flats sent one man straight back to St. John's College, Cambridge, which had presented him to that living. Thorpe-le-Soken had no resident Vicar, 'my health not permitting me to live so near the sea'. A Rector of East Mersea thought that 'the great damps . . . make it impossible for any but the natives to live there'. Others shunned coastal residences for family reasons, a Rector of Tolleshunt Knights being concerned for his young wife's health, a Rector of Foulness for his family's very lives. These refugees from the coast usually chose residence in a town or pleasant villages like Dedham, Colchester, Maldon, Danbury, Rayleigh or Ingatestone, each of which in consequence had a strong clerical presence.

Essex tithes did finance contributions to scholarship in a wide range of subjects. The work of Morant and John Howlett is well known, but there were a number of other scholars holding Essex livings.[13] Richard Biscoe, of North Weald Bassett, wrote on the veracity of The Acts, a Rector of Netteswell on *Ethics,*

13 *D.N.B.*, *passim.*

Figure 2.   Maldon Vicarage.
Mainly fifteenth century with some painted wall decoration surviving.

(John F. Buchan)

Figure 3.   Waltham Abbey Rectory.
Sixteenth century with seventeenth century additions.

(John F. Buchan)

Rational and Theological and a Rector of Stapleford Tawney on Ecclesiastical History. Thomas Rutherford, of Shenfield, was Professor of Divinity at Cambridge, where he taught Physics and wrote *A System of National Philosophy* and *Institutes of Natural Law*. A Rector of Bradwell became Professor of Astronomy at Cambridge, while Peter Elmsley, incumbent of Little Horkesley, became Professor of Ancient History at Oxford, wrote commentaries on the works of Euripides and Sophocles and edited the plays of Euripides and *The Acharnians* of Aristophanes. Another distinguished Classicist, a Rector of Lawford, conducted research into the Attic Orators, besides publishing an important commentary on Athenian inscriptions. Others secured administrative posts, a Rector of Colne Engaine the Headmastership of Christ's Hospital and both the Rector of Littlebury and the Rector of Hadstock the Vice-Chancellorship of Cambridge. From this massive scholarship and administrative experience Essex villages benefited little because, as a result of them, they saw so little of their nominal parsons. A Rector of Birchanger could not live in that village, 'being a Public Lecturer to the University of Oxford and a Fellow of a College there'. Two Fellows of All Souls found little time for the parishes of Barnston and South Weald respectively. A Vicar of Great Chishall lived in Cambridge because at Great Chishall 'the profits are so small as would starve me without the benefits I receive by living in Cambridge'. Peter Elmsley rarely visited Little Horkesley because he resided either at Edinburgh, where he wrote for the *Edinburgh* and the *Quarterly Reviews*, or at Oxford where he was President of a college. Exceptions were Thomas Twining, who held Fordham, White Notley and St. Mary's-at-the-Wall, Colchester, and remained in Essex, while editing and translating Aristotle's *Poetics*, and, of course, Philip Morant.

Absentees' usual plea was that they employed a curate to conduct one Sunday service and to christen, marry and bury the parishioners, an arrangement which the Bishop would normally sanction. Curates, at £30 a year in 1700 rising to £50 in 1800, were not easily found, especially for uncongenial parishes, and, even when appointed, could themselves become absentees. A Rector of Peldon could not persuade curates to live in Peldon — 'they will not live here, though they at first engage to do so, but will get to Colchester'. A Rector of Rettendon lamented, 'should I send ever so many curates thither, they would all serve me in the same manner and stay no longer than till they could get some other subsistence in a better country'. The curate of Ovington did not live in that parish, but preferred the pleasant Suffolk town of Clare. Curates were sometimes non-resident because the parsonage failed to meet their requirements. When visiting their parish, they could be grudging in their commitment, meeting only the barest requirements of their office. Curates, too, could themselves be pluralists, holding two or even three curacies, such as those of Rawreth and North Benfleet; Ridgewell and Great Yeldham; Mucking and Thorndon; Little Clacton, Frinton and Great Holland.

The cause of this dereliction of duty, it has been suggested, was the self-indulgence and pretentiousness of genteel society, from which the clergy, as partners in that society, could hardly remain immune. Their association with the affluent was further strengthened by the patronage system, a feature of the clerical world to which there is no space in this article to do full justice. Some Essex clergymen were already genteel enough by birth, but not a few, having risen from commerce, industry or the professions,[14] assumed gentility with all the insistence of new arrivals. All three of Easthorpe's eighteenth century Rectors came from workaday middle-class families. Rectors of Ashdon, Lawford, Netteswell, Sutton and White Roding had as fathers, a brewer, a barber, a wool-sorter, a maltster and a doctor respectively. Among a group of twenty-nine other Essex clergymen whose parentage is recorded, while one had a gentleman for a father and eleven had a clergyman, seventeen had sprung from trade, farming, handicrafts and the professions. All alike maintained their right to an income that would enable them and their families to live appropriately and they believed, with reason, that their Bishop, in acknowledging this right, thereby approved their tenure of two or more livings.

Absenteeism could be excused because the parsonage was too mean for a gentleman to dwell in. One Rector of Aldham was non-resident because of 'the extreme unfitness of the Glebe House for the residence of a clergyman'. Aythorp Roding lacked both parson and curate because 'there is no place fit for a gentleman'. At White Colne the parsonage was 'a mere cottage wherein the poorest people have been . . . used to live'. At Lindsell it was 'only a poor cottage', at Cold Norton 'a mere mud cottage', at Shellow Bowells 'a very mean thacht house', at Margaretting 'a crazy structure'; and more to the same effect. In 1790 the Woodham Walter rectory was judged inadequate for a family with

14 A. R. West, *A History of Easthorpe*, 1989, 13; *D.N.B.*, biographies of 29 clergymen holding Essex livings.

servants, and servants could be numerous; the Vicar of Henny had four, the Vicar of Wickham St. Paul's five and the Rector of High Laver six.[15] To improve their parsonage became a pre-occupation for many, such as a Rector of Peldon, who wished 'to keep up my manner of life'. Wicken Bonhunt's Rector spent £300, others much more. By 1772 a new County History[16] was able to commend many clergymen for helping to enhance the rural scene by such re-building. Thus at Sheering 'the present incumbent is making great improvements in the parsonage and the lands belonging to it', a new vicarage at Writtle was now 'pretty and neat', while at Broomfield the parsonage had become 'a commodious gentleman's seat'. This spate of Georgian building and re-building was part of a wider movement by the county's gentry, in which the clergy, as part of that society, readily participated. Their new buildings, standing close to those of the secular gentry, furnished visual proof of their own gentility. Thus at Great Braxted:

> 'A very elegant seat called Braxted Lodge ... commands a most agreeable prospect of the neighbouring country. Charles Buxton, Esq., has a very good house with spacious gardens well watered and abounding with many elegant buildings that render it a most agreeable summer residence. And the Rev. John Cott, the rector ... has pointed his parsonage with brick; so that these houses, standing within sight of each other ... render this as agreeable a spot as any in the whole neighbourhood.'

Parsonages might rival minor country houses; that at Theydon Garnon contained a hall, 'two handsome parlours, kitchen, seven bedrooms, coach-house, stables for eight horses, pleasure and kitchen gardens, fishponds and six acres of pasture'.[17] All these pretentions cost not a little, obliging the clergy both to seek additional sources of income, and to try to enhance existing ones.

Clerical incomes did appreciate after 1750, as agricultural productivity rose. Curates gained nothing, the modest increase in their stipends being counterbalanced by increased prices. Vicars, who held only a single living, were somewhat better-off than curates because agricultural progress did add a little in real terms

15 *Chelmsford Chronicle*, 20 April, 1798; 11 May, 1798; 15 June, 1798.

16 P. Muilman, *A History of Essex by a Gentleman*, 1769–72, vol. 1, 207, 308, 380.

17 *Chelmsford Chronicle*, 1 April, 1774.

to the Small Tythes on which they depended. However, many, probably most, vicars had more than one source of income. Hatfield Peverel's Vicar, who had to watch the increasingly lucrative Great Tithes of that large parish accruing to the lay impropriator, the owner of Hatfield Priory, also held the Vicarage of nearby Ulting. In 1772 Great Maplestead's Vicar received only £90 a year from that parish, with £17 for a Good Friday sermon, but he also acted as curate of Little Maplestead.[18] The Vicar of Feering was Vicar of Mundon and chaplain to the Earl of Talbot. The Vicar of Great Saling, who also held the Donative of Bardfield Saling, in 1767 recorded 'total year's profit of Great and Bardfield Saling, £128. 18. 6.'[19] an income probably larger than that of any local farmer, other than the occupant of Saling Hall, and about six times the earnings of a farm worker. Rectors prospered as they ensured that their Great Tithes, almost always taken in money, rose at least commensurately with prices and agricultural output. They carefully noted any development on farms that could justify upward revision of tithe agreements. One Rector of Rayne raised his tithe revenue from Old Hall from £19 to £31. 10. 0. and sought a further increase by proving that it contained more acres than its occupant would admit. He increased one farm's payments by nearly 25% and another's by nearly 100%. The total income from tithe and glebe in Rayne rose from £154 in 1755 to £235 in 1785 and £385 in 1804.[20] Annual tithe receipts increased at Great Parndon in 1717–80 by 84%, at Downham in 1721–1800 by 148%, and at Little Tey in 1763–1800 also by 148%.[21] Expectations rose. Tithes for sale were now often designated 'improveable', the contemporary euphemism denoting any prospects of increasing gain. In 1777 the tithes of Tolleshunt Major were advertised as 'capable of great improvement'[22] and in 1781, when the advowson of Layer Breton, that is the right of presentation to its living, was for sale, the advertisement stressed that, though tithes and glebe currently yielded only £150 a year, they were both 'very improveable, being capable of an immediate 40% increase'.[23]

Pluralism and absenteeism were only one product of clergymen's gentility. Another was a tendency to view

18   E.R.O., D/P 83/3/1.

19   E.R.O., D/P 297/3/1.

20   E.R.O., D/P 126/3/2.

21   E.R.O., D/P 184/8/1; D/P 257/3/1; D/P 38/3/1.

22   *Ipswich Journal*, 10 May, 1777.

23   *Ibid.*, 11 August, 1781.

parishioners, large landowners excluded, as descending in a downward social gradation from themselves. When in 1778 his Bishop enquired about 'families of note' in his parish, a description which he interpreted as meaning families of wealth or rank, the Vicar of Boxted replied that his parish consisted of 'the only genteel family, Mrs. Cook and her daughters, widow and children of my predecessor; four or five substantial farmers, several small farmers and butchers; and most of the rest labourers'. The Rector of Rivenhall could see 'one family of note . . . The rest are all farmers'; thé existence of labouring families escaped his notice. Ashen had 'no family above the rank of ordinary farmers', while at South Ockendon 'there are no families of distinction. There are seven farmers, all of low extraction and illiterate. The rest are little tradesmen and common labourers. There are two farmers, both of whom have been servants.' Contempt for labourers was predictable but it is surprising that farmers, a class from whose work and enterprise the clergy were then profiting, could be seen as they were in these verses,[24] dedicated by William Cowper to his close friend, W. C. Unwin, Rector of Stock, in the evident belief that Unwin would find their sentiments quite acceptable:

'The Yearly Distress, Tithing Time at Stock

Now all unwelcome at his gates
    The clumsy swains alight
With rueful faces and bald pates
    He trembles at the sight.

And well he may, for well he knows
    Each bumpkin of the clan
Instead of paying what he owes
    Will cheat him if he can.

One wipes his nose upon his sleeve
    One spits upon the floor
Yet not to give offence or grieve
    Holds up the cloth before.

Oh, why are farmers made so coarse
    Or clergy made so fine?
A kick that scarce would move a horse
    May kill a sound divine.

Then let the boobies stay at home;
    'Twould cost him I dare say,
Less trouble taking twice the sum
    Without the clowns that pay.'

24 *The Works of William Cowper*, 1835, vol. 8, 173-5.

Figure 4.   Dagenham Old Vicarage.
Early seventeenth century with 1665 additions.

(John F. Buchan)

Figure 5.   Sandon Old Rectory.
Five-bay, two storey house built in 1765.   (John F. Buchan)

Noncomformists in particular were dismissed as low-born and ignorant. Those at Debden were 'only two Quakers of low degree', those at West Tilbury 'the lowest and most worthless orders of the people', those at Great Baddow 'of no quality', the Feering Baptists 'of the inferior class' and Stock Methodists 'all of the lowest order'. Upminster Methodists were also 'of the lowest order of the people' and the Rector saw it as an occasion for ridicule that 'a carpenter is their teacher'; in the artisan economy of the time it was not unlikely that this teacher was also a carpenter's son. Birdbrook's Nonconformists were dismissed as illiterate, South Ockendon's as ignorant. It was commonplace for Nonconformists to be accused of such stupidity as not to know why they dissented or what denomination they followed.

It is difficult to find any Essex rural clergyman of this period referring to the families of farmers, artisans, shopkeepers or labourers as people with whom it would be pleasant or instructive to consort. The poor were completely disregarded as possible friends; when mentioned, it was often for their shortcomings. A Vicar of Aveley thought them 'very dissolute'. W. C. Unwin, of Stock, found the village 'in a state of notorious depravity and was commended for 'his exertions to curb the libertinism of the poor'.[25] Asked by the Bishop to name any parochial problems, the curates of Fobbing, Foulness and Fryerning could think only of the people's proneness to adultery, while the curate of Margaretting noted calf-jobbers' bad language. Holding the attitudes they did, many clergymen could never have enjoyed frank and friendly relations with most of their parishioners. Nor do surviving sermons suggest that in the pulpit they spoke to the hearts of the plebeian majority. Steeped in theological and classical learning, their elegant periods may have excited some admiration but can have given little spiritual inspiration to their humbler hearers. A Stanford Rivers Rector's obituary described his preaching:

> 'His deportment was graceful, his countenance benign, his voice agreeable, his articulation clear, his action expressive and his delivery elegant.'[26]

He also published an essay on 'Delicacy'. In 1801 the Revd. John Howlett, of Dunmow, a close student of local village life, when discussing the possible effect of tithe commutation on social harmony, conceded:

25 The Revd. F. W. Austen, *Rectors of Two Essex Parishes*, 1943, 323, 328.
26 *Chelmsford Chronicle*, 7 July, 1775.

'The most powerful cause of moral and religious
influence in a clergyman is the affection of his
parishioners. Of the affection we at present possess so
very little that a commutation of tithes could not
possibly diminish it.'[27]

Resistance to tithes was never stilled, since every year some
farmers tried to evade them or reduce their value, and some
clergymen sought to increase them. Their collection was always 'a
battle', wrote one Rector of Rayne,[28] and it prompted a Rector of
Peldon to complain that 'the farmers have a great deal more of the
serpent, but nothing of the dove'. A Weeley Rector was so
troubled by evasions that he asked Philip Morant's advice on how
to combat them; his was a troublesome parish where one farmer
took the parson to the High Court and another allegedly contrived
'a combination' against payment.[29] At Takeley an attempt by the
Vicar to increase the level of tithes provoked a challenge to his
whole authority; his version was as follows:

'This has induced such violent irritation . . . that no
patience or charity on my part can allay it. They will not
mend the road, the only road, to the church, which is
also impassable, nor repair the Bible or Prayer Book,
that are in a shameful state, though frequently impor-
tuned so to do, and they have lately built a Vestry Room
in the Church, in which, while settling the parish
business, they indecorously Smoke and Drink.'

Such concerted defiance cannot often have been offered but acts
of individual resistance were many.

There was also resentment at the clergy's assumption that
they were entitled to demand church attendance, to catechise all
the young and generally supervise the village. No longer legally
obliged to attend church, parishioners often stayed at home,
especially on Sunday mornings. At Downham the Rector found
that 'the most pressing persuasions were ineffectual'. At
Birdbrook there was open defiance, due to 'the deeply rooted
prejudice of the people against . . . the discipline of the Church'. A
Wicken Bonhunt Rector's 'good words and threats' were not
enough to bring children to be catechised in church; at Newport,
too, parents were reluctant to submit them to the ordeal. A

27 J. Howlett, *An Enquiry Concerning the Influence of Tithes upon
     Agriculture*, 1801, 61.

28 E.R.O., D/P 136/3/2.

29 D. J. Brown, *A History of Weeley Church and Village*, 1981, 6–7, 21.

Moreton Rector lamented that 'the prejudice of the many, especially the common people against receiving the sacrament seems almost invincible', this despite his publishing a tract on 'Damnation'. Aveley's Vicar met retaliation:

> 'They will not attend the church. I have done all I can in public and in private, but No. Some even affronted my predecessor when he has spoken to them . . . They have told him that, if they were paid as he is, they would come, too. I have met with insults also.'

Noncomformists had a more principled case against the whole Anglican establishment but, grateful for toleration while still apprehensive of harrassment, they now avoided conflict. Essex Quakers had once defied the tithe system, as their Books of Sufferings testify, yet even they largely abandoned what they had learnt was a hopeless struggle; Morant's sole Quaker parishioner was paying him by 1766. Nonconformists, too, resented the compulsion to finance a religious sect to which they were opposed, but even in their more militant times they had rarely been found at the Quaker's side. By 1766 Little Baddow Congregationists were expressly commended by the Rector for regular payment. The Anglican supremacy was invincible, being upheld by the aristocracy and gentry, including Whig reformers, none of whom in Essex raised their voice against it. In their turn Essex clergymen emphasised their own value to the political establishment, especially when addressing congregations of the powerful. An Assize sermon in 1726 had urged Christians to support 'one of the best constitutions of civil government, as well as one of the best establishments of religion, that ever Mankind enjoyed since the World stood'.[30] At the other end of the social scale Great Bursted Benefit Club members were urged to be loyal to 'the King under whom you are godly and quietly governed, and to the glorious constitution of the country'.[31] The French Revolution elicited even more vehement Anglican support for British institutions and British inequalities. Another Assize sermon warned against 'selfish, seditious views' and commended 'that wise subordination which the Almighty has established' and 'the inequalities in station and circumstances which . . . ought to be cheerfully submitted to'.[32] Some sought to associate Nonconformity with

30 *The Revd. Mr. Cox's Sermon at Assizes*, 1726, 25.

31 The Revd. J. Thomas, *Sermon to Members of Three Benefit Clubs*, 1822, 19.

32 P. T. Burford, *An Assize Sermon*, 1794, 5, 9.

(John F. Buchan)

Figure 6.   Great Baddow Old Vicarage.
Five-bay, two storey house with Roman Doric porch, c.1725.

Revolution. The Little Baddow Rector in 1810 had 'never known a Dissenter yet but was not ill affected to the Government' and the Rector of West Tilbury, himself a Baronet, wanted the withdrawal of Toleration from Nonconformists, who were 'to the dishonour . . . and danger of Church and State'. A Great Bardfield mob, probably with a Churchwarden's complicity and possibly the Vicar's connivance, drove Methodist preachers out of the village by brute force, accusing them of supporting the French Revolution.[33] Furthermore, many clergymen were now becoming Justices, until in the early nineteenth century they comprised a quarter of the Essex Magistracy.[34]

Such powerful forces were ranged in defence of the Anglican supremacy as to render it seemingly invincible, at least until the 1832 Reform Act, the perils of which it easily eluded. Its survival at that time, however, it owed partly to its own self-reform, faint preludes to which were observable in Essex in 1781–1800. James Penn, Vicar of Clavering, in 'A Sleepy Sermon' analysed the current state of religion:

> 'In a few years we shall have neither virtue nor religion. The rich practise little of either, they are respectable without it. The middling people ape the vices of their superiors and have a taste for gaiety and extravagance. The poor cannot attend to spiritual matters, being taken up in keeping themselves and their families from starving.'[35]

In a sermon on the greed of genteel society he said:

> 'The altar is not without its share of this vice. The acquisition of more livings than they can discharge which, after possession, are seldom, if ever, visited, proves it.'[36]

Another critic was W. L. Phillips, Vicar of North Shoebury. His Visitation Sermon at Danbury was described by a contemporary as follows:

> 'This excellent, cheerful, social, worthy man laid open the improprieties, bad examples and illiberal conduct of

33 *The Triumph of Religious Liberty over the Spirit of Persecution*, 1795, *passim*.

34 W. White, *History, Gazetteer and Directory of Essex*, 1848, 41–3.

35 J. Penn, *Sermons and Tracts*, 1777, 3–6.

36 *Ibid.*, 88–90.

the clergy in general . . . The parsons could scarcely sit it
out and afterwards had at him in the public papers, but
he gave them as good . . . He printed the sermon which, I
think, lashes the tribe very deservedly.'[37]

The sermon seems not to have survived but the newspaper
controversy throws some further light.[38] One correspondent wrote
that 'the four classes in which the preacher was pleased to rank his
brethren were the licentious, the idle, those who were professionally ignorant and the time servers'. Another conceded that
'there was some truth in his sermon' but argued that 'the truth is
not always to be spoken at all times'. A third deplored the voicing
of such sentiments 'before a congregation consisting chiefly of a
class of men too apt to despise a *parson* and who are happy if they
can pick a hole in a black coat in which every spot is conspicuous
and is sure to be magnified by the generality'. Those referred to
can only have been the Churchwardens, who attended on Visitation days. As substantial farmers,they were large tithe-payers
and, being responsible for ensuring the performance of a Sunday
service in their parish church, were the first to be blamed for a
perfunctory performance by some curate in a hurry to be gone or
for the absence of any service at all. There is further evidence of
Churchwardens' resentment and of parsons' awareness of it.
Others identified as likely to have enjoyed the sermon were
'gentlemen of fashion and frivolity' and 'those who look upon
religion as priestcraft and the clerical body as an incumbrance
upon society'. It would seem that there did exist groups critical
of the ecclesiastical system whose viewpoints were rarely afforded
publication.

By 1800 more Essex clergymen were voicing self-criticism. A
Moreton Rector contrasted clerical neglect with 'the zeal of the
Dissenting teacher'. A Birdbrook Rector admitted 'the formerly
neglected state of many parishes, the want of pious, zealous
Churchmen'. A Rector of Great Horkesley urged colleagues to
refrain from blaming Nonconformists for their own unpopularity;
they had only themselves to blame, he thought. A Vicar of Wix
understood why Nonconformity had flourished in that village
when the church had been left in ruins, while the Rector of Little
Baddow attributed the support for local Nonconformity to his own

---

37 A. F. J. Brown, *Essex People, 1750–1900*, E.R.O. Publications No. 59, 1972,
    37–8.

38 *Chelmsford Chronicle*, 15 June to 20 July, 1787.

predecessor having been 'a drunken sot'. Such candour reflected some willingness to correct abuses. Reform was not swift and an enquiry into the state of Essex education in 1807[39] showed how few clergymen were yet seriously affected, but by 1830 the rapid expansion of Anglican schools was providing firm evidence of a new evangelical spirit alive in many villages.[40] Meanwhile, rural Essex itself had been changing and, to those who ruled it, its social condition now seemed so troubled and at times so menacing as to require an active clergyman in every parish and therefore an end to pluralism and absenteeism.

39 E.R.O., D/AEM 2/4.

40 See National Society for the Education of the Poor in the Principles of the Established Church, *Annual Reports*, 1821–1830.

Figure 1. Claybury Hall from the south-west in 1978.

The east wing was added in the mid-1890s, and the tower (c.1890) of the hospital appears over the tree tops. Otherwise this landscape — including tree cover — has changed little over the years (cf. Figure 2).

(Photo: Author)

Claybury and the Survival of the Golden Woods.

HERBERT HOPE LOCKWOOD

'I will lift up mine eyes unto the hills'

FROM MANY PARTS of Woodford and Ilford and even further afield a long low ridge of woodland can be seen above the suburban roof tops. A pinnacled Gothic tower peers over the trees — more prosaically the Victorian water-tower of the massive Claybury Mental Hospital which hides its twenty-seven million bricks behind these woods. And glimpses can be had from some angles of the older Claybury Hall, a more modest Georgian building nestling beneath the final fold of woodland above the valley of the Roding.

The hospital — or asylum, as it was then called — took its name from this mansion when it was built by the London County Council one hundred years ago.[1] And the woodland is called Hospital Hill Wood — yet, strange to relate, it is not so named from the mental hospital which it has sheltered for a century, but from a medieval institution called Ilford Hospital which owned it long ago. But the woods themselves are older than all these and once bore yet another name.

Now is a good time to record what is known of their history because their future may be in the balance. The mental hospital, built to house two thousand patients (there were 850 still there in 1985), has been declared redundant. Its miles of echoing corridors and vacant wards are already under offer by the Waltham Forest Health Authority, who also own Claybury Hall with its park and woodlands.[2]

---

1 *V.C.H. Essex*, v, 194–95; G. E. Tasker, *Ilford Past and Present*, 1901, 148–49; R. Jones, 'L.C.C. Asylum at Claybury, etc.' *Journal of Mental Science*, xliii, 1897, 47–58.

2 This may be misleading: at the time of writing there are still some 400 in-patients and it now seems unlikely that the final closure can take place in 1993 as originally planned, and likely that the Hospital will celebrate the centenary of its opening in 1893 (information from Eric Pryor — former Assistant Director of Nursing Services).

Figure 2. Claybury Hall from the south-west — engraving 1797.
This house was built in 1790–91 of 'white', gault brick from Woolpit. The terrace in the front of the house was known as 'the Rose'.
Note the horses and cart in the foreground following the old right-of-way.

(L.B. of Redbridge Library Service)

The Manor of Barking and the Forest of Hainault

The history of this whole area may be said to begin in the year 666 when Erkenwald (Eorcenwald), later Bishop of London, founded the Abbey of Barking for his sister Ethelburga (Aethelburh) who became its first abbess. His diocese of London was then co-terminous with the kingdom of the East Saxons. The foundation grants to the Abbey by Hodilred (Oethelred), kinsman of Sebbi, king of the East Saxons, and by King Suidfred (or Suebred), the son of Sebbi, gave that monastery the entire manor of Barking which, in modern terms, comprised Barking, Ilford and Dagenham — some twenty-nine and a half square miles (18,800 acres).[3]

The river Thames formed its southern boundary and it stretched inland five to six miles from where the first gravel terrace rose above the marshes to the wooded ridge of which we first spoke. The western spur of this clay ridge, sometimes called the Havering Ridge, where Claybury now stands, rises to around 230 feet above sea level, and the end still called Hainault Forest, where it runs eastward into Havering, touches 300.

The foundation grants, in the form in which they have come down to us, do not actually name the western boundary. Coming nearer to modern times we know that the western bounds of manor and parish followed the river Roding for much of their course — not the modern main stream of this river, however, but the western channel known in the Ilford area as the Aldersbrook and further south as Back River. This is significant because on a geological time scale the river has tended to migrate eastward, occluding its former channel to the point that sections have disappeared in modern times, with some help from man, leaving only traces like the parapets of former bridges. But a tenth century charter describes the boundary of [East] Ham with Barking as running even then, 'along the *old* Hile' (*andlang ealdan Hilae*) — Hile being a former, possibly Celtic, name for the Roding (hence Ilford). So even in the later Saxon period it looks as if the boundary were an old one on the way to fossilisation.[4]

So it is all the more interesting that in the north-west corner of the manor this boundary forsook the river altogether and

---

3 C. Hart, *The Early Charters of Barking Abbey*, 1953, esp. 35–43, 'Topography'; C. Hart, *The Early Charters of Eastern England*, 1966, 117–45.

4 *V.C.H. Essex*, v, 184–85; P. H. Reaney, *Place Names of Essex*, 1935, 94; H. H. Lockwood, *Where was the First Barking Abbey*, 1986, 9, fig. 7; O.S. 6″ Map, 1894–96, sheets XLIV, XXXIV.

followed a straight line up Roding Lane North and across the flank
of the Claybury spur before turning east parallel to the ridge-line.
And in 1969 the West Essex Archaeological Group, excavating
where the boundary crossed Claybury, showed that this straight
section was the line of a Roman military road which, ignoring
details of the natural terrain, ran through Chigwell on to Dunmow.
And they found some evidence that this road continued in use,
though much pot-holed, throughout the middle ages.[5]

This alone might warn us against imagining that the Saxon
newcomers found a virgin landscape here. But, in fact, the major
Roman road from London to Colchester, on the line of the present
A118, bisected the manor.[6]

Nevertheless the indications are that this was always an area
of dispersed settlement. Even by the beginning of the nineteenth
century the only significant nucleations were the small town of
Barking, which had grown up in the south-west corner as a river
port by the gates of the monastery, the village of Ilford where the
Roman highroad crossed the Roding, and a few hamlets. Sub-
urbanisation arrived like a flood at the end of the century but even
then the northern quarter was little affected until the 1930s.[7]

Moreover there is no doubt that the area was also heavily
wooded in the early medieval period. In the mid-sevententh
century the parish of Barking alone (i.e. the manor less Dagenham
—about 12,300 acres) still had at least 2,610 acres of woodland,
whilst field names like 'frith' and 'reden' testified to former
woods.[8] All of this, apart from about 150 acres, lay to the north of

5 L.R., 2/214, Bounds of Manor, 1609; F. B. Harvey, 'The Route from London
  to Colchester', *The London Archaeologist*, I, no. 6, 1970, 127–29; 'Excavation
  of the London to Dunmow Roman Road at Claybury', 1969, MS notes by F. R.
  Clark (W.E.A.G.).

6 *V.C.H. Essex*, iii, 1963, 24–25; I. D. Margary, *Roman Roads in Britain*,
  1967, 246.

7 Chapman and André, Map of Essex, 1777, sheets XVI, XXI; O.S. 1″ Map,
  1805, Essex; *V.C.H. Essex*, v, 185–86, 267–70.

8 This estimate of 2,610 acres comprises 1,510 acres of wastes of the forest and
  1,100 acres of enclosed woodland. The rounded figure 1,510 is based upon
  1,400 from the Tithe Award of 1847 (E.R.O., D/CT 18), plus sixty enclosed
  after 1663 to endow 'New Chapel' (see below) and fifty for Allotments to the
  Poor in 1832. This could still be an underestimate (see note 16 below). The
  figure 1,100 is calculated mainly from the 'Companion' to the Parish Tithe
  Map, 1666 (Hatfield House, Cecil MSS, Essex (Ilford Hospital), 1/17a), the
  c.1750 copy of this Map (E.R.O., D/P 81/3/16), and the Vicars' Tithe Books,
  1669 (E.R.O., D/P 81/3/110) and c.1750 (E.R.O., D/P 81/3/15).

the Romford Road (the A118). In part the explanation was ecological because northward the London Clay eventually surfaces from beneath the lighter terrace gravels with their pockets of fertile brickearths to produce heavier and less easily worked soils ('three horse land'). In fact the northernmost sector was known generally in the middle ages as 'la Claye', from which derived the manorial names of Claybury and Clayhall and many field-names.[9]

But the road itself was a legal rather than a geological boundary. From the time of the Norman kings down at least to the eighteenth century the preservation of woodland owed as much to the operation of Forest Law as it did to ecology and economics. The area became the eastern part of the great Royal Forest of Waltham — hence the ancient name of Estholte for Hainault Forest to distinguish it from Epping Forest on the west of the Roding. And the old Roman road through Ilford was made the southern boundary of the Forest until the Disafforestation of 1851.[10]

The original object of Forest Law was the preservation of the 'vert and venison', of the beasts of the royal chase and of their food and cover. James I was the last monarch to take real 'delight and pleasure' in the hunt. But ulterior objectives of extra-parliamentary revenue for the Crown and timber for the Royal Navy still kept part of the ancient machinery creaking along almost up to the time when public interest in recreational facilities and the environment provided a new and sufficient motive for preserving the forest and its wild life.[11]

Forest, in the old legal sense of an area subject to Forest Law, included settlements and farmland as well as woodlands. But fences there must not be of such a height as to restrict the freedom of movement of the deer. And woodlands, even though private property, were subject to inspection by the officers of the forest, whose licence was necessary for felling trees. Though such licences were required and given in the normal course of woodland

9 *V.C.H. Essex*, v, 184; O.S./Geological Survey sheet 257 (Drift).

10 W. R. Fisher, *The Forest of Essex*, 1887, 21–22, 394, 401; M.R., 801; E.R.O., Q/RDc 42B. For Estholte *v.* Reaney, 1935, 2.

11 As well as being royal hunting grounds, the forests were an important source of royal revenue at the height of the middle ages — C. R. Young, *The Royal Forests of Medieval England*, 1979, 122–34. For policy in the seventeenth and eighteenth centuries — Fisher, 1887, 36–52, 239–41; *V.C.H. Essex*, v, 291–92. The nineteenth century change of attitude is a major theme of Sir W. Addison, *Portrait of Epping Forest*, 1977 and *Epping Forest*, 1991 — it came too late to save much of Hainault.

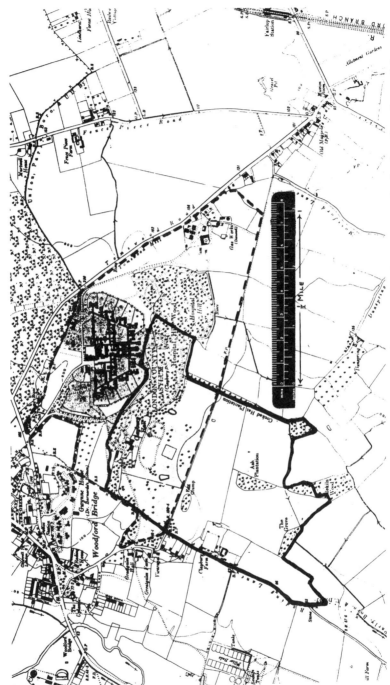

Figure 3. The solid black line indicates the boundaries of the original Claybury estate: the broken line those of the present Claybury Hospital grounds (these latter differ — particularly on the south and south-west sides — from those conveyed in 1886). (The base map is the O.S. six-inch, 1921 edition (1:10,560))

management, they did not extend to 'stubbing and grubbing'; licences to actually clear woodland in this manner were rarely given before the late seventeenth century.[12]

Forest, in the modern sense of a large stretch of continuous unenclosed woodland, was then termed 'wastes of the forest' and its limits were marked by a woodbank and fence of oak pales. Indeed this may have been the original sense of 'forest', deriving from a word *foris* meaning 'outside'. The final course of the fence in Barking is clearly shown on Thurston's Map of 1851 and the positions of some of the gates, or 'hatches' are indicated still by the names Fullwell Hatch, Aldborough Hatch and Marks Gate.[13]

The rights of common pasture in these 'wastes' and of taking limited quantities of wood (estovers) for fuel and repairs to fences and buildings were some compensation to forest dwellers for the many restrictions they endured. And coupled with geographical factors they tended to bias the farming not only towards arboriculture but towards animal husbandry.[14]

In addition to three large groves held in demesne well to the south of the forest fence, the Abbess as Lady of the Manor of Barking was owner — subject to the stringencies of Forest Law — of all the wastes of the manor.[15] In 1617 the royal surveyors recorded the wastes of the Forest which had passed into the hands of the King at the Dissolution as containing 3,260 acres (excluding the heathland at Little Heath and Chadwell Heath), 1,615 of which lay within Barking parish. This last figure includes thirty-two and a half acres at Tomwoods Hill within the wastes of the Forest, but there is reason to suppose that the whole north-western corner of the manor including Claybury lay beyond the fence in the early middle ages.[16]

---

12 Fisher, 325 and ff.; E.R.O., D/DMs 049 and 050 contain sixty-seven Warrants to View in the seventeenth century and all are for felling; the first licence for clearing I have come across in Hainault was granted in 1737 for a thirty acre coppice at Bunting Bridge (Guildhall Library, D'Oyley MS 1377).

13 Fisher, 4 note; E.R.O., Q/RDc 42B.

14 *V.C.H. Essex*, v, 291; Fisher, 257–58, 261, 283–87, 299–305; L.R.R.O., 198, 23–27.

15 C47-58-1-30.

16 E.R.O., D/P 81/3/110 *rear*, fo.22. The alternative method of estimating regressively by adding approximations of fifty acres for Tomswood Hill and ten for 'Robinson's Corner' to 1,510 acres (see note 8 above) would give 1,570 acres for the wastes of the forest in Barking c. 1617. The difference of forty-five acres (1,615–1,570) is perhaps a little large to ascribe to errors in surveying alone but it is below 3%.

The Clearing of Claybury.

Around the middle of the twelfth century, the Abbess Adeliza (Adelicia) founded the Hospital of Ilford. She endowed the infirm poor of 'Ileforde' with — amongst other things — 'in perpetual alms all our assart in Estholte namely 120 acres' (*in perpetua elemosina totum essartum nostrum de Hestholte scilicet centum et viginti acras*). This was confirmed by a charter of King Stephen (1135–54), granting 'to God and to the holy church of St. Adelburga of Barkinge all that assart of Estholt for the maintenance of the infirm of the Hospital of [blank] of Ileford' (the copy held by the Hospital has 'c.xx.acr.' in the margin).[17]

We do not know the exact circumstances or calendar date of Stephen's grant to Barking; but we have other evidence that he was generous to the church in matters of Forest Law, if only because of the weakness of his political situation and the laxity of administration during the troubles of his reign. The Convent was obviously concerned to safeguard their foundation of the Hospital since all the terms of Adelicia's endowment were repeated by the Abbess Matilda (1175–99), daughter of Henry II, and confirmations also obtained from Gilbert (Foliot), Bishop of London (1163–87) and from Hubert (Walter), Archbishop of Canterbury (1193–1205). Incidentally, these twelfth century grants show the fallacy of the belief later prevalent that Ilford Hospital was founded as a leper hospital; the brethren are described simply as poor and infirm.[18]

An assart was of course a clearing made by felling and 'grubbing' out the roots of the trees permitting cultivation of the land. The name 'Claybury' could not have applied at this stage for the simple reason that in Middle English the element 'bury' would have indicated that a court or manor house already existed there. It first occurs, as we shall see, in the fifteenth century although the name could well have been in use for some time because all earlier examples of 'bury' names in Barking were those of demesne manor-houses of the Abbey (e.g. Eastbury, Loxfordbury, etc.). So is there sufficient evidence anyway for identifying the twelfth century assart as the later Claybury estate? No previous historian has done so to my knowledge, and I must confess that I was not confident enough to make the identification back in 1965 when I

---

17 E 368/449 m.i; Cecil MSS, Essex (Ilford Hospital), 1/6, fo.5–5v; *Idem*, fo.5v.

18 Young, 1979; Cecil MSS, Essex (Ilford Hospital), 1/6, fo.5; *Idem*, fo.3.

contributed to the section on Claybury in the *Victoria County History of Essex*, Vol. 5.[19]

Since then a great deal of fresh light has been thrown on this question from the archives in the possession of Lord Salisbury, former Master of the Ilford Hospital, at Hatfield House. But the key lies in an agreement made in 1219 between the Abbess Mabel of Bosham and the Hospital, witnessed by the Bishop of London and many local notables, confirming and increasing their endowments. (Incidentally this is the earliest document to mention 'leprous brethren'.) Amongst additions were all the tithes both great and small 'of *their own lands* at the Clay'.[20] Now the earliest extant Hospital Rental, with the double dating 1384–85 and 1401, has an item of 33s. 4d. which the next Rental of 1493 says is the rent 'for Cleyberry lands'. And the parallel Tithe Lists show the Hospital as entitled to the tithes of 'a place called Cleyberye' in 1384–85 and 1401, and 'of all Cleyberry lands' in 1493.[21]

The identification of Claybury with the twelfth century assart is therefore established in general terms. But we should be able to go further since we now have detailed Parish Tithe Surveys and Maps for Barking going back to the mid-sevententh century (*v.* Fig. 6) which confirm that Claybury lands were all within the Hospital Tithing, but nearly all adjacent lands tithed to Gaysham Hall. And we know that tithe boundaries did not normally alter with changes of tenancy of land. On the accompanying plan (Fig. 3), these boundaries have been transferred onto a modern map and should show the extent of the original freehold of Claybury and so of the assart.

Do they indicate the same, or similar, area? This question raises some interesting problems. Well before the 1860s, when the first accurate cadastral survey was made for the Ordnance Survey 25″ Plans, the boundaries of the Claybury estate had been greatly extended as a result of the extensive purchases of adjoining lands by James Hatch at the beginning of the nineteenth century. The same difficulty applies to the survey accompanying the Tithe Award of 1847; but in this case the tithing boundaries are given

19 E. Ekwall, *Oxford Dictionary of English Place Names*, 'burg'; *V.C.H. Essex*, v, 191, 194–95.

20 Cecil MSS, Essex (Ilford Hospital), 1/6, fo.26v–27v; E.R.O., T/P 93/4 (Smart Lethieullier's MS, History of Barking, *Appendix*, unpaged).

21 1384–85 and 1401 — Cecil MSS, Essex (Ilford Hospital), 1/6, fo.2–2v; Valence P.L., MS, 'Fisher *v.* Wight' — Schedule fo.42v; 1493 — *Idem* fo.44; E.R.O., T/P 93/4 (Appendix, unpaged).

and older field divisions indicated where necessary by dotted lines. The area assigned here to the Hospital Tithing is 173¼ acres. The earliest extant Parish Tithe Survey of 1666 (based on a Manorial Survey of 1652) gives a comparable measurement of 176½ acres for the same area.[22]

There is, it must be admitted, one snag. The earlier survey also added nineteen and a half acres tithing to the Hospital on the north of Claybury, which the Master of the Hospital later exchanged with the impropriator of the Gaysham Tithing. However there is no evidence that the tenant of Claybury was ever assessed for tithe to the Hospital on so large an acreage as 196 acres. On the contrary, the earliest detail of Claybury lands in the Hospital's records, probably dating from the late sixteenth or early seventeenth century, adds up to only 157 acres. And a conveyance of 1767 describes the freehold estate as 160 acres.[23]

But the central problem would seem to be, not minor differences explicable mainly in terms of the improvements in surveying in modern times, but in the major discrepancy between the 120 acres of the original assart and the later tithe surveys. Yet there is a highly plausible explanation for the difference. There is very little doubt that the twelfth century assart would have been measured in Woodland or Forest acres not in the later Statute acres. Now the Woodland acre was based upon a larger perch measuring variously eighteen, twenty, or twenty-four feet whilst the latter used the standard perch of sixteen and a half feet. And 120 Woodland acres measured by a twenty foot perch would be equivalent to 176⅓ Statute acres. Surprising therefore though the conclusion may be, there is a strong probability that our plan actually shows the boundaries of the medieval assart.[24] An alternative possibility will be discussed below (see p. 102).

Several interesting deductions follow. In the first place, it is plain that the long west side of the assart rested on the former Roman road where it crossed through the forest. This would have

22 E.R.O., D/CT 18 (J. Mills); Cecil MSS, Essex (Ilford Hospital), 1/17A, fo.1 (Fookes).

23 The tithes handed over to Gaysham were from nos. 4 and 5 on the Parish Tithe Map — probably originally part of Little Golders; Cecil MSS, Essex (Ilford Hospital), 1/6, fo.25v; E.R.O., D/DDa T35.

24 R. E. Zupko, *Dictionary of English Weights and Measures*, 1868, 4, 120–22; Fisher, 1887, 321; Assuming the eighteen foot perch were used the equivalent would be 143 Statute acres; if the twenty-four foot perch had been used it would be 254 acres.

facilitated access and cartage. By the nineteenth century, the Claybury estate had expanded further west into Woodford but these lands were copyhold additions.[25] The original 'infirm brethren' were obviously in no position to undertake the long and arduous task of forest clearance themselves, or even to farm the cleared land. At an early stage it must have been let, probably on a long lease, and eventually it became freehold subject to a quit-rent of £1 13s. 4d (1 pound and 1 mark).

The Heart of the Woods

But it would not have been economical for any tenant to clear the woods from the south-facing clay scarp in the north of the estate. Properly managed these would have yielded timber and wood as well as providing pasture for swine, and perhaps sheep as in later times. The sixteenth-seventeenth century note of Claybury lands mentioned above calls them 'The great Wood Leasewe [pasture] next to Spittle hill'.[26]

This description is explained by the map (Fig. 5). Only the eastern part of the nineteenth century Hospital Hill Wood was called Spittle [i.e. Hospital] Hill in earlier centuries. And it was in Vicar's Tithing not that of the Hospital, so it could not have been part of the original Claybury. Yet it was owned by Ilford Hospital — hence the name — until the end of the eighteenth century when it was absorbed into the Claybury estate by James Hatch. On the Tithe Award Map of 1847 only a dotted line marks the division between these woods and nowadays the remains of the boundary ditch can easily be missed.[27]

But, most interestingly, this division is still apparent to the ecologist. Between 1978 and 1981, Dr. Peter Ellis with the assistance of members of the Epping Branch of the British Naturalists Association undertook a plant survey of the woodland. His starting point and findings were well summarised in a letter to myself.

'I noticed the exact correspondence of its southern margin on modern maps with that shown on Chapman

25 Greater London Record Office (= G.L.R.O.), (M), D/A4/1 — 2nd schedule includes Gales Field and a strip near Park Gates — Manor of Woodford — enfranchised 1879.

26 Cecil MSS, Essex (Ilford Hospital), 1/6, fo.25v.

27 E.R.O., Sage Collection, History of Barking, II, 390; E.R.O., D/P 81/3/16, sheets 1 and 3, no. 11; E.R.O., D/CT 18 (nos. 2550, 2550a); Personal observation.

Figure 4.   A page from the sketch-book of Walthamstow naturalist Edward Forster depicting the outskirts of Hainault Forest near Claybury, October 1779. In the woodland here he first identified the woodrush named after him.

(L.B. of Barking and Dagenham Library Service. Photo: Author)

and André's map of 1777. This I took to mean that the wood had been more or less undisturbed for two centuries at least, and probably throughout historical times ... It quickly became clear that the distribution of plant life in the wood was very uneven and that plants characteristic of old woodland were mostly to be found in the western portion. As we progressed we found that the division was remarkably sharp when certain plant species were considered, and that the line of division was in the region of the drainage ditch . . . The table summarises the distribution of some common plant species; of these the hornbeam, wild service tree, wood anemone, wood melick and yellow archangel are plants characteristic of old woodland and uncommon outside it. The fascinating thing is that the ecological division of the wood appears to correspond with a difference in the two portions as they appear on Chapman and André's map of 1777.'[28]

These findings have been reinforced by the work of the London Wildlife Trust, who now manage the woodland. The density of wild service trees proves unusually high. Some fifteen more indicators of ancient woodland can be added to the eight employed by Dr. Ellis. These include Forster's woodrush for which this is the 'type locality'.

Both portions are undoubtedly ancient woodland but the eastern portion is more open woodland with more exotic plantings such as red and turkey oaks. There are traces of the summer house on the summit which appears on the first Edition 6″ O.S. map of 1862/71 and of rhododendron bushes which must date from the same period. But the management practices which account for the peculiarities of this section must have originated at an earlier stage and, unfortunately, the archives of Ilford Hospital at Hatfield House have yielded very little on this property. Unlike the woodland further east in Hainault Forest, the trees here show only occasional signs of pollarding and this fits in with other evidence that these woods were not subject to common of pasture before Disafforestation.[29]

28 Letter dated 17 October, 1981 in my possession.

29 Evidence submitted by London Wildlife Trust re. Unitary Development Plan of London Borough of Redbridge, Policy LP EN 41, D413 (September/ October 1991) — esp. Appendix 2 'Claybury Flora' by the London Wildlife Trust and Passmore Edwards Museum; Personal communications from Clive Griffiths (London Wildlife Trust, Redbridge Group).

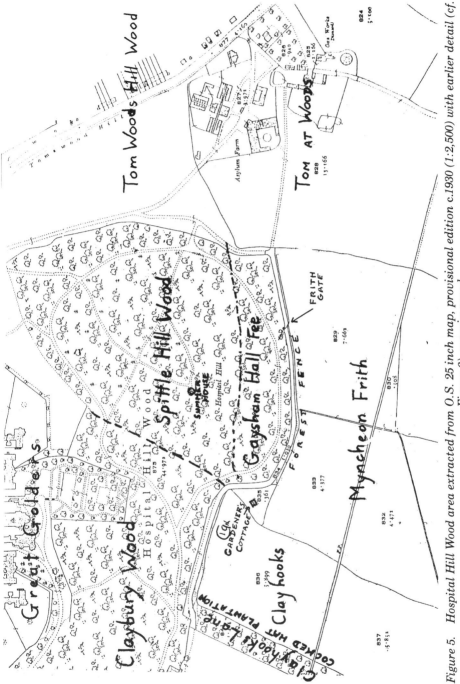

Figure 5. Hospital Hill Wood area extracted from O.S. 25 inch map, provisional edition c.1930 (1:2,500) with earlier detail (cf. Figure 6) superimposed.

When the trustees of the Claybury Estate were arranging to sell the lands in 1886 to the Justices of Middlesex for a Lunatic Asylum and it was agreed that the Marquis of Salisbury as the Master of Ilford Hospital should be paid £50 to release an annual payment of £1 13s. 4d., the speculation was that this had been some sort of a rent for the woods, 'but the hereditaments out of which the same was payable cannot now be accurately identified'. However, whilst the historian can now identify these as Claybury, the origins of the Hospital's separate title to the twelve acres of Spittle Wood are more obscure. The wood is first referred to by name in the Chantry Certificates 1546–48, so it must go back into the Middle Ages. Bamber Gascoyne giving evidence as Master to the Commissioners for Woods and Forests in 1793 claimed it 'by virtue of a Grant from the Lady Abbess of Barking to the Hospital', but offered no details.[30]

Another dotted line on the 1847 map indicates that the south-east margin of Spittle Hill was also a separate woodland at some time (cf. Fig. 5). This is clearly shown on the seventeenth century manorial and tithe maps with the name of Gaysham Hall Fee, which means that it was a detached portion of the demesnes of Gaysham Hall away to the south. The Tithing also supports this description. But even on the seventeenth century tithe map (or on the eighteenth century copy which has survived) the boundary of this seven acre wood appears only as a broken line and there is now no trace of it on the ground. If our knowledge of the medieval history of the manor of Gaysham were less fragmentary we might know more about this and another smaller parcel also named Gaysham Hall Fee further north.[31]

The Fields of Golders

These woods so far described — Claybury Wood, Spittle Wood and Gaysham Hall Fee — formed the belt of ancient woodland which still survives. The lands to the north which became the site of the buildings of Claybury Asylum were called Golders. Little Golders, thirteen and a half acres according to the Vicar's Tithe Map, lay north of Claybury hall, whilst Great Golders, forty-four and a quarter acres, lay north of the surviving woodland. The

---

30 Waltham Forest Health Authority Register of Deeds 47/7, Release of Rent Charge, 21/5/1886; Chantry Certificate E301-20-46; L.R.R.O., 198, (Appendix 15), 97–98.

31 E.R.O., Sage Collection, History of Barking, II, 390; E.R.O., D/P 81/3/16, sheet 3, no. 15; cf. E.R.O., D/CT 18 (no. 2550b).

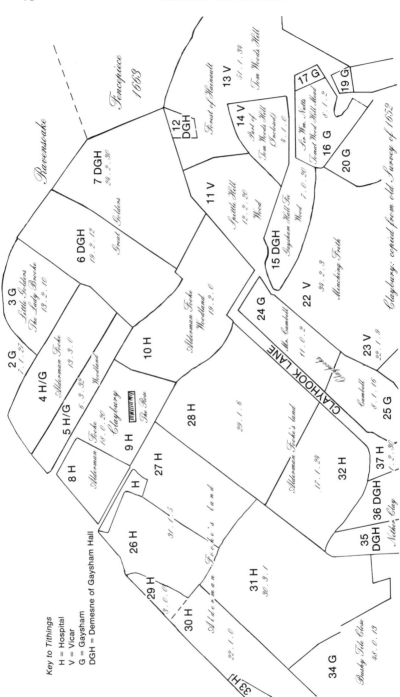

Key to Tithings

H = Hospital
V = Vicar
G = Gaysham
DGH = Demesne of Gaysham Hall

Figure 6.   *Based on a nineteenth century copy of an extract from the Manorial Map of 1652 with additions and amendments by the author from eighteenth century copies of the Parish Tithe Map and 'Companion' of 1666.*

(Essex Record Office and Hatfield House)

earlier forms of this name are 'Goldhurst' and 'Gouldhurst', deriving from OE *gold*, and *hyrst*, wooded eminence — the last element suggesting that it could once have applied also to the woodland further south.[32]

A deed in the archives of Westminster Abbey, *tempo* Edward I (1272–1307), refers to two and a half acres of land in 'Litelgoldhirst' in the parish of Barking abutting east upon the wood belonging to the lordship of Chigwell. So at that date some part of Little Golders had been cleared whilst the rest of Golders to the east was still forested. One of the witnesses, John de Goldingham, was himself the lord of Chigwell; and in 1400, his grandson, Alexander de Goldingham, leased out some of his lands including 'Goldehurste feld' in the parish of Barking, where the term field would suggest some clearance had taken place. And, when Henry FitzSagar of Chigwell and, William, his brother were accused of having burnt twenty acres of heath (*bruere*) of the Abbess of Barking around (*circa*) 'Goldehursthull' in March 1370 'contrary to the assize of the forest', were they burning off scrub in Great Golders?[33]

In a survey of 1617 'of that part of the Parish of Barking w'ch lyeth in ye Forrest of Waltham', John Wroth Esq., then lord of the manor of Chigwell and West Hatch, is shown as holding 'Three *pasture grounds* adjoyning and abutting upon Tomwoods Hill called Great Goulders and Little Goulders' of sixty-nine and a quarter acres. This survey 'taken by Vertue of his Ma'tyes Commission' was one of several preliminary to a scheme for raising royal revenue by accusing forest landowners of unauthorised enclosures. Subsequently Wroth found himself charged with extensive encroachments 'after the Domesdei booke' [*sic*] in his own manor 'Besides certain landes lying within the parish of Barking called Goulders [which] contayne 74 acres'.[34]

Gaysham Hall also had some special interest in Golders. When Thomas de Sandwich died in 1360 he was holding

32 E.R.O., D/P 81/3/16, sheet 1, nos. 3, 6, 7; Various examples of this name are given below. The form 'Gould-' probably reflects the pronunciation *guld*, in use down to the nineteenth century (*Oxford Dictionary of English Etymology*, 1966). The later form 'Golders' also reflects the elision in common speech of the second element.

33 Westminster Abbey Muniments, Deed 1174; Cat. Anct. Ds. I, B 968; E 32/71.

34 E.R.O., D/P 81/3/110 rear, fo.5; SP 14-202-25.

Figure 7.   Richard stands, facing west, on the ancient track of Clayhooks Lane where it turns east along the southern margin of Hospital Hill Wood (Claybury Wood, with Spittle Wood and Gaysham Hall Fee beyond). The woodbank (with intermittent trees) and ditch separates them from the old farmlands of Clayhooks on the right.

(Photo: Author, 1978)

Goldherstland with Gayshams. And in the late seventeenth century Great Golders paid both great and small tithe to the impropriator of Gaysham as though it were, or had been, part of the Demesne of Gaysham Hall. And when in 1842 the descendants of James Hatch bought Gouldhursts (complete with tithes) from John Wight Wight, the owner of Gaysham Hall, it was stated that previously they had only been his tenants.[35]

Anyway, having bought Chigwell and West Hatch in 1800, James Hatch had constructed a new drive from the north to Claybury Hall, which left the Ongar Turnpike and ran through woodland on the line of modern Forest Lane. It crossed the forest tracks which were to become Manor Road and Tomswood Hill Road to emerge past a new lodge into the great clearing that was Golders and curve across to the belt of trees behind the house. Its course is clearly shown on the first edition of the One Inch O.S. of 1805. By 1847 Great Golders (corrupted now to 'Goldens') was entirely arable except for a 'shaw' (fringe of trees) on the south, and it was this large and comparatively level open space which provided the site for the huge mental hospital without further encroachment on the woodland.[36]

The Old Way to Tom-at-Woods

The southern aspect of the Claybury area exhibits a number of relict features of earlier landscapes. The 1652/3 manorial map shows that, south of Claybury Wood, the eastern boundary of the original Claybury estate rested upon another ancient roadway which we know from other sources was called Clayhooks Lane. This, reaching the woodland edge, turned east and, skirting the southern margin of the woods just inside the woodbank which carried the forest fence, arrived at Tomswood Farm. This wood-bank and parallel track are still well-marked features (v. Figs. 7 and 8), although only traces remain of the north-south section — Clayhooks Lane proper.[37]

There are reasons for supposing that this highway or track

---

35 *V.C.H. Essex*, v, 204; *Idem* 224, for a short explanation of the Barking tithings; Cecil MSS, Essex (Ilford Hospital), 1/17A, nos. 6, 7; E.R.O., D/P 81/3/15, fo.20; Waltham Forest Health Authority, Register of Deeds, 47/1, Conveyance, 30/12/1842.

36 See references to New Road and Lodge of James Hatch — Court of Attachments, July 1800, June 1801 — Guildhall, D'Oyley MS 1377; E.R.O., D/CT 78A (no. 741); E.R.O., D/CT 18 (nos. 2589, 2592–94).

37 E.R.O., Sage Collection, 'History of Barking', II, 390.

may be older even than the Claybury assart. Tomswood, or Tom at Woods as it was still called in the eighteenth century, derived its name from the atte Wode family who were its tenants in the later Middle Ages. But the description given in the Barking Abbey Rental of 1456 shows that this settlement was much earlier in origin. In common with most of the old established freeholds in the manor of Barking, e.g. Clayhall, Wyfields and Cranbrook, this tenement 'in Inholte' paid an early type of money rent called a 'gabulum' (gafol, gavel). And it also belonged to the much smaller group of holdings which still paid part of their rents in kind; in this case '3 bushels of oats' (so the farm had included arable at an early date) and a separate payment of 'one ploughshare worth 12d.' for '*a way from the said tenement to the convent*'. And another 2d. was paid for a 'cartegate' — presumably through the forest fence.[38]

At the opposite end, the southward course of this long lane having bent towards the south-west eventually met up with Roding Lane (a little south of where the modern Woodford Avenue crosses). The manorial and parish boundary coming up from the Roding followed Clayhooks Lane for about 220 yards before continuing north to join the line of the former Roman road (*v.* p. 86 and Fig. 3). This again supports the considerable antiquity of this vanished lane, also known here as Marks Hatch Lane. Obviously the lane was gated at this end also and the gate was called Mark Hatch: the 'mark' would be a boundary stone. There is a distinct possibility therefore that the forest fence once followed Clayhooks Lane all the way.

Another interesting, if more remote, possibility also arises. Could the twelfth century assart have extended south of Claybury right down to Marks Hatch Lane? According to the Parish Tithe Survey of 1666 the total area of Claybury (176½ acres — *v.* p. 92 above) plus the land to the south (82 acres — including Bushey Tile Close, Nether Clay and Tilekiln) amounted to 258½ acres. And if the largest Forest perch of twenty-four feet had been used the equivalent of 120 Forest acres would be 254 Statute acres. However, for the near correspondence between these acreages to be regarded as more than coincidental it would be necessary to assume also that the Ilford Hospital had lost control of the eighty-two acres to the south at some very early

38 B.M., Add. MS 45387; E. A. Kosminsky, *Studies in the Agrarian History of England in the Thirteenth Century*, 1956, 176, 353.

period since they tithed to Gaysham and belonged to various owners.[39]

By the seventeenth century the lane was considered to be king's highway. For, in 1631, Sir James Campbell, Lord Mayor of London, who had bought Clayhall a couple of years before, was fined along with others for neglect of Clayhooks Lane which was 'soe straytened and cumbered by reason of the wood being sufred to hang and grow over it wholy it cannot dry but is very dangerous for his Majesty and his subjects to pass through'. Plainly the lane had little value as a thoroughfare and often became overgrown. No trace of this north-south section appears on the Chapman & André map of 1777. In 1784 it sounds as if the tenant of Clayhall had been trying to block off whatever remained because the Barking Court Leet ordered him to 'fill up the cross ditches in the lane leading from Clayhall to Clay Hook and scour his ditch adjoining his own ground'.[40]

When Repton made his report on the grounds of Claybury in 1791 there was already a long slip of woodland running down the Claybury side of the straight stretch of what the Survey of 1806 calls 'The Old Lane'. Later in the century it became known as Cocked Hat Plantation because of the shape of the coppice at its southern end. The northern end still remains, though the trees were felled some years ago, and there are traces of the lane and its ditches and possibly of a woodbank in the now regenerating scrub.[41]

From this point a bridle-path had also linked the ancient east-west track with the Woodford Bridge road (now Roding Lane North). This crossed Claybury within view of the house whose owners tried unsuccessfully to obtain a diversion in the face of opposition from the parish of Woodford. But the construction of the Asylum introduced a new security factor and in 1888 the L.C.C. built a boundary fence of six-foot oak pales along the southern edge of their property. On the outside of this they constructed a new footpath running a straight mile from a stile on the bend of Woodford Bridge Road through to Barkingside on the

---

39 L.R., 2/214, Bounds of Manor, 1609; Court of Swainmote, 1594 (E.R.O., D/DU 403/22, fo.132); E.R.O., D/P81/3/16, sheet 2 and Cecil MSS, Essex (Ilford Hospital). 1/17A.

40 C 99/144; E.R.O., D/DHs M17.

41 E.R.O., T/A 247; Valence P.L., MS, 'Survey of Barking, Essex, 1806'; O.S. 6" Map, Provisional Edition, 1919.

line of the present Ravensbourne Gardens. Thus direct public access to the park and woods was shut off for the best part of a century.[42]

Clayhooks

The name Clayhooks had been applied not only to the old lane but to the land alongside to the east, to which the Parish Tithe Survey of 1666 ascribes an acreage of nineteen and a quarter acres. It appears to have belonged to the manor of Clayhall though sometimes leased with other farms. In 1327, Robert son of William Sparke, the owner of Clayhall, gave the Ilford Hospital 'a croft – – – which lies at le Clay in Barkinge under the wood called Mynchin frith'. In 1379, Robert, Prior and Master of the Hospital granted a hundred year lease to Henry Sparke of Clayhall on 'a croft of arable land lying fallow (friscam) called Lanehoke' in an identical position. This is almost certainly Clayhooks and it shows the land was already under the plough in the fourteenth century and probably took its name from the lane. It is mentioned under the name Clayhooke in the first Hospital Rental of 1384/1401 but not in their subsequent rentals. It was being farmed by Dunspring in the nineteenth century and the fringe of wood down their side of the 'old lane' was called Dunspring Shaw in 1847 — the name Clayhooks being still in use for one of the fields.[43]

Mynchin Frith becomes Dunspring

In 1666, between Clayhooks and the lands of Tom at Woods farm, on the south of Spittle Wood and Gaysham Hall Fee, stretched a large area of fifty-six and three-quarters acres of arable called Minching Frith. From the previous paragraph it will be realised that the medieval version of this name was Mynchin Frith and that it was still woodland in 1379. J. G. O'Leary noticed this name in his *Dagenham Place Names* in 1958 and correctly derived it from *myncen*, OE 'a nun' and *frith*, ME 'a wood, woodland, wooded countryside' giving the meaning as 'Nun's Wood'. But he was obviously wrong in believing that the place was 'on or close to the Dagenham boundary', and less obviously in implying that it was owned by the nuns of Barking Abbey. It was of course within the

---

42 G.L.R.O., (M), MA/RS 1887, 1888; J. Oxley, *Barking Vestry Minutes*, 1955, 170; G. E. Tasker, *Country Rambles around Ilford*, 1910, 14.

43 E.R.O., D/P 81/3/16, sheet 3, nos. 24, 25; Cecil MSS, Essex (Ilford Hospital), 1/17A; *Idem*, 1/6, ff.23, 3, 2–2v; E.R.O., D/CT 18 (nos. 2501–2).

lordship of Barking but the actual owners (feoffees) were the nuns of Stratford-atte-Bowe (at Bromley by Bow — where Chaucer's Prioresse learnt to speak French 'ful faire and fetisly').[44]

The presentments to the Court of Swainmote in 1344 contain an interesting case concerning this woodland. This was a complaint against one Nicholas Hendyman of Barking 'who depastures his beasts by night in Munchenfricht, within the covert of the Forest, and is accustomed at daybreak and also at other times by shouting, to drive the same beasts, chasing away the wild animals of the lord the King by his clamour out of the Forest'. W. R. Fisher, who noted the case in *The Forest of Essex* (1887), was of the opinion that Hendyman was really committing the offence of 'staff-herding' *viz.* following his cattle while depasturing in common in the wastes of the forest. But since it appears that Mynchin Frith was a private wood south of the forest fence, so it is more probable that Hendyman would have paid a rent to the nuns for depasturing there.[45]

It would be interesting to know at what date and under what title the Priory of Stratford-atte-Bowe received this woodland in the first instance. The nunnery was founded about 1100 and few details seem to be available concerning her endowments. Obviously she did not receive Mynchin Frith under that name and it could have been generations before it came into official use (cf. Claybury). However a royal grant of 1246 contains an important clue. This authorised the Prioress and nuns of Stratford to take estovers in *their* wood of 'Goldhurst a la Claye' within the bounds of the royal Forest of Essex without view of the foresters, etc. This could hardly refer to Golders further north and confirms the view embodied in the title of this essay that Gouldhurst, 'The Golden Wood', was the original name for all the woodland in this area.[46]

At the Dissolution the wood called Mynchynfrith, or Myncheon Frith, was on lease and it continued to be leased out by the Crown. By the 1560s part of it was being described, somewhat ambiguously, as a little grove (*groveta*) of land and pasture

44 E.R.O., D/P 81/3/16, sheet 3, nos. 22, 23; J. G. O'Leary, *Dagenham Place Names*, 1958, 70; Medieval ownership, see e.g. L. and P., Henry VIII, xiv(1), 161; Chaucer, *Canterbury Tales*, Prologue.

45 Fisher, 1887, 279, but I cannot agree with his transcription of the herdsman's name from E32/263.

46 Calendar of Patents, 1232–47, 493, *cf.* E32/13 (m.4), E32/14 (m.39) of 1292, E32/16 of 1324.

Figure 8. Richard stands, facing east, on the woodbank south of Gaysham Hall Fee and Spittle Wood. Trees and bushes behind him conceal the site of the c. nineteenth century gardener's cottage. Below left are the old farmlands of Dunsprings (Mynchin Frith); the derelict car illustrates the problems of conservation near the suburban fringe.

(Photo: Author)

containing thirty-six acres. However by 1617 it had become 'One
great arrable ground adjoyning [to Clayhooks] called ye Frith' in
the possession of a well-to-do local landowner, Mr. William Finch
(of Gearies). In another survey of 1616 it is described as 'One close
called Minsing frith'. So another large slice of woodland had
disappeared, though by what warrant is unknown.[47]

The Frith was now the name by which the fields were
generally known although the curious corruption 'Mincing Frith'
occurs as late as a Rate Survey of 1829. However during the seventeenth century this former woodland was incorporated into a farm
called Dunspring. This took its name from Dunspring Grove, a
twelve acre parcel of surviving woodland beside the farmhouse to
the south of Myncheon Frith, which first occurs as Don Springe
Grove in 1616 — it was stubbed by 1750.[48]

The title Dunn Spring Farm is first found on an undated, but
certainly late seventeenth century, plan. This is particularly
interesting because it shows a gate 'goeing into the forrest'
through the Forest Fence on the north of the Frith. There were
probably a number of such small gates but the position of some is
unknown. In contrast to the larger 'hatches' which provided access
for roads and cartways, these were situated on 'ancient riding
ways' which were bridle paths used by the public as well as by
forest officers and doubtless convenient to adjacent landholders
entitled to depasture animals on the waste. Forest Law required
them to keep the riding ways free from obstruction and to provide
'spurgates'. These last were apparently of the type shown in
elevation on the Dunn Spring plan, with a braced vertical member
projecting above the top rail which enabled a horseman to open
the gate without dismounting. By canting the gateposts and using
suitable hinges the gate could presumably be made to swing shut
under its own weight.[49]

The Fencepiece

The other large clearance of woodland before the Disafforestation
of 1851 was the creation of Fencepiece Farm. Measuring fifty-

47 C66/1002 (m.6); L.R., 2/214, fo. 227 [66]; E.R.O., D/P 81/3/110 rear, fo.5;
    E.R.O., D/DHs M29.

48 Valence P.L., Barking Valuation, Terrier 1829, 113; a parallel occurs in the
    name 'Mincing Lane' in the City of London; E.R.O., D/DHs M29; E.R.O., D/
    P 81/3/15, fo.38, no.39.

49 E.R.O., D/DK P1; Fisher, 1887, 331; the interpretation of 'spurgate' is my
    own; many of the Walker maps in the E.R.O. show similar gates.

seven or fifty-eight acres this lay to the east of Great Golders in the parish of Barking but against the boundary with Chigwell and between the forest tracks which eventually became Tomswood Hill and Fencepiece Road respectively. The latter was perhaps the most frequently used route across the forest of Hainault since it joined Fullwell Hatch on the south with Horn Lane Gate on the north leading into Chigwell. Up to the mid-seventeenth century this area was thickly wooded; Strawberry Hill and Ravensoake Hill (the latter largely in Chigwell) being described later as 'the finest part of the forest'.[50]

During the Commonwealth local Puritans had persuaded Parliament to give an acre in the forest for the erection of a chapel at Barkingside 'for the use and encouragement of a Godly and Preaching Ministry there'. The 'New Chapel' was erected near Fullwell Hatch; but after the Restoration the 'godly minister' was expelled, and local inhabitants petitioned the Crown for it to be adequately endowed as a 'chapel-of-ease' to the distant parish church at Barking. In 1663 Charles II agreed to give sixty acres from the wastes of the forest to make 'some competent provision for a Pious and orthodox Priest to officiate'. The Fencepiece was enclosed for the purpose.[51]

500 oaks and hornbeams were said to have been cut down and grubbed up there by 1670. But the project ran into difficulties; as a result of a dispute over the patronage, no curate was appointed and the chapel fell into ruin. The Crown continued to rent out the land, but further clearance was slow. In 1781 nearly twenty acres at the west was still rough woodland and it was reported that 'The land is naturally very poor and will require considerable expense and time to bring it into a tolerable state of cultivation'. In fact, Bamber Gascoyne, in subsequent evidence to the Commissioners, even suggested it be 'again thrown into the Forest' and cited his own profitable management of the nearby Spittle Wood as an example. Nevertheless, the land does seem to have been successfully farmed during the nineteenth century. This may well have been assisted by the construction in 1833 of the new Fencepiece Road on the line of the former forest track. Housing development began here in the late 1930s.[52]

---

50 Chapman and André, Map of Essex, 1777, sheet XVI; L.R.R.O., 198 (Appendix 15), 97–98.

51 V.C.H. Essex, v, 230; Acts and Ordinances of the Interregnum, II, 812; L.R.R.O., 198 (Appendix 4), 61.

52 E32/21 (Presentments of Regarders, no. 93); E.R.O., T/M 177; L.R.R.O., 198

The Ruin of Ravensoake

The remainder of Ravensoake Hill between the parish boundary and Manor Road, part of the manor of Chigwell, retained most of its woodland until even later. It was divided into two sections when the Tomswood Hill road was built, the narrower western strip flanking the north-eastern boundary of the Claybury estate. 'Marvellously pretty is that beautiful stretch of sylvan country covering seventy acres' enthused an Ilford journalist in May 1902 supporting a proposal to preserve Grange Hill Forest, as it was then called, as a detached portion of Hainault. The imminent opening of the Ilford-Woodford Loop line was then increasing land values in expectation of the spread of houses. An article on the 'Reconstruction of Hainault Forest' in the August issue of *Nineteenth Century and After* also supported Edward North Buxton's efforts to include this 'extremely beautiful piece of natural woodland' in his larger scheme. Ilford and Woodford Councils together with the L.C.C. were ready to contribute to the purchase. Nevertheless prolonged negotiations fell through and this woodland was not part of the final Bill which saved the remnant of Hainault Forest for the public in 1903. George Tasker, the Ilford historian, suggested a few years afterwards that the failure was partly due to the L.C.C. having insisted 'upon the right to allow the patients of Claybury to walk in the forest'. Eventually this woodland succumbed to the demands of the twentieth century for high-class housing in a sylvan setting within easy reach of the Metropolis.[53]

The Concealment at Sheepcotes

There remains only one other area of former woodland to consider here, that which lay to the east of Spittle Wood and south of Fencepiece. This is a wood that has passed under several different names and (as in the case of Spittle Wood) there are problems concerning the title under which it was originally held. In the Survey of the King's Woods formerly belonging to the Abbey

(Appendix 15), 97–98; Court of Attachments, 2 June, 1832 — Guildhall, D'Oyley MS 1377; George Gott, who farmed Fencepiece from the 1880s, became a Chairman of the Ilford U.D.C.

53 *Ilford Recorder*, 23 May, 1902; Article signed Robert Hunter, *Nineteenth Century and After*, August 1902, 239–44; *Ilford U.D.C. Minutes*, January–April 1903, 4310, 4349, *Idem*, September 1903–March 1904, 1000; *Ilford Recorder*, 30 October, 1903; G. E. Tasker, *Country Rambles around Ilford*, 1910, 40.

made 1544–45 it is described as, 'a hill or plot of Wood (called) Chepcote Hill with one piece at the Frith Gate and a piece at Great Goldhurst Gate containing in the whole 43 acre set as well with oak as with hornbeam'. Plainly this comprised the two pieces of Gaysham Hall Fee and over thirty acres more; and the name derives from a Sheepcote known to have existed near Tomswood Farm (which also gave its name to a customary cottage and garden erected in the forest — perhaps originally to accommodate a shepherd). Strangely this was the only one of twenty-two woods detailed in the sixteenth century survey which the Woodwards and Keepers were unable to identify for the Commissioners of 1793. Yet the official survey of 1617, previously mentioned, also claims that thirty-two and a half acres of waste and wood called Tomwoods Hill belong to the Lord King (*Rex Dominus*).[54]

On the other hand the Manorial Survey of 1609 states that Thomas Pargeter, the owner of Tom at Woods, equally holds 'by free charter' forty acres of wood called Fernehurstes *alias* Tom at Woods Hill, sometime of John Burr, for which he pays 4s. p.a. quit rent. Moreover the Essex Record Office has an excellent series of freehold conveyances of Tom-at-Woods from 1554 onwards, all of which include sixty acres of wood called by the same name. Yet if we try to trace this title backwards we find that the normally comprehensive Ministers Account of the lands of the dissolved monastery of Barking in 1540 shows John Burre as tenant of Thom-at-Wodes and all associated lands (including the copyhold Shepcott), but no freehold woodlands are mentioned. And we learn from the will of his father, Thomas Burr in 1532, that he held Cleybury lands as well, though no details are given. However a Fine of 1514 shows that he had then just purchased two messuages, forty acres of arable, forty of pasture, and no less than 200 acres of woodland in Barking. No names are given but this could well have included all woods associated with both Claybury and Tomswood. It is worthwhile noticing here that the Burr family were wealthy tanners — they sold the Crown no less than 428 oxhides in 1520 — and oak woodland was the main source of tanbark.[55]

But we must return to our first point; this wood had been

54 L.R.R.O., 198 (Appendix 3A), 52; *Idem* (Appendix 3B), 59; For the Sheepcote see L.R., 2/214, fo.328 [531], and *cf.* earlier B.M., Add. MS 45387, (N), fo.xiii; D/P 81/3/110 rear, fo.22.

55 L.R., 2/214, fo.227 [69]; E.R.O., D/DDa T34; SC 6/964 [287–291]; D/AER 4/ 126; Essex FF 132; *V.C.H., Essex*, v, 241.

enclosed at some period out of the wastes of the forest and it does look as if there were some deficiency of title which became open to question after the Dissolution had delivered the Abbey properties into the hands of the Crown. Probably the owners were lucky eventually to escape the clutches of 'hunters after concealed lands'.

All this could help to explain why in the Award of 1861 under the Hainault Forest (Allotment of Commons) Act which followed disafforestation — Tom Woods Hill (forty-four and a half acres) was the only wood in Barking parish described as 'commonable land situate within the boundaries of the . . . late Forest of Hainault' but *not* 'within the boundaries of the King's Forest or King's Woods'. In view of this and its proximity to Barkingside it would not be surprising if this wood was over-grazed: the earlier name of Fernehursts and the later alias of Thornwood might indicate progressive degeneration of the woodland. Although cleared by the 1860s, in 1886 when the western end was being purchased as part of the Asylum grounds, it was still described as 'Hainault Forest (part of)'.[56]

Repton's Lessons in the Landscape

Before James Hatch took possession of Claybury in 1788 the house and grounds had suffered a period of neglect. By 1791 the house had been rebuilt and Humphrey Repton was called in to give advice upon the grounds. In the Introduction to his 'Red Book' he admits that 'little remains to be done in comparison with what has already been executed'. Extolling the situation of the house and its magnificent view over several counties he lays down his principle that 'When Nature has been so bountiful of charms as in the situation of Claybury, Art can seldom greatly interfere without violating the genius of the place . . . and . . . where Art cannot increase the natural charms, she is only to give comfort and convenience without disturbing what she cannot improve.'[57]

56 Before the Barking Survey of 1616, the Surveyor-General Treswell whetted the appetite of one such 'greedy hunter' by assuring him, 'there wanted £30 of ould rent and two or three woods and lands that he did know which now would come to light' (H. H. Lockwood, 'Greedy Hunters after Concealed Lands', in, *An Essex Tribute*, 1987, ed. K. Neale, p.164) but, suspiciously, Tomswood Hill Wood does not appear amongst the lands of Johnson, the tenant who followed Pargeter (E.R.O., D/DHs M29, fo.95); G.L.R.O., (M), D/A4/1.

57 The chief source for this and the following four paragraphs is E.R.O., T/A 247. The original is also in the care of the Essex Record Office.

Figure 9. 'I shall conclude with a sketch of a scene in the wood, which I confess my skill is as unable to improve as my pencil is with justice to represent', Humphrey Repton, the Red Book of Claybury.

(Waltham Forest Heath Authority. Photo: R. Chapman)

In fact, the only major alteration for which Repton was directly responsible was the re-siting of the drive and the main entrance to the north side of the house (chiefly on the grounds that 'it will be almost impossible for a Lady to get into a Coach on the south side when the wind blows very strong'). Otherwise his recommendations concentrated upon improving the view from the house by destroying all the hedges and siting some additional plantations near the perimeter of the estate to create a 'belt or girdle' of trees 'to unite the present woods'.

A comparison between Repton's plan and the later O.S. plans shows a modified version of this scheme was carried out. Unfortunately the southern portion of the estate was cut off by the arrangements of 1886 and 1887 and the 'girdle' lost by subsequent residential development. However, despite this 'insensitive housing development' (including a twelve-storey block), there is still a splendid view across the Thames into Kent, and a welcome if belated realisation that an 'important landscape asset remains and requires regeneration'.[58]

But it is in his treatment of the main block of woodland that Repton's instinct for conservation of the natural landscape shows most clearly, 'when we enter the Forest-wood, Nature disdains the paltry aid of Art, and shrinks from her intrusion'. He recognises that Claybury Wood is:

> 'doubtless a part of the adjoining forest from which it ought not to be separated. What [Capability] Brown acknowledged of the forest of Needwood, I confess of the little forest of Hainault, it has been the school from which I have drawn the lessons of beauty which I am now called upon to teach others. With an awful reverence for this favorite spot I should tremble at my own presumption if I were to suggest any further interference of Art than such as may enable us conveniently to avail ourselves of its natural beauties.'

Accordingly he confines himself to suggesting improvements to paths, the provision of a small flock of sheep as 'natural gardeners' to keep the turf trimmed and a sunken boundary fence with a small gate. But he also recommended a rustic cottage be erected nearby for security. The boundary fence soon became redundant when Spittle Hill Wood was added to Claybury, but the

58 D. S. Walton, compiler, *Claybury Hospital — Evidence on behalf of Waltham Forest Health Authority to Public Local Inquiry re. L.B. of Redbridge U.D.P.*, 1991, 21, 61, Appendix E 93, Appendix J, sheet 1.

Figure 10. The south aspect of Claybury asylum.

Built between 1889 and 1893, it is seen from the northern fringe of the woodland. The Administration Block is on the right with the Medical Superintendent's house beyond.

(From a postcard, c. 1909)

gardener's cottage built at its southern end just south of the track (*v.* Fig. 8) remained there for much of the nineteenth century.[59]

Troubled Minds and Untroubled Woods

The committee appointed by the J.Ps. of Middlesex in April 1885 'for the purpose of providing an additional Asylum for Pauper Lunatics', having searched in vain throughout Middlesex, reported favourably on the offer of a 'very desirable site' of '250 acres within a mile and a quarter of Woodford station'. They singled out for special mention the farm which 'situated in the lower portion of the property is well suited for receiving the sewage from the Asylum', and the mansion which 'is in excellent repair'. 'If the Lunacy Bill now before Parliament should become law, and the reception of private patients in County Asylums be encouraged, the position of this house is admirably adapted for carrying out this object.' In fact, Tomswood Farm, which had already been included in the estate, became a means of providing fresh vegetables and what we might term 'occupational therapy', as well as a sewage farm and a gas-works. And, with a new wing added, Claybury Hall became the first public institution providing for private patients (30s. per week for those living in London, 40s. for others).[60]

The 'fine views of the surrounding country' came in for special mention, the woodlands did not. But, as already indicated, the broad expanse of Golders field to the north permitted the construction of a massive building covering sixteen acres on 'an attractively created plateau' without destroying any of the remaining woods. Whether they were then perceived as having any therapeutic value for disturbed minds is unknown, though they may well have been so. Anyway, preserved they were, if only as a screen.[61]

We might perhaps deduce something from the fact that Dr. R. Jones (later Sir Robert Armstrong-Jones), the first Medical Superintendent when the completed Asylum was opened by the London County Council in 1893, was a supporter of the campaign for the preservation of Hainault Forest (see above — Grange Hill

---

59 E.R.O., D/CT 18, no. 2548.

60 G.L.R.O., (M), MA/RS 1886; *Claybury Hospital Report*, 1958, *passim*.

61 D. S. Walton, compiler, *Claybury Hospital — Evidence on behalf of Waltham Forest Health Authority to Public Local Inquiry re. L.B. of Redbridge U.D.P.*, 1991, Appendix A 78; Compare O.S. 6" Edition 1, 1862–70 with O.S. 6" Edition 2, 1894–96.

Forest). Conducted walks in the surrounding countryside formed part of the regime for patients even in early days. But when the 1958 Claybury Report was published, its author was explicit, 'Any booklet about Claybury would be incomplete without reference to its grounds, sloping woodland mainly, with hornbeams, oaks, sycamores, elms, beeches and a few maples — majestic and dignified — set among shrubs, bracken and bramble . . . In the spring masses of bluebells nod hopefully. Mosses and lichens, undisturbed through the years, carpet the woods and enchant the eye. Gladness is found there in the summer time. Autumn brings its tinted glories, and the weak sun glisters the snow in winter. At all seasons one may reap

The harvest of a quiet eye'.

Future generations may indeed 'move in these woods with thankfulness' that they have been preserved and cared for by the hospital authorities — the only serious invasion having taken place in the 1920s when Forest House was built as an Admission Ward (currently a Psychiatric Unit).[62]

New Plans and Ancient Woodlands

Claybury Hall was designated a statutory listed building by the Department of the Environment in 1958. But it was not until the 1980s that official interest in the preservation of the grounds was quickened by the Regional Health Authority Strategic Plan to move towards the closure of Claybury Hospital from 1984, and by the preparations begun in 1988 by the London Borough of Redbridge to produce a Unitary Development Plan for the whole borough. And in a surprise move in 1989, the D.of E. notified the D.H.S.S. of their intention of statutory listing the whole of Claybury Hospital (Redbridge had already locally listed the tower) — which they did in June 1990.

A comprehensive study commissioned by the Waltham Forest Health Authority and issued in September 1991 spoke of the 'important woodland and parkland areas . . . where development would be highly visible from outside the site'. It concluded that 'the intrinsic landscape is of great value in both strategic and local terms' and that 'The woods that remain are one of the few fragments of Hainault Forest still existing within Greater London'

62 *Ilford Recorder*, 23 May, 1902; and see other references in note 53 above; information from Eric Pryor re. walks, etc. for patients; *Claybury Hospital Report*, 1958.

as well as being 'of great ecological interest'. These latter have been placed for the time being under the sympathetic management of the London Wildlife Trust.[63]

In their Draft Report of Studies for a Unitary Development Plan, Redbridge argued along parallel lines that the Claybury Ridge, defined as the area of the Hospital and immediately adjoining land, 'has a significance that extends well beyond this borough, although it is also important on a more local level, forming a backdrop to Clayhall and Barkingside in particular and providing a valuable reservoir for wildlife'. Recognising the importance of retaining the area of Ancient Woodland, they declared that 'A significant proportion of the current open space must form part of a new District Park'.[64]

'With an awful reverence for this favorite spot . . .' – Repton

These policies are still in the process of formulation, subject to judicial enquiry and political decisions; actions have yet to follow words. But there now seems a reasonable prospect that some heritage of Claybury and its Golden Woods may survive for a further millenium.

Acknowledgements

I would like to thank the officers of the Waltham Forest Health Authority — particularly Mr. D. Wantling and former officers, Mr. J. Bedford and Mrs. J. Fisher — together with Mr. Clive Griffiths of the London Wildlife Trust, for their assistance in obtaining information. The contribution of Dr. Peter Ellis is obvious from the text. Valuable help was given in the preparation of illustrations and maps by my son Mr. Richard Lockwood, Mr. H. Martin Stuchfield, the Library Services of Redbridge, and Barking and Dagenham, as well as in word processing, by Mr. Bryan Weaver.

63 D. S. Walton, *op. cit.*, 21, Appendix E 96; Information Clive Griffiths.

64 London Borough of Redbridge U.D.P.: Report of Studies — Draft for Public Consultation (December 1989), 475-77; London Borough of Redbridge U.D.P.: — Written Statements Deposited (February 1991), 98.

In the Beginning there was Genealogy

JOHN RAYMENT

I BELIEVE THAT it was Colonel Rodney Dennis, from the College of Arms, who was involved in an exchange of letters to *The Times*, some years ago, in which he gave it as his opinion that, rather than prostitution, genealogy was the oldest profession. Certainly he makes that claim in the opening paragraph of chapter 18 of his book, *Heraldry and the Heralds.*[1]

From the time of the biblical 'begats', there has been a pre-occupation with male descent. The distaff side did not have much going for it. 'The ladies, God bless'em!' indicated, at best, a patronising attitude — and the origins of even that word betray an indulgent male philosophy. There is, of course, a dictionary meaning for 'matronising', but it is by no means the equivalent. In our patrilinear society, from the earliest days until very recently, this attitude has persisted. Genealogy was concerned with descent and inheritance in the male line. Brides were 'chosen vessels' for procreation and the continuance of the line. A dowry was often a necessary incentive, but did little to help the woman feel 'wanted for herself'.

Innumerable wives have been reviled, rejected and even done away with (*vide* Henry VIII), because they could not produce the right kind of offspring — or indeed sometimes any offspring at all. That the male partner might possibly be deficient in some measure, was unthinkable. When, as sometimes occurred, the male line failed (Oh! The disgrace!), and the line came down via a female, it was often kept rather quiet. And only recently did 'family history' take a hold. The idea that 'the lower orders', even 'trade' had a background which could be discovered — and was worth discovering — is a fairly modern idea. Many of the highly respected transcripts and indexes, such as those produced by Colonel Chester in the nineteenth century, are prefaced by notes such as, 'I have taken all, except those of persons evidently of the

1 Colonel R. Dennis, *Heraldry and the Heralds*, Cape, 1982.

humblest rank'! Such selective ideas, aimed no doubt, at reducing the task of copying, demonstrate a short-sighted approach to work which should be comprehensive, and ignore the possibility — even the certainty — of a skeleton in everyone's cupboard. A great deal of 'root-pruning' has been carried out, in the name of respectability.

Family history societies have begun to emerge only in the last few decades. Genealogical societies — some of them — began to widen their viewpoints; the history of a family — which was not quite the same thing — had been, fairly exclusively, the concern of the middle and upper classes. But it was not until 1974 that the idea really took hold.

Let us make this personal and local. In the winter of 1973/4, I was attending a class in Family History at Grays Library, run by Cecil Humphery-Smith, then Director of the Institute of Heraldic and Genealogical Studies in Canterbury. During that course, he asked me whether I was going to the forthcoming Genealogical Conference in April 1974 at Canterbury. 'Oh no', I said, 'I'm only a beginner!'. He was very rude, and I went. A most wonderful weekend. As a tyro, to live in a University Hall of Residence, to meet people whom I had only encountered on the spine of family history books, and to talk 'shop' with one and all, was a new experience, never to be forgotten. On the Sunday we had a discussion. The organisers, who had this up their sleeves all the time, said, 'What we want is more local and county Family History societies'. Pointing at me, 'You live in Essex, don't you? You can start an Essex society!' And I was lumbered. Of course, I had a tremendous amount of help; a committee was formed, Jo-Ann Buck and Noel Currer-Briggs stood by me, and pointed me in useful directions; Derick Emmison (bless his cotton socks) agreed to be our first President, and from being a sort of unofficial Organising Secretary, I was elbowed into being Chairman. I remember that we had almost sixty people at the Inaugural Meeting in the Picture Room at Shire Hall, Chelmsford. It took me a fortnight to write an Inaugural Address; and two weeks to get over the emotional stress — I'd never done anything like it before. But after that it was all exciting, uphill and new.

The Essex Society for Family History was formed in September 1974. At about the same time, there was a meeting of representatives of family history societies, in Birmingham, at which it was decided to form a Federation of Family History Societies, as a parent body for the many emergent societies, and particularly, to act as the host body for the then forthcoming 13th International

Genealogical Conference in London. It was a new life for me. From those beginnings in Grays Library, when Cecil 'chased' me to Canterbury, I was moving in new circles. The Society has grown. From those modest beginnings, it now has a net membership of nearly 1700 members (our membership numbers, which are serial, run to over 3000, but we lose members, as do all societies). We have four officers, a Committee of twelve, five Vice-Presidents (of whom one is Sir William Addison, and three are contributors to this volume), and our Patron is the Lord Bishop of Chelmsford. Derick Emmison was President for three years, Sir William, a member and a strong supporter from the start — it is not only for alphabetical reasons that he is Member No. 1 — was President from 1977 until 1984, by which time the Society had had enough of me as a Chairman and I was promoted. Sir William was also President of A.G.R.A. (Association of Genealogists and Record Agents) from 1985 to 1988 and Vice-President thereafter. While his books, all of them, deal with the historical aspects of one or other subject, the detail shows very clearly that he is fully appreciative of the close relationship between local and family history — which I shall emphasise later on.

To become a County Society with an international membership of 1700, in seventeen years, is a fairly comforting achievement. It is one of the most successful societies in the county. There are monthly meetings — barring certain summer months — on Saturdays. There is a library and a bookstall open for much of the day for the benefit of the 100–200 members and friends who attend. In the afternoon there are lectures, workshops or Q and A panels. People come to use the library, buy a book or two, go out for lunch and a spot of shopping and come back for the lecture. Members hail from all parts of Essex and the U.K. and overseas. Some of these overseas members come to our meetings, if they are researching in this country. Above all, it is a friendly society. At meetings, other than when lectures are taking place, there is a constant buzz of conversation, as members pick each others' brains and, as we often say, 'pin each other to the wall with our grandfathers'.[2] No one, we hope, either member or officer, is ever unapproachable. The beginner's 'Advice Table' is rarely unattended.

We publish a journal, *The Essex Family Historian*, four times a year, which is well thought of and widely read, and

2 Elizabeth Simpson (then Secretary of the Federation of Family History Societies), 1976 or thereabouts, 'I've been pinned to the wall by more grandfathers than that . . .!'.

periodically, a Handbook and list of members. The journal carries news, articles, notes on activities and people, reports of the progress of work in hand and a list of new members and their interests. 'Members' interests' is a valuable reference tool, because suddenly to discover that another member — of one's own or another society — is researching the same name, in perhaps the same village, is quite a thrill. Of course, with the more common names, this may well lead to eventual disappointment, but one never knows. This factor is the driving force in the many 'one-name' groups and societies. Some years ago, one of our members, having 'collected' a number of others who were researching the same name, organised a special 'weekend', out of season, at the guest house which she and her husband ran. And a good time was had by all. The journal also carries a list of books, pamphlets, periodicals and microfiche, published by the Society and by the Federation — some sixty titles — which may be purchased by post.

We have very active branches at Colchester and Saffron Walden, and their Chairmen serve on the main Committee. These cater for members living 'in the sticks'. We have an excellent relationship with the Essex Record Office; Vic Gray, the County Archivist, is one of our Vice-Presidents; Janet Smith, the Senior Archivist, is a visiting guest of the Committee. Our officers have regular meetings with the archivists, and the fullest co-operation results. We are extremely grateful for their excellent services, and we are glad to be able to make occasional financial donations, and to associate ourselves with their projects. We have involved ourselves with the highly successful Essex History Fairs, and have manned stalls there and at other functions, such as the Police Fair at Chigwell. This all leads to publicity and new members, and we have been able to help members of the public with genealogical queries.

In 1978, the present writer, in collaboration with the then Chairman of the Federation, formed and inaugurated five new Societies, North West Kent, East of London, West, Central and North Middlesex. These were started to fill the obvious need, of people who did not wish to travel across London to meetings. The East of London took as its area of activity, Metropolitan Essex, which is in the far south-west of the county. The Essex Society, having its base in Chelmsford, would have found the long lines of communication onerous. The East of London Society thus shouldered a heavy burden, which the Essex society was glad to shed. This highlights an aspect of society work which has caused concern in some quarters. It might be thought that to take over a part of Essex was a form of 'poaching', but it should be clearly understood that although we are proud to have a large and growing membership, we are not in the 'membership league'. To take on an area such as Metropolitan Essex is a heavy responsibility, involving the running of a society, supplying the members with facilities, such as a lecture programme, bookstall, a venue for meeting and all the usual trappings. But, most importantly, the records of the area need attention. Take for example, the monumental inscriptions — there is a large number of parishes, each perhaps with more than one church or chapel, and the inscriptions will have suffered greatly from industrial pollution. There will be a great number of industrial premises, possibly in the process of change or dissolution, and their archives may have to be 'chased' and secured for an under-staffed Record Office. There will be the challenge of transcribing or indexing the Census returns for the area. Parish registers may be crying out to be copied. And all the time, the families who are there, and who were there, should be researched.

Every family history society, every family historian, has a responsibility to the past, to make sure that the records and archives which have survived, are given a chance of being available to future reseachers. There is a duty to the present, in that family historians should be given the best possible chance to use these records; and an obligation to future researchers. Nothing that we do now, must endanger the survival of records. This is particularly important, because there are people who set no value on records; their activities — and sometimes their inactivities — put all history in danger. Someone who has no use for the past, will be of little use to the future.

A passing thought, re past, present and future; everything of history is past — it has happened. Everything of the future has not yet occurred. The bit in between is a minute instant of time, not measurable — an event has happened or it has not. Virtually, there is no present. In my foolish vanity, I thought that I had made an original comment, but; '... the present, like a note in music is nothing save as it appertains to the past and what is to come' (Walter Savage Landor).

On the Essex patch, monumental inscriptions are regularly copied, and to date, the genealogical information on the memorials in more than fifty churchyards and cemeteries have been saved from the jaws of time and the hand of man. Stone has long been regarded as a permanent source of record but filthy

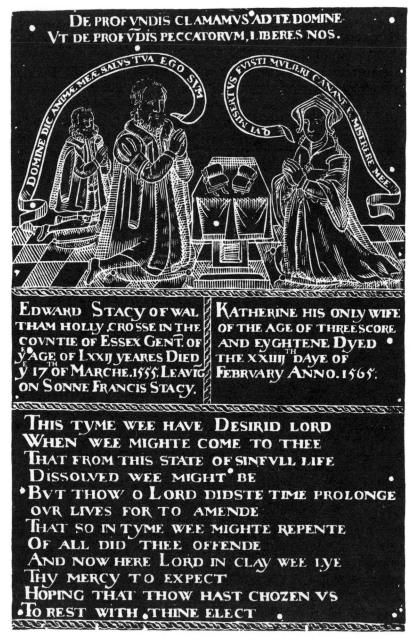

Figure 1. Rubbing reproduced from the monumental brass commemorating Edward Stacy, gentleman, 1555, aged 72, in civil dress, with one son Francis, and wife Katherine, 1565, aged 78, all kneeling on a rectangular plate with inscription and twelve English verses, Waltham Abbey.

(H. Martin Stuchfield)

industrial atmospheres, unsuitable material and vandalism have all done their destructive work. Copies of readable inscriptions have been deposited with the relevant parish or authority, the Society of Genealogists, the E.R.O. and our library. Far more are readable than might first appear, since techniques have been developed to improve legibility.

Enthusiasts among our members have taken it upon themselves to make transcriptions of parish registers, to make indexes of marriages, baptisms and burials, and to make indexes and abstractions of the collection of Marriage Licence documents in the E.R.O. Our past Chairman, the late John Boreham, wrote what was probably the first booklet for family historians on the subject of using the Census.[3] The 1851 Census of Essex is being published on microfiche by the Society.[4] A project is now under way to copy, type and index the surviving pre-1841 Census Returns for Essex — a matter of some forty parishes. The organiser of this project has published three booklets of indexed transcripts of Settlement Examinations for South-east Essex parishes.[5] Another member produced the Federation's first published monograph on the recording of monumental inscriptions.[6] A team of members is currently involved with the indexing of the 1881 Census — a nationwide scheme organised and sponsored by the Genealogical Society of Utah, and masterminded for Essex by our Chairman.

Family history has really taken wing. It has gathered to itself a great multitude of ordinary people, from the well-off to the poorly-off; from the well-connected to those with obscure, even dubious backgrounds. Everyone has the right to learn 'where they came from'; the only bars to research progress (of regress?), apart from the simple non-survival or non-availability of records, are such circumstances as illegitimacy and adoption; even here there are sometimes ways of finding out something of one's background. Not only in this county has this enthusiasm manifested itself.

3 J. M. Boreham, *The Census and How to Use It*, Essex Society for Family History, 1982.

4 *Index of the 1851 Census for Essex: 6 Registration Districts; Colchester, Tendring, Lexden, Orsett, Billericay and Ongar.*

5 J. H. Baxter, *Settlement Examinations, Rochford, Essex, 1728–1830, Rayleigh and Rawreth 1720–1844, Southeast Essex (S. Benfleet, Canewdon, Hadleigh, Prittlewell, Sutton and Lt. Wakering, 1724–1843).*

6 J. L. Rayment, *Notes on the Recording of Monumental Inscriptions*, Federation of Family History Societies, 1981.

From the seven member societies which formed the embryo Federation in 1974, there are now about 150 societies, at home and overseas, dedicated to family history, genealogy, heraldry or 'one-name' studies. Their total membership runs into tens of thousands, although, to be fair, this is a theoretical figure, because many people are members of more than one society.

The Federation itself, from having had only a Chairman and Secretary, now has a President, two Vice-Presidents — ex very hardworking Secretaries — a Chairman (who currently, is also a member of the Committee of our Society — a great linking benefit), a full-time paid Administrator and a Publications Officer — the Federation has an annual turnover in excess of £80,000 from handling some seventy titles — leaflets, pamphlets, monographs, guides, booklets and serial publications. There is an Executive Committee — I was a member for a number of years. The Federation also helps to organise twice-yearly weekend (occasionally four-day) conferences, hosted by one or other of the member societies. Essex S.F.H. hosted the Conference in September 1985 at Writtle Agricultural College, and some of our members have been to conferences at venues all across the country. When I was Record Office Liaison Officer for the Federation I accompanied the Chairman of the time on productive goodwill meetings with the Keeper of the Public Record Office and the Chief Archivist of the Greater London Record Office. From the latter meeting came the promotion of the most useful leaflet *You and Your Record Office — a Code of Practice for family historians using County Record Offices.*[7] The Federation's Executive Committee meeting was once held in the London School of Economics, to which were invited the Registrar General and several of his staff; again, a useful contact indeed.

At the Federation meeting, in Brighton on 4 August, 1974, my proposal, 'That each affiliated society should provide, without charge, to other affiliated societies, one copy of its magazine, list of members or other suitable publication' was carried *nem. con.*. As a result, the Essex S.F.H. has a growing collection of the later issues of the journals of a number of other societies across the country and overseas, which may be studied in our library or, like many of our holdings, may be borrowed for limited periods. Early numbers of these have been deposited in the library of Essex University, where members can use the facilities. Members with

7 *You and Your Record Office — A Code of Practice for Family Historians Using County Record Offices*, Association of County Archivists and Federation of Family History Societies, 1986.

ancestral connections in other parts thus need not, unless they wish, join all the relevant societies; a very great saving!

A close and useful working arrangement has developed between the Federation and the Genealogical Society of Utah. This is the genealogical organisation of the Church of Jesus Christ of Latter Day Saints, the Mormons, who are dedicated to discovering their origins. What is significant, is that they use their funds (several millions of dollars, to date) to ensure that historical records are not left to moulder, but are preserved. They have a programme of microfilming parish records, and giving a copy to the parish, which has been going on for some forty years. Films, over a million reels, are stored in their granite mountain strongroom in Salt Lake City, and copies may be borrowed by ordering via the many genealogical libraries maintained by the Mormons, and studied there using their machines — you do not have to be a Mormon to do this. These are just some of the fruits of what is surely the greatest archive rescue operation ever mounted.

From the family historian's point of view, the most important result of the Mormons' activities, is what is commonly called the 'I.G.I.'. The entries in the parish registers which have been microfilmed so far have been entered onto a great computer database, and the results sorted by country, by county, alphabetically, and by date. This data is then made available on microfiche, which for the uninitiated are postcard-size films each carrying the reduced images of 450 pages (450 'frames'); each frame having sixty entries. A full fiche therefore has some 27,600 entries, relating to baptisms and marriages. The full set in the 1987 English Edition of this, the International Genealogical Index, is a matter of 2,196 fiche; over 50 million entries. Copies of relevant sections of the I.G.I are to hand at many family history societies, including Essex, at all Mormon genealogical libraries and at most County Record Offices and large libraries. Later editions of the I.G.I. contain greatly increased numbers of entries.

Why has family history become so popular? I believe there are a number of factors, which have combined to facilitate its growth. In the first place, the world of genealogical research was largely peopled by academics, scholars, the clergy, and the well-connected. It was an occupation which, as I have suggested above, was exclusive and, to use a trendy word, elitist. Some areas of local history work were, I believe, in a similar position. Up to and including the Victorian period, and after, everyone (nearly) knew his place, and stayed there. Only gradually, as the climate of thought, in such areas as public records, public spending, societies, spare time activities and education, began to liberalise was such a movement possible.

The time was beginning to ripen. More and more people were being offered early retirement, redundancy was becoming a well-known word, and the attractions of sport were not for everyone. This occupation/hobby/pastime/obsession offered a chance to nibble at an academic pursuit, to visit relatives and gossip, to visit libraries and record offices and delve, to make discoveries and to make mistakes. What an attraction! And to join a society where everyone was of a like mind, and never said, 'Oh, shut up about your old grandfather!'. To develop an interest into a speciality, and be able to offer advice to newer members! Perhaps to carry out some indexing or transcription work, to be a valued member of a society, even to write a monograph or a magazine article, and be quoted! Which, I wonder, is preferable; to be an unswerving specialist — to know everything (everything?) about a subject, or to have a working knowledge of one or two subjects, and a happy acquaintance with many? This was a new field.

But genealogy was still there. It was necessary. No family history can be undertaken without having first built a family frame, a scaffold, a family tree. Genealogy is the starting point, and whereas in earlier days, when it was thought to be the aim and end, it was now realised that all the members of the family had an influence on the family; all the circumstances, social, financial, political and so on, were important in order to colour and shade the family portrait. So that the genealogy had to be investigated. But after that was done (and, in truth, it is never 'done' but always being developed), the family history, the 'leaves on the tree', the embroidery, if you will, could be happily sought, and attached to the main. Family history can be what genealogy never was, 'All things to all men'.

In my own researches, as the illustrations serve to show, I have discovered that my great grandfather William was a hotelier in London Wall, a Common Councillor, as well as a Freeman of the Loriners' Company and of the City of London. He was thus invited to the ceremony of the visit of Queen Victoria to Epping Forest in 1882. My father, an early amateur photographer, had to obtain permission to pursue his hobby in Epping Forest.

Why has the Essex Society for Family History been success-ful? Its officers and committee have done a first-class job, but so have the members. And, behind it all is a hidden circumstance.

Essex, from its position in the country, has, over the past centuries, nay, millenia, been a kind of transit camp for people who, in their hordes, came over from the Continent. Invaders, coming to conquer us; whether they did or not, some of them left their seed. Evaders, escaping religious persecution abroad, came over in their thousands and settled, for a time or permanently; they left, and are still leaving, their genes to mix with ours. Ours? We are them! Traders have visited us from very early times, and sailors always leave something behind.

During the ages of Britain's gradually civilising existence, people have been coming to these Islands, and have left them — always by sea. Until the coming of aircraft, there was no other way. In the period since our separation from the Continent, very few people travelled here casually. Twenty miles of choppy water, and the need to hire a boat and crew, would have deterred all but the determined. It follows then, that many of those elements of ancestry which we in this country tend to treasure, were drawn from the bold and the brave, the obdurate and the tolerant, the freethinkers and the bigots, the opportunists and the business men, the raiders, persuaders, evaders and traders.

But the bold captured the affections of the local girls — and

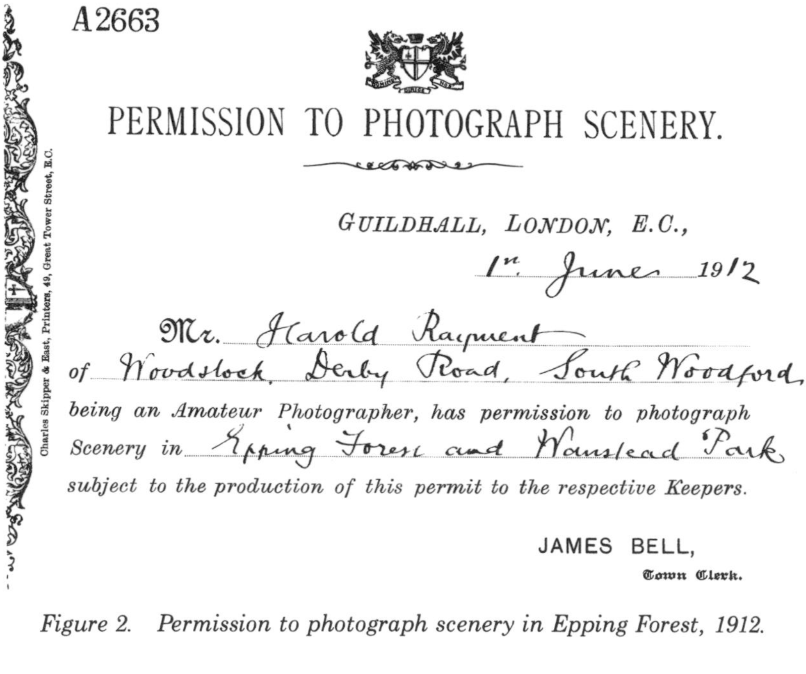

A 2663

PERMISSION TO PHOTOGRAPH SCENERY.

GUILDHALL, LONDON, E.C.,

1ˢᵗ. June 1912

Mr. *Harold Rayment*

of *Woodstock, Derby Road, South Woodford,*

being an Amateur Photographer, has permission to photograph

Scenery in *Epping Forest and Wanstead Park*

subject to the production of this permit to the respective Keepers.

JAMES BELL,
Town Clerk.

Charles Skipper & East, Printers, 49, Great Tower Street, E.C.

Figure 2.   Permission to photograph scenery in Epping Forest, 1912.

Figure 3. Invitation: Visit of Queen Victoria to Epping Forest, 1882.

probably left them; the obdurate contributed a sturdy country obstinacy with a tolerance sometimes at the root of freethinking. The bigots mostly kept their own counsel — except when they were laying down the law; the business men 'made a fast buck'; the traders raided and the raiders traded. The persuaders — missionaries — spread their word, and their seed, and traces of all these remain. The evaders brought their tools — if they could — and their skills, to upset the balance of labour and trade, but to enrich the·techniques and thought of their chosen industry, to the ultimate benefit of the country.

But the Continent was always the loser. Intolerance and persecution have helped to denude nations of their skilled artisans, men of energy, adaptability and imagination, who are the lifeblood of any truly developing nation. However insular we may declare ourselves to be, we are indebted to 'bloody abroad' for much of our country's virtue. Even a cursory glance at *An Alphabetical Index of Patentees of Inventions, 1617–1852*[8] reveals that a substantial proportion of the names listed have a Continental flavour, reflecting a profound influence on the direction of the Industrial Revolution.

This county of ours, on the route to London, either via the Thames or the East Coast ports, has perforce become a mongrel breeding ground par excellence. All manner of men and their mates settled in Essex, and though some moved on, what a people they have produced! Our Society membership, therefore, has arisen from that marvellous, mixed, mongrel population. Not only have we a rich and complicated ancestry to draw on, but we have all kinds of folk to call on when we want things done. And we are rarely disappointed. Movements of these kinds — out of the country — were the result of evaders seeking a new life in America; this country is not innocent of intolerance and persecution. Following them, and still following them, traders sailed to and from those rich productive shores. And, over the centuries, missionaries and colonists have sought to spread the influence of the Bible and increase the number of red patches on our schoolroom maps. So the Essex Society for Family History has a strong overseas membership.

It is possible that the 'busy-ness' of an active family history society could be quantified by estimating the 'total population' — both 'in' and 'through' — the relevant area over, say, the last 300

8 B. Woodcroft, *An Alphabetical Index of Patentees of Inventions, 1617–1852*, 1854, Evelyn, Adams and Mackay, 1969.

years. The numbers of souls who were 'hatched, matched, and despatched' might be relatable to the potential membership and to the potential 'work to be done' in terms of record rescue and transcription. Perhaps this index could be called the 'people throughput'.

The growth and success of a family history society will, I think, depend not only upon the enthusiasm and activity of its committee and members, but more fundamentally, on the relationship between its 'people throughput' and the social development of the area. Societies in places with a high throughput, such as the metropolitan fringes, might not thrive because the area was not yet 'residential' enough to support and provide the necessary administration. Societies with a mixed 'town and country' or a 'town and suburbia' coverage, might have a more responsive membership to call on.

It has been suggested to us that 'family history is family history, and local history is local history — never the twain shall meet'. This is a narrow-minded idea, and is just not true. For a local historian, studying a village, say, or an industry, to do so without considering the people who lived in the village or the people who founded and ran the business, would be a nonsense. Similarly for a family historian to attempt an account of his or her family without investigating — if possible — the family residence, the family business, the various workplaces and so forth, would produce a very poor story. Family history is about people and places; local history is about places and people. Where's the difference?

And it is worth emphasising that family history, in its role of an extension to, and elaboration of, genealogy, is an indispensable tool for the proper study of local history. As stated above, the two are inseparable, and mutually supportive, but I feel sure that the local history world may not appreciate fully, the extent to which the family historians have improved the availability of records. All across the U.K., as in Essex, parish registers have been transcribed and indexed, along with monumental inscriptions, census returns, settlement certificates, wills, marriage licences and many other classes of material. All of which serves to make the 'nuts and bolts' of local history, as well as of family history, that much more usable.

The 'family history people' do not just 'beaver away', they publish! On hard copy, microfilm and microfiche. And when all is said and done, research is all very well, but if no one can read it, what's the use of all that work! Never mind that it is not finished, no historial account is ever truly finished, nor can it be! Local historians have also been particularly prolific publishers. Two prime examples — among many — of the way in which local and family history are shown to be but two sides of the same coin, are Patricia M. Ryan's *Woodham Walter, A Village History*[9] and *Annals of Ashdon, No Ordinary Village* by Robert Gibson.[10]

It is interesting to look at our membership figures. At a rough guess, the Society has around 40% males and 60% females. At meetings we attract numbers of married couples, but the figures indicate that 'The ladies, God bless 'em' have plenty going for them now. And members bring their friends to meetings — sometimes they are induced to join, but it is an open meeting — the Charity Commission insist upon it.

When the Essex Society started, meetings were held in the evening, at the Quaker Hall, Chelmsford, by the Rainsford Road interchange. This venue was soon found to be too small, and we moved, by the good offices of Donald Jarvis, one of our Vice-Presidents, to Christ Church, the United Reform Church complex in New London Road. Here was everything we could wish for, meeting rooms, catering facilities, comfort, car park. We started in one of the smaller rooms, and I recall that very soon, on the occasion of an Annual General Meeting, we suddenly discovered that we could not all sit down in the room. 'Everyone pick up your chair, and up we go to another room', fortunately vacant! So we have progressed, and now we have our meetings in the Assembly Hall, with a limit of 200, our library in another, our bookstall in the room vacated above, and our copy of the I.G.I. with our microfiche readers, in the smallest. No, not 'the smallest room'. Progress, progress.

Why has family history become so popular? I believe that we have always been curious about the past, especially our own. Great numbers of people have, for various reasons, moved about the country, and about the world. Long distance travel has become so easy, but homesickness never really goes away. Where did I come from? Which house did we occupy? What did grandfather do? Or even, who was my father? Curiosity also has a persistence. And the realisation that it is now much more acceptable to dig into the past, that it is reasonably easy, provided

9 Patricia M. Ryan, *Woodham Walter, A Village History*, Plume Press, 1989.

10 R. Gibson, *Annals of Ashdon, No Ordinary Village*, Essex Record Office, 1988.

certain rules are followed, and that the skeleton in the cupboard never looks so bad when the cupboard door is open. It is also a fact that a bit of roguery in the family makes it easier to trace — as well as rather more exciting. That great-grandfather was a love-child just seems to make it all rather more romantic. And aren't we just a little bit proud to be able to confess that an ancestor was hanged, for something that nowadays is regarded rather more indulgently? If you had an ancestor who was a goody, who never did anything out of the way, who wasn't talked about, or got his name in the paper, then he won't be remembered, hasn't left any mark, and as far as you are concerned, did not exist. History is the story of the past. If an event was not recorded or remembered, then it did not happen.

There is another force, seeming to influence the activities of family historians. A kind of magnetism draws some of us, we think, back to those places where our roots lie. I have felt a definite affinity with Ipswich, and fully expect, one day, to find that a part of my family hails from there. I am not alone in this. Fuller, in *Abel Redivivus*[11], writes, 'There is a secret lodestone in every man's native soil, effectually attracting them home again, to their country, their centre'. Thus quotes William Addison in *Worthy Dr. Fuller.*[12] Sir William knows all about the fascination of history, and the obsession of family history.

Part of the fascination of family history lies in the unexpectedness of discovery. If I may misquote Paul Valery, with my own version, 'The trouble with our studies, is that the past is never what we think it is going to be!'.

11 T. Fuller, *Abel Redivivus*, 1651.

12 W. Addison, *Worthy Dr. Fuller*, Dent, 1951.

John Round of Danbury Park[1]

W. R. POWELL

THE TRAVELLER WHO turns off the Chelmsford bypass towards
Maldon soon finds himself crossing Sandon bridge into Main
Road, Danbury. As he ascends the hill he reaches the gate of a
well-wooded park, with a notice announcing that this is Danbury
Park Conference Centre. A long drive brings him to a red brick
mansion in an exuberant Tudor style, with an episcopal shield of
arms surmounting the main entrance, and a royal arms higher up
on the portico tower. From 1845 to 1890 this was Danbury Palace,
residence of successive bishops of Rochester and of St. Albans,
and it now belongs to the Anglia Polytechnic. But it was built in
1832–4 by an Essex squire, John Round.

By the early nineteenth century the Rounds were well
established among the leading families of this county. They were
all descended from John Round (*d.* 1718), who had come up to
London from Stratford-on-Avon, married well, and became
Solicitor for the City.[2] His son William (*d.* 1772), also a solicitor,
inherited from an uncle the Birch Hall estate near Colchester,
which has remained in his family down to the present day. William
had three sons. James, the eldest (*d.* 1806), became a banker at
Colchester, and by his marriage acquired Colchester Castle and
Holly Trees House. The second son, William, died in the Black
Hole of Calcutta in 1756. The youngest son, John (*d.* 1813), of St.
Martin's House, Colchester, was called to the Bar and became
Recorder of Colchester. He married Catherine, daughter and heir

1 This paper was completed in August 1991. I am grateful to Miss L.
Charnwood, assistant manager, for access to Danbury Park Conference
Centre, and to Mr. K. Smith, ranger, for the guided tour of Danbury Country
Park. Unless otherwise stated, the paper is based on John Round's diaries,
1819–49: E.R.O., D/DRh F25. Round summarized his own career on the
flyleaf of his diary for 1849.

2 For the Round pedigree see: *Visitations of Essex*, Harl. Soc., 1878, ii, 699–
702; J. Foster, *Our Gentle and Noble Families of Royal Descent*, 1883,164–6;
Burke's Landed Gentry (1952), 2204–6; E.R.O., D/DRh F11. All these
sources contain research by J. H. Round.

of Edward Green and widow of the Revd. Richard Daniel, who brought him the manor of St. Clair's Hall in St. Osyth. John Round, builder of Danbury Park, was their only son.

John Round was born on 8 March, 1783, and grew up at Colchester. When he was nine years old he went as a boarder to Queen Elizabeth's Grammar School at Dedham. The school, founded in the sixteenth century to provide free places for poor children from the Dedham area, had been enlarged in the mid-eighteenth century to take private pupils, and flourished under the mastership of Thomas Grimwood (1736–78) and his son the Revd. Thomas Grimwood, D.D. (1778–98).[3] John Round's later career shows that he had received a good education. On leaving Dedham at the age of sixteen he became a pupil of the Revd. Samuel Parlby at Stoke-by-Nayland, Suffolk, before going up to Balliol College, Oxford, in 1801.[4] Balliol was then beginning the rise to pre-eminence which culminated under Jowett. John Parsons, Master 1798–1819, and also Bishop of Peterborough (1813-19), was one of the reformers responsible for Oxford's examination statute of 1800. John Round was thus one of the first men to come under the new statute, graduating B.A. in 1805 and M.A. in 1808. He remained devoted to Balliol all his life, often revisiting the college, and sending his three sons there. The family's links with Balliol were further strengthened by John Round's cousin James T. Round (1798–1860), who was the first man from the college to win a double-first, and who became a fellow in 1822 before returning to Colchester as rector of St. Runwald's, and later of St. Nicholas' and All Saints', with his home at Holly Trees.[5]

Soon after coming down from Oxford, John Round qualified as an Essex magistrate, and was appointed as a deputy lieutenant. He also served for a time as an officer of the Colchester Volunteer Regiment.[6] In 1812, at the age of twenty-nine, he was returned unopposed as one of the two Tory M.P.s for the borough of Ipswich. In 1818 he was elected high steward of the borough of Colchester, a post which he held until his death. He retired from

3 *V.C.H. Essex*, ii, 538–40.

4 For Parlby see J. Foster, *Alumni Oxonienses*, 1715–1886, 1071.

5 *V.C.H. Oxford*, iii, 85; Foster, *Our Gentle and Noble Families of Royal Descent* (1883), 167.

6 In 1803 he held the rank of Captain, and his cousin Charles Round was a lieutenant-colonel in the same regiment: *Officers of Gentlemen and Yeomanry Cavalry and Voluntary Infantry of U.K.*, 1804, 237.

Parliament in the same year, and although he was again a candidate for Ipswich in 1820, he was narrowly defeated, and he never contested a seat there again.

Round had inherited from his father the family house in Colchester and two Essex farms, from his mother St. Clair's Hall, and from her sister, Mrs. Mary Meade, a property in Staffordshire. In 1815 he married Susan Constantia, daughter of George Caswall of Sacomb Park, Hertfordshire. Susan traced her descent from King Edward III, through John of Gaunt, Edmund Beaufort, first Duke of Somerset (d. 1455), Mary Boleyn (sister of Henry VIII's queen), and John Wilmot, Earl of Rochester (d. 1680). Besides royal blood, she brought her husband a substantial dowry, with greater benefits following the death of her father in 1825 and that of her mother in 1829. Her only brother, George, went mad in 1816, and died in 1826. Susan and her three sisters thus succeeded, as coheirs, to the Sacomb Park estate, which was sold in 1825 for £100,000, and to their mother's estates in Essex and Suffolk. From her mother Susan inherited the manor of West Bergholt, near Colchester, and a farm at Mount Bures. She also benefited under the will of her aunt, Diana Caswall, who died in 1830. John and Susan were thus a wealthy couple. In his diary for 1824 he noted 'Estimate for an income of £3,000'. Even if this was anticipating Susan's share of Sacomb Park, it probably did not include her later inheritances.

Throughout their married life John and Susan spent much of their time in London, which was convenient for his Parliamentary and professional work. In 1819 they bought the lease of 25 Albemarle Street, Piccadilly, and they occupied this house until 1830, when they took over the lease of 33 Davies Street, Berkeley Square, formerly the home of Diana Caswall. John was a director of the Amicable Insurance Society, he had banking interests,[7] and he was later a shareholder in the Eastern Counties Railway. As a Churchman he was one of the founders of King's College, London, in 1828, and he was prominent in the Church Building Society, and the Clergy Orphan Society. Unlike his father he never qualified professionally as a lawyer, but he sometimes served on special juries in the courts of the Exchequer, King's Bench, and Common Pleas, and on grand juries at the Essex Assizes; and in 1814 he was granted the honorary degree of D.C.L. (Oxford). John and Susan moved in the best society, numbering among their closest friends

7 In the Chelmsford Savings Bank (see below) and probably also in the Colchester bank of Round, Green and Co.: cf. P. W. Matthews and A. P. Tuke, *History of Barclays Bank*, 1926, 149–51.

Sir Robert Peel, the first baronet,[8] who was godfather to their second son, Lord Kenyon, a lawyer,[9] and Lord Bridport, Irish peer and Tory M.P.[10] Besides lawyers and politicians, their circle included many Church dignitaries, including Charles Manners Sutton, Archbishop of Canterbury (1805–28), his successor William Howley (1828–48), and Charles Blomfield, Bishop of London (1827–56).

John and Susan Round had three sons, John, Frederick Peel, and Edmund, and two daughters, Constantia and Eliza. They employed about a dozen servants, including two nursery maids and a governess, and sent the boys away to school from the age of seven or eight. But during the holidays there were often family outings, special treats and games at home. On young John's eighth birthday, for instance, his father took him to see the Diorama — a forerunner of the cinema — in Regent's Park. On another occasion (17 January, 1825), 'the children amused themselves with a pantomimical performance in the dining room. John was Harlequin, Frederick — Columbine, Edward — a clown, and Missy a flower girl.' In the following year a pony was bought for the children to ride during their seaside holiday.

In 1827, with ample funds now available, John and Susan laid out £7,000 for a house in Brighton, 15 Brunswick Terrace. The Terrace, 'a fine piece of scenic architecture in the Carlton House manner', still stands on the seafront at Hove, looking out across the Channel towards France. It had been built in the early 1820s for the fashionable residents of George IV's Brighton.[11] The Rounds' decision to buy number 15 had been prompted by their doctor's advice that little Frederick, who was delicate, should be sent to school in Brighton. With eight main bedrooms, there was plenty of accommodation for a growing family, and there were spacious reception rooms. John and Susan gave dinner parties there two or three times a week, and occasional large balls. Their Twelfth Night party in 1828 was attended by 100 adults and 80 children. Among the guests were 'the Duke of Devonshire, Countess Desart, Countess Lindsay, Lady Ashbrook, Rothschilds, Wellesleys, Lords Compton, Beauclerk, &c.'. The family remained in Brighton until 1829, when Susan's mother

---

8   1750–1830: *D.N.B.*

9   George Kenyon (1776–1855), Baron Kenyon: *Complete Peerage*, vii, 187.

10   Samuel Hood (1788–1855), Viscount Bridport: *Complete Peerage*, ii, 318.

11   W. S. Mitchell, *East Sussex* (Shell Guide), 88, pl. f.p.81; *cf.* S. Muthesius, *The English Terrace House*, pls. f.p.24; A. Dale, *Fashionable Brighton 1820–60*, 118f.

died. They then decided to settle in Essex, and early in 1830 they
bought the Danbury Place estate.

Danbury Place had belonged to Sir Walter Mildmay (*d.* 1589),
Chancellor of the Exchequer under Henry VIII and founder of
Emmanuel College, Cambridge, who is said to have built 'a fine
seat' there. It descended through the Mildmay and Ffytche
families to Elizabeth, Lady Hillary, eldest daughter of Lewis
Disney Ffytche and wife of Sir William Hillary, Bt.[12] After Lady
Hillary's death in 1828 her sister Sophia was anxious to buy
Danbury Place. She had married John Disney of The Hyde,
Ingatestone, the gentleman archaeologist who later became the
first president of the Essex Archaeological Society. For over a
year Disney negotiated for the property with Lady Hillary's
executors.[13] In July 1829, when his surveyor visited Danbury
Place, the house was ruinous, with rain pouring through the roof in
many places. In August Disney was considering making an offer,
but he did not secure the property. At the end of that month the
whole estate, including two farms in Woodham Walter, was put up
for auction.[14] Most of it was not then sold, but two months later
John Round appeared on the scene.

Round probably had greater resources than Disney, and he
was certainly more businesslike. He visited Danbury Place for the
first time on 21 October, and on 8 December he made a successful
offer of £21,000 for the house and park, together with Lodge farm,
Woodham Walter. On 1 May, 1830, he received the report of an
architect, 'Mr. Good' — probably Joseph H. Good — stating that
Danbury Place was too dilapidated to preserve.[15] Round then
invited both Good and Thomas Hopper to submit designs for a
new house. He would already have been familiar with the work of
both men. Joseph Good was surveyor to the Commissioners for
New Churches, and his recent private work included additions to
the Royal Pavilion at Brighton. Hopper had since 1816 been
county surveyor of Essex, and he had designed several public and
private buildings in the county.[16] On 24 May John Round visited

12 Morant, *Essex*, ii, 19; *D.N.B.* (Sir W. Mildmay); Chapman and André, *Map of
    Essex*, 1777; M. Hopkirk, *Danbury*, 16–9; *D.N.B.* (Sir W. Hillary).

13 E.R.O., D/DQc 2/3: Letters of J. Disney re Danbury Place. For Disney
    see *D.N.B.*

14 E.R.O., D/DOp T27.

15 For J. H. Good see H. Colvin, *Biog. Dict. Brit. Architects*, 350–1.

16 For Hopper see: Colvin, *op. cit.*, 433–5; N. H. Burton, 'Thomas Hopper', in
    Architectural Outsiders, ed. R. Brown, 1985, 114-31. Miss N. R. Briggs
    kindly drew my attention to Mr. Burton's paper.

Figure 1.   Danbury Park: Engraving of entrance front by G. Virtue, 1835, from Thomas Wright's History of Essex.

Paul's Cray Hall, near Bromley in Kent, which Hopper had designed, and on 5 June he accepted Hopper's plans for Danbury.[17] After that events moved fast. Round raised £7,000 by selling one of his Essex farms — Rundells at Latton — and on 14 July he and Susan met Hopper at Danbury, inspected the park, and 'fixed on a site for our house, put up poles for distances'. The old house was demolished in August, and on 14 September John Round noted in his diary 'Mr. Hopper met us in the park at 4 o'clock. Dear John laid the first stone of the new building amidst the cheers of the workmen. May it please God to prosper the undertaking in which I have engaged.' The privilege of laying the foundation stone was a holiday treat for the 14-year-old John, the son and heir: next day he went back to school at Harrow.

The new house, called Danbury Park, was built about 100 yards east of the old one. According to Thomas Wright, whose *History of Essex* was then in the course of publication, it was 'intended to be erected from a design by Mrs. Round'.[18] This statement, which has influenced some later writers,[19] almost certainly exaggerates Susan Round's part in the work. She was a talented artist and, it seems, a forceful person, and, with her husband, had many consultations with Hopper over the design and construction of Danbury Park. She may well have suggested the architectural style, and the eclectic Hopper would have been happy to fall in with her wishes, but there is no doubt that the detailed planning was his. In 1845, when the Rounds put the house up for sale, it was said to have been 'designed and completed under the superintendence of an architect of great eminence'.[20] The particular choice of style may — as Mr. Neil Burton suggests[21] — have been influenced by that of old Danbury Place, which was an imposing Tudor house of two storeys and attics, with crenellations to the first floor.[22] But Danbury Park was by no means a copy of Danbury Place, and, indeed, Hopper incorporated in it features which he was using at that time in designing

17 On 21 November, 1831, John Round visited Boreham House, near Chelmsford, a house which Hopper had recently extended.

18 Wright, *op. cit.*, i, 128. The engraving of Danbury Park (f.p.128) includes the figures of a woman and three boys, probably Susan Round and her sons: see Figure 1.

19 Notably N. Pevsner, *Buildings of Essex*, 1965, 155.

20 E.R.O., *Sale Cat.*, B2895.

21 N. H. Burton, 'Thomas Hopper', 124.

22 *Excursions through Essex*, 1818, 30.

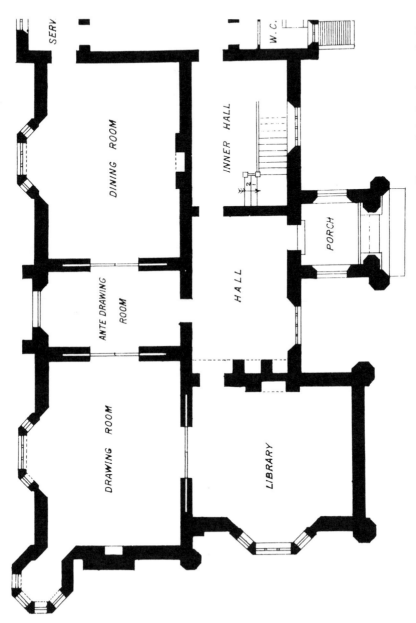

Figure 2.   Danbury Park: Ground floor plan showing main reception rooms. From a Sale Catalogue of 1892.
(Essex Record Office)

Margam Abbey, and which had been suggested by Tudor originals at Melbury House in Dorset and East Barsham Manor in Norfolk.[23] It is worth mentioning, however, that some use was made of 'old materials' — presumably from Danbury Place — in the new house.[24].

While Danbury Park was being built the Rounds lived mainly in their London home, 33 Davies Street. During the following years they rarely occupied their Brighton house, but let it on short tenancies to well-connected visitors, including Princess Lieven (1830), the Marquess of Thomond (1831), Viscountess Deerhurst (1839), the Earl of Rosse (1841), Lord Carew (1842), and Baroness Braye (1843). Ten guineas a week was a typical rent. Danbury Park was ready for occupation by 17 July, 1832, when John Round wrote: 'Unpacked a waggon-load of furniture. Much alarmed by an accident that happened to dear Edmund, which might, but for the mercy of Heaven, have terminated very calamitously. He had been trying some experiment with gunpowder, which exploded and injured his face, but happily not his eyes. Mr. Foaker was sent for and came express. He applied a lotion of lime water, and prescribed quiet and a dark room.' After this involuntary housewarming the family settled down proudly in their new home, and on 1 August gave their first dinner party there. The Bishop of London and Mrs. Blomfield came in September for a short visit, and in the following June the Rounds lent the house to Lord Kenyon's eldest son for his honeymoon. Some structural work and much internal carpentry, papering and painting still remained to be done, and it was not until May 1834 that all was complete. From 1833 the house was insured for £8,000.

Danbury Park was one of the most notable houses built in Essex in the nineteenth century, with a grand suite of reception rooms and twenty-six bed- and dressing-rooms.[25] It is a three-storey building of dark red brick, which, according to a writer of about 1861[26] was designed to appear

> '. . . not merely in good imitation of the Elizabethan style, but to have been really erected in the 16th century. This is chiefly the effect of artificial means employed at the time of its erection to give it the hue of antiquity — followed up by the sobering course of the

23 N. H. Burton, op. cit., 122–6.

24 E.R.O., D/DRh 25/14, 24 February, 1832.

25 For detailed description see: E.R.O., Sale Cat. B13, 1892.

26 D. W. Coller, People's History of Essex, 1861, 238–9.

last quarter of a century.[27] The building, with its
minarets, pinnacles, and tall, clustering, chimneys,
which are in excellent keeping with the present character of the place, has a very imposing appearance. The
entrance at the west front stands boldly out from a
recess, and presents a fine specimen of old English
architecture. The door leading from the porch to the
vestibule is of solid oak, four inches in thickness,
studded with octagon-shaped pegs, and chastely
panelled. From the vestibule, the ceiling of which is
finely panelled, access is obtained to the principal suite
of apartments — first the library, 26 feet square ... Next
is the drawing-room, 28 feet by 21, but appearing much
larger from the base of a small octagon turret forming a
part of it; and adjoining these the ante and dining-room,
the latter 30 feet by 21; the height of these rooms is 16
feet; and the floors are of polished oak; and the ceilings
are panelled in a style of great richness, a space of about
four feet in the centre of each being filled with husks and
seedlings intertwining each other, and bound together
with a ribbon. The whole of this suite of apartments
communicate with each other by means of large folding
doors, which either swing back or run into the walls, and
with their panelling of pure white and gilded mouldings,
they have a chaste appearance. A beautiful effect was
produced during Mr. Round's occupancy, by huge
mirrors fixed in the wall, extending nearly from ceiling
to floor, so as to reflect the green woodlands or the white
wintry scene of the park without ... The principal staircase is of oak . . . The prospect from the roof of the
palace is truly magificent . . .'[28]

To decorate the interior of the house the Rounds employed
George Morant and Son of New Bond Street, London, one of the
leading firms of the day.[29] In the reception rooms were hung family
portraits: 'Sir Peter Lely's portrait of the Rolts . . . the Earl of

27 For the artificial colouring see E.R.O., D/DRh F25/15, 14 May, 1833.

28 For more exact measurements of the reception rooms see E.R.O., *Sale Cat.*
B13. For the staircase see Figure 3.

29 E.R.O., D/DRh F25/15, 13 and 19 October, 1833; E.R.O., *Sale Cat.* B2895.
For George Morant and Son see: *Country Life*, lxvii, 1930, 694–6; J. Fowler,
and J. Cornforth, *English Decoration in the 18th Century*, 1974, 29, 47, 204. I
am grateful to Miss N. R. Briggs for information on Morant and Son. That
firm did further work at Danbury Park in 1843.

Sandwich . . . Timothy Caswall by Sir Joshua Reynolds', and in John Round's study, prints of 'Mr. Pitt, the Bishop of Peterborough, Mr. Hart Davis, Lord Wynford, and the Earl of Eldon'.[30] At least one of the fittings seems to have come from old Danbury Place. This appears from John Round's diary for 6 September, 1833: 'Agreed that Mr. Wray should find a chimney-piece for the library, cost £20, to match the one intended for the drawing-room brought from Italy by Sir William Hillary.' Both these chimney-pieces still survive, in the rooms mentioned. They are made of stone, with allegorical figures in relief.

The house has not been greatly altered since 1834. An episcopal chapel (now the Conference Centre library) was added in 1850, at the south-east corner of the house.[31] The exuberant exterior of Danbury Park, which amused Pevsner in the 1950s,[32] has since then been toned down by the removal of many of the chimney clusters and pinnacles. Internally, the main reception rooms are now separated by permanent partitions in place of the original folding doors, and false ceilings have been inserted below the panelled ceilings. The drawing-room, at the north-east corner of the house, has been enlarged to include the adjoining anteroom.

During the building of the house the park was being remodelled with new plantations, which seem to have been mainly in the north, near Main Road, and in the south by the lakes. On 1 March, 1831, it was decided to bring over 150 young oaks from John Round's manor of West Bergholt, and on the following day American plants were ordered from a Chelmsford nursery — possibly to start the 'American Garden', which was later a feature of the park, north-west of the main lake.[33] On 1 August, 1833, 'our boat *Majestic*' was launched on the main lake by the six-year-old Eliza Round. Two months later Danbury parish vestry agreed to Round's proposal that the Chelmsford–Maldon road, which then curved southwards for half a mile along the northern edge of the park, should be diverted to follow a straight course further north, and that was done in the following year, at John Round's expense,

30 E.R.O, D/DRh F25/15, 18 and 19 November, 1833. The Rolts and Timothy Caswall were ancestors of Susan Round. 'The Earl of Sandwich' may be an error for the Earl of Rochester, whose sister was another of her ancestors. Hart Davis was a close friend of John Round. Lord Wynford, formerly a Tory M.P. and judge, was related to Susan through the marriage of his son.

31 E.R.O., D/CC 2/2.

32 N. Pevsner, *Buildings of Essex*, 1965, 155.

33 Illustration in the 1892 *Sale Cat.*, E.R.O., B13.

thus enlarging the park and taking the road farther away from the house.[34] The parish lost nothing by the change, since Round owned the land on both sides of the old road, though the new road was slightly shorter and steeper than the old one. The landscape gardening was directed by Susan Round, while her husband ensured that the park produced an income from hay-making, cattle-grazing, sheep-farming, forestry, and fishing. By 1836 there was also a herd of deer, and on 4 January, 1836, John Round dressed his first haunch of venison.

There have been so many alterations to the park since the Rounds' time that it is difficult to distinguish their work. The north-east area of the old park is now a camp site, the central area comprises the house and grounds, with the new buildings and car parks of the Conference Centre, while Danbury country park occupies a narrow belt along the southern fringe,including the lakes. The country park contains some features from the Rounds' time, notably the ice-house near the western lake, the ha-ha which protected the formal gardens from the deer, and the rhododendrons and a solitary Arizona cypress surviving from the American Garden.[35]

As squire of Danbury, John Round was not a great landowner, but he rapidly became a leading figure in the county. Already high steward of Colchester, he was appointed a commissioner of sewers in 1832, served as high sheriff of Essex for the year 1834–5, and in 1835 became chairman of Chelmsford petty sessions. He was a member of the Chelmsford Beefsteak club,[36] and a director of the Chelmsford Saving Bank.[37] In 1837, after a short but vigorous campaign, he was elected as one of the two Conservative M.P.s for the borough of Maldon. He retained the seat in 1841, holding it until the 1847 general election, when he retired. He paid £500 election expenses in 1837, and in the following year was pressed by his constituency agent for a further £200.[38] In 1841 his agent again submitted a bill for £700.[39] Since Round

---

34 E.R.O., D/DRh F25/15, 26 October, 1 November; F25/16, 10 January; E.R.O, Q/RHi 4/83.

35 I am grateful to Mr. K. Smith for information on these features. For the gardens see also 'Danbury Park' in *My Garden Illustrated*, March and April 1920.

36 E.R.O., D/DRh 25/15, 30 August, 1833 etc.

37 *Ibid.*, F25/16, 28 February, 1834 etc.

38 *Ibid.*, F25/20, 19 and 31 May, 1838.

39 *Ibid.*, F25/23, 13 December, 1841.

received 407 votes in 1837 and 436 in 1841, it appears that each vote cost him more than £1, and it is therefore not surprising to find from another source that bribery was then being openly practised at Maldon elections. After the 1852 general election the winning candidates for the borough, both Conservatives, were unseated on petition,[40] and a Royal Commission was appointed to investigate corrupt practices there. John Round was not a candidate in 1852, but the Commission reported that at each contested election during the past thirty years there had been large-scale bribery. Before 1847 'a system had prevailed of issuing to all voters who applied for them tickets of the value of 15s. each for a "plumper", and 7s. 6d. each for a split vote, and which tickets could be exchanged for goods of that amount at any of the shops in the neighbourhood'.[41] Round was not called before the Commission, and its report contains only a few passing references to him. From the evidence given by other candidates concerning their election expenses between 1826 and 1852, it seems that his expenses in 1837 and 1841 were relatively low. If Round did make payments to voters he could have pointed out that many of them, franchised as freemen, lived outside the borough, and were being compensated for the cost of travelling to the poll, and for loss of earnings. To a man who had first entered Parliament under the Regency that would not have seemed corrupt, but by the 1850s stricter views were prevailing. It must also be admitted that both in 1837 and 1841 Round had been the running-mate of Quintin Dick, the most unscrupulous of the politicians investigated by the Royal Commission.

As member for Maldon, John Round was on most issues a loyal supporter of Sir Robert Peel. Although he had been a close friend of Peel's father, he was never on intimate terms with Sir Robert himself, but he was able to exploit the family connection in 1842 by obtaining a government post for his son Frederick. On the Corn Law issue Round was a firm Protectionist, yet he voted for the ministry on several crucial divisions in 1846, including that of 25 June on the Irish Coercion Bill, in which Peel was at last defeated.

The Rounds remained at Danbury until 1845. They loved the place, but the years there were clouded by domestic troubles, and

40 *McCalmont's Parliamentary Poll Book, 1832–1918*, eds. J. Vincent and M. Stenton, i, 192.

41 *Royal Commission on Corrupt Practices in the Borough of Maldon* [1673], H.C., 1852–3, xlviii.

at last by catastrophe. Susan was seriously ill for several months in the winter of 1835–6. The youngest child, Eliza, died in 1837, aged ten. Two years later Constantia, then fifteen, suffered from 'hysteric spasms', and in 1841 young John (Johnny) was attacked by an alarming illness in particularly distressing circumstances.

Johnny Round seems to have been a personable but somewhat indolent young man. He had spent five years at Harrow, receiving satisfactory reports until his last year, when he got into serious trouble of some kind, and left under a cloud.[42] In 1834 he went up to Balliol College, where Richard Jenkyns, an old friend of his father, was now Master. After graduating in 1838,[43] Johnny enrolled as a student of the Inner Temple, his father paying 100 guineas in tuition fees,[44] but he was never called to the Bar. In April 1840 his father presented him to Queen Victoria at a royal levee, as 'Mr.John Round junior, West Essex Yeomanry Cavalry'. The West Essex was a Volunteer regiment formed in 1830 to protect the government's munition works at Waltham Abbey and Enfield during the Reform Bill agitation.[45] Johnny served in it until 1846 or later, reaching the rank of captain.[46]

In June 1841 Johnny became engaged to Mary Anne, only child of John Francis Maubert of Beulah Hill, South Norwood, Surrey.[47] A week later the Round family went up to Oxford to see him take his M.A. It was a particularly happy weekend. The Master of Balliol entertained them to a dinner party, at which 'Constantia played on the concertina — much admired by the Bishop of London'. During the following weeks the Round and Maubert families exchanged visits in London, and Mary Anne, with her parents, spent a fortnight at Danbury Park. But on 20 August Johnny, who had been staying at Beulah Hill, was brought back ill to Davies Street in Mr. Maubert's carriage, and 'his dear Mother sat up all night with him'. He soon recovered, but on the 30th John Maubert abruptly terminated the engagement. 'All our

42 E.R.O, D/DRh F25/15, 29 September, 1833 and later entries.

43 *Harrow School Register 1800–1911*, 26.

44 *Ibid.*; E.R.O., D/DRh F25/20, 14 January, 1838; F25/21, 26 October, 1839.

45 J. W. Burrows, *Essex Units in the War, 1914–19, iii: Essex Yeomanry*, 1925, 71.

46 E.R.O, D/DRh F25/27; J. Foster, *Our Gentle and Noble Families of Royal Descent*, 1883, 161.

47 *Cf.*, *Pigot's Directory of London*, 1832–4, 186: Stockbrokers, Maubert and Co., 4 Shorters Court, Bank; *Kelly's Directory of Surrey*, 1845, *s.v.* Norwood, Gentry.

feelings were necessarily deeply grieved', wrote John Round, 'though full justice was rendered by Mr. Maubert to my son's character and conduct'. He immediately got in touch with his solicitor and with the family doctor, Thomas Davies, who examined Johnny and prescribed for him. On 5 September there was a meeting between Dr. Davies, Mr. Maubert, John and Johnny Round. An exchange of letters then confirmed the Mauberts' decision. On 10 September John Round wrote, 'Melancholy day. My spirits, which had hitherto been kept up by enforced excitement, gave way — I was quite unnerved.'[48]

It is clear that the Mauberts broke off the engagement because they had doubts about Johnny's health, arising from his illness on 20 August. The nature of the illness is not stated. Its symptoms must have been alarming: perhaps Johnny fainted or had a fit. In 1843 he consulted a Dr. Latham, probably Peter Latham, a leading heart specialist,[49] and in 1845 he is said to have fainted from a bilious attack,[50] but there is no other evidence of heart trouble, and he lived to be seventy-one.

Immediately after the termination of the engagement the Round family went off to Paris for two months. On their return Johnny received a curious consolation prize, brought by Mr. Maubert's butler: 'a handsome gold watch, of which his acceptance was requested, in testimony of Mr. Maubert's sincere regards.'[51] Eighteen months later Mary Ann Maubert married Captain Plantagenet Cary, R.N., brother and eventually heir of Viscount Falkland. She died childless in 1863, at the age of forty-four, too soon to become a viscountess. Her husband died at South Norwood in 1886, leaving £104,000.[52]

By the end of 1841 John Round himself was suffering a breakdown, no doubt brought on by worry over Johnny's health and prospects. He had for many years been afflicted by varicose ulcers in his legs, and erysipelas in his face, and in June 1842 he had a slight stroke, with temporary loss of speech. By then the family was spending less time at Danbury. Both Frederick and Edmund had come down from Oxford and were working in London, and in July Johnny left England on a long continental

48 Charles Gray Round, M.P. of Birch Hall sent John a kind letter of sympathy which he received on that day.

49 E.R.O., D/DRh F25/25, 20 and 31 March, 1843. For Latham see *D.N.B.*

50 E.R.O., D/DRh F25/28, 28 August, 1845.

51 *Ibid.*, F25/23, 26 November, 1841.

52 *Ibid.*, F25/25, 27 April, 1843; *Complete Peerage*, v, 254–5.

tour. John Round's diary for 1844 has not survived. But in January 1845 he and Susan decided to dispose of both Danbury Park and 33 Davies Street, and to make their permanent home in Brighton. Danbury Park was bought by the Ecclesiastical Commissioners as the residence of the Bishop of Rochester, whose diocese had just been extended to include Essex.[53]

On 26 May, soon after contracts had been exchanged on Danbury Park, Susan Round and Constantia went up to London to attend Queen Victoria's drawing room. Having booked into Raggett's Hotel, Dover Street, Piccadilly, they went out to the theatre. Returning to the hotel at midnight, they were sitting down to supper in their second-floor rooms when fire broke out below. Constantia escaped down a fireman's ladder, but her mother, who had collapsed on the stairs, was 'literally burnt to cinders'.[54] John Round, Johnny, and Edmund had been staying that night at rented chambers in St. James's Square. On learning of the fire they rushed over to Dover Street, but could only watch the hotel burning. The fire engines were slow to arrive, and one of the firemen was drunk. Another macabre touch was added to the tragedy a day or two later, when the landlord of the hotel, claiming that the tenant — who had died in the fire — owed him four years' rent, attempted to seize all property found in the ruins, including jewels belonging to Mrs. Round and Constantia. Susan Round's remains, identified with difficulty, were buried in Danbury churchyard on 31 May. On the following 6 August her husband 'left Danbury finally . . . my sufferings during the day were great'.

After Susan's death John Round postponed his plans to settle in Brighton. During the next two years he spent long periods abroad, mainly in Paris. Constantia was usually with him, and was often joined by her brothers. In 1848 and 1849 the old man spent the early part of each year at 15 Brunswick Terrace, from which Constantia was married in May 1848 to Captain Henry Story, R.N., 'a nephew of Lord Ashburton and of Sir Thomas Baring, Bt.', as her father noted proudly in his autobiographical notes. Edmund, who in 1846 had married Lousia, daughter of Charles G. Parker of Springfield Place, was living at Springfield Lyons near Chelmsford. He had been called to be Bar, but had recently become a partner in the Essex bank (Sparrow, Tufnell and Co.) at Chelmsford.[55] Frederick was an official at the House of Lords.

53 E.R.O., *Sale Cat.* B2895; E.R.O., D/DRh F25/26; *Essex Review*, xxxvii, 17, lvii, 8.

54 *The Times*, 27–31 May, 1845 (reports and inquest).

55 See also P. W. Matthews and A. P. Tuke, *History of Barclays Bank*, 157.

Johnny remained with his father, occupied with part-time soldier-
ing and sketching. Like his mother he was a talented artist, and in
1847 he published a volume of lithotints entitled *Continental
Scenery: views of Germany, Switzerland &c. Part I.*[56] John
Round presented a copy of the book to the Carlton Club, to which
he and Johnny both belonged, and another to Sir Robert
Peel.[57]

On 17 February, 1848, John Round gave a dinner-party at 15
Brunswick Terrace which included 'Miss Horace Smith'. This was
Eliza, eldest daughter of Horace Smith, the poet, writer, and
patron.[58] The Smiths had settled in Brighton in 1826, and from
1840 had been living at 12 Cavendish Place, about five minutes
walk from Brunswick Terrace. Horace was a generous friend and
advisor to literary men, including Shelley, Thomas Hood, Leigh
Hunt, Lord Lytton, Thackeray, the critic Richard Ford, and the
actor-manager Charles Kean.[59] He died in 1849, but Eliza and her
sisters, Rosalind and Laura, maintained their father's literary
salon at Cavendish Place,[60] and about that time, if not before,
Johnny Round must have met Laura Smith. Unlike Mary Ann
Maubert, Laura was not an heiress, but she was intelligent, lively,
and well educated.[61] According to one of her friends she 'had a
good deal of combativeness and irascibility, *no* sentiment, and a
great deal of prudence and adhesiveness'.[62] Johnny and Laura
were married in 1853, and made their home with his father at 15
Brunswick Terrace, where their son John Horace, historian,
genealogist, and president of the Essex Archaeological Society,
was born in 1854.

In 1849, with his active life behind him, John Round entered
in his diary a brief *cursus vitae*. He had for many years been a
deputy lieutenant and a magistrate of Essex, and high steward of
Colchester. For shorter periods he had served as high sheriff of the
county and as a commissioner of sewers. As a Member of Parliament, a Churchman, and a higher graduate of Oxford, he had been

56 London, Dickinson and Co. No later parts are known to have been published.
   For press notices see E.R.O., D/DRh Z13.

57 E.R.O., D/DRh F25/28, 5 and 15 May, 1847.

58 For Horace Smith and family see A. B. Beavan, *James and Horace Smith*,
   1899, and *cf.*, *Athenaeum*, 1 and 15 April, 1899; *Essex Review*, xx, 1911, 74–
   87.

59 E.R.O., D/DRh C1 to C140: letters to Horace Smith and family.

60 W. Gérin, *Anne Thackeray Ritchie*, 1981, 235.

61 E.R.O., D/DRh F12: Laura to Johnny Round [1860].

62 *Ibid.*, F11: Laura to Johnny Round, 21 January, 1858.

Figure 4. Danbury Churchyard: Tomb of John Round and his wife Susan.

(Photograph by Avril H. Powell, 1991)

Figure 3. Danbury Park: Detail of main staircase.

(Photograph by Avril H. Powell, 1991)

active also beyond Essex. He owed his position mainly to his social standing. Born into a landed family long established in the county, he had, like his father and grandfather, married an heiress, while his wife's family tree included at least ten heiresses, going back to the fifteenth century. John's marriage may have had genetic drawbacks, for he and Susan have no descendants living today, but it was a happy one. Susan, talented and capable, seems to have been a brilliant hostess. Besides entertaining frequently at home, she was in 1836 one of the chief organisers of the Winter County Ball at the Shire Hall in Chelmsford, when '201 attended, including the principal families in the county'. Her social skills must have contributed much to John's success, by securing his place among the small group of friends and relations who in those days ruled Essex.

Besides being well-connected, John Round was business-like and serious-minded — 'a safe pair of hands' in modern parlance. In the public service he seems to have been a reliable executive rather than a leader. Though not himself a lawyer, he had several friends in the profession, including judges, and he acquired much legal experience. As well as officiating as a magistrate, he served on special juries in the central courts, and on the grand jury at Essex Assizes, often dining with the judges on such occasions. His legal activities might be worth examining in greater detail, in the wider context of public order and law-enforcement in early-nineteenth-century England. In particular, it would be interesting to know more about the selection of jurymen at that period, and about their relationship with the judges.

John Round died in 1860, and was buried with his wife in Danbury churchyard. Young Horace Round, who visited his grandparents' grave about twenty years later, reported to his father:

> 'I found the railings of the tomb covered to the very top with creeper, and there were remains of copious blooms on the clematis. The mass of green made a great feature in the churchyard, and the view was really lovely, the air being extremely clear . . . Then we drove down to the Palace, and, the family being away, went right through the house and grounds.'[63]

63 E.R.O., D/DRh F13, probably written September 1880. The Rounds' tomb still stands in Danbury churchyard, though it is sadly decayed, and the inscriptions are barely legible. See Figure 4.

Essex Quarter Sessions and its Chairmen, 1760–1815

NANCY BRIGGS

DURING THE EIGHTEENTH century, the chairman of Essex Quarter Sessions was named at the previous session. These nominations were recorded in the sessions books, which, up to 1782, also give the name of the Chelmsford inn at which the justices were to dine, usually the Saracen's Head, near the Sessions House or Shire Hall, although the Black Boy, further down the High Street, was used in July 1768 and April 1782.[1] Some leading magistrates found it convenient to take the chair at a particular time of year. The Epiphany Sessions was chaired by George Wegg, 1761–63, 1766, and by Thomas Berney Bramston, 1780–82, 1792–94, 1801–04. John Wolfe chaired the Easter Sessions in 1800–02 and 1804–08. Trinity Sessions was chaired by Bamber Gascoyne, 1774–77, and by Richard Baker, 1791–95, 1797–1800, 1802, 1805–08. At Michaelmas Sessions Thomas Cowper presided between 1780 and 1784, John Henniker (later Henniker Major) between 1790 and 1793, and John Silvester between 1806 and 1813 (see Appendix). Unlike the position in Gloucestershire, there seems to have been no suggestion of the desirability of having a permanent chairman, although in 1809 it was agreed that Thomas Gardiner Bramston should take the Epiphany session and Charles Callis Western that at Easter annually. At Michaelmas 1814 Bramston raised the possibility of the justices considering 'some permanent arrangement' after Silvester's resignation; his 'very handsome offer . . . to take upon him the Office of Chairman of the Quarter Sessions in future twice a year' was accepted.[2]

The chairman's duty was to 'keep order, give the charge to the Grand Jury, and pronounce the sentence of the Court'.[3] Legal qualifications were considered desirable, but not essential, for the office. James Round, who took the chair at short notice on 9

1 E.R.O., Q/SMg 19–32.

2 Moir, 1969, 91, 104; E.R.O., Q/SO 20, 498; Q/SO 23, 107; Q/SBb 437/18.

3 Moir, 1969, 91.

January, 1770, was applauded by George Wegg, who was not present, 'for his Spirit and Goodness to his Country in not suffering our Quarter Session to be adjourned for want of a Lawyer to preside, but . . . got thro' the business very well'. On this occasion, the eleven lay justices included Thomas Berney Bramston, who was to take the chair on many occasions between 1773 and 1809.[4] At a later date, Richard Baker, a prominent member of the Inner Temple, who took the chair between 1789 and 1809, wrote to the clerk of the peace in connection with John Silvester's nomination in 1806:

> 'We both know, how highly important it is to the Community at large, that the Justice of the Country should be administered by Honorable Men, and able Lawyers . . .'[5]

A number of chairmen were professional lawyers, Chester Moor Hall (1703–71), chairman between c. 1756 and 1767, now best known as the inventor of the achromatic telescope, was a Bencher of the Inner Temple. His monument in Sutton church describes him as 'a judicious lawyer . . . and a magistrate of the strictest integrity'.[6] Charles Gray (1696–1782) was chairman between c. 1757 and 1775; he was Treasurer of Gray's Inn and Recorder of Ipswich, 1761–76. He had a large practice as a barrister and was steward of many local manors.[7] Charles Collyer, chairman between 1762 and 1769, also acted as steward of manors in North Essex.[8] Sir Anthony Thomas Abdy (?1720–75), who took the chair on two occasions during the gaol controversy and advocated taking out a *mandamus* to enforce the execution of the gaol act in 1771, took silk in 1765. His practice was in chambers dealing with family and landed property business, rather than at the bar. As member of parliament for Knaresborough, 1763–75, he specialised in legal questions and supervised the drafting of the *nullum tempus* bill in 1768.[9] George Wegg was associated with Thomas Mayhew, the Colchester attorney; he practised mainly in the ecclesiastical courts, but became recorder of Colchester and

4 E.R.O., Q/SO11, 371; E.R.O., Colchester Branch, D/DRg 4/36; see Appendix.

5 E.R.O., Q/SBb 405/21.

6 Ranyard, c. 1880, 3, 5–7.

7 Namier and Brooke, 1985, ii, 534–35; Sier, 1948, 17–21.

8 E.R.O., D/DU 133/161, 163, 164; D/DC 41/136.

9 Namier and Brooke, 1985, ii, 1–2; E.R.O., D/DBe 01; see Appendix.

Ipswich.[10] George's half-brother, Samuel Wegg (1723–1802) who took the chair between 1776 and 1794, was a Senior Bencher of Gray's Inn and Prothonotary of the Court of Common Pleas.[11] Thomas Cowper, chairman between 1779 and 1784, practised from the Temple.[12] John Wolfe, chairman between 1799 and 1813, practised from Lincoln's Inn and acted as a manorial steward for Thomas Fuller of Wood Hall, Arkesden, before purchasing the estate *c*. 1789.[13] John Silvester, whose nomination was backed by Richard Baker, 'devoted himself to the profession of the Law', becoming Common Sergeant of London in 1790 and Recorder in 1803.[14] Writing to Baker in July 1806, he expressed willingness to take the chair at Michaelmas Sessions, 'tho' I must decline the compliment that the County of Essex can not find a Chairman better fitted to sustain its duties than myself'.[15] When forced to resign in 1814 as a result of the act postponing the date of the Michaelmas sesion until after 11 October (54 Geo.III, c.84), he asked the clerk of the peace to thank his fellow magistrates 'for the many instances I have received of their marked kindness and attention'.[16]

Some of the gentry taking the chair on a fairly regular basis had received a legal education, but appear never to have practised. Bamber Gascoyne, who took the chair between 1761 and 1780, was called at Lincoln's Inn in 1750.[17] His knowledge of the law led him to offer to give T. B. Bramston a charge in January 1770, when he was trying to persuade him to take the chair during the gaol controversy.[18] He had earlier written to John Strutt in June 1763, exhorting him to 'think how uncomfortable a man must appear whilst he is delivering down and explaining the laws of the Kingdom, and adjudging men's liberties thereby, to be anxious many suspect his knowledge, his judgment and integrity'.[19] In resigning as chairman in 1781, he referred to his 'advance in years,

10 Bensusan-Butt, 1981.

11 Round, 1895, 19; Venn, 1922-54, i, pt. iv, 358.

12 E.R.O., Q/JL 6.

13 E.R.O., D/DC 41/464; D/DZw 26, 27; D/DAd 121; Q/RSg 4, 73.

14 *G.M.*, 1822 (1), 370-71.

15 E.R.O., Q/SBb 405/22.

16 E.R.O., Q/SBb 437/10.

17 Namier and Brooke, 1985, ii, 486-91.

18 E.R.O., T/B 251/7.

19 E.R.O., T/B 251/7.

which adds no strength to Legal Judgment'.[20] His reputation in this respect had spread beyond Essex to Gloucestershire, where the anonymous author of *The Magistrate's Assistant* (1784) dedicated to Gascoyne 'This Summary of those Laws which uniformly regulate his conduct as a Magistrate . . .'. Thomas Berney Bramston had a brilliant career at Oxford and was called to the bar in 1757, subsequently serving as Bencher, Reader, and Treasurer of the Middle Temple.[21] John Henniker, who took the name of Major in 1792, had been called to the bar in 1777, but was better known as a politician and antiquary.[22] Samuel Bosanquet, who took the chair between 1799 and 1805, had studied law, but confessed to the clerk of the peace before taking the chair for the first time that he depended on his goodness 'to arrange all things in such order and to give me such instructions as will enable me to go through with propriety'.[23]

It has been calculated that clerical justices constituted about a quarter of the qualified magistrates on the Essex bench, *c.* 1784–1807, but this active group never provided a chairman, unlike the Revd. John Foley, who chaired the Gloucestershire sessions between 1796 and 1800 in conjunction with a practising barrister.[24] Apart from professional lawyers, like Charles Grey, the son of a successful glazier, Essex chairmen were drawn from the ranks of the gentry.[25] Pre-1700 families were represented by Thomas Berney Bramston and his son, Thomas Gardiner Bramston, of Skreens, Roxwell, Sir Anthony Thomas Abdy, 5th Baronet of Felix Hall, who succeeded to the Albyns estate on the death of his cousin, Sir John Abdy, in 1759, and Charles Callis Western of Rivenhall Place and Felix Hall, Kelvedon.[26]

Others came from the ranks of the new smaller gentry one generation away from commerce or still involved in the City. Bamber Gascoyne (1725–91) was the son of Sir Crisp Gascoyne (1700–61), Lord Mayor of London and a brewer in Houndsditch, who acquired estates in Barking. Bamber inherited his first name

---

20 E.R.O., Q/SBb 304/7.

21 Craze, 1955, 107; Namier and Brooke, 1985, ii, 111.

22 Venn, 1922–54, ii, pt. iii, 330–31.

23 Lee, 1966, 69–76; E.R.O., Q/SBb 377/56.

24 King, 1984, chapter 6, *passim*; Moir, 1969, 91, 104 n.39.

25 Sier, 1948, 17.

26 Addison, 1973, 1, 29, 198–99; *Essex*, iv, 226; Briggs, 1989, 15; Smith, 1901, 1.

Figure 1.   Bamber Gascoyne (1725–1791), one of the leading justices serving as Chairman of Quarter Sessions. The engraving, published in 1783 under the title 'The Bon Vivant', is based on J. Sayer's caricature of 1782.

(Essex Record Office)

and seat at Bifrons from his grandfather, Dr. John Bamber, and
was determined to become a country gentleman, both in Essex
and Lancashire, although he was not liked in Essex and never held
a parliamentary seat there after his defeat at Maldon in April 1763.
Gascoyne made improvements to Bifrons, probably to the designs
of William Hillyer, and directed the restoration of Barking church,
c. 1769–71; he 'is said to have been moved by the wish that God's
house should be at least as handsome as his own'. When member
for Midhurst in the autumn of 1765, he was away playing the
squire, with 'amusements of the field in the morning' and cards in
the evening. Both he and his father were verderers of Epping
Forest. John Hanson, writing in 1796 after Gascoyne's death,
described how this noted 'bon vivant' brought an immense
cauliflower to the Chelmsford Florist Feast and laid claim to the
first prize; the joke was 'long remembered as truly characteristic
of old Bamber Gascoigne'. He took his duties at the Admiralty
seriously, but this did not prevent him being 'one of that festive
Society held at Dagenham Breach which during Lord Sandwich's
presidency at the Admiralty had éclat as well as merriment, the
Admiralty barges being frequently employed in carrying the
company to the Breach'.[27] Richard Baker (1742–1827) was the son
of Richard Baker, a rich London merchant of Stepney Causeway.
Between 1743 and his death in 1751 the elder Baker acquired
about 1,500 acres in South Essex; less than half his estate, valued
at over £50,000, consisted of agricultural land. His son first
became chairman in 1789, by which time a further 750 acres had
been added to the estate centred on Orsett Hall.[28] Samuel
Bosanquet II (1744–1806) inherited the Forest House estate in
Leyton from his father, Samuel Bosanquet (d. 1765), a London
merchant of Huguenot descent. Samuel II became High Sheriff of
Essex in 1770 and was also a verderer of Epping Forest, but
devoted much of his time to the Bank of England, of which he
became Director in 1792.[29]

A certain amount about procedure at Quarter Sessions can
be ascertained from the order books and sessions bundles. Unlike
Gloucestershire, where the Revd. John Foley's charges to the
Grand Jury were printed in 1804, no charges by Essex chairmen

27 Addison, 1973, 82; Briggs, 1989, 17, 20–21; Namier and Brooke, 1985, ii,
    486–91; Brown, 1972, 58; *Essex*, v, 194, 213-14, 227, 228, 289; Colvin, 1978,
    418.

28 Collins, 1978, 17–18.

29 *Essex*, vi, 189; Lee, 1966, 69–76.

have been recorded.[30] Before taking the chair on Tuesday, 14 July, 1795, Richard Baker wrote to the clerk of the peace, advising him of his intention 'to be in court very punctually at 11, but I think your Advertisements should require all persons having business to transact to attend at 10'. Those concerned with the House of Correction were to attend at 8 a.m. on Wednesday, as he wished to discharge vagrants from the House. Should business not be finished by Wednesday at 8 p.m., he felt that county business should be adjourned for a week, 'as it will certainly be proper for me to get thro' all the business where witnesses are to attend, to save them a double journey'. The court in fact resolved to adjourn until 14 August 'after the present necessary Business of this Sessions shall have been gone through'. Baker remarked that, in July 1791, he had contrived to finish the whole business by dinner time on the Wednesday, 'but since that period, the County business has so multiplied upon us, that the same thing will never be done again'. He intended to try the traverses, misdemeanours and petty larcenies, time permitting, but had taken the precaution of informing the Chief Baron that he might have to leave them for him to try.[31] Part of the increase in county business can be ascribed to factors within Essex, such as the increase in the number of county bridges, extensions to the County Gaol (1787–94) and the rebuilding of the Shire Hall (1789–91). Reports from committees on these and other subjects, such as vagrancy, the administration of the gaol, and the method of keeping the county accounts, would be received and discussed in court.[32] Outside pressures on Quarter Sessions were to increase during the French Wars; for example, adjournments in November 1796, March and April 1797 dealt with the raising of men for the army and navy; a committee was set up to deal with allowances for militiamen's families.[33]

It is perhaps surprising that Samuel Bosanquet, taking the chair for the first time in October 1799, supposed that 'if the chair be taken at 12 o'clock, it will be in good time', revealing himself 'unacquainted with the usual routine of the business'.[34] However, in March 1801, the clerk of the peace warned John Wolfe 'that we made 4 days of it last Session and I fear that we can hardly expect

30 Moir, 1969, 91, 184.

31 E.R.O., Q/SBb 360/47; Q/SO 16, 71.

32 Briggs, 1984, 303–04; Briggs, 1989, 17; E.R.O., Q/ACm 1.

33 E.R.O., Q/SO 16, 323, 391,392; Q/ACm 1.

34 E.R.O., Q/SBb 377/56.

to be let off for much less at the next'.[35] The record of this session, held on 14 April, 1801, gives the wording of an advertisement to be issued on the conduct of future sessions. The session was to be held at the Shire Hall on a Tuesday, at 11 a.m., when the court was to be opened. At this time Chief Constables were to make their returns; both the Grand Jury and persons bound by recognisances to give evidence on bills of indictment were to be sworn. After the reading of the proclamation, the charge was given to the Grand Jury by the chairman. The court was then to be adjourned to an upstairs room opposite the Grand Jury room to do County business; accounts were not dealt with until Wednesday morning. Meanwhile, the Grand Jury was proceeding with the criminal bills of indictment, which were returned as 'billa vera' or thrown out. Counsel and attornies were preparing for appeals, which had to be notified to the clerk of the peace before the afternoon opening of the court. Magistrates and their clerks would have had to send recognisances and examinations to the clerk of the peace at the latest by the morning of the day preceding the session. The court was to be adjourned to the Crown Court at 5 p.m. on Tuesday, 'or as early an Hour after as the County Business will permit', to resume general business. Persons wishing to take oaths or qualify for offices could attend at the first opening of the court on the Tuesday or any time on Wednesday morning.[36] These regulations were amplified by those printed in 1824. The court was still opened by the chairman at 11 a.m. on a Tuesday. After oaths had been taken and the chief constables sworn, the court then adjourned to the room over the Crown Court for the clerk of the peace to give details of county business; if the justices considered that such business would take more than three days including the opening day, the court would appoint two or more justices and recommend a chairman to sit apart on the following day to deal with specific business. Committee reports would be received and discussed in any convenient order, but individual justices could also give notice of business, which would be taken in the order it had been notified to the clerk. Appeals were heard on the second day; counsel were to address themselves exclusively to the chairman 'from whom alone the opinions of the court can be received as such'. Insolvent debtors were also dealt with on the Wednesday. The Crown Court was also held on the second day; vagrants' cases preceded the trial of indictments.[37]

35 E.R.O., Q/SBb 383/44.

36 E.R.O., Q/SO 18, 73; Moir, 1969, 91–95.

37 *Orders*, 1824, 23–24, 27–31.

No chairman could carry out his duties without taking notes in court, although, unfortunately, no notebooks survive for the period; the dispersal of the Bramston MSS. is to be regretted. Some 'Chairman's Minutes' for Michaelmas 1773 cover several cases including that of Thomas Wood of Great Burstead, miller, charged with having a false balance. Eleven witnesses were called; the surveyor of weights and measures was cross-examined; two of Wood's servants gave evidence that he kept a set of brass weights 'to try the others by' and other witnesses testified to the effect of weather on the scales, which were only an ounce out. Wood was discharged.[38] Thomas Gardiner Bramston specifically refers to his notebooks in July 1814; he had received a petition from the brothers of a man convicted in January of riot at Aveley, forwarded by the Home Secretary, who required information on the state of the prisoner's case as it had appeared at the trial. The request had arrived as Bramston was leaving for a holiday in Bath, but he was able to call on 'the friendly assistance of Mr. Gepp in going over to Skreens' to make a search for the book, so that Bramston could 'refer to my notes taken at the trial'.[39] His obituary referred to the way in which 'in his public character as a magistrate he distinguished himself by his unwearied vigilance and anxious exertions for the public benefit.[40]

*   *   *   *   *

The controversy over the siting of the county gaol, which raged between 1767 and 1772, reveals much about some of the leading justices, particularly Bamber Gascoyne, whose correspondence with John Strutt has been preserved.[41] As early as April 1767, Gascoyne was worried about the issue being raised at the Easter sessions; he thought that it should be done at the Midsummer sessions 'when all the gentlemen of the county do and can attend'.[42] In October a committee was appointed to employ a surveyor and to report on whether rebuilding of the gaol was necessary as a result of the Grand Jury's presentment at the last Assizes. The committee membership consisted of Sir William Maynard, Sir William Mildmay of Moulsham Hall, John Luther, Charles Gray, Bamber Gascoyne, Chester Moor Hall, Charles

38 E.R.O., Q/SBb 274/14; Q/SPb 15, f.6; Q/SMg 21.

39 E.R.O., Q/SBb 437/7.

40 *G.M.*, 1831 (1), 273.

41 Briggs, 1989, 17; E.R.O., T/B 251/7.

42 E.R.O., T/B 251/7.

Figure 2. The County Gaol, Chelmsford, built to William Hillyer's designs between 1773 and 1777, after controversy at Quarter Sessions, 1769–1772, as to its siting. This view of c.1810 shows the Gaol as altered and enlarged by John Johnson between 1782 and 1796; the House of Correction, 1802–1806, is at the left end of the Gaol. (Essex Record Office)

Collyer, John Bullock, Thomas Berney Bramston, William Round, Archibald Douglas, John Strutt, Charles Smith, William Wright, William Mills, James Round, John Whittle and the Revd. John Tindal, rector of Chelmsford.[43] At the committee meeting, Mildmay and Tindal supported the surveyor's scheme to rebuild on the original site by the river, albeit enlarged. One or two members suggested the use of a different site, so Mildmay, Bullock and Tindal concurred with the majority decision to examine the White Horse site, at the top of Chelmsford High Street, near the Sessions House, although it was not on the market.[44] By April 1768 it was decided to reconsider the original site and to commission a report from James Paine.[45] Gascoyne considered at the end of September 1768 that an act to rebuild the gaol would be absolutely necessary; he told Strutt that he would 'try to bring a justice or two to act with us'.[46] The committee did not wait for Paine's report, recommending in October that the present site was unsuitable, because it was unwholesome for the prisoners, dangerous to the county and impracticable from the nature of the foundations. The clerk of the peace was to advertise for plans and estimates for 'a spacious and commodious Gaol', whilst a new committee sought a new site.[47]

By April 1769 the choice of site had changed to the Bell inn at the top of the High Street, near the conduit. The parliamentary committee on the petition for a gaol bill met on 13–17 April, but then adjourned for two months. The issue was supposed to be referred to a general meeting of the county, but Abdy was prevented from calling it. Gascoyne took the chair in July, when the court passed a motion by some of the bill's managers for Dance to survey the Bell site and also the Brickfield at the upper end of the town, owned by Mildmay.[48] Gascoyne wrote jubilantly to Strutt that next session would see the end of the gaol business, but thought that he and Bramston should meet Dance at Bifrons; plans were to be laid for a new court house on the Bell site as well as a gaol.[49] Gascoyne was absent when Gray took the chair in

---

43 E.R.O., Q/SO 11, 243.

44 *Fair State*, 1771, 2; E.R.O., Q/SO 11, 256.

45 *Fair State*, 1771, 2; E.R.O., Q/SO 11, 268.

46 E.R.O., T/B 251/7.

47 *Fair State*, 1771, 3; E.R.O., Q/SO 11, 301–02.

48 E.R.O., Q/SO 11, 328, 345–46; Q/SBb 258/17; *Fair State*, 1771, 5, 6.

49 E.R.O., T/B 251/7.

October 1769. Both Dance and Paine reported in favour of the old site; Mildmay insisted that Paine's report on the unsuitability of the Brickfield should be read out, but made a conditional offer of the site, if Dance's further survey found it preferable to the old site. Gascoyne wrote indignantly to Strutt, accusing him of being 'planet struck' and advocated the use of an experienced surveyor to refute Dance's scheme by providing a plan for a gaol on the Bell site. However, Quarter Sessions in January 1770, with James Round in the chair, decided on the Brickfield site, after some justices had prevented Dance from making comparisons with the original site. Dance, when questioned by the House of Commons committee, categorically stated that 'the *Old Situation was more convenient* and in every respect *more eligible* than the Brickfield'. An act was accordingly passed to authorise the purchase of additional ground adjoining the existing gaol.[50]

The author of *A Fair State of all the Facts concerning the Dispute about a proper Situation for the Common Gaol of the County of Essex*, published in 1771, considered it a matter of 'great surprize' that after a mass of evidence, including that of surveyors and medical men, had been produced to procure the act, 'a Majority of Justices assembled at the Quarter Sessions [on 10 July, 1770], consisting of a number of Gentlemen from the Neighbourhood of Barking and Stratford, should contrary to the Opinion of many of the most respectable Justices of the County' decide to postpone the execution of the act and set up a committee to apply to parliament to amend it.[51] The writer was referring to a number of justices from the London end of the county, headed by Bamber Gascoyne and his brother, Joseph, their friends, John Keeling and Anthony Todd, and, possibly, Samuel Bosanquet.[52] Gascoyne would also have been supported by T. B. Bramston, John Strutt and the latter's brother-in-law, the Revd. Charles Phillips. There is evidence from the Strutt MSS. that Gascoyne had been planning some sort of coalition. As early as September 1768, he was trying to bring one or two supporting justices to the next sessions. He was hoping to 'have many justices from these parts and all with us' at the Easter sessions in 1769, when those present, apart from Keeling and Todd, included John Leapidge and Ynyr Burges, both of East Ham. The following October, Todd was the only one to attend of the three from the

50 E.R.O., Q/SO 11, 368, 375; *Fair State*, 1771, 6, 7; E.R.O., T/B 251/7.

51 *Fair State*, 1771, 1, 8; E.R.O., Q/SO 11, 420.

52 *Essex*, v, 213; vi, 189, 252.

area who were planning to do so. It was Todd who gave Gascoyne a report on the sessions held on 9 January, 1770, when James Round excelled himself as chairman.[53] 'The most respectable Justices of the County', who in July 1770 favoured putting the gaol act into execution, probably included Charles Gray, William and James Round, John Jolliffe Tufnell of Langleys and the Revd. John Tindal.[54]

The division between the two factions at this session may explain why the committee to apply to Parliament to amend the act did not consist of named justices, but of all those present in court, plus any others who wished to attend the first meeting on 30 July; there was a quorum of seven.[55] This committee was accused of going beyond its terms of reference; it proposed by a majority of one vote to apply to repeal the act and to recommend the purchase of the White Horse site and the building of a new sessions house in addition to the gaol.[56] Gascoyne had been instrumental in getting William Hillyer to survey the old gaol, the Bell and the White Horse. The new gaol was to be on the White Horse site and designed in such a way as to be free from objections as to its being dangerous and obnoxious to the towns-people, who were in favour of it remaining at the other end of the High Street. The assize house was to be between the old sessions house and the churchyard, a site which was eventually chosen for the Shire Hall. Gascoyne obtained the support of the Lord Lieutenant, Lord Rochford, for the project and for Hillyer's designs. Quarter Sessions, with Gascoyne in the chair, approved the scheme on 2 October, 1770.[57]

A month later, a meeting was held at the Black Boy of about 1,600 landowners, including Sir William Mildmay, farmers and occupiers of land liable to pay tax to concert measures for opposing the removal of the gaol from its site by the river to the White Horse and 'the erecting several unnecessary Buildings at a very great Expence to the County'. The erection of the gaol on the White Horse site would deprive farmers of convenient accommodation on market days and produce a risk of spreading 'Gaol

---

53 E.R.O., T/B 251/7; Green, 1910, 87; *Essex*, v, 14; E.R.O., Q/SO 11, 321, 362.

54 E.R.O., Q/SO 11, 406; *cf.* voting record, 16 July, 1771, Q/SO 12, 59.

55 E.R.O., Q/SO 11, 420.

56 *Fair State*, 1771, 8.

57 *Fair State*, 1771, 8; E.R.O., T/B 251/7; Q/SO 12, 4–5. For Hillyer, see Briggs, 1984, 300–01.

Distemper'. A petition was to be presented to Parliament, in conjunction with the inhabitants of Chelmsford, putting forward arguments which it was hoped would 'outweigh the private piques or Malignity of 3 *Justices* of the peace, expending upwards of £1000 County Money to support their Arbitrary Measures'.[58] However, during January 1771 Gray, Bramston and Gascoyne met to settle the petition to Parliament; the hearing began on 15 February and was adjourned on 16 April for a week. John Strutt gave evidence in favour of rebuilding the sessions house; business was frequently halted by the noise of carriages and droves of cattle. Members of the grand jury had no room to retire to and had to adjourn to a public house. Strutt also seems to have been behind the printing of the evidence given to the House of Commons committee.[59]

Matters came to a head at Quarter Sessions on 16 July, 1771, with Gray in the chair. John Luther moved a motion to carry the original act (10 Geo. III) into execution by purchasing lands adjoining the present gaol; this was lost by seventeen votes to twenty-seven. The Earl of Rochford's motion to petition to repeal the act and to obtain a new act to build a new gaol on the White Horse or any other convenient site was passed by twenty-seven votes to ten. Unusually, the order book records the names of those voting. Gascoyne's supporters included those present in July 1770, with the exception of Bosanquet, who was absent; John Pardoe of Leyton also voted with this group. Richard Benyon of Gidea Hall was one of Luther's prominent supporters.[60] Benyon continued to be involved in the ultimately successful attempt to enforce the orginal act. This was achieved by a committee, including Luther, Sir Anthony Abdy and Lord Waltham of New Hall, Boreham, who called a meeting at the Black Boy on 18 November, 1771, 'to concert measures for enforcing the performance of the Act' and preventing 'the misapplication of the County's Money'. Benyon agreed with Abdy 'that the best and least expensive method of proceeding will be to move the Court of King's Bench for a Mandamus'. At the sessions in January 1772, it was decided to seek counsel's opinion to show cause why the writ should not be issued. The writ was actually obtained by Major-General Philip Honywood and, as a result, Quarter Sessions was obliged in July

58 E.R.O., D/DBe 01.

59 E.R.O., T/B 251/7; *Several Petitions* [1771], 16.

60 E.R.O., T/B 251/7; D/DBe 01; Q/SO 12, 59–60; *Essex*, v, 208; vi, 186–87.

1772 to obey the order of the higher court and put the act in execution.[61]

Charles Gray took the chair at the last two sessions at which the siting of the gaol was the main issue. After serious food shortages in the spring of 1772 led to riots in various parts of Essex, Gascoyne showed himself ready to do his duty by taking the chair at the Easter sessions at the request of the clerk of the peace. Gray, Sir Anthony Abdy, already a martyr to gout, and George Gent had already declined. Gascoyne wrote to the clerk that he supposed 'somewhat is expected at this Sessions to be done touching the late Riots; it is an unpopular and Critical matter and therefore left for me. Had there been any stir about building a Goal (*sic*) you would have Justices in numbers, but the *Peace and honour* of the County is not of Consequence.'[62] The sessions was attended by twenty-two justices, not far short of the attendance of twenty-five in April 1769 when the gaol was on the agenda. The higher attendances of thirty-one in July 1770 and forty-four in July 1771 may have been partly influenced by the time of year as well as by the gaol controversy.[63] The court decided in April 1772 that all rioters, apart from the three who pleaded guilty, were to be prosecuted at Quarter Sessions or Assizes.[64] On this occasion Gascoyne, who was sometimes inclined to bid 'adieu to county business', obviously concurred with the views of the author of *The Magistrate's Assistant* on the difficulty of persuading gentlemen to 'dedicate some Portion of their Leisure Hours to the Preservation of public Peace, and to the Maintenance of good Order and Decency among their Neighbours'.[65] These remarks, however, could equally well apply to all those justices who served as chairmen of Essex Quarter Sessions during the period under review.

61 E.R.O., D/DBe 01; T/B 251/7; Q/SO 12, 94, 137, 146; Green, 1910, 85.

62 E.R.O., Q/SBb 269/1, 5, 37, 47; Brown, 1969, 131.

63 E.R.O., Q/SO 11, 321, 406; Q/SO 12, 1, 46, 107.

64 E.R.O., Q/SO 12, 124; *Ch. Ch.*, 1 May, 1772; Brown, 1969, 131.

65 E.R.O., T/B 251/7.

APPENDIX

Chairmanship of Essex Quarter Sessions, 1760–1815

	Epiphany	Easter	Trinity	Michaelmas
1760	John Comyns	George Wegg	Charles Gray	Chester Moor Hall
1761	George Wegg	Bamber Gascoyne	Charles Gray	Chester Moor Hall
1762	George Wegg	Bamber Gascoyne	Charles Collyer	Charles Gray
1763	George Wegg	Charles Collyer	Chester Moor Hall	Charles Gray
1764	Charles Collyer	Bamber Gascoyne	George Wegg	Charles Gray
1765	George Wegg	Chester Moor Hall	Charles Collyer	Charles Gray
1766	George Wegg	Chester Moor Hall	Bamber Gascoyne	Charles Gray
1767	Charles Collyer	Chester Moor Hall	Charles Gray	Charles Collyer
1768	Charles Gray	Charles Collyer	Bamber Gascoyne	Charles Gray
1769	Charles Collyer	Sir Anthony Abdy	Bamber Gascoyne	Charles Gray
1770	James Round	George Gent	Sir Anthony Abdy	Bamber Gascoyne
1771	Charles Gray	George Gent	Charles Gray	Charles Gray
1772	Charles Gray	Bamber Gascoyne	Charles Gray	Charles Gray
1773	Charles Gray	Charles Gray	Charles Gray	T. B. Bramston
1774	John Conyers, jun.	T. B. Bramston	Bamber Gascoyne	Bamber Gascoyne
1775	Charles Gray	James Round	Bamber Gascoyne	T. B. Bramston
1776	Samuel Wegg	T. B. Bramston	Bamber Gascoyne	Samuel Wegg
1777	Bamber Gascoyne	T. B. Bramston	Bamber Gascoyne	Samuel Wegg
1778	T. B. Bramston	Samuel Wegg	Bamber Gascoyne	Samuel Wegg
1779	Thomas Cowper	Samuel Wegg	Bamber Gascoyne	Thomas Cowper
1780	T. B. Bramston	Samuel Wegg	Bamber Gascoyne	Thomas Cowper
1781	T. B. Bramston	Samuel Wegg	T. B. Bramston	Thomas Cowper
1782	T. B. Bramston	Samuel Wegg	T. B. Bramston	Thomas Cowper
1783	Samuel Wegg	T. B. Bramston	Samuel Wegg	Thomas Cowper
1784	T. B. Bramston	T. B. Bramston	T. B. Bramston	Thomas Cowper
1785	Samuel Wegg	Samuel Wegg	T. B. Bramston	T. B. Bramston

	Epiphany	Easter	Trinity	Michaelmas
1786	T. B. Bramston	Samuel Wegg	T. B. Bramston	John Henniker
1787	T. B. Bramston	Samuel Wegg	John Henniker	T. B. Bramston
1788	Samuel Wegg	John Henniker	T. B. Bramston	T. B. Bramston
1789	John Henniker	Samuel Wegg	T. B. Bramston	Richard Baker
1790	John Henniker	T. B. Bramston	Richard Baker	John Henniker
1791	T. B. Bramston	T. B. Bramston	Richard Baker	John Henniker
1792	T. B. Bramston	Samuel Wegg	Richard Baker	John Henniker-Major
1793	T. B. Bramston	John Henniker-Major	Richard Baker	John Henniker-Major
1794	T. B. Bramston	Samuel Wegg	Richard Baker	T. B. Bramston
1795	John Henniker-Major	T. B. Bramston	T. B. Bramston	T. B. Bramston
1796	John Henniker-Major	T. B. Bramston	Richard Baker	John Henniker-Major
1797	Richard Baker	William Selwyn	Richard Baker	Richard Baker
1798	T. B. Bramston	William Selwyn	Richard Baker	T. B. Bramston
1799	John Wolfe	T.B. Bramston	Richard Baker	Samuel Bosanquet
1800	T. B. Bramston	John Wolfe	Samuel Bosanquet	Samuel Bosanquet
1801	T. B. Bramston	John Wolfe	Richard Baker	Samuel Bosanquet
1802	T. B. Bramston	John Wolfe	John Wolfe	Samuel Bosanquet
1803	T. B. Bramston	Richard Baker	Samuel Bosanquet	Samuel Bosanquet
1804	T. B. Bramston	John Wolfe	Richard Baker	T. B. Bramston
1805	Samuel Bosanquet	John Wolfe	Richard Baker	Richard Baker
1806	John Wolfe	John Wolfe	Richard Baker	John Silvester
1807	T. B. Bramston	John Wolfe	Richard Baker	John Silvester
1808	John Wolfe	John Wolfe	John Wolfe	John Silvester
1809	T. B. Bramston	T. B. Bramston	John Wolfe	John Silvester
1810	T. G. Bramston	C. C. Western	T. G. Bramston	John Silvester
1811	T. G. Bramston	C. C. Western	John Wolfe	John Silvester
1812	T. G. Bramston	C. C. Western	John Wolfe	John Silvester
1813	T. G. Bramston	C. C. Western	T. G. Bramston	John Silvester
1814	T. G. Bramston	C. C. Western	John Wolfe	T. G. Bramston
1815	C. C. Western	T. G. Bramston	John Wolfe	T. G. Bramston

Bibliography

Addison, 1973 — Addison, W., *Essex Worthies.*

Bensusan-Butt, 1981 — Bensusan-Butt, J., *George Wegg and East Hill House, Colchester*, typescript, 1981.

Briggs, 1984 — Briggs, N., 'The evolution of the office of county surveyor in Essex, 1700-1816', *Architectural History*, xxvii, 297–307.

Briggs, 1989 — Briggs, N., *Georgian Essex*, E.R.O. Publication, no. 102.

Brown, 1969 — Brown, A. F. J., *Essex at work, 1700–1815*, E.R.O. Publication, no. 49.

Brown, 1972 — Brown, A. F. J., *Essex People, 1750–1900*, E.R.O. Publication, no. 59.

Ch. Ch. — *Chelmsford Chronicle.*

Collins, 1978 — Collins, E. J. T., *A History of the Orsett Estate, 1743–1814*, Thurrock Museums Department, Publication no. 2.

Colvin, 1978 — Colvin, H., *A biographical dictionary of British Architects, 1600-1840.*

Craze, 1955 — Craze, M., *History of Felsted School, 1564–1947.*

Essex, iv — Victoria County History, *Essex*, iv, 1956.

Essex, v — Victoria County History, *Essex*, v, 1966.

Essex, vi — Victoria County History, *Essex*, vi, 1973.

Fair State, 1771 — *A Fair State of all the Facts concerning the Dispute about a proper Situation for the Common Gaol of the County of Essex.*

G.M. — *Gentleman's Magazine.*

Green, 1910 — Green, J. J., 'Chapman and André's Map of Essex . . .', *Essex Review*, xix, 78–88.

King, 1984 — King, P. J. R., 'Crime, law and society in Essex, 1740–1820', Cambridge Ph.D.

Lee, 1966 — Lee, G. L., *The Story of the Bosanquets*, 1966.

Moir, 1969 — Moir, E., *Local Government in Gloucestershire, 1775–1800*, Bristol and Gloucestershire Archaeological Society Records Section, viii.

Namier and
Brooke, 1985

Namier, L. and Brooke, J., *The House of Commons, 1754–1800.*

Orders, 1824

Orders, Rules and Regulations of the Court of General Quarter Sessions . . . of the County of Essex . . .

Ranyard,
c. 1880

Ranyard, A. C., 'Chester Moor Hall, the inventor of the achromatic telescope', reprinted from *Astronomical Register, c.* 1880.

Round, 1895

Round, J. H., 'Pedigree of Wegg', *Genealogist*, N.S., xi, 19.

*Several
Petitions*
[1771]

The Several Petitions and Evidence laid before Parliament for and against obtaining a Bill to remove Chelmsford Gaol.

Sier, 1948

Sier, L. C., 'Charles Gray, M.P., of Colchester', *Essex Review*, lvii, 17–21.

Smith, 1901

Smith, C. Fell, 'The Western Family of Rivenhall', *Essex Review*, x, 1–22, 65-80.

Venn, 1922–54

Venn, J. and J. A., *Alumni Cantabrigienses.*

Wills of Elizabethan Essex Clergy

F. G. EMMISON

THE SUBJECT MATTER which I offer to a long-term friend is fitting, I trust, because it tallies with three of his numerous activities. Among his early books was *The English Country Parson* (1947); his many chairmanships included that of The Friends of Essex Churches; as a Fellow of the Society of Antiquaries he would have loved to handle the books bequeathed in these wills.

There were seven courts in which the wills of Essex clergy could be proved. The local courts were those of the Archdeacons of Essex, Colchester and Middlesex (Essex and Hertfordshire Jurisdiction), of the Bishop of London's Commissaries (London Jurisdiction, and Essex and Hertfordshire Jurisdiction); abstracts of the last court are being published in *Essex Wills, 1558–1603*, volumes 8–12; the rest have already appeared in volumes 1–7 and in *Elizabethan Wills of South-West Essex*.[1] Other wills were proved by the Bishop's Consistory Court (now preserved in the Greater London Record Office). Testators living in the diocese of London with property worth over £10 in more than one diocese or of higher social status had their wills proved by the Prerogative Court of Canterbury (now in the Public Record Office); such wills made between 1558 and 1603 by Essex clerics are herein briefly abstracted and discussed.[2] The only omissions are five clerical testaments of negligible interest.

The wills cover a period of great upheaval in religious affairs, especially in Essex. The diocese of London, which embraced Essex, bore the brunt of the unrest because of the strong element

---

1 F. G. Emmison, ed., *Essex Wills*, vols. 1–7, E.R.O., 1982–92; vols. 8–12 (F. G. Emmison and K. J. Neale, eds.), awaiting publication; F. G. Emmison, *Elizabethan Wills of South-West Essex*, Kylin Press , 1983.

2 Photocopies, purchased and presented by The Friends of Historic Essex of all (approximately 1,000) Elizabethan P.C.C. wills of Essex testators, with index of personal names, may be seen at E.R.O. Over 300 detailed abstracts in F. G. Emmison, *Elizabethan Life: Wills of Essex Gentry and Merchants*, E.R.O., 1978.

Figure 1. A nineteenth century engraving of Dedham.

(Essex Record Office)

of Puritan dissent. The penal provisions of the Acts of Supremacy and Uniformity, passed soon after Elizabeth's accession, and her dislike of over-zealous preachers of unorthodox doctrines led to her proclamation against them (see wills nos. 2 and 22). Soon began a general persecution of the Puritan clergy, and those of Essex were most exposed.

Some free-thinking opposition was seen in the University of Cambridge, which was largely Protestant. It arose partly from its ancient privilege of licensing a number of preachers, which resulted in the appointment of 'church lecturers'. Of these, the non-beneficed Dr. Edmund Chapman at Dedham was the active moderator of the 'Classis' movement involving about sixty ministers of Essex and Suffolk (no. 22). In 1575, John Aylmer, Bishop of London, began to show extreme anti-Puritan hostility, evinced later by his searching visitation of 1584. Its severity drew an appeal by twenty-seven Essex ministers to the Privy Council for 'protection' from persecution, but ejection or silencing of nearly fifty clerics ensued. A number of councillors, headed by Cecil, Lord Burleigh, expressed their anxiety in a long petition to Aylmer.[3]

> 'Hearing of late of the lamentable estate of the church in Essex, that is, of a great number of learned preachers there suspended ... and of certain appointed ... neither of learning nor of good name, and ... a great number occupying the cures being notoriously unfit . . . or chargeable with great faults, and drunkenness, filthiness of life, gamesters, haunting of alehouses and such like ... we do most earnestly desire that the people may not be deprived of the pastors being diligent and learned . . .'

Details of such clerics were almost certainly taken from a long survey of 'unpreaching ministers in Essex', listing their names and delinquencies or inadequacies, compiled by some hundreds of laymen from various areas in Essex and submitted to the Privy Council. Patently partisan, it was printed by Davids[4] in full without comment.

This introductory note to the wills is desirable in the context of the almost complete absence of our testators' names from the

---

3 T. W. Davids, *Annals of Evangelical Nonconformity in Essex*, 1863, 77, 79, 83.

4. *Ibid.*, 88–126.

lists of unworthy ministers. The truth is that our clergy were mostly high-ranking incumbents (notably Dr. Wattes, no. 10) with rich benefices, probate of whose wills would normally fall within the P.C.C. jurisdiction. Many of these men were connected, if only indirectly, with the leaders of the diocesan hierachy. None was apparently ever charged with a clerical offence[5], Dr. Chapman's office being exceptional. It is of course a fact that the names of those who lived orderly but mundane lives were generally absent from court and other archives. Historians and genealogists are consequently deprived of useful biographical details, collateral knowledge, and scandal! Hence, wills of such people have an importance as they may be informative beyond the facts found in routine records. More importantly, in the present aspect, they go some way towards modifying the unpleasant allegations publicised by Davids and later writers using the biased survey. Several of our testators endured some form of disapproval (nos. 2, 17, 20, 22).[6]

It is interesting that the incumbent of a parish close to Colchester left a bequest to the strictly religious Flemish immigrants there (no. 8). If charity and scholarship are deemed worthy criteria, both are disclosed in a number of the wills. Generous gifts to the poor appear (especially nos. 5, 6, 8, 13, 16, 22), but very few legacies to their own churches; somewhat unusual is the 'profit' from a ewe towards the repair of a church (no. 9). In addition to general bequests of books, five wills specify the titles (nos. 6, 12, 15, 19; those in no. 10 being too numerous to copy). Cambridge is remembered by four *alumni* (nos. 6, 8, 10, 16). New England historians will find two items of interest (nos. 10, 14).

The wills appearing below are given in narrative form, the dates and extracts using modern style. Because of space restrictions, legacies, etc. of cash, household goods, livestock, and the like are mostly omitted (but not those in no. 6); students of Tudor social life have ample material in the books cited herein, together with the abundant detail in *The Description of England*[7] by the

---

5 F. G. Emmison, *Elizabethan Life: Morals and the Church Courts*, E.R.O., 1973.

6 Details of academic careers are of course obtainable from Venn, *Alumni Cantabrigiensis*, 1922; very few Essex clergy graduated at Oxford. Lists of the Essex clergy (somewhat incomplete) with dates of institution appear in R. Newcourt, *Repertorium Ecclesiasticum Londinense*, ii, 1710.

7 G. Edelin, ed., *William Harrison's Description of England*, Cornell University, 1968.

contemporary social historian, William Harrison, rector of
Radwinter near Saffron Walden (1558–93), and *Elizabethan Life:
Home, Work and Land.*[8] Unfortunately it is not easy to compare
the farming activities of clergy and laity.[9]

1. *John Mason, rector of South Fambridge and of Ashingdon; will dated 6 November, 1559; proved 22 June, 1560.*

Instituted to South Fambridge in 1530 and Ashingdon in 1555.
Wishes to be buried in the former chancel. Two unidentified
'priests', John Ayre and Robert Thomson, are to get his 'fox-
furred gown and best short gown'. His ample household goods
include a 'singleside gun'.

2. *John Gregill (or Gregyll), vicar of Barking; will dated 12 December, 1559; proved 22 December, 1559.*

Instituted in 1524. He was one of several Essex clerics forbidden
in December 1558 to engage in unorthodox preaching, and soon
afterwards had a short spell in the Fleet prison on suspicion of
papacy. He had been presented to Barking by the abbess and
convent of Barking, and he also held three non-Essex benefices. In
1559 he apparently conformed and was re-instated to Barking.[10]
He asks the parson of St. Andrew Undershaft, London, (of which
he was rector) to make a funeral sermon and another on his
month's day, adding 'to the poor people at my month day 40s. in
money and 20s. in bread, drink and cheese'. 'My executors shall
leave in the vicarage wherein I dwell, to remain to the next vicar, a
featherbed, on condition that he shall nothing demand of my
executors for dilapidations of the vicarage.' His interment is to be
'at the entering in at the chancel within the door'.

3. *Peter Wilie, former chantry priest of Chelmsford; will dated 31 January, 1565; proved 18 March, 1566.*

Wilie (Wyley or Wyleigh) never held a benefice. At the Dissolution
of the Chantries, he was chaplain of Mountney's chantry *alias* the

8 F. G. Emmison, *Elizabethan Life: Home, Work and Land*, E.R.O., 1976,
   reprinted 1991.

9 The same difficulty was found by F. W. Brooks, 'The Social Position of the
   Parson in the 16th Century', *Journal of British Archaeological Association*,
   3rd series, x, 35.

10 *Acts of the Privy Council, 1558–70*; J. Strype, *Annals of the Reformation*,
    1709–31,i, 65; E.R.O., T/A 333.

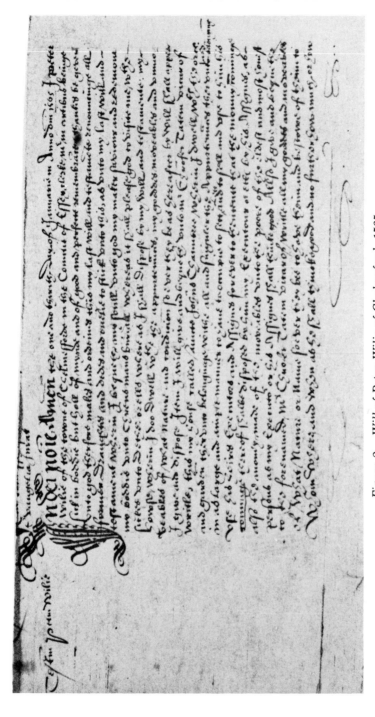

Figure 2. Will of Peter Wilie of Chelmsford, 1565.

Former priest of the chantry chapel in Chelmsford churchyard, he also taught at the grammar school there, about to be re-founded.

(Essex Record Office)

[Editor: In 1968-70 the Friends of Historic Essex purchased from Somerset House negative photostats of the whole series of nearly 1,000 Essex Wills proved in the Prerogative Court of Canterbury, later presented to the Essex Record Office (T/A 816). Abstracts of 339 of them were printed as *Elizabethan Life: Wills of Essex Gentry and Merchants* (E.R.O., vol. 71, 1978). Wilie's will is reproduced and indicates that those who wish to consult them will find the entire series remarkably legible.]

Blessed Mary's chapel in Chelmsford churchyard. It possessed the small manor of Benedict Otes in Writtle, endowed to provide a priest to say mass in the chapel. The chantry certificate, 1548, reads that 'Peter Wyleigh clerk, Master of Arts, aged 56 years, and hath none other promotion, and of good conversation, and teacheth a grammar school there and hath done this sixteen years and more, is now incumbent thereof'; it adds that he 'celebrateth mass in the chapel'. The commissioners also state that 'a grammar school hath been continually kept with the revenues', that his wages are £9 12s. a year, and that 'the school is very meet and necessary to continue and it is needful and necessary to have an assistant to serve the cure in the parish church'.[11] Although re-endowed with other local lands, the school was as elsewhere sychophantically called 'King Edward VI Grammar School'. The ex-chaplain subscribed to the Act of Supremacy in 1559. By his will, he wishes 'to be buried in Writtle churchyard before the new chapel of Mr. Carpenter in the east'. It concludes: 'To Mr. Christopher Tatem, vicar of Writtle, my house called St. John's Chantry, wherein I dwell, to occupy and sell to the intent that the money be disposed to the poor of the eldest and most honest persons. I make him my sole executor. To Mr. John Royden, parson of Little Waltham, 6s. 8d., whom I make supervisor'.

4. *William Ryche, vicar of Stebbing; will dated 3 November, 1568.*

Newcourt's[12] list for Stebbing is a blank between 1524 and 1568, when John Durden was instituted 'on the death of the last vicar' (unnamed). By his very brief nuncupative will he gives 40s. towards his church repairs and 13s. 4d. to the poor; he prays to be buried at the north door of the church. Letters of administration were granted, 6 January, 1569.

5. *Edward Watkynson, rector of North Benfleet; will dated 6 May, 1570; proved 13 Febuary, 1571.*

Instituted 1556, he was also rector of Ramsden Crays, 1541-71. Apparently a bachelor, his long will reveals charitable legacies to the poor of both parishes and of Ramsden Bellhouse, South Benfleet, Rayleigh and Rawreth, totalling £5, and to the hospitals of Moulsham in Chelmsford and Mile End in Middlesex 6s. 8d. each. He also gives 20s. for repairs to North Benfleet church and

11 *Victoria County History, Essex*, ii, 511-2, etc.

12 R. Newcourt, *op. cit.*, ii, 557.

3s. 4d. towards amending Battles Bridge nearby. Edmund Tyrell, his patron, receives £3 6s. 8d., and James Sumner, rector of Rawreth, gets his best silk hat.

6. *Hugh Taylor, rector of Danbury; will dated 26 August, 1572; proved 15 October, 1572.*

Instituted 1568, he was also rector of Woodham Ferrers, 1549–61 and of Rettendon, 1561–72, and had been curate at Chelmsford about 1534. In a very long and interesting will, he directs a modest burial in Danbury churchyard, 'not coffered but in an honest sheet', with 40s. to the poor that day; he insists on an abnormal number of funeral sermons. 'To Robert Pearson (rector of Cold Norton) £6 to make 6 sermons in Rettendon, 6 in Woodham Ferrers, 4 in Danbury, and 4 in Chelmsford; to Mr. Sympson the elder (there were four contemporary Thomases in Essex) £3 to make 4 sermons in Rettendon, 4 in Woodham Ferrers, and 4 in Danbury; to Mr. Sympson his brother 40s. to make 4 sermons in Chelmsford and 4 in Writtle; all of which sermons shall be made within 2 years after my death'. Debts totalling £10 owed to him are to go to the poor of Chelmsford and £3 to Maldon and Writtle. Alms to the poor of Harley (in Shropshire) probably indicates his birthplace; to which he adds £4 'to the poor of the Cross church in Shrewsbury, to be delivered by my cousin Thomas Taylor of Clifford's Inn in London'. He not uncommonly remembers the poor prisoners in Newgate, Ludgate, Marshalsea and the King's Bench; each gaol gets 40s. Then more generosity. 'In consideration that I have received a yearly benefit out of the benefice of Woodham Ferrers, to the poor there £20 to be bestowed in shirts, smocks and some sheets or else in some wood, to be given to the poorest 20 nobles (£6 13s. 4d.) immediately after my death, so yearly until the £20 be bestowed. To the poor scholars of Cambridge £10 to be distributed by the advice of the Vice-Chancellor where most need is'. Finally, his goods are to be sold and the money given to the poor of the same four Essex parishes by the discretion of Gilbert Annand (vicar of Boreham) who gets his chamlet cassock. Edward Bynder, 'curate' (of Danbury?), the first witness, will be able to wear his master's black gown, cloak and hat and his chamlet doublet. Among the numerous bequests of household goods, clothes, coins, etc., Richard Garten will get 'my stillatory (still) and all my glasses for waters'; Thomas Somerfield, his sister's son, 'my best bedstead in my great parlour with the best featherbed, my best gelding with saddle, bridle, boots and spurs, a bow and a sheaf of arrows, and 40s.'; and Mr.

Barnarde 'my great hog, and my bees'. The most interesting asset is his library, whereof 'to Mr. Robert Pearson all St. Augustine's Works in 10 books; and if it shall please him to buy any of my books not bequeathed he shall have them better cheap before another. To Mr. (Robert) Monke (rector of Woodham Ferrers) Althanasius' Work in one book and two small books in parchment coverings, one of Virgilius, the other of Theodoretus. To Mr Harry Hais (of Rettendon?) Peter Martin upon the Kings in two books, and I desire him to help my executors to sell the rest not bequeathed. To Mr. Gylbert Annand of Boreham Musculus' Commonplaces and a New Testament of Erasmus' translation with bovyons (meaning?) and clasps. To Mr. Person (i.e. parson) of Sandon an Exposition upon the Proverbs called Lodovynis' Lavaterus. To Mr. Carter (William, vicar of Walton-le-Soken?) a book called Gwalter upon the Acts. To Mr. John Wallinger my Bible in English. To Mr. Richard Parker (vicar of Dedham, 1582–90?) my Geneva Testament. To Mr. William Hamon, my scholar, Elliott's Dictionary with my other books in the church. To John Bynder, my scholar, my Callapyne in my study and all my grammar books, and such as be taught in grammar schools that be found in my study I will be given to poor men's sons that go to grammar school'. The will is a remarkable memorial to a man of education, scholarship and thoughtful charity.

7. *Robert Freman, rector of Ashen; will dated 7 September, 1573 (nuncupative); proved 24 September 1573.*

Instituted 1563. He was also rector of Ridgewell (1562–69?). In a very brief will, directing burial in Ashen chancel, he bequeaths to his brother-in-law Thomas Pannell, a Cambridge student, £20 and such of his books as he desires, and six unnamed books to several kinsmen.

8. *George Lucas, rector of Arlesford; will dated 2 December, 1572; proved 11 December, 1572.*

Instituted 1568. His neighbour Mr. (John) Wilton (rector of Little Bentley) gets a French crown for a funeral sermon. The poor scholars of St. John's, Cambridge, have 5s. Four seam (quarters) of his malt is to be sold to buy the poor parishioners a cow, the profits of which are to remain to their use 'for ever'; and the poor of Thorrington likewise get a cow. Some cash goes to the poor of Brightlingsea and Elmstead, with 'my taffeta hat to the poor folks' of Wivenhoe! Of interest is a bequest of 10s. 'to the congregation of persecuted strangers and Christians at Colchester', i.e. the

Dutch church there. The first witness is Mr. (Edward) Burges, (rector) of Wivenhoe, 'preacher' (1572-89), the suffix being complimentary.

9. *Thomas Buelye, rector of Great Stambridge; will dated 8 November, 1575; proved 26 January, 1576.*

Usually spelt Bewley, he was instituted in 1570. Also rector of Southchurch (1562-76), he had been rector of Wanstead (1558-62), presented by Lord Rich a month after Elizabeth's accession. To be buried in Great Stambridge chancel. To the patrons of his livings, the archbishop of Canterbury (Southchurch), he leaves an old ryal, to Thomas Shaa (Stambridge) an hogshead of wine, and to Lord and Lady Rich each an old ryal. Owning himself the advowson of a prebend in Chichester cathedral, he gives the next presentation to Stephen Barwick of Southchurch, charging him to be 'mindful of my goodwill towards him and therefore to continue faithful and friendly to my wife and children'; Barwick was to become rector of Hadleigh in 1578. The poor of Great Stambridge and Southchurch receive 26s. 8d., and for the repair of each church 'an ewe sheep and the profit thereof, if any good man will give the pasture, if not, to the stock of each 3s. 4d.'. He leaves unspecified books in his 'book chamber' to his son. The overseers are Shaa, Barwick and Nicholas Wardall (rector of Hawkwell, no. 14).

10. *Dr. Thomas Wattes, archdeacon of Middlesex, dean and rector of Bocking; will dated 23 May, 1577; proved 3 August, 1577.*

A long and important will, but concerned little with Bocking. The peculiar of Bocking included a number of parishes in Essex and Suffolk, Bocking being the head of the jurisdiction of the archbishop of Canterbury, whose commissary was the dean of Bocking. The deans were mostly learned men, of whom John Gauden, bishop of Worcester and dean and rector of Bocking, was to be regarded later as the author of the *Eikon Basilike*. As rector, Dr. Wattes had in 1570 succeeded Dr. John Calfhill (who was also archdeacon of Colchester). His status in the Church hierarchy accounts for his 'especial good lord and master and trusty friend, the lord Edmund (Grindal), archbishop', being co-executor (with his wife), receiving in remembrance his best silver tankard double gilt, and for other 'good friends', Alexander Nowell, dean of St. Paul's and John Mullyns, archdeacon of London, each having a piece of silver parcel gilt. His burial is to be in St. Paul's, 20 marks being given to poor prisoners in the London gaols and another 20 marks to Christ's Hospital in London. His Bocking house is mentioned thus: 'I will that no glass at the manor house of the parsonage of Bocking set up by Mr. Cafeld (Calfhill) or by me shall be removed but remain for my successors in consideration that he shall seek no trouble against my executors for dilapidations'. By a codicil dated the next day, his library in his London study 'and such other of my books at my house at Bocking as my good lord archbishop of Canterbury shall think meet' are bequeathed to 'the common library within the college called Pembroke Hall in Cambridge'. The catalogue comprises thirty titles of religious and classical works. The other Bocking items are: 'to Katherine my servant at Bocking 20s.', and 'to John Key the ploughboy to help him to a new master 40s.' (six London servants get bigger legacies). Among the remaining provisions is this intriguing sentence: 'To William Cowell of London hosier the lease which I had of him of the house of Adam Wynthrop, and I forgive him £15 which he oweth me for the lease, and to his wife, my cousin Luce, for her pains she hath taken with me, £10'; the last phrase normally refers to care during sickness. Such a distinctive name as Adam may perhaps refer to the father of John Winthrop, destined to become 'the father of New England' and the first Governor of the Colony of Massachusetts (see also no. 14). John was born at Groton Manor near Sudbury, Suffolk, in 1588. Did Adam previously live in London, or was his own father the Adam of our will?

11. *Giles Buskyll, rector of Orsett; will dated 17 July, 1579; proved 14 December, 1579.*

(Mis-spelt 'Bluskell' in Newcourt; 'Buskell' elsewhere in the will.) Instituted 1560 on the deprivation of his predecessor, he was also rector of St. Lawrence Jewry, London (1551–66) and rector of Little Thurrock (1567–79). He wills that his wife Joan 'do not marry anyone who hath been my servant nor any other single man, if so the use of my lands and the bringing up of my son and daughter' are to be given to two named leading London citizens. Clearly a fairly wealthy man by his substantial cash legacies and his silver gilt goblet, he leaves unspecified land in Harleston, Suffolk (his birthplace?) to his son. To be buried in Orsett church.

12. *Richard Wyn (or Wynne), rector of Chingford; will dated 18 September, 1583; proved 3 July, 1584.*

(Recorded as 'Gwyn' at the institution of his successor.) Instituted

1564, he was also rector of Toppesfield (1556–?). To be buried in Chingford chancel, the poor then to get £3, also £3 'in wheaten bread'. As tokens of remembrance he leaves £5 each to Henry Leigh gentleman and to 'my mistress, Mistress Joan Leigh widow' (the Leigh family were patrons of the benefice). There are several other large cash bequests, such as to 'Mr. Roger Loyde of the Queen's Yeomen of the Ewry 2 angels' and to 'John Wyn my sister's son, servant to my Lady Walsingham' 20s. The books he passes on are: 'To Robet Leigh (or Lee) gentleman, Cooper's Dictionary', and to his brother Thomas Fowle, vicar of Chigwell (1571–89), four commentaries on the gospels and epistles.

13. *John Twydall, rector of Thorrington; will dated 25 August, 1584; proved 22 December, 1584.*

Instituted 1565. To be buried in the chancel, he leaves 10s. to the poor of Thorrington, and 20s. to those of St. Martin-within-Ludgate, London, while devising his leasehold house at London, which he leaves to his wife. The Master and Fellows of St. John's, Cambridge, the patrons, receive 40s. His library is thus distributed. 'To my brother Wall (surname) Musculus' Commonplaces in Latin and Calvin's Institutions in Latin; to my brother(-in-law) Humphrey Cole Gualter on the Small Prophets; to the son of Mr. (Thomas) Simson (vicar of Ardleigh) two books called Conciliationes Locorum treating of the Evangelists and Acts of the Apostles'. His best gown goes to Samuel Osborne, parson of Alresford. Other legacies include 'the bed in the great parlour at Thorrington and my dagger'. He ends: 'I earnestly request my Lord's Grace the archbishop of Canterbury, my singular good lord and master, to be supervisor, and as a small remembrance a gold ring with a death's head in it, price £3'.

14. *Nicholas Wardall, rector of South Fambridge; will dated 3 December, 1586.*

Instituted 1581, he was also rector of Hawkwell (1565–86).His plate (2 silver salts, silver bowl, and stone cruse covered with silver) and legacies including £100 to one son, reveal substantial possessions. He leaves to the poor of Hawkwell 20s. and of Fambridge 13s. 4d., and his riding cloak to his curate, Christopher Capon. Letters of administration, 22 December, 1586, were granted to Edward Fourd during the minority of his children, the executors. A testator of the neighbouring parish of Vange (1586) had wished him to preach two funeral sermons. One of the overseers is 'Mr. John Fourd of Rochford', a few miles away. Is he possibly the 'John Forth (a variant of Ford) of Great Stambridge (next to Rochford) gentleman', who made his will in 1613? If so, he could be the father of Mary the only child of John Forth of Great Stambridge who became the first wife of the renowned John Winthrop senior (see no. 10).

15. Dr. Edmund Sheirebrooke, rector of Ashdon; will dated 23 September, 1589; proved 9 January, 1590.

(Also spelt S(h)e(a)rebrooke.) Instituted 1565.[13] His name appears later among the signatories to two petitions from members of Cambridge University to Sir William Cecil in favour of Thomas Cartwright, the Puritan divine and preacher.[14] He gives Henry Imanson (evidently a carpenter) £5 and 'such walnut tree board and plank as is rough and unwrought, with such oaken and ashen board as may be helpful in his occupation', also timber for repairing the 'houses (outhouses) belonging to the parsonage, for the avoiding of dilapidations and for my funeral'. The well-endowed rectory in fact has the status of a manor, and the glebe terrier of 1610 undoubtedly indicates a large parsonage with two barns, a dovecote and several outhouses. The present rectory includes work of c. 1600. Bequests embrace 20s. to the poor of Ashdon and Hadstock and 10s. each to Radwinter and Bartlow, all adjoining places. He remembers 'every one of those children for whom I answered at their baptisms' with 5s., and forgives 'Mr. Huyt parson of Blickling in Norfolk' a £5 debt. Jasper Hooll, his curate,[15] receives 'the priest's chamber wherein he dwelleth, the orchard, and two little houses betwixt the churchyard and the orchard, which I bought to the intent that he makes assurance of the chamber'. He also gets 'the Works of Musculus or the Works of Peter Martir at his choice' and the rector's best bed, one cassock and a gown. At death, all tithes due 'from those (ac)counted poor men by the curate's judgement' are not to be collected.[16]

16. Matthew Richardson, rector of Ovington; will dated 29 July, 1594; proved 26 September, 1594.

Instituted 1575. After providing for burial in the chancel and

13 'He was university preacher in 1562 (*sic*) but was deprived of this position in 1566' (Angela Green, *Ashdon: A History of an Essex Village*, 1989, 163).

14 *Ibid.*, 'A parishioner, William Trappes, stated that he considered Shearebrook's curate, Mr. Hoole, was "no minister", and that he would not come to church unless "Mr Doctor" did preach himself'.

15 Angela Green, *op. cit.*, 153.

16 Angela Green, *op. cit.*, 158.

giving £4 for meat, drink and bread at his funeral, he gives 'to have a new pulpit and seats in the chancel £4, to be done within a year after my decease', also 'towards the mending of the highways in Ovington £3'. There are legacies of 40s. each for a remembrance to eight clerics in various parts of Essex. After Ellen his wife's death the rent of £4 from his purchase of freehold land is to go to Magdalene College, Cambridge, to help six poor scholars, to whom he also gives the sum of £6 13s. 4d. Further noteworthy almsgiving reads, 'I bequeath to be always employed in a stock of barley to be made into malt £10, yearly distributed among the poor people of Ovington by four or two at the least of the chiefest inhabitants, who shall take sufficient bond for the safe keeping of the stock of £10, so as by God's permission the £10 may remain to the poor for ever'. And to each of Belchamp St. Paul and two adjacent Suffolk parishes he gives 40s. This remarkable will also discloses generosity to a number of friends.

17. *Robert Bankes, rector of Moreton; will dated 11 July, 1590; proved 23 August, 1591.*

Instituted in 1548, he was deprived in 1554, but restored *c.* 1560. He is the only cleric in our series who figures in the survey of 1585: 'Mr. Banckes, canon of Christ Church in Oxon, who by reason of age is not able to preach, not distinctly to read, yet he provideth none among his people to do good. Witness, Robert Oyley' (who has not been identified); he is also one of the three incumbents thus recorded as non-resident; but he willed to be buried in Moreton chancel. He witnessed the will of a parishioner in 1574, but little else is known of him. The advowson had been granted by the Crown to Lord Rich, who had originally presented Bankes, as he did again in happier times.

18. *Peter Wentworth, vicar of Great Bromley; will dated 1 September, 1592; proved 14 September, 1599.*

The patron was William Cardinall, a local J.P., at his institution in 1581; but he himself, a member of the Wentworth family of Gosfield, had owned the lay parsonages of Gestingthorpe (1582–99), which he passed to his wife, and of Long Melford, Suffolk. He was also vicar of Gestingthorpe (1588–91), in the chancel of which he desired to be buried, as well as rector of Abberton (1578–91), having resigned both. He devises freeholds in Coggeshall and in Shotley just over the River Stour in Suffolk. 'All my books' (no details) at Melford and Bromley are to be divided between his sons. Newcourt presumed that he was the author of *An Exhor-*

tation to Queen Elizabeth and a Discourse of the true and lawful successor (1598);[17] he was chaplain to Lord Darcy and published a sermon on certain Psalms (1587).

19. *Edward Williamson, rector of Bulphan; will dated 9 June, 1598; proved 5 August, 1598.*

Instituted 24 Febrary, 1593, he succeeded his father Edmund (1581–92). He gives his 'loving mother 1 of my best kine, the new-made chest, 3 joined stools, and the new trundle bed' and his brother(-in-law) his best gown and cloak and the two volumes of (Foxe's) Book of Martyrs. His wife Anne is residuary legatee of cash, cattle and the two houses in Cranham and Corringham. His body is to be 'decently buried'.

20. *Thomas Howell, rector of Paglesham, clerk; will dated 2 January, 1600; proved 1 April, 1600.*

Instituted in 1578, he had also been rector of Great Stambridge (1588–89). Making no provision for burial, three gold rings, one 'with the Turkey (turquoise) stone in it', and 'the great pair of virginals' (the sole reference to a musical instrument), pass to his two daughters. If they become orphans, his overseer, a Paglesham yeoman, is to give security for their maintenance to 'my loving friends Mr. (Ezechiel) Culverwell (rector of Great Stambridge), Mr. (Arthur) Dent (rector of South Shoebury) and Mr. (William) Negus (rector of Leigh)', all three well-known Puritan preachers; Culverwell and Negus were both to be deprived in 1609. It is not surprising therefore to find that Howell calls himself 'clerk', not rector, in 1600, for he had perhaps been in trouble with his superiors in the previous year, having either ceded or been deprived according to Newcourt.

21. *John Debank, rector of Bradwell-next-the-Sea; will dated 20 March, 1602; proved 2 September, 1602.*

Instituted 1563. The timber-framed north wing of the present well-known rectory, of early sixteenth century date, is the Parsonage House of the will, to which the fine Adam-style extension was to be added two centuries ago. A rich benefice, the testator is concerned with the advowson, which will be held by his son Thomas and Humphrey Cole, vicar of Tillingham: 'to the right worshipful Dr. (William) Tabor, archdeacon of Essex, one presentation of the parsonage of Bradwell, and I give authority to my

17 T. W. Davids, *op. cit.*, 98n.

executors to present him for the first avoidance thereof according to my promise to him, on condition that he will be resident thereon, nothing doubting but that he will have as great a care of my charge and flock as I myself would have had, if God had spared me any larger life'. Is Debank devout or sactimonious? Certain it is that the archdeacon was duly instituted rector within little more than a month after Debank signed his will, when suffering from mortal sickness. His urgent wish having been effected, one may speculate what lay behind this unusual arrangement. The rector's clerical neighbour Cole is given £5 and a cancelled debt, and his son, Debank's godson, gets 40s. towards maintenance at school. The widow, Jane, will be able to display good plate: 'a double bell salt cellar of silver and gilt, 12 silver spoons marked with letters of my name, 2 beakers or tuns of silver of the biggest or longest, 1 of the 5 silver tuns or lowest cups, a standing gilt cup with a cover, 1 gilt bowl out of a nest of bowls, a bowl of silver that is not gilt, and 2 of the lesser bowls of silver and gilt'. The executors are Dr. Tabor and Cole and Thomas; the supervisor is another neighbour, Anthony Turrell, parson of Dengie; but they are given no funeral directions. Debank's name crops up in a bizarre story found in earlier Essex Assize records. A Bradwell labourer, indicted for having on 4 April, 1592, seditiously and publicly declared, 'The earl of Derby keepeth the crown of England and the earl of Shrewsbury hath had three children by the Queen of Scots at Stafford Castle, and this is no good government which we now live under, and it was merry in England when there was better government, and if the Queen die there will be a change, and all those that be of this religion now used will be pulled out'. And with these words he struck Debank on the head with his cudgel. The court ordered him to be pilloried in market time with a paper above his head for scandalous words;[18] such crazy sayings were not rare at the time.[19]

22. *Dr. Edmund Chapman, church lecturer at Dedham; will dated 12 May, 1601; proved 10 February, 1603.*

In some of the towns and villages with a zealous Puritan laity, 'church lecturers' were appointed by them to afford spiritual instruction. Their unorthodox activities led to various disputes with some beneficed clerics and anti-extremist laymen. Such ministers concentrated on biblical study, preaching, prayer and

18 F. G. Emmison, *Elizabethan Life: Disorder*, E.R.O., 1970.

19 *Ibid.*, 10, 41–59.

holy 'exercises'. Arising from such principles came the Classis Movement of the 1580s. The leading member of the Dedham 'Classis',[20] which drew its clerical members from the Essex–Suffolk borders, was undoubtedly Dr. Chapman, Richard Parker, vicar of Dedham, acting as secretary.[21] Chapman's name occurs in the petition to Cecil on behalf of Cartwright in 1586 (see no. 15).[22] More is known about Chapman than of any of the beneficed clergy whose wills we have considered. This remarkable man's career began as a sizar of Gonville Hall, Cambridge, in 1554.[23] He became B.D. in 1569, D.D. in 1578, and a canon of Norwich cathedral, where his singing in some services aroused Archbishop Parker's indignation; he was deprived about 1576 for nonconformity. He was a preacher at Bedford and London. He was appointed lecturer at Dedham in 1570, and was succeeded by 'roaring John Rogers', whose vigorous preaching resulted in the epithet. In the opinion of Dr. Rendall, the late vicar of Dedham, Chapman secured for the ministry of the Word an influence hardly, if anywhere, surpassed in England'. His intense desire to promote the education of poor children is evinced by an 'order agreed by Mr. Dr. Chapman, Mr. Parker, and the ancients of the congregation of Dedham' in 1585, when they were to be taught to read English. He is remembered by a fine alabaster and marble tablet in the church.[24] Because of the special interest of Dr. Chapman's will, an abstract follows:

> 'To Susan my loving wife for her life half my goods, plate, and English books, and my houses and lands in Dedham and Ardleigh, with remainder to my son Peter at 21, and if she die before then my executors shall receive the rents and profits towards the good bringing up and preferment of my children and the performance of my will. To my son John all my other books for his better encouragement of his study. To my daughter

20 *Essex Review*, 1st series, xviii, 46; xxviii, 144; xxix, 9; xxx, 112.

21 F. G. Emmison, *Elizabethan Life: Morals and the Church Courts*, E.R.O., 1973, 193.

22 T. W. Davids, *op. cit.*, 94n.

23 Venn, *op. cit.*, ii, 321.

24 William Bettes, rector of Wivenhoe, left in his will (1570) a small sum to the poor of Dedham, which may suggest his having been there for a short time, but the bequest was more likely due to the influence of Chapman, who was a witness. (F. G. Emmison and K. J. Neale, eds., *Essex Wills*, vol. 9, no. 31, E.R.O., awaiting publication).

Susan £200 at marriage or 20. My executors shall collect
the rents of my messuage in Bread Street in London
until John is 24 and shall bestow the rents towards the
preferment of my children; and for their greater benefit
I give my executors power to let it for 21 years after the
end of the present lease for the yearly rent of 40 marks
or such reasonable sum as they can get, which rent John
shall enjoy at 24, and in the meantime they shall pay him
towards his maintenance 20 nobles. To my children
equally a moiety of my goods and plate at the said ages.
Towards the augmentation of the stock of the poor of
Dedham where I dwell £5, when in the judgement of my
executors it shall be well and strongly confirmed and
established, to the benefit of the poor for ever. To my
brother Nicholas Chapman a ring of gold of the value of
20s., his son Thomas 20s., and my cousin Edmund
Chapman, son of Nicholas, 20s. To my nephew Dan-
nocke 10s. to be bestowed in a "gimmal" (ring) of gold.
To my old man Peter Peele 20s. to help to pay his debt to
Mr. Moore. To Mr. Moore being in Cambridgeshire 10s.
The residue of my goods to all my children equally
(praying God to bless them all). Executors: Mr. John
Hare of London esquire, Mr Osborne of Hawkstead (co.
Suffolk) esquire, and Simon Fenn of Dedham clothier,
and for their pains and for a small token of my love
£3 6s. 8d. apiece. Witnesses: Richard Collins notary
public "and his two servants." '

The legacy of £200 is a criterion of ample material
possessions. During his ministry he had received numerous cash
bequests from devoutly grateful testators of Dedham and several
neighbouring villages who had been inspired by his religious
teaching; for example, a double ducat from a Langham widow for
revealing 'the rich treasure of the Word'.[25] A curious sidelight is
found in connection with the offence of 'harbouring' an unmarried
mother. Ralph Cox of Dedham in 1599 had not brought his
daughter, delivered of a bastard three or four years past, 'to
punishment, which was concealed by Dr. Chapman and the
churchwardens'.[26] One would not have thought he would have
overlooked the delinquency.

25 F. G. Emmison and K. J. Neale, eds., *Essex Wills*, vol. 11, no. 1433, E.R.O.,
    awaiting publication.

26 F. G. Emmison, *Elizabethan Life: Morals and the Church Courts*, E.R.O.,
    1973, 27.

Ham House Estate, Upton, West Ham and its People

FRANK SAINSBURY

THE ESTATE IS still there at Upton although the house has gone. An ivy-clad cairn of stones that once marked its site has also gone. Its 'people' are now the people of Newham at large and the notice boards at the main gates provide the clue to the last chapter of the estate's story covering over four centuries.[1]

That story records Elizabethan and Jacobean gentry, a Commonwealth Justice, Restoration and Georgian baronets, a naval officer of rank and — for the last hundred years of private ownership — two Quaker names of national note.

It is worth pausing at 'Quaker names' — Upton, on rising ground towards the north of West Ham, was a more prosperous part of the parish and, until approximately one hundred years ago, remained a neighbourhood of larger houses in their own grounds. From around the middle of the eighteenth century it attracted noted Quaker families of means — Cockfields, Gurneys and Frys, Listers, Dimsdales — with a Meeting at Plaistow established in the early days of the Society. Apart from the eighteenth/ nineteenth century seat of the Pelly family, Ham House was its principal estate.

It had several names — The Grove or Grove House, Rookes Hall, Upton House and, finally, Ham House. 'Upton House', which name seems to have been confined to the middle of the eighteenth century, has caused confusion with the other Upton House on the opposite side of Upton Lane and the birthplace, in 1827, of Joseph, Lord Lister the famous surgeon. Unfortunately more than one biography of that pioneer of antiseptic surgery erroneously illustrates the eighteenth century engraving of Ham House as his birthplace.

The estate was originally only about one third of the extent of the present 'West Ham Park' under the charge of the Corporation

---

1 The basic facts are in *V.C.H., Essex, VI*, 53, 72 and Katharine Fry, *History of the parishes of East Ham and West Ham*, 1888 (= *Fry*), 230–37. There are two errors in *Fry*: p.231, Robert Rooke was William's kinsman, not son; and on p.237, 'Mrs. Katharine Fry' should read 'Mrs. Elizabeth Fry'.

Figure 1.   Ham House (then Upton House) in the days of Dr. John Fothergill.   (Newham Public Libraries)

of the City of London and, to quote the *Victoria County History*, 'appears to have originated as a small tenement called Grove House or The Grove later Rookes Hall'. The same source indicates that Ham House is said to have been rebuilt in the eighteenth century and described as a large two storey building with eighteenth century exterior. The half 'H' plan, however, suggests that it may have been of earlier origin.

The Rookes

William Rooke, son of William, succeeded to the small estate in West Ham on his father's death in 1559. He apparently enlarged the property and died in 1597 holding Grove House and twenty-eight acres of land at Upton, with other small properties in West Ham. It became known as 'Rookes Hall' and, after the death of William's widow Ann, the estate passed to a kinsman — Robert Rooke.

A former Churchwardens' register of charities held at the Local Studies Library, Newham gives among the early parish benefactions:

> 'Willm. Rookes of Upton, Gent. did by his last Will dated the 5th of March, 1596 charge all his Estate in the Parish . . . with an Annuity or Yearly Rent of Five Pounds for ever . . . unto the Churchwardens of this Parish, they to distribute the same in bread amongst the Poore by 2s. worth every Sunday in the forenoon.'

This was among the larger of seven bequests to the poor of West Ham recorded for the last twenty years of the sixteenth century.

There is a monument to Robert Rooke by the organ in West Ham parish church which indicates that the family were of some long standing in the parish. It represents Robert in plate armour kneeling with his two wives, with four sons and three daughters kneeling below and, lying below them, an infant in swaddling clothes. It is inscribed:

> 'Here lyeth ye body of Robert Rookes Esre Captain of ye trained Band of this hundred descended from ye antient family of Rookes of this parish . . . He had 2 wives and 7 children and dyed the 5th of October 1630 in [*] year of his age.'

* The figure of age is unclear and the monument also seems to have credited him with his kinsman William's benefaction for it reads 'who hath given yearly contribution   poundes to ye poor

of this parish for ever'. A later hand has incised a rather crude 'not' between the 'hath' and the 'given' and filled in the number of pounds with some form of pitch or enamel.

Robert was succeeded by his son Robert and, according to the references cited, the house and estate remained with the Rookes until it was sold to Sir Robert Smyth of Upton in 1666.

I have been unable to verify, however, that the Rookes remained in possession of such a principal property much after the death of the first Robert in 1630. When King Charles I levied 'Ship Money' on the County of Essex in 1636[2] the name of Rooke(s) does not appear among the sixteen principal contributors from West Ham. When, as mentioned later, the parishioners met in 1653 for the appointment of a registrar, no 'Rooke(s)' appears among the forty-four principal inhabitants who appended their names as consenting. When King Charles II levied his tax on hearths in 1662[3] no 'Rooke(s)' appears among the nineteen taxed for the (then) Upton Ward of the parish.[4] Incidentally, a Smyth is so listed and for the largest house in the Ward. The Rooke monument has been damaged at some time. Were they Royalists?

The Smyths[5]

There was no such doubt regarding Robert Smyth. He was obviously the most important man in the parish during the Commonwealth. The manor of West Ham had been granted by King Charles I to his wife, Henrietta Maria. During the Interregnum it was seized and sold by Parliament and Smyth bought the manorial rights and held courts 1650–59. About the same time he acquired a half-share in the manors of East Ham and West Ham Burnells which continued with the family until 1798 — that is long after they had ceased other local association. The Ham House estate was associated with these manors until it was sold off separately in 1761. He was an Alderman of the City of London and a Justice for the County of Essex, being High Sheriff in 1642. He was active in the proposed Presbyterian organisation of the County in the 1640s

2 E.R.O., Ship Money:T/A4.

3 E.R.O., Hearth tax: Q/RTh 1.

4 Soon after the Restoration the Upton Ward of the parish was merged with the larger Church Street Ward.

5 The Smyths appear in *V.C.H., Essex, VI*, 1, 12, 64, 68, 96-97, 114, 118 and, unless otherwise stated, this section is based thereon.

and named an Elder but, in the words of Dr. Harold Smith:[6] 'For Essex we have the constitution on paper; it is by no means clear whether it ever worked'. He was also a member of the Parochial Inquisition of 1650 set up to enquire into the value of ecclesiastical benefices but the commissioners and jurors were also able to recommend new parishes or unions of parishes.

Robert Smyth sat as a Commissioner at Romford in September 1650 when the abortive suggestion was made for the parochial separation of Great Ilford from Barking and the absorption of Little Ilford into Wanstead and Great Ilford.

The West Ham parish registers have a very good example of the election of a lay 'register' in 1653 and of the lay conduct of weddings 1653—59. 'Alderman Robert Smith Esquire Justice of the Peace' heads the list of parishioners consenting to the election and administers the oath to the appointee — Edward Lawford. Smyth also conducted over seventy weddings during the period concerned, including that of his daughter Anne to William Palmer the founder of the endowed school at Grays Thurrock.[7]

At the Restoration the manor of West Ham was restored to the Queen Dowager but, as with many who had maintained the fabric of affairs during the Commonwealth, Robert Smyth continued in favour with the new administration — being knighted on 25 August, 1660, and created baronet of Upton on 30 March, 1665. He died in 1669 and was buried at West Ham. The baronetcy survived through the family until 1852.[8]

The Smyths do not figure much in parochial affairs after the Commonwealth. The second Sir Robert was Auditor of the parish accounts 1672/3 and Surveyor of Highways for the Church Street Ward in 1676 but they do not appear in the index of names in Vestry Minutes thereafter.[9] This second Sir Robert was of little more than local note but his brother James, knighted by King Charles II, was Lord Mayor of London in 1684. There is a large monument to him in the south chapel of West Ham parish church.

6 Harold Smith, *The ecclesiastical history of Essex under the Long Parliament and Commonwealth*, [c.1931], 193f, 236, 250f, 340f.

7 See also: H. E. Brooks, 'William Palmer of Grays Thurrock', *Essex Review*, 34, 171–86.

8 C. J. Parry, compiler, *Index of baronetage creations*, 1967.

9 The early parish registers of West Ham are deposited with the Archaeology and Local History Centre, Passmore Edwards Museum, Newham and the Vestry minutes and other Vestry records with the Local Studies Library, Stratford Public Library, Newham. Acknowledgement is made to both these institutions. The registers and the minutes have both been indexed.

It looks a little unfinished — as if there ought to have been a statue. It records two daughters and James's son — also James — who was created baronet of Isfield in Sussex by George I in 1714. There is a tablet in the chapel to the grandson of this James — Sir Hervey Smyth, who was aide-de-camp to General Wolfe at Quebec. Upon Hervey's death, without issue, in 1811 this second baronetcy became extinct.[10]

The family acquired the manor of Berechurch Hall, south of Colchester and other manors in north Essex and their later story is told in the article 'The Smyth family of Berechurch Hall' in *Essex Review*, xxiv, 178f.[11]

Katharine Fry's History is not precise on the date at which the Smyths relinquished the Ham House estate . . . 'The Smyth family sold the estate, after it had been in their possession nearly a century, to Admiral Elliot, who is said to have brought the cones of cedar trees from the Levant, and to have planted them in his garden . . .'. A check through the Overseers' account books for the Church Street Ward of the parish gives the following chronology:[12]

'1749   Sir Trafford Smyth
1750   Henry Smyth (presumably Sir Trafford's uncle
          and brother of the third Sir Robert)
1751   A Mrs. Lemmon
1752   Captain George Elliott'

Admiral Elliott[13]

Apart from the fleeting Mrs. Lemmon (1751) Admiral Elliott's is the shortest tenure in this long history — 1752–62. He came of a Scottish family, was made a Lieutenant in the Royal Navy in 1740 and served on the *Superb* and on the *Rippon* on the Jamaican

---

10   J. and J. B. Burke, *General and heraldic history of the extinct and dormant baronetcies*, 1841.

11   The descent of the family is a little unclear at one point in this article. See also a reference to the eighteenth century James Smyth, *Essex Review*, 50, 17–18.

12   West Ham Parish, *Overseers' Account Book, 1749–1762*, in the Local Studies Library, Stratford. Unfortunately the pages of this account book after 1752 do not give the same detailed list of ratepayers, year by year.

13   I am indebted to the Maritime Information Centre, National Maritime Museum, Greenwich, for references to John Charnock, *Biographia navalis . . . volume V*, 1797 and *The commissioned sea officers of the Royal Navy*, upon which this section is based.

station. The captain of the latter vessel became ill, Elliott was sent to sea in command and captured a Spanish frigate. This made his career.

He was promoted captain of a sloop and then of the captured frigate itself (which had been brought into British service) and became Commander-in-Chief of the station.

He returned to England at the end of 1744 and in 1747 was made captain of the *Newark*, a newly launched vessel of eighty guns. After this he appears to have retired from active service and this would possibly coincide with his arrival at Upton. He was Overseer for the Church Street Ward in 1759 and his signature appears in the Vestry Minutes.

In 1762, the year of his sale of the estate to Dr. Fothergill, he was put on the superannuated list with the rank and half pay of rear-admiral and lived principally at Copford in Essex until his death in 1795. For some years he enjoyed the nominal office of 'general of the mint' in Scotland — a sinecure worth £300 a year.

We come now to over a century of Quaker ownership of the estate distinguished by two men of national — if not international — note: Doctor John Fothergill, physician and botanist, owner 1762–80 and Samuel Gurney, banker and philanthropist, owner 1812–56.

Doctor John Fothergill

A major source is *Dr. John Fothergill and his friends: chapters in eighteenth century life* by Doctor R. Hingston Fox, published by Macmillan in 1919.[14] It is worth quoting the last paragraph of his introductory chapter:

> 'Dr. John Fothergill and his friends took a worthy part in the advances of the eighteenth century. Fothergill touched life at many points. As a physician, he helped to bring into English medical practice the new spirit of Natural medicine. As a man of science, he extended the boundaries of knowledge, and brought the riches of the animal world and even more of the vegetable world to light. As a lover of justice and of liberty, he had strong sympathy with the American people: he did what he

14 The major original source is John Coakley Lettsom, *Memoirs of John Fothergill, M.D.*, 4th edition, 1786 (= *Lettsom*). His preface cites further biographical sources. I have preferred Fox's more direct account (= *Fox*) and, unless otherwise stated, this account is based thereon.

Figure 2. Dr. John Fothergill from the painting by William Hogarth.
(Newham Public Libraries)

could to aid their growth, and he essayed to stand with Franklin in the breach, to stay the onset of the war of separation. As a philanthropist and a social reformer, and as a pioneer in education, he was a shining example to his age. Lastly, as a member of the Friends, during the Quietist phase of the Society, he took a leading part in shaping its policy and influence on both sides of the Atlantic.'

As our main concern is with Fothergill's botanic garden at Upton we commence with Fothergill the botanist. Botanic Gardens had already developed in England from the herb garden of the Barber Surgeons and the gardens of the College of Physicians to Kew Gardens established by the Dowager Princess of Wales in 1760.

Fothergill had already commenced collections of shells, corals and insects[15] but was encouraged to concentrate on botany by his fellow Quaker Peter Collinson. Collinson had met and formed a friendship with Linnaeus on the latter's only visit to England. Collinson's trade as a woollen draper or mercer with a large American connection put him in touch, eventually, with John Bartram, a Quaker farmer of Philadelphia — a self-taught botanist who travelled widely in search of new trees and shrubs and laid out his own botanic garden in 1728. Collinson and his friends supplied Bartram with funds and specimens from England and every year the American put on board ships sailing for England a number of bales and boxes from his collections.

Collinson, in turn, distributed to like-minded friends, including several noblemen like Essex's own Robert, Lord Petre with his plantations at Thornwood.

Thus encouraged, Fothergill at first chose a sheltered plot of land on the Surrey side of the Thames but learned that a tenant-at-will depended on its produce. He therefore gave up this project and, it is said, made a present of the intended purchase money to the man's family.

Then, Zachariah Cockfield, a Quaker shipowner of Elmhurst at Upton, West Ham and a patient of Fothergill, introduced him to the Upton estate which he purchased in 1762.

On purchase, the estate was only the thirty or so acres of the Rookes' time but Fothergill enlarged it to around eighty acres — that is covering more than the extent of the modern West Ham

---

15 The extent and value of Fothergill's other collections are described in *Lettsom*, 54f.

Park. He bought land up to the Romford Road with a carriage entrance and its two octagonal lodges remained long after his time.[16] To quote from the account of Hingston Fox:

> 'Here he planted a flower garden, surrounded by shrubberies and a wilderness of trees. A piece of water wound its way through the midst, its banks lined with exotic shrubs. Evergreens gave the aspect of spring even in midwinter. A greenhouse and hothouses, then less common than now, opened by a glass door from one of the villa sitting rooms, and extended for about 260 feet. Here oranges and myrtles blossomed freely, amidst some 3,400 species of plants brought from warm countries. Nearly as many more species flourished on the open ground, whilst the forest trees of North America and China, rare oaks, firs and maples throve in the adjoining plantations . . . In order to enrich his garden Fothergill entered into correspondence with persons in far countries, and enlisted the aid of sea-captains and travellers. He thus obtained large quantities of plants and seeds from China, Hindustan and others of the East Indies, the West Indies, Siberia and the newly discovered islands . . .'

Sir Joseph Banks, a contemporary President of the Royal Society, wrote:[17]

> 'Those whose gratitude for restored health prompted them to do what was acceptable to their benefactor, were always informed by him that presents of rare plants chiefly attracted his attention, and would be more acceptable to him than the most generous fees.'

One interesting story is of the 'barrels of earth from Borneo'. A sea-captain was ill with yellow fever in the London docks and no one would go near him. Partly out of compassion and partly to study the disease Fothergill went on board, cared for him and cured him. He would take no fees but asked the captain on his next voyage — which was to Borneo — to bring back two barrels of earth from as many points as possible. When the captain got there he feared the ridicule of his crew and left without the earth. His

16 *Fry* indicates that although the driveway was long disused the lodges remained until about the 1850s.

17 Quoted by *Lettsom*, 41.

conscience smote him, though, and he turned back and did as Fothergill had asked. Fothergill had a bed of burned mould prepared in his hothouse and the contents of the barrels spread over it. The story concludes: 'in due time there came up many sorts of new and curious plants, some of which have been introduced into English gardens'.

Sir Joseph continues:

'In my opinion, no other garden in Europe, royal, or of a subject, had so many scarce and valuable plants. That science might not suffer a loss, when a plant he had cultivated should die, he liberally paid the best artist the country afforded to draw the new ones as they came to perfection: and so numerous were they at last, that he found it necessary to employ more artists than one[18] . . . His garden was known all over Europe, and foreigners of all ranks asked, when they came hither, permission to see it . . .'

It is not clear to what extent Fothergill actually resided at Upton. Five years after taking the estate he moved from the City to Harpur Street to a new house in what was then a new road (Off the modern Theobalds Road).

Tuke, another biographer[19] records:

'The removal from White Hart Court to Harpur Street did not lessen his work . . . again and again we find both the Doctor and his sister speaking in the strongest terms of the hurry and fatigue of his busy life.'

Tuke also tells us:

'At Upton, of which Fothergill says "there is a forest on one side, not populous, and a Meeting", he sought occasionally for a little quiet from the excessive hurry of his London life; but it was too near to afford him the relief he needed. Importunate patients could send to him, and he could not resist their appeals. So we find him writing from Upton . . . 1764, to his brother Samuel

18 *Fox*, 199, indicates that these paintings, 2,000 in number, were purchased by the Empress Catherine of Russia after Fothergill's death for £2,300 but this may be a misreading of *Lettsom*, 55, which *could* refer to paintings of other of Fothergill's collections.

19 James Hack Tuke, 'A sketch of the life of John Fothergill' (= *Tuke*) reprinted from the *Proceedings of the Centenary of Ackworth School*, 1879. Quotations are from 34, 40, 41.

> Fothergill at Warrington . . . "One day it came into my
> thoughts, unsought for, to retreat a few months next
> summer into Cheshire" . . .'

So he took Lea Hall some four miles from Crewe and retired
there for about two months each year from 1765–80, the year of his
death. 'Hither I bring down', he told a friend, 'a great cargo of
letters'; and many more soon followed him. His correspondents
were in most parts of the civilised world. It was here that much of
his writing work was done in botany, in philanthropy and in
politics, and especially in the concerns of his own Society. Here,
too, he composed many of his medical papers. He discouraged
practice and made it a rule to take no fees whilst he was away,
leaving his wealthy patients to the care of others. But he devoted
one day each week to give his advice *gratis* to the poor at
Middlewich.

According to Tuke:

> 'Later he says "I am in treaty to let Upton. I find it
> embarrassing in point of time, though managed with
> frugality, expensive. I shall preserve the liberty of the
> garden and part of its produce, but quit all use of it for a
> lease of seven years. What seeds I receive will be taken
> care of, and I contribute to the support of the
> gardens." '[20]

Tuke, who was writing in 1879, continues:

> 'He had, in fact, found that he could rarely visit his
> beloved garden, and Lea Hall, and the change to Harpur
> Street had prevented the need of another country
> house. The writer well remembers, when a boy, on his
> first visit to Upton, being shown by the late Samuel
> Gurney many of the rare shrubs in the garden; and also

20 I have been unable to confirm from any of the printed sources that Fothergill
actually carried this proposed leasing into effect. With the help of the
Overseers' rate collection books for the Church Street Ward (The Local
Studies Library, Stratford, holds a broken series of these orignal books late
eighteenth/early nineteenth century.), Michaelmas 1779 and Lady Day 1802,
I have made the reasonable supposition that Fothergill leased about two
thirds of the estate to John Gray the 'eminent gardener' of Fulham (*Lettsom*,
39) and was rated for the other third which most likely included the house.
Fothergill's portion was purchased by Sheppard in 1786 or 1787 and the
portion leased to Gray in about 1801–02. This would also account for the
apparent discrepancy between *V.C.H., Essex, VI*,72, 'In 1786 or 1787 Ham
House was acquired by James Sheppard' and *Fry*, 233, 'About the year 1800
it became the property and residence of Mr. James Sheppard'.

being told the tradition that Dr. Fothergill had so little time to visit the place by day-light that he used to come down in the evening and go round the garden to inspect his favourite plants with a lantern.'

Understandably much space has been devoted to the garden at Upton. A brief biographical note and an account of his work as a physician: John Fothergill was born of yeoman stock at Carr End, Wensleydale, Yorkshire on 8 July, 1712. Carr End, built by his great-grandfather, John Fothergill, was a plain stone farmhouse which remained in the family for nearly two hundred years. This John Fothergill was convinced as a Quaker probably on the occasion of George Fox's first journey through the Dales. Our John's father made three missionary journeys to America on behalf of the Friends.

John's brother, Samuel, spent two years in America 1754–56 and visited nearly all the Meetings in the northern and many of the southern colonies. He was one of the foremost Quaker preachers of the century. Samuel and our John jointly contributed the article on Quakerism to the first edition of the *Encyclopaedia Britannica.*

After grammar school at Sedburgh, Yorkshire, John was apprenticed to Benjamin Bartlett, a Quaker apothecary of Bradford and gained good experience visiting and prescribing for patients. Bartlett was so satisfied with him that he released him after six years to enable him to go to University.

As a Dissenter, Fothergill was barred from Oxford and Cambridge and — much more fortunately at that time — went to the Anatomical School at Edinburgh which followed the modern trends of Leyden and attracted students from at home and abroad. Here, he was encouraged to become a physician and took his M.D. He came to London and spent two valuable years at St. Thomas's Hospital and, after a tour abroad, settled at White Hart Court in the City near a famous Meeting House and surrounded by the houses of Quaker merchants. Through his compassionate treatment at St. Thomas's he had already become known to the poor and they brought him experience if not money. He would say in later life (somewhat deprecatingly): 'I climbed on the backs of the poor to the pockets of the rich'.

He had not been long in practice when a major opportunity arose which made his reputation. A virulent form of scarlatina (or a type of diphtheria?) had taken a heavy toll in London 1747–48. He made a careful study of the complaint and devised his revolutionary and successful regimen. His *Account of the sore-throat attended with ulcers* went through six editions in his lifetime and established his name. It was translated into almost every European language. His secret was a thorough training at Edinburgh, reliance on personal observation and emphasis on diet as a means of cure — as against the traditional nostrums and bloodletting which had still held sway.

He was now numbering the famous amongst his patients — including John Wesley who, in 1753, showed signs of 'consumption'. *Wesley's Journal* has the entry: 'Doctor F. — told me plain . . .'. 'Dr. F.' prescribed country air, milk, horse riding and rest from the evangelist's incessant work. The horse riding part was carried out, anyway.

Fothergill's published medical works were largely confined to short papers embodying his observations on diseases encountered in the course of his extensive practice and were read before the Medical Society of Physicians of which he was one of the founders and later President. They included studies of tubercular meningitis, hydrophobia and angina pectoris. At the time of the influenza epidemic in mid-century he printed his *Sketch of the late Epidemical Disease* on five pages with wide margins and circulated among his colleagues for comment and return.[21]

He was an early advocate of inoculation against smallpox, approved the methods of his friend Thomas Dimsdale and advised him on his publication which went through seven editions and various translations. The Empress Catherine of Russia sought to halt the ravages of smallpox which was excessively fatal in her country and decided to have the Imperial family inoculated as an example. The Russian minister in London consulted Fothergill who recommended Dimsdale for the mission to St. Petersburg. Dimsdale's undertaking and its complete success are a separate story. It brought him a barony of the Russian Empire and a present of £10,000.[22]

Fothergill's public repute as a physician spread through Great Britain, North America and the Indies. It was said that 'Dr. Fothergill, London' would find him.

Returning to Hingston Fox's introductory chapter (quoted above) we can only summarise his many other interests. Fothergill

21 Fothergill's papers are gathered in one volume, *The works of John Fothergill, M.D., with some account of his life* by John Coakley Lettsom, 1784 (= *Fothergill's Works*). Original editions of *Lettsom* and *Fothergill's Works* are held by the Local Studies Library, Stratford.

22 Chapter IX of *Fox* gives a good account.

was much involved in Quaker endeavours to resolve the disputes in and with the American colonies.

Fothergill had first contact with Benjamin Franklin when, through Fothergill's advice and assistance and with a preface in his hand, the American's experiments in electricity were published and made his name in the scientific world of their day. Correspondence followed and they met and became firm friends when Franklin came to England in 1757 to try to settle disputes over the governance of the Quaker colony of Pennsylvania. Franklin records: 'I went to visit Dr. Fothergill, to whom I was strongly. recommended, and whose counsel respecting my proceedings I was advised to obtain'. The Pennsylvania question was soon overshadowed by the tension building up in the colonies over the intransigence of the home government.

Having family connections and numerous correspondents in North America, Fothergill was better able to foresee the consequences of government policy. He published anonymously in 1765 *Considerations relative to the North American colonies*[23] which pleaded the cause of the colonists, combatted the general ignorance at home of American affairs and advocated the repeal of the Stamp Act. (The Act was repealed in the following year and there was a period of comparative calm.)

From 1770, however, North's policy of taxation, repression and military occupation led to the inevitable rupture. In the period 1774–75, before Franklin left England for good, Fothergill and his Quaker friend David Barclay co-operated with Franklin in the drawing up of the latter's *Hints for Conversation, upon the subject of terms that may probably produce a durable union between Great Britain and her colonies.*[24] They were intended to be submitted to important persons on both sides but were never seriously considered.

In March 1775, not long before the war of separation commenced, Fothergill with three Friends acting on behalf of the English Quakers presented a petition to King George III for a peaceful settlement. As Hingston Fox says: 'The Friends often exercised their long established right of approach to the sovereign direct: Fothergill was generally chosen to head the deputation ... and the king thought well of the Quakers'. Although the king gave audience to the Quakers (and did not on this occasion to the Lord Mayor and Aldermen of London) their petition had no effect on

23 Printed in *Fothergill's Works*.

24 Printed as 'Appendix A', *Fox*, 393f.

the outcome. At one point in the conflict Fothergill offered to go with Barclay to act as mediators if the home government was willing to send them — but this came to nothing. The disappointing thing was that at the conclusion of the conflict some of the agreements were in line with Franklin's, Fothergill's and Barclay's original points.

As to social policy, Fothergill worked with John Howard on prison reform, particularly in connection with health in prisons, gave evidence with him before the House of Commons which led to an Act of 1774, and was appointed in 1779, one of the Commissioners under an Act for the erection of penitentiaries and embodying reforms for the gainful employment of prisoners.

He was before his time in many other instances. He advocated public baths, public cemeteries, the national registration of births and deaths, the establishment of an international court of justice and the abolition of slavery. He was interested in the development of canals and made a number of suggestions for the better planning and safety of the metropolis.[25]

As a philanthropist much of his generosity was unobtrusive: 'For many of his patients he would take no fees and to the close of his life he set apart some time for attending the poor without charge'; 'After prescribing for a poor patient he would give a sum "to defray the cost of medicines" '; 'Or at a final interview, when he seemed to be feeling the pulse, he would slip into the hand a banknote'.

Lettsom expressed another aspect of Fothergill's generosity: 'Men of more genius than fortune found in him a liberal patron'. His support of Franklin's electrical experiments have already been mentioned. Nearer home, the *Natural History of Birds* of George Edwards, the eighteenth century naturalist with West Ham connections, owed much to Fothergill's help.[26]

In his last years he was the prime mover in the establishment of the Quaker school at Ackworth in Yorkshire and completed the codification of Quaker discipline adopted on both sides of the Atlantic.

At Fothergill's death in 1780 his collections were largely sold — principally to his Quaker friend and biographer John Coakley

25 Described in *Lettsom*, 111–26.

26 Edwards was born at Stratford and died in retirement at Plaistow, West Ham. The original set of seven volumes of his *Birds* followed by his *Gleanings in Natural History* are held by the Local Studies Library, Stratford.

Lettsom — although some of the greenhouses and many of the fine trees he planted remained. *Hortus Uptonensis; or, a catalogue of stove and greenhouse plants in Dr. Fothergill's garden at Upton, at the time of his decease* occupies thirty-five quarto pages of the *Works* cited at note 21.

From 1780 to 1786 the property remained in the hands of his executors. In 1786 or 1787 the estate was sold to the Quaker, James Sheppard; upon his death in 1812 it was purchased by his son-in-law Samuel Gurney and we enter on the last chapters.

Samuel Gurney

The chief sources for Samuel Gurney are the *Dictionary of National Biography* and a somewhat pious biography by Mrs. Thomas Geldart — *Memorials of Samuel Gurney* published by W. and F. G. Cash in 1857.[27]

He was born of Quaker parents at Earlham Hall, Norwich in 1786 and his birth place is now the administrative headquarters of the University of East Anglia. His father, John Gurney, was a prosperous wool stapler and worsted spinner and later a banker and had distinguished children. Four — Samuel himself, Joseph John and Daniel, with their illustrious sister, Elizabeth Fry, all appear in the *Dictionary of National Biography* (a record for siblings ?).

Unlike his younger brother Joseph, Samuel had no pretensions to scholarship and, after school, his father apprenticed him to Joseph Fry, Quaker tea merchant and banker of Mildred Court, Poultry in the City. Joseph had married Samuel's sister Elizabeth and was the son of William Storrs Fry who had owned Plashet House, East Ham since 1787. The Fry family and the Sheppards were therefore well-to-do neighbours and co-religionists and, in due course, Samuel married the young Elizabeth Sheppard at the Barking Meeting House in 1808. They settled first with Elizabeth's parents at Ham House but after the birth of their first child moved to North End, East Ham — the northern suburb of the, then, comparatively sparsely populated parish. As already indicated, Samuel moved back as owner of Ham House in 1812 and they spent the rest of their married life on the estate.

A new financial procedure known as bill-broking had developed in the first decade of the nineteenth century, led by the

27 The Gurney family has a number of references in the index to *V. C. H., Essex, VI*, and a full account is given under 'Gurney of Walsingham Abbey and Sprowston Hall' in *Burke's Landed Gentry*.

Figure 3.   Samuel Gurney.

firm of Richardson and Overend, and Samuel's father set him up in business with them. His business acumen and the wealth he inherited from his father-in-law and then his father enabled Samuel to advance in the firm which became Overend and Gurney and, for some forty years, was said to be the greatest bill discounting house in the world. It expanded into lending money on a variety of securities and during a banking crisis in 1825 Gurney tided many other firms over their difficulties with loans. He became known as the 'banker's banker' and, at his death, his firm held some eight million pounds in deposits.

Elizabeth Fry now briefly enters the story.[28] Her husband, Joseph, had inherited the Plashet House estate on his father's death in 1809; they moved there from Mildred Court and it was from Plashet that Elizabeth commenced her campaign for prison reform in 1813. In 1828 one of the banking concerns with which Joseph Fry was connected failed and they were obliged to give up Plashet.

There was, and still is, an enclave on the modern Portway frontage of the Ham House estate which Samuel Gurney also owned and he made it possible for the Frys to move to the house in its grounds in their somewhat reduced circumstances. In the Frys' time it was called 'Upton Lane House' but later 'The Cedars' and it survived until 1960. By a little irony the home of the Quaker reformer is now covered by the modern buildings of a Territorial Army HQ. A plaque at the foot of the flagstaff commemorates the connection of the place with Elizabeth Fry.

To return to Samuel Gurney. In some ways he mirrored the wide interests of his eighteenth century predecessor, John Fothergill. He supported the work of his sister Elizabeth, brother Joseph and brother-in-law Fowell Buxton for the improvement of prisons, the reform of the criminal code, the abolition of slavery and the improvement of the lot of negroes. He had interest in the Niger Expedition, 1841, Fowell Buxton's project to introduce commerce into Africa by legitimate means. The experiment ended in disappointment and saddened Buxton's latter days but lessons were learnt of benefit to later endeavours.

From 1848, Gurney was a patron of the infant colony of Liberia. There was opportunity to purchase the territory of Gallenas, a notorious slave market near the north-western frontier, and add it to Liberia. Gurney subscribed half the purchase money and a town was named in his honour.

---

28 Elizabeth Fry is only incidental to this essay. See under her name in Part II of the 'Bibliography' volumes of the *V.C.H. of Essex*.

Figure 4. Ham House in the days of Samuel Gurney.

(Newham Public Libraries)

He was a staunch opponent of capital punishment when people could still be hanged for forgery and there is the well known story of an employee of Gurney's firm who committed a forgery by which substantial loss was sustained. The culprit was brought before Gurney who said, 'We have thee under our power, and by the law we must hang thee — but we will not do that; so (opening the private door) be off to the continent, and beware of ever returning'. The incident caused considerable trouble to Gurney and there was even fear of his being prosecuted for letting the man go but it had some effect in securing a change in the law.

In 1849 Gurney made a philanthropic tour of Ireland, ravaged by the famine and gave an unostentatious relief. 'Unostentatious' was the mark of his considerable generosities.

Like Fothergill, he was also interested in education and was treasurer of Fothergill's Ackworth School for over forty years. From 1843 until his death he was national Treasurer of the British and Foreign School Society — the 'umbrella' body of the 'British' schools as opposed to the 'National' schools of the established church.

He left £5,000 in his will in trust for the British school at Stratford, later replaced by the Bridge Road Board school. Subsequent deeds were replaced by a Scheme made by the Minister of Education in 1955 and the endowment is now known as 'Samuel Gurney's Educational Foundation' and applied to secondary or higher education.[29]

In 1855 he became ill and doctors recommended a visit to the south of France. He took a large house at Nice and then moved to Menton. Finally he became so weak that it was decided to return to England by easy stages but he died in Paris on 5 June, 1856. He was brought back to England and buried in the Society of Friends' burial ground which still exists (though closed) at Barking. His niece, Katharine Fry, records that there was a procession of eighty-eight carriages to the funeral.

Soon after his death local people wished for some memorial to him and several suggestions were made — a library and reading room, baths and washhouses, a dispensary or almshouses. Finally, the present obelisk in the centre of Stratford Broadway was agreed and inaugurated in September 1861.

29 Scheme No. 3771P, sealed 20 April, 1955.

The Public Park

Now — what of the Ham House Estate, Upton?

Samuel's eldest son and heir, John Gurney, survived his father by only three months and his son — another John — was living at Sprowston Hall, near Norwich and had no wish to come to Upton. For a time other members of the family — including Lady Buxton — lived in the house but, by the end of the 1860s, it was obvious that the Gurneys would wish to dispose of the property and there was some danger that, like other private estates in West Ham, the approximately eighty acres of the estate would be covered with houses. (Towards the end of his life Samuel had begun to dispose of some of his land holdings in Forest Gate and, in 1872, John Gurney was to dispose of the Hamfrith estate and later the rest of the Woodgrange estate.)

There were three endeavours to save the estate as an open space for the people and a full account is given in Dr. Gustav Pagenstecher's *The story of West Ham Park* published locally with a second edition in 1908. Dr. Pagenstecher, formerly tutor to the younger members of the Gurney family, was John Gurney's agent for his West Ham property.

The first endeavour was commenced in August, 1868 by Mr. Charles W. Tanner, a member of the West Ham Local Board of Health and sometime Churchwarden of West Ham. Hearing that the estate was on the market he called on Dr. Pagenstecher and asked the acreage and price. The reply was 'About 80 acres and a reserve price of £30,000'.

Tanner pressed the desirability of its becoming a public park and asked if Gurney would reduce the price in that event. Gurney had already expressed a desire in this direction so an appeal for contributions towards purchase was placed in the local paper — the *Stratford Express*. Tanner placed the matter before the Local Board which referred it to its General Purposes Committee and, at a meeting of 17 November, 1868, the Committee supported the proposition and directed that Gurney be asked a price. Gurney said: '£25,000 if for use as a public park' and then later added that, in the event of the estate's being so purchased, members of the Gurney family would donate between £5,000 and £6,000.

The General Purposes Committee recommended an approach to the Government for a contribution or a loan at preferential rates and, on 8 January, 1869, a deputation led by John Meeson, Chairman of the Local Board, was introduced to the Under Secretary at the Home Office by Andrew Johnston, an Essex M.P. The Under Secretary was favourable but requested more details and these were sent by the Clerk of the Board. No reply was received but the proponents heard through the M.P. that the Government was favourably disposed.

Then there was the first hint of setback when two months later a deputation headed by Thomas Crow[30] of Stratford petitioned the Board to take no further action in the matter. Although the Chairman of the Board ruled that such a petition was inconsistent with the decision already taken, these opponents were to win the 'first round'.

A reply was received from the Government to the effect that it would be prepared to lend the required amount — repayable over a period of fifty years at terms favourable to the ratepayers. John Meeson nevertheless thought it wise to refer the matter to the Parish Vestry which still had competence in such matters and the Local Board Clerk asked the parish officers to convene a Vestry Meeting.

The Vestry met on 29 April and Mr. Tanner moved, and the Revd. John Curwen seconded, a resolution recommending that the Local Board of Health effect the purchase of the estate under the terms of Mr. Gurney's and the Government's offers. Mr. Thomas Crow and Mr. James Scully (a 'stormy petrel' in several local incidents) moved and seconded an amendment that the Local Board be requested to break off all negotiations on the subject and not to reopen them. This amendment was carried by a large majority.

Mr. Tanner and a supporter then demanded a poll which was fixed for 3/4 May. The Revd. John Curwen, Major Banes (later one of West Ham's early M.Ps.) and others used the brief interval to address meetings in support of the public park idea but the poll resulted in 1,081 votes for Crow's amendment and only 293 against. This effectually ended any possibility of action by the Local Board.

The demolition of Ham House in 1872 and signs that John Gurney might be selling the estate moved the supporters of the park project to a second effort independent of the Local Board. A public meeting was held in August 1872 and a committee appointed, but nothing was accomplished.

Early in November that year Mr. John Barber, who had been one of the prime movers of this second effort, consulted Dr. Pagenstecher as to what might *still* be done to save the estate from

30 Thomas Crow was the head of a family involved in the religious, political and educational life of West Ham in the nineteenth/twentieth century. A typescript biography is held by the Local Studies Library, Stratford.

the builders. Pagenstecher read to him several letters from John Gurney in which he had said that, although an offer of £27,500 had been made to him, he would rather see the estate preserved as a place of public resort. As the parish had already decided that no charge should fall on the rates the only alternative was to raise the money by subscriptions, which he (Mr. Gurney) would be glad to head with a substantial sum . . . provided that the matter was taken up by substantial people and likely to be carried through. At Dr. Pagenstecher's suggestion a meeting of wealthy and influential residents was convened at the West Ham Town Hall on 22 November, 1872, which appointed a Committee which, by subsequent enlargement, included a cross-section of clergy, ministers, industrialists, businessmen and other local notables. J. C. Whitworth, the Editor of the *Stratford Express*, gave considerable aid by occasional leaders and by publishing all appeals and subscription lists free of charge. Encouraged by the composition of this Committee, John Gurney renewed his offer of sale for £25,000 and increased the contributions by the Gurney family to £10,000 — leaving only £15,000 to be found.[31]

A public meeting was held at the Town Hall in January 1873 and £2,000 was raised but then the project hung fire. Jeremiah Self, the Clerk to the West Ham School Board, who had acted as Secretary resigned and Dr. Pagenstecher was reluctantly persuaded to take his place. He suggested the happy thought of an appeal's being made to the City Corporation as they had large sums available from the Coal and Corn dues for the preservation of open spaces.

Pagenstecher and a colleague waited on the Lord Mayor of London who referred them to Mr. Deputy Bedford, 'an enthusiast in the cause of preserving open spaces'. Deputy Bedford proved his worth and advised a petition to the Common Council of the City. A memorial was drawn up and presented to the Court of Common Council by Bedford and, as a result, a deputation was asked to appear before them. The local Committee was encouraged by the reception the deputation received and redoubled its efforts — raising a further £1,000.

The City's offer was initially somewhat disappointing — only £2,000 — and with considerable hardihood Dr. Pagenstecher replied to Mr. Deputy Bedford:

'Dear Deputy Bedford. Your offer of £2,000 is no use; you might just as well offer half a crown. Nothing less

---

31 Although it is not always made clear, this £10,000 included a sum of £1,000 initially given by Andrew Johnston, M.P.

than £10,000 will do, for we are a poor lot here, and it is quite impossible for us to raise the money still wanting for the purchase of the park.'

In the meantime Gurney had received a private offer of £30,000 for the estate but generously extended the time limit he had set for the 'Park Committee'. Including a generous £500 from the Directors of the Leather Cloth factory in Stratford the local appeal had now reached £4,000.

What Pagenstecher described as his brevity and impudence had its effect. The Court of Common Council took legal advice that it could apply a fund set up under the Metage-of-Grain Act, 1872, and accordingly offered the sum of £10,000, provided that Pagenstecher would personally guarantee the £1,000 now required. The bells of West Ham parish church rang out to signal this resounding success. Pagenstecher entered into a bond for the £1,000 — courageously pledging his credit in the hope that the sum would be forthcoming in further subscriptions.

He collected £300 and then conceived the idea of appealing to Quakers throughout the country in view of the associations of the Society with Ham House. A letter in their periodical *The Friend* brought many responses from members of the Society with memories of Samuel Gurney or Elizabeth Fry and, by March 1874, the result stood at £600 . . . but there it stopped, with £400 still to be found by Dr. Pagenstecher under his bond.

In some desperation he appealed to Mr. James Duncan, a sugar refiner in Silvertown before Tate and Lyle, who had made several benefactions in the south of West Ham. To Pagenstecher's great relief and delight Duncan immediately gave him the required £400. Charles Tanner, Gustav Pagenstecher, Mr. Deputy Bedford and James Duncan should be included in the 'people' in our title.

The money raised, arrangements were made for the conveyance of the Park to the City Corporation and its opening to the public. The ceremony took place on Monday, 20 July, 1874, and the Local Studies Library at Stratford in Newham has a copy of the programme for the day bound up with a copy of Pagenstecher's history of the park.

All West Ham was *en fete*. The route from Bow Bridge to the Park was decorated and triumphal arches had been erected at the bridge and the park gates. The Lord Mayor's procession which consisted of twenty-five carriages, headed by the City Marshal on horseback, was received at Bow Bridge by John Meeson, the Chairman of the Local Board. Bands of Volunteers played them to the park where Mr. John Gurney delivered the title deeds of the estate to the Lord Mayor who, after suitable speeches, declared the grounds open to the public.

The prefatory speech of the City Solicitor is worth quoting in concluding this account of the Ham House Estate:

> '. . . the Corporation of London has from time to time, in its long history embarked on many matters for the public weal, but the ceremony of that day added for the first time a public recreation ground. In 1872 the Corporation found themselves in possession of a very ancient franchise, yielding them a large revenue, in connection with the metage of grain arriving in London. Such, however, were the customs and exigencies of trade, that the measuring of grain had now become obsolete, and the Corporation with the consent of Parliament, had made an arrangement by which the sums they should henceforth receive from that source would be applied, as occasion arose, to the preservation of open spaces for the people in and around the Metropolis. The case of West Ham was the first that was brought before them and they acceded with complete unanimity to a grant of £10,000, by which that splendid estate would now for all time, become the property of the people . . . the Corporation had the royal licence to hold it on behalf of the people . . .'

Not only has the City Corporation held the estate on behalf of the people but it maintains it without any charge on the local rates.

The park is controlled by a Committee of Management. The original composition was eight representatives of the City Corporation, four representatives of the Gurney family and three representatives to be appointed (then) by the 'Vicar, Church-wardens and Overseers of the parish of West Ham'. A scheme of the Charity Commission, 1991, has reinterpreted this last phrase as 'One by the incumbent for the time being or priest for the time being in charge of the present benefice of West Ham, and Two by the Council of the London Borough of Newham'.[32]

In recognition of his efforts Dr. Gustav Pagenstecher was one of the original appointees of the Gurney family and was made Vice-Chairman of the early Management Committee.

32 Charity Commission Scheme CD(Ldn2), 206, 948 A/1 supplied by courtesy of the Town Clerk's Office, Corporation of London.

The Haddocks of Leigh

A. C. EDWARDS

IN 1565 THE ancient port of Leigh on the Thames estuary was described as 'a very proper town, well-furnished with good mariners, where commonly tall ships do lie'.

Leigh was certainly 'Well furnished with good mariners'. There was the amazing Elizabethan, Andrew Battel, who set out for the River Plate in 1589, but soon found himself on the other side of the Atlantic and at the beginning of fantastic adventures in central and south-west Africa, which lasted until 1607. There were the well-known Leigh families of Goodlad and Salmon and their numerous interconnections. Above all, there was the famous family of Haddock, which can be traced back to 1327.

Not much is known of its early history, although there is that interesting figure brass in Leigh church, with its inscription in Latin:

> Hic jacet Ricūs Haddok & Christina ac Margareta ūxes
> ei' & Johēs Haddock, filius dictor' Rici & Cristine, ac
> Alicia, ux' dc̄i Johēs; qui q'dm Ricūs obiit 11 die
> Novembr' Aᵒ Dᵉi MCCC Liij, qr' āibus p'pciet' de'

The Haddocks remained at Leigh until 1707, when their house was sold and the family moved to Kent, although, for some time, later members of the family were buried at Leigh.

Its great period was the second half of the seventeenth century and the first half of the eighteenth, when it produced two admirals and at least seven captains of the Royal Navy. Obviously it was one of those naval families to whom this country owes so much — a family which gave long, honourable service. The surviving letters and papers show them to be a keen, lively lot, with what Dr. Johnson calls 'a bottom of sense'; and, in addition, they had a strong sense of 'family' — and they liked the minor good things of life. Not least, one or the other of them was always in the forefront of stirring and important events; this gives a pleasing point to main maritime occasions.

Figure 1. Admiral Sir Richard Haddock, 1629–1715.
(National Maritime Museum, London)

The earliest known naval captain was a Richard Haddock, who commanded the *Victory* in 1652 and received a reward of £40 for good service. Two of his sons served in the navy: Richard was in command of a fireship in the action off the Dutch coast in May 1673, during the Third Dutch War; William, his elder brother, commanded the *America* with distinction in the First Dutch War and was presented with a gold medal. At least three of Captain William's sons were naval officers. Richard was the most distinguished. He became Admiral Sir Richard Haddock, and a good part of this essay will be devoted to him. William served under Richard in Cromwell's war with Spain, 1657–8. Joseph served under Richard in those bitter, slogging actions off the Dutch coast in May–June 1673. Later, Joseph was in command of *The Princess of Denmark* on the East India Station, and took part in the events which led up to the founding of Fort William (Calcutta) in 1670.

But, to return to the great Sir Richard Haddock, 1629–1715. Most, of the surviving letters are his or written to him. Several were written to his father, Captain William Haddock, during the war with Spain. In the first of these, from the *Dragon* off Dungeness, 30 May, 1657, his affection for his father is obvious; he was greatly piqued because he missed his father passing by in the *Hannibal* on his way to the Mediterranean. Then he continues:

'. . . Sir, my wife desires you, please, on your arrival at Venetia, to buy for her a foiled stone of the measure I conceive was given by her sisters to Brother Andrew at Leigh; as also a pot kettle and 2 stewpans, one lesser than the other; as also a jar from Leghorn, with what other things necessary for a house, to the value of £3 or £4 in all, which shall thankfully be repaid . . . my Lord Protector hath denied the government under the title of King, and, since, it's established to him in the title he now bears.'

He was obviously anxious to pass on all scraps of news, so he adds a postscript:

'. . . since the writing the above lines, I have received orders to go over and ride before Dunkirk, and to take command of that squadron there. This day is arrived happy news, General Blake's burning and sinking 16 sail of the King of Spain's galleons and ships at Santa Cruz, most welcome and true.'

Figure 2. Battle of Sole Bay, 1672.

This victory of Blake's on 20 April was the great man's last exploit. He died on 17 August when in sight of England on the voyage home.

From 1661 to 1666, Richard Haddock was in the Mediterranean. Then, in 1666, he commanded the *Portland* in the attack on Vlie and Schelling.

A later group of letters and papers concerns the murderous action in Sole Bay in May 1672, during the Third Dutch War. The first of these was written to his wife on 14 May. He was then Captain of the *Royal James*, the flagship of the Earl of Sandwich, Admiral of the Blue, and second-in-command under the Duke of York. Richard knew that action was bound to come and was anxious to put his affairs in order.

> '. . . I desire my Cousin Goodlad, the draper, to receive three pounds for thee of Cousin Boys, which is due April last; and pray when the bond is due of Mr. Welsted and Temple, go to them and receive the interest, £9, and desire them to let me have £100 or more if possible, to supply my occasions; thou knowest the employment I am in is very expensive . . . pray let me know what is done with the money in Brother Hurlestone's hand and Brother Thornburgh; I know they will be very kind. I have here enclosed sent thee my will, which have made for all good respects. I desire thee to keep it by thee, sealed as it is. If God Almighty, in His providence should take me out of this life, you will find I have not failed of my promise to thee . . .'

The next letter was written on 21 May, near Sole Bay. The Dutch had been sighted, but the winds were against action:

> 'Had it pleased God yesterday to have given us fair weather, God assisting, we had given a good account of our actions; our men brisk and brave and very ready and willing to fight. The Earl of Bristol on board with us. I think a fourth part of the nobles of England in the fleet. His Royal Highness, the Duke of York, is very zealous to engage the Dutch, God sending a good opportunity and water enough under our keels.'

Then he remembers the little good things:

> 'I had almost forgot to desire thee to return my thanks to Capt. Grantham for the barrel of muscadine he brought me from Mr. Wilkinson of Messina, and for a chest of

> Florence he sent me from himself, with several other
> things, all which I received, with a chest of Florence for
> my Lord Sandwich. Pray pay him three pounds for it — I
> shall receive it here of Mr. Lowe, my Lord's servant.'

His description of the battle on 28 May is given in his report
to the Duke. He was in the thick of it. He took one ship which
attempted to board him. He was attacked by another. Then, while
he was below having the remains of a toe cut off, the *Royal James*
was attacked by a fireship. It blew up; the Earl of Sandwich and
most of the company were lost, but Richard Haddock, with his
nine toes, jumped overboard and was saved. It was after this
action that he was presented to Charles II, who took a silken hat
from his own head and placed it on Richard's — a signal
honour.

Then came letters and papers describing the two actions off
the Dutch coast in May–June 1673. There is his journal, which
runs from 11 May to 29 June. He was captain of Prince Rupert's
flagship, the *Royal Charles* off Dungeness, when the King and
Duke came out in their yachts from Rye, dined on board on the
17th and supped on the 18th. The King's yacht was appropriately
named the *Cleveland*. The first action was fought in the Schoon-
velt on 28 May — 'a smart brush' as he describes it to his wife in a
letter of the 29th. It certainly was a hammering match, with the
Dutch getting perhaps the better of it. Then Richard
continues:

> 'My brother Joseph very well; was with me last night
> after the battle. My uncle, Richard, very well; he hath
> burnt his ship; was fair to burn De Ruyter within his
> length, when they shot his masts about his ears, for
> which endeavoured service the Prince hath given him
> one hundred pounds and gratified also his Officers, etc.
> I suppose we shall not attack them in that place again.
> Our greatest care was to keep clear of the sands in that
> narrow hole, our ship so tender with a sail that we fought
> with the water coming into our lower tier of ports, which
> was very disadvantageous — could not give that service
> intended of us . . .'

The *Royal Charles* was certainly an unsatisfactory ship; and
so Prince Rupert and Richard Haddock transferred to the *Royal
Sovereign* on 3 June and the morning of the 4th in time for the
second action that afternoon and evening. This was another
gruelling, stubborn contest. Both sides were well-matched; then,

eventually, the Dutch drew off. The English followed, but finally decided they were too battered and too short of powder; so they made off for the Nore buoy. On the 11th, the King and Duke came out from Sheerness, supped on board and dined there the next day. After that, Prince Rupert pushed off for a week at Blackheath with his mistress, Mrs. Howe.

Later that year, Richard was made a Commissioner of the Navy, and in July 1675, he was knighted. In 1682, he was made Commander-in-Chief of all ships in the Thames and Narrow Seas. In 1683 he became Commissioner of the Victualling Office. He became Comptroller of the Navy in 1689, a post he held until his death. In 1690, he was one of the joint Commanders-in-Chief of William III's expedition to Ireland. Earlier, he had been M.P. for Shoreham, 1685–7. He died on 26 January, 1715, in his eighty-sixth year and was buried at Leigh.

Long before that, however, there are certain letters which need to be noticed. The first is a letter to Sir Richard from his eldest son, Richard, written four days after Russell's magnificent victory at La Hogue in 1691 — there had to be a Haddock there! It was written on 23 May in 'the Hook', as all English sailors called La Hogue:

> 'Honoured Sir, this is to acquaint you of our engaging with the French, and of our having got the victory. We met them at sea, May 19. There was about 60 sail. We fought them from 11 to 9 at night, since which we have been in pursuit of them. There is run ashore at Sherbrook [Cherbourg] bay Tourville with three more capital ships, which are now burned. Cousin Tom Heath burnt Tourville; and have chased 14 sail more in the Hook, where we are now. Sir Cloudisley Shovell is going in with the 3rd rates and fireships to destroy them. We have been so unfortunate to lose Rear-Admiral Carter in the fight. I am very well and have received no wound; only a small splinter hit me in the thigh, but did no damage, only made it black and blue. I would write more particularly, but the vessel, I hear, is going away presently; having no more at present, but only my duty to yourself and my mother.
> I remain, your dutiful son Richd Haddock.'

The next, a nice interlude of 4 July, 1694 — a letter from a lady for Sir Richard:

> 'Your good nature, Sir, hath drawn upon you the gossip-

ing of a company of women. My sister desire we may drink our punch with you tomorrow, in the evening, about six o'clock, if it is not inconvenient to you. I should have sent to you today, but was prevented. However, Sir, it may yet be adjourned for a longer time if you are otherwise disposed. The doctors are sending me to Tunbridge ere long, so that a warm foundation before drinking those cold waters will not be amiss for, Sir, your obliged humble servant
Isabella Chicheley'

She sounds an Isabella well worth knowing!

There are two delightful letters from Sir Richard to Richard, full of news and affection:

'Navy Office, this 27 Nov. 1702

Dear Sir,

I have yours of yesterday's date from the Downs, which brings us the joyful tidings of your safe arrival there. Your long passage from Newfoundland put us in great fear of your welfare, and particularly your mother hath been a month or 5 weeks crying for you and your brother Nicholas's safety; but blessed be God you are both come well home. Your brother, now with us, came up from the Downs by leave from his captain, and hath behaved himself with so much bravery and courage that he hath gained the good report of the Duke of Ormonde, his Capt., etc. both in the action at Rota and St. Mary Port [Cadiz] and Vigo, and was the first man that boarded one of the galleons at Vigo . . . God Almighty hath blessed the forces of her Majesty and her Allies, both by land and sea, in a wonderful manner, for which we lately had a public day of thanksgiving in this City. The Queen, House of Lords, and Commons, with the Bishops, Judges etc., came to St. Paul's Church, where, after sermon *Te Deum* was sung.

Since your leaving England, two of our Board are dead, vis. Mr. Southern and my good friend, Commissioner Willshaw, who died 23 September last. Your cousin, Anna Babb that was in one of our almshouses at Stepney, is likewise dead, and my poor Cousin Lockwood's son-in-law Cousin Hodges, died at Gosport, since his arrival from Vigo, who waited a tender on the

Duke of Ormonde's ship. *We* are all in good health, praised be God, and do kindly salute you.

I am, your most affectionate father
Richard Haddock'

The second letter, of 10 December, 1703, written fourteen days after the great storm, shows the old man's relief on receiving:

'to our great joy, the account of God Almighty's wonderful preservation of you in the late most dreadful storm, which no man living can remember the like.'

This was the storm which blew the first Eddystone lighthouse and its designer Henry Winstanley of Littlebury into the sea. Sir Richard gives an account of some of the disasters and ends:

'Pray God send you with the King of Spain well out of that place and over to us.'

The 'King' was the Archduke Charles, the Allied candidate in the War of Spanish Succession.

Young Richard was at the capture of Gibraltar — of course a Haddock would be there! His father's friend and kinsman, Captain Whitaker (later, Rear-Admiral Sir Edward Whitaker) wrote from the *Devonshire* in Gibraltar Bay a few days after the event. His letter does not add to knowledge of the capture, but the last sentence of the penultimate paragraph is worth quoting:

'This was the manner we took Gibraltar, which I hope we shall maintain.'

The final paragraph gives particular pleasure:

'I hope, Sir, you'll excuse the trouble I give, but, believing that everybody here writes at the time upon the occasion, I could not forbear giving my very good friend, Sir Richard, this particular account of the whole matter, which I don't doubt that Capt. Haddock will give you much the same account. Pray please to favour my spouse with a line or two, fearing mine should miscarry. My humble service to my good lady and all your good family. I beg you'll make use of this as far as you shall think fit, it being a true account of the whole matter, I am

Your most hearty humble servant and kinsman to serve whilst,
Edwd Whitaker.

P.S. This was writ all in a hurry, so that I hope you'll excuse me.'

Figure 3. Admiral Sir Nicholas Haddock, 1686–1746.
(National Maritime Museum, London)

Not much more is known about young Richard. In 1707 he had the misfortune to be surprised by the French when convoying the Archangel merchant fleet and to lose fifteen ships. This did not seem to comdemn him in the eyes of his superiors, for he was appointed to the *Resolution* in the following year; but he seems to have retired soon, probably through ill-health. However, many years later, in 1734, he reappears as Comptroller of the Navy, and held the post for fifteen years. He died in 1757.

His brother, Nicholas Haddock, 1686–1746, became a distinguished admiral. He entered the navy, 19 May, 1699, as a volunteer in the *Portland*, under his kinsman, Edward Whitaker. He was present at the attack on the treasure fleet at Vigo, 12 October, 1702; indeed, as Sir Richard proudly stated in that letter to Richard, Nicholas was the first to board one of the galleons, an attack which was to become part of sea lore. He was in the *Royal Anne* at the relief of Barcelona by Peterborough in 1706 and sent a letter home to his father, describing the action. Later, there was a typical Haddock touch in another letter from Spain:

> 'I desire your excuse for this bad scrawl and blotted paper, but I write with a pen made with an old razor that I find in the house Im quartered in.'

In 1707, when only 20, he was given his first command, the *Ludlow Castle*. Later, off Cape Passaro, 1718, he led the van, disabled four Spanish ships in succession and contributed largely to Admiral Byng's total destruction of the Spanish fleet. His letter to his wife is a good example of considerable understatement:

> *Grafton*, at sea, about 10 leagues
> from C. Passaro, August 4th, 1718
>
> My dear Fanny,
>
> The *Superb* being ordered from the fleet with the Admiral's letters, I send this to tell you I am well. Five days ago, we had a battle with a Spanish fleet off of Cape Passaro, on the Island of Sicily, in which several of their ships were destroyed. The *Grafton* had her share in that action, and the Admiral has been pleased to make me great compliments on my behaviour that day. I shall soon be ordered to be refitted at Port Mahon, the ship requiring it(!). I had fifty men killed and wounded. Among the former was L^t. Bramble, who was appointed by the interest of Sir Charles Wager. I'm sorry for him, he being a good officer. My cousin Haddock chased towards the shore after part of

the Spanish fleet, when they separated, with 4 or 5 other ships whose signals were made for that purpose, and they are not yet come into the fleet. However, I doubt not but he is well, the ships that they were sent after being of the smaller sort.

My dear, please send to Mrs. Harris to tell her that her spouse[Captain Barrow Harris of the *Breda*] is well. He dined aboard me the day after the action; he was one of the ships engaged. Just before we sailed from Naples, I received your letter and am glad to hear yourself and the little boy are well. I give my love to all friends and remain, my dear Fanny

Your most affectionate husband
Nicholas Haddock'

In 1733, he was made Commander-in-Chief, Nore. In 1738–41, while protecting British commerce, he took two Spanish prizes to the value of two million dollars. His work in the Mediterranean led the Italian merchants of London to present him with a magnificent gold cup. Eventually, be became Admiral of the Blue.

As he lay dying in 1746, he spoke those splendid words which were often quoted, once by Nelson:

'My son, considering my rank in life and public affairs for many years, I have left you but a small fortune, but it is honestly got and will wear well; there are no seamen's wages or provisions, nor a single penny of dirt money in it.'

But any essay on the Haddocks should end by going back to the tough indomitable Sir Richard, whose vigour even old age could not dim. First, a letter written at the age of eighty to the Commissioners of the Admiralty. It is a safe bet that my Lords of the Admiralty rarely receive similar letters today!

'25 July, 1709

Gentlemen,

In the year 1672, I commanded as Captain of the *Royal James* under the Rt. Honble the Earl of Sandwich in the Sole Bay fight. The said ship, after a vigorous defence was burnt by the Dutch; in which action I was wounded, the cure of which cost me in surgeons, apothecary, nurses, etc. betwixt four score and a hundred pounds. I have been so remiss and negligent as not to demand satisfaction for my reimbursement. Do pray the favour of the Board I may have a bill made out, what you will think convenient, having been out of my money now 36 years.

I likewise, in the year 1690 (being one of the Commissioners for Victualling) was taken into custody at Portsmouth, and brought up a prisoner from thence by order of the House of Commons, and remained, as such, a considerable time in the hands of Mr. Topham, the sergeant-at-arms to said House, under pretence of poisoning the fleet, then at sea (under the command of Admiral Herbert, now Earl of Torrington) with guts in our beer and gauls in our beef; and with great difficulty obtained to be bailed.

I must not call it an injustice in that august assembly what they did to me; but it cost me about a hundred pounds to Mr. Topham for his fees, and to lawyers soliciting the House of Commons, with expenses of entertainment when in custody; for satisfaction of which I presume the Board will not think fit to allow me, except directed to do so by the Lord High Admiral, for which shall make application to him; but for my cure I doubt not the favour and justice of the Board in ordering a bill to be made out.

I remain, Gentlemen, your very humble servant
Richard Haddock'

'Very humble servant'! This recalls the end of one of Wellington's letters:

'I remain your humble and obedient servant
Wellington
You know damn well I'm not!'

Finally, Sir Richard's last recorded letter — to his grandson, Richard Liddell:

'Clapham 28th May, 1712, Wednesday
Dear Grandson,

I came yesterday to this place, and according to my promise, do answer yours of 18th instant, from Christ College in Oxford. It happens to be this day 40 years ago that I was burnt out of the *Royal James* in the Sole Bay fight against the Dutch. Am well pleased to find the efforts you intend to make yourself in Westminster Hall. It is like the saying of your Uncle Nicholas, who doubted not to be as great as Sir Cloudisley Shovell was; and he pushes very fair for it.

Your father and family went to Wakehurst (Sussex) Saturday last; took Betty and Fanny Clark down with them; got well thither. Your Uncle Richard, the week past, hath been very ill with a fever and ague, which kept me from thence longer than I designed; is now under the advice of Dr. Radcliffe, who gave me leave to come down hither, promising his care of him; and was downstairs when came away.

With my hearty prayers for your health and welfare, I am

Your most affectionate grandfather
Richard Haddock'

The Haddocks were an incomparable tribe, a closely-knit family; all men of Leigh, Essex men, Englishmen; tough, fearless, able, kind, affectionate, an indispensable breed. It is on men like these, in the navy and in other vital places, that the safety of this realm has depended — and still depends today.

*   *   *   *   *

This essay is based mainly on the *Correspondence of the Family of Haddock 1657–1713*, edited by E. Maunde Thompson, Camden Misc., Vol. VIII. Sir Edward Maunde Thompson, 1840–1929, was a palaeographer and a director of the British Museum. He was created a K.C.B. in 1895.

Epping Forest

ROBERT MITCHELL

SIX THOUSAND ACRES of woodland lying green and golden in the sunshine or even white and magical in the snow, surely represent permanence. In fact it is not like that at all.

The Forest is a living changing thing and change has been occurring ever since the glaciers last came south about 14,000 years ago. The ice sheet split on the hill north of Epping. The two arms gouged out the valley of the Roding and the Lea, forcing up a ridge of heavy clay between. With the retreat of the glaciers, a desolate land of tundra remained, the clay ridge now carrying the gravel and glacial till left behind. The English Channel was still a few thousand years away. The animals of Europe came freely across — mammoth reindeer, arctic fox — the denizens of a bleak, unfriendly land. The glaciers moved steadily northwards and around 8000 years ago the waters broke through at the Straits of Dover. Britain had become an island. The warmth of the sea and the disappearance of the glaciers produced a climate where trees replaced the shrubs and bushes of the tundra and a cool but temperate regime prevailed.

Neolithic man was living in the Forest 4000 years ago. He built, with logs, a causeway almost on the line of present day Lodge Road, which connects the Epping Road to the gates of Copped Hall. In so doing they blocked a small stream which caused a bog to form which remains today. A boring taken from the bog gave a core which, amongst the humus, contained pollen produced during those four thousand years. Examination of the core enabled the sequence and frequency of trees, during the period, to be determined. The core was examined at 10 cm intervals except at critical depths when examination was made at 5 or 2.5 cm intervals. Treatment with potassium hydroxide, hydrofluoric acid and acetolysis solutions removed the humus, silicates and cellulose respectively. Slides were prepared from pollen concentrates and counts expressed as percentages of the whole tree pollen count.

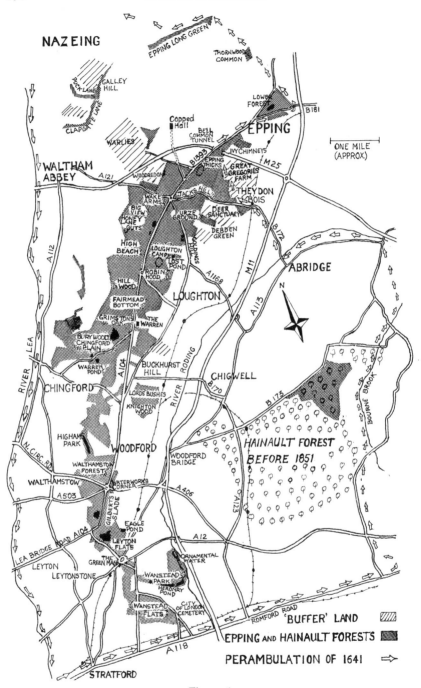

Figure 1. (Drawn by Harry Bitten)

The lowest zone, carbon dated to 2340 B.C. — late Neolithic and early Bronze Age — was from depths of 170 to 120 cm. It showed, consistently, lime (tilia cordata) oak and hazel with traces of beech, birch, pine, elm and alder. The similarity, at this level, to the results from a bore taken on Hampstead Heath, probably indicates that human intervention had not then, significantly altered the tree cover. The pollen count is adjusted according to the circumstances of regeneration. The basic count for lime is doubled for it is insect pollinated making the pollen under-represented, while birch with its tiny multitudinous seeds is reduced to a quarter. The corrected count gave a temporary complete lime domination reaching 96% around A.D. 500, just before its first decline.

The zone above, lasting from A.D. 600 to 840, shows the first lime decline to 50% making this essentially a Saxon phenomenon. Pioneer beech appeared and together with increased oak (to 20%) and birch (to 30%) replaced the lime. An increase in willow and alder at this time indicates a change from open water to fen and an increase in heathland. The complete lime domination in zone one which showed the highest figures anywhere, may have been fairly local. The decrease was probably due to clearance as the Anglo-Saxon invasion put pressure on the population as the invaders came along the Thames, Roding and Lea valleys. There was probably a retreat towards the front ridge and clearance partly by burning as the charcoal deposits show. Lime gives excellent leaf fodder and fibre while the base rich soils it favours are well suited for cultivation after clearance.

Zone 3 starting at A.D. 840 shows lime declining at an increased speed to 3%. The main beneficiary was beech, which having increased to 26% in the earlier zone, now moved to over 60%. Birch also declined but hornbeam, the Forest's special tree, first appeared, while oak remained fairly constant. From then we see the tree mix which has lasted until today. Open woodland increased to the greatest percentage ever attained though some open water and fen persisted. Thereafter, birch first advanced to domination but subsequently declined to about 20% today. Lime finally disappeared and hazel followed. Beech now dominates and tends to increase while oak, dominant in certain areas, is just over 10% overall. Hornbeam, although considered the typical Epping Forest tree only constitutes some 2–3% of the whole.

The dramatic changes in tree cover call for an explanation. Since the Forest is entirely post-glacial, the climatic changes are unlikely to have been sufficient to cause such changes. The first clearance of limes correlates with the Anglo-Saxon invasions around A.D. 600. The penetration of the area by the Anglo-Saxons is shown by the frequency of their place-names which still persist in the area. The second clearance which exterminated the limes coincided with the Danish invasion. The extra pressure on the land resulted in increased use of the ridge and marginal lands. After this clearance, lime did not return and beech was the main beneficiary. So the nature of the Forest which was to provide the conquering Normans with their hunting was established. The next eight hundred years until it became 'the people's forest' were to see human intervention — management is too kind a word —cause changes as great as those that had gone before.

There had long been human occupation. Neolithic man had caused the bogs from which we learn so much. Around 500 B.C. Iron Age man built his two great forest earthworks — Ambresbury Banks and, one and a half miles south-east, Loughton Camp. The former, well known, standing within sight of the main Epping Road, south of Epping, is the bigger. It covers 12½ acres and had an earth wall 12′ high and an 8′ deep ditch so presenting a 20′ wall to any invader. But was it meant to repel invaders? The enormous amount of work involved in making such a construction with the tools of the time, indicates an important use. A number of excavations have failed to find any evidence of this. In fact the lack of any quantity of artefacts or coins suggests only very intermittent use. A driftway connecting the Thames valley with East Anglia may have been run along the forest ridge. The forest earthworks may have been connected with this track, possibly for protection of cattle. Caesar mentions that the British built such enclosures in times of tribal warfare. It is also suggested that they were look-out posts, Loughton to the south-east, Ambresbury to the north-west in days of much less tree cover. All such explanations seem inadequate to explain the vast effort involved in building them and the lack of any evidence of continuous use. Two such look-out posts in such close proximity seems to be a luxury.

The earthworks and the Forest generally abound with legends of Boudicca. After the death of her husband, Boudicca assumed the leadership of the tribe — the Iceni — possibly centred near Thetford. In those non-feminist days this did not suit the Romans who sent over an army to deal with the matter. Boudicca was both defeated and personally humiliated, and the Romans behaved with great brutality. Soon afterwards she set out for revenge. Colchester was an undefended city of retired Roman soldiers. This she took, burnt down and repaid the brutality. The ample wine cellars were available to Boudicca's army. When she set out for London it had lost much of its discipline. The road to London passed close to Epping Forest. Some soldiers would undoubtedly come through the much larger forest of those days. Possibly Boudicca herself passed through. Her exact movements are uncertain but after burning down London she turned north to St. Albans which suffered equally. The Romans now intervened again and the final battle was fought. The exact site is uncertain; matching the topography with the description of Tacitus suggests a position near Mancetter which is close to Nuneaton. The British were massacred. The fate of Boudicca is unknown. Tradition generally has a basis in fact so I believe Boudicca had a connection of some sort with the Forest — but not the final battle.

Whatever the exact nature of Iron Age and Iceni penetrations of the Forest they had no noticeable effect on the tree structure nor did the Romans. The Anglo-Saxons and the Danes were very different as shown by the extinction of the lime in the Forest and the increase of open woodland as they cleared areas for living and cultivation. The Anglo-Saxon and Danish kings certainly hunted in the Forest and to Canute is attributed the first forest laws made about A.D. 1020. The texts of these are now thought to be medieval forgeries and it was William I who created the first real forest administration. On arrival he decreed himself to be the legal owner of all land giving him hunting rights and allowing rents to be charged.

England was then an entirely agricultural and pastoral society. Such decrees affected the very basis of society and could have caused unrest. It is possible that it was as a compromise that the commoners were allowed to keep the rights of grazing, pannage and lopping to a greater extent than allowed elsewhere. The word 'forest' was a Norman-French introduction, though its use then was different from today. A 'forest' was essentially an area subject to the Royal hunting laws. Hunting was normally in areas of tree cover, grassland and heath and it was to such areas that the name was applied. The extent of tree cover was irrelevant. When land was 'deforested' it was no longer subject to the hunting laws.

To administer the hunting laws and, especially to collect the fines imposed, a series of officials was appointed. The chief officer was the Lord Warden, a Royal appointment which became hereditary to the de Veres, the Earls of Oxford. It was a position of great status, worthily upheld over centuries. In 1709 this was transferred to Sir Richard Child who spent £100,000 on the gardens of Wanstead House which he owned. It passed by inheritance to Earl Tylney and Viscount Wellesley — the latter the 'wicked William' of the Duke of Wellington's family, who destroyed Wanstead House. He encouraged and profited by the enclosures he was meant to prevent.

Below the Lord Warden came the Lieutenant of the Forest. These largely ceremonial officers were assisted in the day to day running of the Forest by the Deputy Warden. Under him were the Master Keepers — often of lord of the manor status, Underkeepers, Regarders, Woodwards and Reeves. All had special areas of forest to control or duties to perform. Named lists of these officers exist going back to 1250, but only the Reeves survive today. They are responsible for marking the cattle with the parish mark of their origin. Today, only about four farmers exercise their right of grazing and as all of them come from one parish — Waltham Abbey — the task is a simple one. Recently at a meeting of Verderers and grazing farmers it was agreed that cattle should carry a small ear button coloured to identify the owner.

Parallel with this administrative structure there was a judiciary led by the Verderers of whom there is also a nominal list back to 1250. The title is French reflecting the Norman influence but it is possible that they existed back to the time of Canute. For Waltham Forest they were elected for life by the freeholders.

The Verderers' Court — the oldest in the land after the Coroners — was the first Court of Attachment or Woodmote. The court dealt with evasions of forest law which were largely punished by fines. More serious crimes were within the jurisdiction of the Swainmote, also presided over by the Verderers with a jury of freemen, though this court could not sentence. Sentencing was done by the Chief Justice in Eyre who came out every two or three years, those awaiting sentence being remanded on bail. Many of these officers were officially unpaid but the incidental advantages were great. The Lord Warden was also the Keeper of the Royal Park and mansion at Havering-atte-Bower. He also received all fines imposed for offences against forest laws.

Only two Verderers have been dismissed for misconduct over the centuries. Their crimes are unknown but considering what many Verderers did with impunity, they must have been very unpopular or excessively sinful. The Verderers' elections usually cost about £500 in the money of the day. In a bitter election battle of 1798, the poll lasted 14 days and the two candidates, bringing electors from all over the County spent £7,000 and £10,000 each. The £10,000 spender won. Even in those days he would have had difficulty in recouping that. Local prestige counted for much but surely not £10,000.

The severity of the imposition of the laws varied over the centuries from strict and harsh when the Sovereign was a keen hunter, to chaos and eventually impotence when royalty lost interest. The financial position and greed of the royal master, who ultimately benefited from the fines, also affected the severity with which they were imposed.

The forest boundaries changed frequently reflecting the strength or weakness and, again, the greed of the monarch. William Rufus, son of William I, inherited the Forest from his father and maintained it unchanged. We know he was a keen hunter for he was killed on 1 January, 1100, while hunting in the New Forest. No doubt he also visited Epping Forest. Henry I, a strong king, inherited from Rufus and added to it, seizing adjacent lands. His successor, Stephen, weak in any case, was subject to many troubles, not least matrimonial. He attempted to placate his enemies with gifts of land as the country sank into a state of chaos.

Henry II, ginger headed and compulsively active, was a devotee of hunting and frequented Waltham Forest. Not surprisingly he took back all the land that Stephen had given away. Hunting probably helped his lonely last years when he was estranged from his sons, Richard and John. Richard, of the lion heart, became a victim of his own bravado and died in France from an arrow wound. However, he did give to Waltham Abbey the land on which Copped Hall was to be built. John, who had governed the country in his brother Richard's absence, operated the forest laws in an oppressive manner. This was one of the causes of the Barons' revolt which led to Magna Carta. As a result some land was returned but, more importantly, the forest laws were eased. It was in John's reign, in 1205, that the name Waltham Forest first appears.

In the succeeding reign of Henry III, following a perambulation in 1225, the Barons, perhaps still savouring their success against John, presented the King with demands for boundaries and a charter of liberties, which so enraged him that he cancelled the whole charter.

Fifty years later Edward I declared new and enlarged boundaries. He was much engaged in wars in Scotland and building castles in Wales. It was probably his absences which compelled him in 1300 to restore the boundaries of the 1225

Figure 2.   Queen Elizabeth's Hunting Lodge, Chingford.

perambulation. During these two centuries of turmoil, the good or welfare of the commoners seems never to have been considered. There followed a period of neglect and stability. Perhaps the Wars of the Roses engaged the energies of royalty and nobility alike.

With the Tudors interest returned, at least intermittently. Henry VIII in his younger days was a gifted athlete and caused the building of the Great Standing as his forest hunting lodge. But he died in 1545 only two years after initiating the building. Only with the accession of Elizabeth, after the years of neglect of Edward VI and Mary, did the Forest truly live again and Henry VIII's hunting lodge took her name.

The story that she received there, the news of the defeat of the Armada is probably apocryphal for in 1588, the date of the Armada, the lodge was in a sad state after the neglect following Henry's death. It was in 1589 that Elizabeth initiated a thorough repair and renovation. Certainly she used the Great Standing to watch the hunting of the deer from the deer park in Fairmead.

James I brought his fanatical love of hunting with him from Scotland. He often breakfasted in Copped Hall, having already enjoyed a hunting session. He also regarded it as a source of income and imposed fines and punishment whenever possible. He even had a special gaol built at Stratford to house first offenders.

Charles I was always short of money. It was this which caused him to attempt the exactions which prompted the Civil War. The Forest did not escape for he enlarged its boundaries, partly by the perambulation of 1641, and then exacted rents and dues for the land he had stolen. This behaviour offended all classes and by causing great antagonism was another minor cause of the war which followed.

Cromwell, though not personally involved with the Forest, was sympathetic to its interests. The Long Parliament passed an Act authorising the selling of the Forest against Cromwell's wishes. He adopted the traditional strategy, setting up a Commission of Enquiry and no more was heard of the scheme. During the Commonwealth the Forest deteriorated as the Civil War soldiers were released. Many were destitute and took to the Forest. They made their way as highwaymen and by poaching the deer which they sold as venison. After the Restoration, Charles II took little interest in the Forest as such. However Samuel Pepys, as Navy Secretary found it a useful source of oak for the rebuilding of the Navy. Timber could be floated down the Roding and across the Thames to Deptford.

Some of the great houses were already built. Copped Hall, just north of the Forest, had been built by Thomas Heneage, Treasurer to Queen Elizabeth. He married the Countess of Southampton, mother of Shakespeare's patron and it was at this wedding that the specially written *Midsummer Night's Dream* was first performed. Shortly after his accession Charles II stayed at Copped Hall. Later, William III went there under less favourable circumstances taking refuge in the house when nearly kidnapped by highwaymen while crossing the Forest.

At the southern end of the Forest, Wanstead House had been built by Sir Joseph Child into the greatest house in the land, where royalty and the nobility were regularly entertained. Much of its grounds have now been incorporated into the Forest. As I write (October 1991) the fate of the grounds of Copped Hall hang in the balance. It could go for private development or be incorporated into the Forest for permanent public enjoyment. The issue is yet to be decided.

William III was a keen huntsman but he had built Het Loo, his splendid hunting Lodge in Holland and it was from there that he preferred to ride. Royal interest now finally waned and the Forest deteriorated. The Hanoverians had neither the figures nor the enthusiasm for hunting and considered it somewhat undignified. As always royal indifference led to neglect of the forest laws. Many of the Verderers responsible for upholding the laws in the late eighteenth and most of the nineteenth centuries were, at least, negligent. Many factors were increasing the pressure on the land and illegal enclosures occurred, some perpetrated by the Verderers themselves. In addition the Lord Warden was the dissolute Wellesley-Pole whose extravagance had led to the destruction of Wanstead House.

Illegal enclosures continued with the Verderers' Court unable or disinclined to halt them. The 60,000 acres of the 1641 perambulation were reduced to about 7,000 by 1800 and were still being rapidly reduced. By 1851, the son of Wellesley-Pole had recovered the Wanstead Park estate and he instructed his tenant of Aldersbrook Farm to enclose thirty-four acres of Wanstead Flats. This led to a ceremonial breaking down of fences, but he claimed hereditary Lord Warden's rights and the enclosure was upheld. In 1854, the Corporation of London bought part of Aldersbrook Farm to provide a cemetery. By so doing they became commoners of the Forest — which was to prove crucial. In 1871 another twenty acres of Wanstead Flats, adjacent to the cemetery was enclosed. Notice served by the Corporation and a mass meeting failed to have the fences removed so the Corporation instituted legal proceedings.

Meanwhile at the northern end of the Forest a struggle was occurring at a different level. Loughton was the main area where lopping rights were still exercised. A controversy between the Willingale family and the Revd. Maitland, the lord of the manor, about the exact timing of the lopping resulted in three of the family going to gaol.

By now Epping Forest had become more than a local issue. Edward North Buxton supported the Willingales who continued to fight which would have been impossible without his influence and financial support. In the south the Corporation was now fully involved. In April 1871 the House of Commons passed a resolution in favour of preserving Epping Forest as an open space. The resolution was treated with contempt by the Government. This so incensed Mr. J. T. Bedford, a courageous and persistent member of the Court of Common Council of the Corporation of London, that he got a resolution passed by the Corporation commanding the City to secure the future of the Forest. The City Corporation passed this unanimously but the Government refused to listen. So the Corporation took it to the Courts to establish precisely what rights the public had over the wastes of the Forest.

The concern of the Corporation was not without a basis. As London developed as a centre of commercial activity many of the merchants and financiers moved eastwards into splendid houses where they could enjoy the rural surroundings. This was particularly evident in the northern part of the Forest from where they could coach to their businesses daily. Later, many of the houses would change to other uses and some of the grounds be incorporated into the Forest.

Before proceeding with the action, a Verderers' Court was called but proved impotent and resigned. This clear demonstration of the breakdown of the legal processes of the Forest ensured that the action would go forward. After three years of preparation the case came before the Master of the Rolls. Twenty-three days of hearings later, the decision was unanimously against the enclosers. The decision rested largely on inter-commonage. The commoners had the right to graze throughout the Forest, not only on the lands of their own lord of the manor. Buying out the rights of his own tenant did not give the lord of the manor control. The commoners of other manors still had the right to graze his land and therefore he could not enclose. All land enclosed since 1851 had to be returned. An arbitrator, Sir Arthur Hobhouse, was appointed to decide doubtful cases and there was no appeal against his decisions. What a splendid way to get disputes settled.

The City bought out the nineteen lords of the manors for a little over £250,000 and the lopping rights for £8,000. Enough of the £8,000 was left over to build Lopping Hall which still stands in the centre of Loughton. It was opened, somewhat inappropriately, by the Revd. Maitland, one of the foremost illegal enclosers.

In 1882, Queen Victoria visited the Forest and dedicated it to the use of the people for ever. She also renounced the royal hunting rights which still existed even though they had not been exercised for a long time. She could not give the land of the Forest for she did not own it but only the hunting rights. The land had belonged to the lords of the manor whom the City had bought out for hard cash. The Epping Forest Act was passed in 1878 without opposition. For a short period land could be exchanged with the Arbiter's approval and Wanstead Park and Hill Wood (between High Beach and Fairmead) were obtained in this way.

The Act completely changed the form of the administration. The Verderers lost their legal powers and forest laws and customs ceased except for the right of commoners to graze cattle and to pannage, the feeding of pigs, but the latter is no longer exercised.

The Act vested the Forest in the Corporation. The administration has as its head the Ranger, appointed by the Sovereign. The present Ranger is Prince Richard, Duke of Gloucester. The management is the responsibility of the Epping Forest and Open Spaces Committee consisting of twelve members of the Court of Common Council and the four Verderers. The Verderers are elected every seven years by the commoners, who are those living in the Forest parishes and owning not less than half an acre free of buildings.

The Act imposed on the Conservators the duty to keep the Forest unenclosed and unbuilt and to maintain it as an open space for the enjoyment and recreation of the public. No land may be sold but by Act of Parliament may be taken for roads or similar purposes, although an exchange of land must be made. The Act also required the 'natural aspect' to be preserved. For over a millennium man has occupied and adapted the Forest to his use. Any definition of 'natural aspect' must be subjective. The Act's instruction to protect 'the timber and other trees, pollards, shrubs, underwood, heather, gorse, turf and herbage' is, at least, definite.

When Wm. D'Oyley, a Loughton surveyor, was appointed the first Superintendent, many problems faced him. Much of the land was an inaccessible swamp. As a first priority access was improved with a new road from the Queen Elizabeth Hunting Lodge to the Epping Road. Connaught Waters was created to drain Fairmead, a strategy that was followed elsewhere. Lopping, gravel extraction and deer poaching all continued illegally but were gradually stopped or, at least, decreased by more keepering.

About 500 acres of overcrowded trees were thinned each year, but in other parts, especially those areas in the south, previously enclosed, the trees had been largely destroyed. 56,000 trees were planted, some in the pollard-devastated areas in the north. Most were the typical forest trees, oak, beech and hornbeam but a magnificent avenue of black Italian poplars was planted across Wanstead Flats and is there today. A row of poplars planted across Woodford Green had to be felled in 1966 as dangerous.

After 1879 the Superintendent was Alexander McKenzie who, with his son and grandson, were the Superintendents from 1879 to 1949. The work of Alexander McKenzie was much criticised but gradually the results proved the correctness of his methods. Many ponds were cleared, the biggest being Wanstead Park's ornamental waters. Meanwhile the area of the Forest was growing. Gifts or purchases had added Oak Hill, Highams Park, Yardley Hill and Bell Common and the total area approached 6,000 acres.

The railway had been extended to Chingford and, later, to Loughton. Chingford Plain had become an almost permanent fair and large numbers of people came regularly to the Forest. To cater for these crowds the great teetotal restaurants, the Retreats, were built. The biggest was Rigg's Retreat at High Beach, claiming to serve 3,000 people with tea at the same time. Until the first World War cycle meets also attracted great numbers. They used the Retreats as a focus for their rides to which many came in fancy dress. The Forest was now established as a centre for popular pleasure and amusement. How this fitted to the preservation of the 'natural aspect' is doubtful.

After 1878 pollarding ceased and with the exceptional initial planting the Forest gradually returned to a more normal forest appearance. But was that the 'natural aspect'? The

precise aim of management has always been difficult to define
for there is no final decision. The aim must be to manage the
Forest so that it looks unmanaged and to arrange the progression from grassland and heather through scrub into mature
trees to look like the unassisted work of nature. At the same
time the interests of those seeking recreation whether riding,
golf or just walking must be considered.

It must also be remembered that this is a Site of Special
Scientific Interest which imposes a duty to consider the
interests of scientists, biologists, botanists, entomologists,
each of which believes their interest should predominate. But
especially must be considered the right to peace, quiet and
seclusion in the inner recesses of the Forest for those who seek
it and many do. The recent creation of three large non-
intervention areas caters particularly for the latter as well as
the fauna of the forest, perhaps its weakest aspect.

The path of progress has not been smooth from the devas-
tated 1878 Forest. The initial work was not really complete
when the first World War took away the men who would have
undertaken the Forest management. The Forest moves on a
fifty-year cycle and arrears were hardly complete when war,
with its urgent demands, again came. A few bomb craters and
remains of tank traps alone remain to recall those days. Since
then the cycle has turned again and maintenance is on a steady
basis, no longer struggling to overcome unavoidable neglect.

The cycle is not an unchanging one however for the Forest
is always changing and so are the aims of management. The
demand for more and bigger roads and ever increasing facilities
for cars has coincided with alarms about pollution. And
pollution, holes in the ozone layers and potential greenhouse
effects all caused concern, but acid rain was the greatest
concern. The Conservators commissioned a report from Dr.
Oliver Rackham on acid rain. He found it had caused no
material damage and so halted a campaign built up, no doubt,
on genuine concern but inadequate evidence. He did find areas
of 'group damage' affecting beech but this was due to mainly
natural factors, especially as the beech here was very near the
margin of their range. Overall he gave the Forest an
excellent report.

Difficulties remain nevertheless. The need for human
intervention and management has been greatly increased by the
lack of grazing animals. The restriction of cattle to only half the
year and the reduction in their numbers; the coralling of the deer

Figure 3. The Fallow Deer, Epping Forest.

— considered necessary to protect them from poaching and road accidents; the loss of most rabbits; have all demanded human attention to preserve the 'natural aspect'.

But all is not gloom. Reintroduction of pollarding including experiments to determine the best methods, forgotten in a century of disuse, is helping to restore the grasslands. A balance between the slowly increasing heather and a variety of grasses is being sought. Scrub, good for grazing, around the grasslands could create an area attractive for deer. Possibly this is now happening and deer are gradually returning. Rabbits are surprisingly important and their resurgence is also helping to control the grass. So far there is no sign of disease returning. But especially the deer, both black fallow and muntjak are gradually, very gradually, increasing their number and spreading their range. The three non-intervention areas, introduced at the suggestion of the Nature Conservancy Council, should help to provide suitable breeding areas. Improved grass cutting methods will improve the quality of the grass and encourage the wild flowers.

Horse rides and the damage which inevitably occurs in wet weather cause controversy. Varying covers, including shale, for the rides may reduce the damage. Only experiments and time will determine the result. The management structure and the organisation of the information services are under review. The Corporation feels, with some justification, that the extent of its support, financially and otherwise, is not generally appreciated. It is attempting to remedy this by improved publicity. The preservation of the boundaries of the Forest and its protection from encroaching development, remains of paramount importance. The Conservators never surrender land except in exchange and seek continuously to extend the Forest.

There are problems, and difficulties will undoubtedly arise. The reassurance is the determination of the Conservators only to act in the best interests of the Forest. The unanimous support and good will of all who live around and use the Forest is the final guarantee that the Forest will continue to prosper.

*   *   *   *   *

Note:

For much of the information on changes in tree cover, I am indebted to *Woodland Continuity and Change in Epping Forest* by C. A. Baker, P. A. Mosey and Patricia M. Oxford.

The Essex Landscape in Morant's Time and Today

OLIVER RACKHAM

This paper is adapted from the Morant Lecture, delivered to the Essex Society for Archaeology and History in Colchester Castle on 22 June 1990.

Philip Morant (1700–1770)

MORANT WAS A Jerseyman who came to Essex. He was Vicar of Chignall Smealy, Shellow Bowells and various other places, but is remembered less for his services to the church than for his distinction as an historian. In 1748 he published *The History and Antiquities of the most ancient Town and Borough of Colchester.* Ten years later there appeared his yet greater work, *The History and Antiquities of the County of Essex.*

Morant was also the author of books on national history, but it is these on Essex that have made him famous. Although seemingly specialised, they became famous to the point of being honoured with a parody.[1] Morant comes near the beginning of the great flow of published volumes of texts and abstracts of public records, which was to continue throughout the next century but, in our degenerate times, shows signs of drying up. I say 'degenerate times' advisedly: one cannot lift his three mighty volumes, their 1381 folio pages crammed with detail, without a sense of awe that he should have been able both to write them and to find a publisher. How often is such a feat achieved in these days of a well-ordered Public Record Office and of typesetting on a computer?

Morant is still the most essential source for anyone working on the history of the Essex landscape. To find out the history of a wood, one turns up Morant to see whether he says anything about it, or what documents there are that might mention it. Morant's value is in these references: he seldom says anything about the landscape directly. He is an historian's historian: information

---

1 *The History and Antiquities of the Ancient Villa of Wheatfield, in the County of Suffolk.* Ex fumo dare lucem, Cooper, London, 1758.

Figure 1. Hadleigh, photographed by an unknown German pilot on 31 August, 1940. This picture catches almost the moment when the suburbs of Southend, eating into the Hadleigh woods, were stopped by public protest. The wood to the east of centre, Barnes Wood or Hadleigh Great Wood, anciently a property of St. Paul's Cathedral, had just become 'Belfairs Nature Reserve'. Belfairs Wood, lying to the east, had suffered the comic fate of having a golf-course bulldozed into it. This wood had once belonged partly to Prittlewell Priory. To the north lies Pound Wood, which had belonged to Westminster Abbey, and to the north-west is West Wood, also a property of St. Paul's. All these woods had complex medieval and earlier histories which had been forgotten by Morant's time. Between Pound and West Woods lies the settlement of Daw's Heath, which was a real heath until c.1800. In the south of the picture lies Hadleigh Castle, and farther south still the railway crosses the enwalled Hadleigh marshes.

Since 1940 the houses have only slightly increased. The old woods, now mostly public places, are little altered. Much new woodland has sprung up, especially around Hadleigh Castle.

interests him only if it has been written down. Archaeology was then only beginning to be a source of evidence. The error of trying to write landscape history without doing fieldwork was to continue long after Morant's time; it is still prevalent today, although there is no longer any excuse for it.[2]

In Morant's time one gets a more direct view of the Essex landscape as a whole than is possible earlier. Although the maps in Morant's books contain little relevant detail, the Essex Record Office contains a magnificent corpus of contemporary and earlier large-scale maps — a collection which can hardly be rivalled anywhere outside Sweden. Shortly after Morant's death, Chapman and André published their atlas of Essex.[3] These maps can be compared with the first edition 25-inch Ordnance Survey of the 1870s: some of the Essex sheets, which appear to record every hedgerow and wood-pasture tree, are the finest productions that the O.S. has ever achieved. A later, comparable, source is the aerial survey, covering most of Essex, commissioned by Adolf Hitler, flown in the 1940s, and now preserved in the United States National Archives in Washington[4] (Figure 1).

Essex Then and Now

It might be thought that Essex would have changed more than most counties, owing to urbanisation and development in the last hundred years. However, a surprisingly small proportion of Essex, less than fifteen percent, has changed radically; and even where it has, a surprisingly large proportion of the distinctive features of the landscape survive among the development.

Readers will not need to be told of the expansion of London and its satellite towns: of Southend, Canvey Island, Grays Thurrock and the Hams. To some it may yet come as a surprise to open Chapman and André and find that London still stopped well short of the Essex–Middlesex border, or that 'South End' was still a handful of houses forming one of the 'ends' of Prittlewell. More than three-quarters of Essex, however, still has the same settlement pattern as in Morant's time: a land of dispersed settlement,

2 O. Rackham, 'The countryside: history and pseudo-history', *Local History*, 14, 1987, 13–17.

3 J. Chapman and P. André, *A Map of the County of Essex*, London, 1777; reprinted several times by Essex Record Office.

4 Enquiries to: Cartographic Branch, U.S. National Archives, Washington, D.C., 29408. The reference to Figure 1 is GX 10404/F857/016, and to Figure 5 is GX 10381 SG050.

of hamlets and scattered farms and a labyrinth of lanes. It is more like Herefordshire than either is like Cambridgeshire — for reasons, still dimly understood, which were operating a thousand years before Morant.[5]

The rural road map of Essex is almost identical today to what it was in Morant's time. The only important change is the addition of a couple of hundred miles of modern main road. This began in the 1830s with the making of the Epping New Road, which split Epping Forest from end to end; a disaster which would hardly be allowed today.

The Agricultural Landscape

The story of the English countryside is not one of continual change, but of brief upheavals separated by long intervals of stability. Morant lived at the beginning of one of the great upheavals, the Enclosure-Act movement which created much of the landscape of *middle* England as we now see it. Enclosure Acts, as we shall see, had a calamitous effect on some of the rarer features of Essex, but they left the ordinary landscape unaltered.

Essex, nine-tenths of it, is one of the Ancient Countryside counties.[6] It has never been a land of villages set in great communal fields. The pattern of hamlets and isolated farms, hedged fields, and innumerable lanes goes back far beyond Morant's time. It is shown, for example, in the maps of Earl's Colne by Israel Amyse in 1593[7] and implied by the hundreds of medieval buildings in the hamlets and farms. In much of south Essex it seems to go back to the Iron Age.[8] There were, of course, many piecemeal alterations (Figure 5) before the catastrophic destruction of hedges through the farming fashion of the 1960s and 1970s. However, the great majority of the roads and hedges that survive are well over 250 years old (Figure 2). Morant, returning today,

5 O. Rackham, *The History of the Countryside*, Dent, London, 1986, especially Chapters 1 and 9.

6 O. Rackham, *Trees and Woodland in the British Landscape*, 1st ed., Dent, London, 1976, 17.

7 E.R.O.

8 W. Rodwell, 'Relict Landscapes in Essex', *Early Land Allotment*, ed. H. C. Bowen and P. J. Fowler, *British Archaeological Reports, British Series*, 48, 1978, 89–98. P. J. Drury and W. Rodwell, 'Settlement in the later Iron Age and Roman periods', *Archaeology in Essex to AD 1500*, ed. D. G. Buckley, *CBA Research Report*, 34, 1980, 59–75.

would instantly recognise most of Essex; he would be completely lost in Cambridgeshire.

The typical Essex hedge is of a mixture of trees and shrubs such as hazel and maple, runs in an erratic course, and is set at intervals with pollard trees; in contrast to the Enclosure-Act hedges of Cambridgeshire, which run in straight lines, are flimsy hawthorn-rows, and were planted at a time when pollard trees had gone out of fashion.

In Morant's time hedgerow trees, both timber and pollard, flourished as never before or since. For example, a survey of Little Coggeshall in 1734 records 4061 trees (mainly elm, oak, ash and maple) on 603 acres of farmland; at Woodham Ferrers in 1771 there were 920 trees, mainly oaks, on about 200 acres of farmland.[9] Farmland trees tend to prosper when farming does not. There was a decline in the late eighteenth century, continuing into the mid-nineteenth. Hedgerow trees increased again in the late nineteenth century, to be the victims of agricultural prosperity, and then of Dutch Elm Disease, in the third quarter of the twentieth.[10]

In the extreme north-west, a few Essex parishes had classic Midland-type open-field layouts, all of which were abolished by Enclosure Acts after Morant's time. For example, the western half of Saffron Walden had such a transformation in 1823; the eastern half lay within Ancient Countryside and was unaffected.[11] (Embryonic open-fields were once widely scattered in Essex, but only on an experimental scale.)

Heaths

Essex has lost its heaths so completely that some readers may not realise they ever existed. In Morant's time, heaths and rough grassland were not much less extensive than woodland. Examples are the great ring of heaths around Colchester, or Tiptree Heath and its neighbours. Small heaths went almost to the south coast at Mucking and Orsett.

In Morant's time, heaths and commons were fully used for pasturage by the people living on their edges; but it was becoming fashionable to disapprove of them. They were the chief target of the Enclosure-Act movement in Essex. For us there can be few

9 E.R.O., D/Dc E/15/2–3; D/Ra E1.

10 O. Rackham, *The History of the Countryside*, Dent, London, 1986, chapter 10.

11 D. Cromarty, *The Fields of Saffron Walden in 1400*, Essex County Council, Chelmsford 1966.

Figure 2. An Essex lane: Poor's Lane in Hadleigh, between Barnes Wood (Belfairs Nature Reserve) on the left and Dodd's Wood on the right. This is one of the many ancient roads which have never been tarred. On each side it has a woodbank, made in medieval or Anglo-Saxon times to mark the boundary of the wood. April 1986.

more depressing comparisons than between Chapman and André's map in 1777, when all the heaths were in use, and the first edition Ordnance Survey sixty years later, when nearly all had been abolished and destroyed. The effect was to add a little to Essex's stock of poor-quality farmland. The 'improvers' did not know when to stop — they seldom do.

Odd corners of heath escaped here and there, perhaps because Enclosure-Act commissioners had scruples about depriving poor commoners of rights for which they could not adequately be compensated. However, heathland needs to be maintained by grazing, and is difficult to preserve on a small scale. Nearly all the remaining heath became overgrown with trees; it has lost its distinction as heath without gaining distinction as woodland.

The Coast

Morant lived at a time when the local sea-level was rising relative to the land, as it still is rising. In the middle ages, many marshes, such as Foulness Island, that had once been tidal were enwalled and made into farmland. The last great enwalling was of Canvey Island by Dutch 'adventurers' in the 1620s.[12] By Morant's time, this development was nearing its limit, and it was becoming difficult to retain those marshes that had already been embanked. The famous Dagenham Breach, when a surge broke through a medieval sea-wall on 29 October, 1707, proved to be only just within the power of eighteenth century technology to repair.

Since then, the land has sunk by some three feet more. Although this can be coped with by raising the sea-walls and by pumped drainage, the situation has become more precarious. The great surge of 31 January, 1953 drowned some 120 people in Essex, and resulted in the loss of some enwalled areas such as Bridgemarsh Island. It will not be the last.

Salt-marshes used to be a special feature of Essex. Up to Morant's time, along with heaths, they were the principal pasture for sheep. They are now much reduced, squeezed between the sea-banks and rising sea-level.

Fresh or brackish marshes, behind the sea-walls, are notable both for plant and animal life and for antiquities, for example, the successive stages of medieval enwalling, the earlier 'Red Hills' resulting from Roman salt-boiling, or the winding creeks of the

12 B. E. Cracknell, *Canvey Island: the history of a marshland community*, Leicester, 1959.

Figure 3.   A giant coppice stool of chestnut, dating from well before Morant's time. West Wood, Thundersley. April, 1986.

original saltmarsh. Like the heaths, but at a later date, these have been destroyed before they were fully appreciated. On Canvey Island, development and industrialisation have taken their toll. Much elsewhere has been lost to arable farming, notably Wallasea Island, where the entire internal landscape of the island, within the perimeter wall, was destroyed in the 1960s.

In Morant's time, a hazard of Essex coastal life was malaria, carried by the brackish-water mosquito *Anopheles maculipennis* subspecies *atroparvus*. It disappeared in the nineteenth century; nobody really knows why — the destruction of the marshes was too late to be the cause.[13]

Woodland

In Morant's time, most of the woodland in Essex was a permanent feature, dating from time out of mind. Woods were valuable property, regularly managed by coppicing. Most of the trees (the *underwood*) were cut down at regular intervals of years and allowed to grow again from the stools (Figure 3) to yield an indefinite succession of rods and poles, used for hurdlework and other specialised uses, but also as a source of energy in the form of logs, faggots and charcoal. In Essex, a major use of underwood was for salt-marsh sea-defences.[14] Scattered among the underwood were *timber* trees, mainly oaks, allowed to grow until they were big enough for use as beams and planks. Woods had definite boundaries, usually defended by earthen banks which formed part of the conservation of the wood (Figure 2).

For Morant, all this would have been something familiar which had always been done. Many of his medieval documents give details of such management; he pays little attention to it because he takes it for granted. We now know that similar woodmanship goes back to the Neolithic period.[15]

In historic times, Essex has not been a very wooded county. The original wildwood, which would have covered everywhere except the salt-marshes, was grubbed out long before the records begin — in the Iron Age or earlier. Domesday Book suggests that about twenty percent of Essex was woodland or wood-pasture,

13   S. P. James, 'The disappearance of malaria from England', *Proceedings of the Royal Society of Medicine*, 23, 1929, 71–87.

14   O. Rackham, *Ancient Woodland of England: the woods of South-East Essex*, Rochford District Council, 1986, 40.

15   O. Rackham, *Trees and Woodland in the British Landscape*, 2nd ed., Dent, London, 1990.

much like the average of France today.[16] Shortly afterwards, with a greatly rising population, much of this too was grubbed, a process which was halted by the Black Death in 1349.

By the fourteenth century, woodland was valuable land and was carefully defined and conserved. Most of the woods then existing were still there in Morant's time. Many are still extant today: Hadstock Wood, Hempstead Wood, Soane or Bullock Wood in Colchester, Wall and Monk Woods next to Hatfield Forest, Norsey Wood in Billericay, Tile Wood in Thundersley, to take a few examples at random.

It must be emphasised that the destruction of woodland is not a one-way process. Any piece of Essex, if not continually cultivated or grazed, turns into a wood. This is a common and most important process, and is still going on especially in the south. The new or *secondary* wood, however, will not be the same as the original: it may, for example, be an oakwood with brambles where the nearby ancient wood is a limewood with oxlips.

In the middle ages, the main product of woodland had been underwood. Timber trees were much smaller than we expect today; the majority of those preserved in medieval buildings are little more than oak poles.[17] In Morant's time, and indeed all through the eighteenth century, there were some Essex woods in which this tradition was still maintained. There was also the beginning of the transition to the modern practices of regarding timber more highly than underwood, and of allowing oak-trees to grow bigger.[18]

Woodland since Morant's time — North-West Essex

In two parts of the county it is possible to go into more detail. In the north-west, there was some readvance of woodland in the post-Roman period. For example, the area now around Stansted Airport was the second most extensive wooded area in Essex in 1086. Excavations in advance of extending the airport showed that this area, far from being untouched wildwood, had a long history of Roman and earlier settlement: most of the 1086 woodland must have been secondary. This woodland was again grubbed out,

16 O. Rackham, *Ancient Woodland: its history, vegetation and uses in England*, Edward Arnold, London, 1980, 123.

17 O. Rackham, *Ancient Woodland of England: the woods of South-East Essex*, Rochford District Council, 1986, chapter 6.

18 O. Rackham, *Ancient Woodland: its history, vegetation and uses in England*, Edward Arnold, London, 1980, 148–49.

except for the woods of Hatfield Forest (which, too, contains Roman and earlier sites) and some neighbouring medieval woods.[19] The same story is told by archaeological survey in Elmdon and neighbouring parishes, which reveals Roman occupation on the sites of later woods since grubbed up.[20]

Medieval grubbing-out is documented, to some extent, in the records of Colchester Abbey, which had lands near Hatfield Forest. By 1350 the distribution of woods was almost the same as in Morant's time. The Ordnance Survey of 1805 shows that, in the present Uttlesford District, there were 286 woods, most of them ancient, covering four and a half percent of the land area. In the mid-nineteenth century, during a brief period of agricultural prosperity, there was a third phase of destruction, reducing ancient woodland to three percent of the area.

Very little changed between 1870 and 1950. Then came a fourth phase of destruction, in which ancient woodland was seized and destroyed, not only, as previously, by farmers to add to their arable land, but by foresters to make plantations. By 1980 I reckoned that ancient woodland covered less than two percent of Uttlesford District. In general, it is the smaller woods that have survived (Figure 4).

Woodland since Morant's time — South-East Essex

South-East Essex tells a different story. This whole corner of the county is covered with the remains of a ancient, semi-regular grid of roads, hedges and fields, probably planned in the Roman period or earlier. The wooded, and once also heathy, hills between Rayleigh and Rochford stand out as a gap in the grid. There can be little doubt that this area was set aside as non-agricultural land by whoever made the grid. This arrangement still obtained in 1086: Domesday records not much more woodland than there was in Morant's time. There had been no post-Roman expansion of woodland. Parts of the woodland in the hills belonged to lowland places up to eight miles away.

The post-Domesday grubbing of woodland seems not to have happened in South-East Essex. In the later middle ages woodland increased through hedges being allowed to expand into

19 O. Rackham, *The last Forest: the story of Hatfield Forest*, Dent, London, 1989, chapter 2.

20 T. Williamson, 'The development of settlement in north west Essex: the results of a recent field survey', *Essex Archaeology and History*, 17, 1986, 120–33.

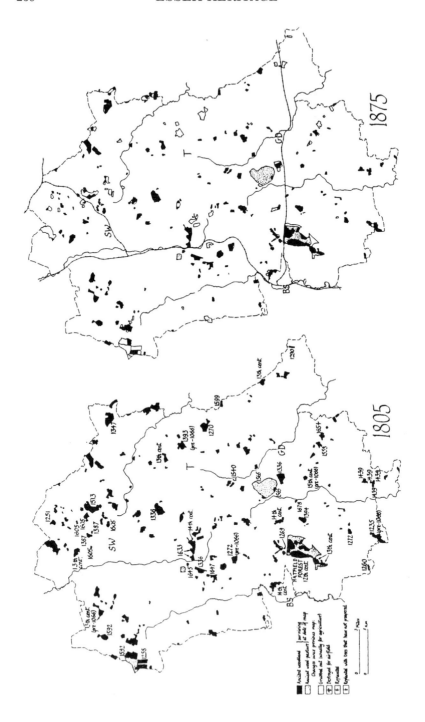

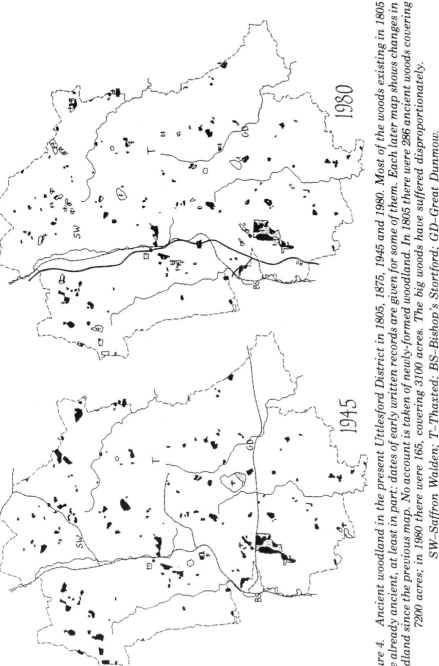

Figure 4. Ancient woodland in the present Uttlesford District in 1805, 1875, 1945 and 1980. Most of the woods existing in 1805 were already ancient, at least in part: dates of early written records are given for some of them. Each later map shows changes in woodland since the previous map. No account is taken of newly-formed woodland. In 1805 there were 286 ancient woods covering 7200 acres; in 1980 there were 165, covering 3100 acres. The big woods have suffered disproportionately.
SW–Saffron Walden; T–Thaxted; BS–Bishop's Stortford; GD–Great Dunmow.

(These maps first appeared in O. Rackham, The History of the Countryside.)

belts of woodland. Much of this increase was again grubbed out in the late seventeenth and early eighteenth centuries. This affected mainly the small and middle-sized woods. The great woods of the Rayleigh–Rochford area were much the same in Morant's time as they had been for at least a thousand years.

Shortly after Morant's time there was another phase of grubbing. Nearly one-third of the woodland of South-East Essex was destroyed between 1805 and 1820. This did not happen at all in North-West Essex; here it was possibly the action of a few eccentric landowners. In contrast, the mid-nineteenth century phase of destruction here consumed remarkably little woodland. There were two further phases of destruction, in the 1930s (Figure 1) and again from 1945 to 1970. Unusually, these losses were more to development than to agriculture, and not at all to forestry.[21]

The result in each area is that rather less than half the ancient woodland that Morant might have known is still there, but for a different set of reasons at different periods. The North-West Essex story is more typical of the country as a whole than the South-East Essex story. Woods survive in the most unexpected circumstances: for example, in the Grays–Thurrock area, full of huge quarries, there are fourteen ancient woods, dating from long before Morant, remaining on patches of undug and unbuilt-on ground.[22]

Plotland

A curious feature of South-East Essex are the *plotland* woods. The idea of plotland began with the Socialist philosophy of the early nineteenth century ('Three Acres and a Cow'): land was to be parcelled into smallholdings, on which factory workers were to find a new and happier livelihood as peasants. In Essex this was put into effect much later, mostly after World War One ('a Land Fit for Heroes'). Thousands of acres of poor and difficult land were divided into three-acre plots with little houses on them. Some of these have come up in the world and now have conventional houses ('Exclusive Wooded Grounds'). A few are still much as originally intended, although the cow has usually turned into a horse. But many hundreds never prospered: the houses rotted

---

21 O. Rackham, *Ancient Woodland of England: the woods of South-East Essex*, Rochford District Council, 1986, chapter 4.

22 O. Rackham, 'Woodlands and their management', *Landscape History and Habitat Management*, ed. J. MacConnell, South Essex Natural History Society, 1977, 17–21.

away and the site, like all derelict land, turned into woodland. These woods (already visible in the 1940 air photographs) are a considerable addition to the woodland of south Essex.[23]

Plotland is an excellent habitat and a fascinating monument of social history. It preserves fragments of old grassland with rare plants, and also hedges from the previous, sometimes Roman or Iron Age, field system. Two Country Parks, in Langdon Hills and Rochford, have been made out of plotland.[24]

Wood-pasture

Wood-pasture is the combination of trees and grazing animals. The shade of the trees is bad for the pasture; the livestock are liable to eat the regrowth of the trees after felling. Wood-pasture management therefore differs from that of woodland, and involves compromise between the two interests. Usually it includes going to the extra trouble of pollarding the trees — cutting them, not at ground level, but about ten feet above ground so that the animals cannot reach the young shoots. Pollards are of special significance because cutting prolongs their lives; like all ancient trees, they are important not only as historical evidence but for the special habitats for animals and plants which they provide.[25]

In Morant's time, wood-pastures of various kinds were widespread in Essex. Chapman and André map them scrupulously, using a different symbol from that for woodland. Epping Forest, for example, being a wood-pasture, is differentiated from the woods which abutted on it.

Wooded commons

The original wood-pastures were wooded commons, going back to Anglo-Saxon or prehistoric times.[26] Many were still being grazed by cattle and sheep in the eighteenth century, especially in the Danbury area.

23 O. Rackham, *Ancient Woodland of England: the woods of South-East Essex*, Rochford District Council, 1986, 26–34.

24 *Woodland walks in South-East Essex: Grove Woods*, Rochford District Council, 1987.

25 P. Harding and F. Rose, *Pasture-woodlands in Lowland Britain*, Institute of Terrestrial Ecology, Monks' Wood, 1986. O. Rackham, *The last Forest: the story of Hatfield Forest*, chapter 11.

26 O. Rackham, *The History of the Countryside*, Dent, London, 1986, chapter 6.

Figure 5. Little Easton Park as Hitler saw it on 10 May, 1940. The park, with celebrated ancient trees, was much as it had been in Morant's time; the airfield had not yet begun to destroy it. The wood to the south, which still survives, is about one-half of the medieval Dunmow High Wood. In the south of the picture is Stane Street, the Roman or Iron Age road, now the A120, with the Dunmow railway (now extinct) parallel to it. The photograph reveals some grubbing-out of hedges (very unusual for the time) around the road and railway. (There is some thin cloud in the northern part of the picture.)

Most wooded commons suffered the fate of heaths, being destroyed by Enclosure Act after Morant's time. A few survived but lost their trees. Curtis-Mill Green, Navestock, still has oaks, but they are a plantation, not the original ones. The best survivor is Gernon Bushes, continuous with (but not part of) Epping Forest; it now belongs to the Essex Wildlife Trust, which is experimenting with re-pollarding the ancient hornbeams.[27]

Parks

At about the time of the Norman Conquest, the wood-pasture scene was transformed by the addition of deer to the other wood-pasture animals. Sometimes this was done on private land by the making of parks. A park, in its original sense, is a piece of land on which the owner keeps deer, confined by a special deer-proof fence (the *pale*). Unknown to Morant, Essex had what may have been the prototype of all English parks: Ongar Great Park, mentioned in a will of 1045. This park was presumably for the native red deer. About 1100 the fallow deer, a more suitable animal, was introduced probably from Sicily. Parks were multiplied to reach a total of about 160 in Essex, including the royal parks of Havering, Rayleigh, Writtle and Hatfield Broad-oak.[28]

Medieval parks functioned mainly as deer-farms; few of them were long-lived. By Morant's time, most of them had long been given up; the survivors included Writtle Park. Henry VIII set a new fashion of emparking in which hunting, or the supply of deer for hunting in other parks, was the main objective. Although Henry's own parks of Nazeing Wood and in Epping Forest did not long outlive him, the fashion was copied in the landscape parks attached to great houses. Several of this Tudor generation of parks survived into the eighteenth century: for example New Hall, Markshall and Little Easton.

In Morant's time the fashion of emparking was again revived. Picturesque landscape, which had been a factor in the creation of most Tudor and some medieval parks, now became the dominant

---

27 N. Coombs, 'Notes on re-pollarding hornbeam at Gernon Bushes Nature Reserve', *Pollard and Veteran Tree Management*, ed. H. J. Read, Corporation of London, 1991, 49.

28 O. Rackham, *Ancient Woodland of England: the woods of South-East Essex*, 191–92, 198. O. Rackham, *The last Forest: the story of Hatfield Forest*, Dent, London, 1989, 80–81. O. Rackham, *Ancient Woodland of England: the woods of South-East Essex*, Rochford District Council, 1986, 18–20.

motive.[29] A few of the bigger Essex parks were by known designers. At Audley End, the park by Lancelot 'Capability' Brown preserved little if anything of the previous park of Walden Abbey. This was unusual: most park designers were well aware of the virtues of ancient trees and earthworks, and carefully preserved such relics of the previous landscape. These were not necessarily descended from a medieval park: at Thorndon, for example, the park still preserves the pollards from a wood-pasture common.

Time has not dealt well with Essex parks. Chapman and André's map shows about sixty-five parks, of which twenty-seven appear to be still extant. However, a park has always been a precarious enterprise, and this is perhaps the normal survival rate over two centuries. However, the mere continuation of a park does not mean that its features have survived. Landscape parks in Essex are a nineteenth as well as an eighteenth century fashion. The full story has yet to be told, but the Victorians certainly made many new parks: Warley Place had, in its day, one of the most celebrated gardens in England. They also Victorianised existing ones. Combined with the twentieth century fashion for 'improving' (destroying and re-seeding) old grassland, this has the effect that in Audley End park, for example, there is not much now to be seen even of the eighteenth century.

There were three major disasters in the mid-twentieth century. Ongar Great Park, probably the first park in all England, of which much had survived despite centuries of disuse, was unknowingly grubbed out in the agricultural boom of the 1950s. Little Easton Park (Figure 5) was made an airfield in World War Two, and what remained was grubbed out later. Markshall Park, probably Tudor, with its wonderful oaks cherished by generations of the Honywood family, survived the war only to be destroyed to no purpose afterwards, despite having been bequeathed to the nation for preservation by its late owner.

There are, nevertheless, still a few ancient parks in Essex, where one can see something of the trees and herbage, and the remains of yet earlier landscapes, that Morant could have seen. These include South Weald and Thorndon Parks, with their fine pollard oaks and hornbeams; and the park of New Barrington Hall in Hatfield Broad-oak, with its immense pollards round the boundary that are probably inherited from Hatfield Priory.

29 O. Rackham, *Trees and Woodland in the British Landscape*, 2nd ed., Dent, London, 1990, chapter 8.

Forests

A Forest was a tract of land on which the king, or some other great magnate, had the right to keep deer. It differed from a park in that there was no pale, and the deer (usually fallow) stayed from force of habit. Forests were not, as commonly misstated, 'reserved to the king for hunting'. The king's deer were added to the other land-uses and did not replace them. Most Forests were also commons, on which commoners had rights of pasturage and sometimes woodcutting. Forests might or might not be wooded, although all those remaining in eighteenth century Essex were.

The heyday of Forests was long before Morant's time. There had been five in Essex, or six if one counts Wintry, north of Epping, as a separate Forest. Colchester Forest had been frittered away into private hands in the sixteenth century, but Waltham or Epping, Hainault, Hatfield and Writtle Forests still existed in the eighteenth century largely unchanged since the thirteenth. (The belief that Forests were once much larger is a myth: scholars have mistaken the area within the jurisdiction of the Forest courts for the actual area of the Forests themselves.)[30]

Not only the physical fabric but the ancient institutions still lingered about some of them. In Epping Forest the Crown still kept deer on other people's land, and drew a little revenue from persons fined for breaches of Forest Law. Had Morant visited Hatfield Forest, he would have met Daniel Gilbey, the Forester, dressed in Lincoln green, riding to four large hounds. In both the common rights (pasturage and woodcutting in Epping, pasturage only in Hatfield) were fully, some said excessively, exercised. Epping Forest, although still a long ride outside London, had, as Sir William Addison has shown, acquired a richness of literary and historical associations which made it the most famous Forest in England.[31]

Essex had examples of the two kinds of wooded Forest management. Epping and Hainault were non-compartmented Forests. Areas of trees were intermingled with *plains* — grassland and heath — but not demarcated from them. The trees were exposed to browsing animals all the time, and in consequence

30 O. Rackham, *Trees and Woodland in the British Landscape*, 2nd ed., Dent, London, 1990, chapter 9. O. Rackham, 'Archaeology and land-use history', *Epping Forest — The Natural Aspect?*, ed. D. Corke, *Essex Naturalist*, NS 2, 1978, 16–75.

31 W. Addison, *Epping Forest: its Literary and Historical Associations*, Dent, London, 1945.

were pollarded by the commoners and landowners. Hatfield and Writtle were compartmented Forests. Here the tree'd areas were definite coppice-woods (seventeen at Hatfield, eight at Writtle) with woodbanks separating them from the plains and from each other. They were felled by the wood-owners and then fenced for nine years to keep deer and livestock away from the regrowth. The plains, accessible to livestock at all times, also had trees, which were pollards.

The Age of Reason did not understand Forests. They were represented as the 'nest and conservatory of sloth, idleness and misery'.[32] They were supposed to keep the hangman busy: the Black Act of 1723, directed at Forest criminals, had created fifty new capital offences. To get rid of Forests was one of the chief aims of the enclosers; but those in Essex survived late. Hainault Forest was enclosed by Act in 1851, and most of it promptly destroyed by special machinery. The modern conservation movement began with public concern to avert a like fate from Epping Forest. Hatfield Forest had its Enclosure Act in 1857, but, exceptionally, passed into the hands of the Houblon family, who loved and maintained it as a kind of super-park. Writtle Forest had been taken over in one piece by the Petre family, its landowners.

Although, uniquely, three of Morant's Forests and a fragment of the fourth have come down to our time, their complex cultural and ecological fabrics have not escaped the upheavals. Epping Forest was saved by the Epping Forest Act of 1878, but its subsequent history is a story of lost opportunity. The early Epping Forest Conservators inherited a unique and stable cultural landscape of pollard trees, heaths, bogs and plains; this they abandoned and tried to turn the Forest into an ordinary beechwood. Pollarding was suppressed, grazing allowed to decline, and the open spaces to become overgrown. The consequences are still working themselves out in excessive shade, loss of heather, loss of rarer plants, dying trees, and too much compaction from visitors' feet and horses' hooves on the bare ground. Hatfield Forest was given by Edward North Buxton and his family to the National Trust in 1924. Its story is happier. The Trust, although it did not until very recently fully understand or appreciate the Forest, did at least try to keep up most of the land-uses as in the Houblons' time; with the result that Hatfield is now the best preserved of all the wooded royal Forests of England.

A change which would greatly surprise Morant is the huge

32 C. Vancouver, *General View of the Agriculture of Hampshire*, 1794, 496.

increase of deer. There are now more deer in Essex than there have been for a thousand years. Their depredations have grown to become a constraint on the management of woodland, not only in the Forests (which by definition have had to live with deer) but in the countryside at large.

Conservation and the Future

It is no accident that the Essex landscape has come relatively well through the upheavals of the twentieth century. 'Improvers' do not know when to stop, but they can be told. Halfway back to Morant's time, the Commons, Footpaths, and Open Spaces Preservation Society began the modern conservation movement by frustrating the destruction of Epping Forest.

In the 1930s, Southend Town Council were pioneers in another direction, purchasing Hadleigh Great Wood, which is now England's longest-running coppice-wood nature reserve (Figure 1). They were reluctant pioneers, persuaded to that decision by pressure of public opinion, including (it was said) methods unusual in a democracy.[33] Most of the other South East Essex woods are now public open spaces, and Rochford District Council has recently set the highest standards in the conservation and management of ancient woodland.

For sixty years, Essex County Council has been active in the conservation and understanding of the landscape. It pioneered the system of Tree Preservation Orders. It has been very active in archaeology and the conservation of ancient buildings, especially the great barns. It acquired and maintained Garnett's Wood and one-third of Chalkney Wood as a public open space. It has produced excellent publications on the landscape and its meaning. The most recent initiative is the scheduling of Historic Landscapes for special protection, the first being Writtle Forest.

Among other conservation bodies, the Essex Wildlife Trust has numerous nature reserves in woodland, saltmarsh and other places. Almost all of them perpetuate fragments of the eighteenth century countryside.

If the immediate prospects seem bright, this is in large part the work of Colin Ranson, who for many represented the Nature Conservancy Council here. Few have loved and understood Essex as he did. The days that he spent in marshes and plotland, in

33   O. Rackham, *Ancient Woodland of England: the woods of South-East Essex*, Rochford District Council, 1986, 34–35.

woods and searching for fragments of heath, in lecture-hall and farmhouse kitchen — and in committee-room and public inquiry and in the inevitable pushing of paper — all this brought to public attention things that would otherwise have been swept away unthinkingly. He particularly favoured conservation schemes in farmland and the re-coppicing of ancient woods, both of which now prosper. He died in 1989 leaving his work unfinished, but at a point from which others could carry it on. *Si monumentum requiris, circumspice.*

Since his death, there have been four notable initiatives on sites that Colin loved and regretted. The Forestry Commission has begun the task of rehabilitating as an ancient wood its part of Chalkney Wood, perhaps the most notable of the Essex limewoods, once thought lost to coniferisation. Lawrence Sisitka, with the help of his specialist colleagues in the National Trust, has drawn up a management plan for Hatfield Forest, recognising for the first time all the details which make the Forest one of the most important of the Trust's historic properties. The City of London Corporation has resumed experimental re-pollarding in Epping Forest. Finally, to mention what to Colin was an utterly lost cause, the Thomas Phillips Price Trust, with the collaboration of Simon Leatherdale of the Forestry Commission, are making strenuous efforts to rehabilitate Markshall.[34]

The conservation of Essex will need all the help that it can get. Pressures increase for development connected with Stansted Airport, especially on the historic landscape around Hatfield Forest. Proposals for golf-courses proliferate — hardly destructive in themselves, but they include buildings and roads which are unlikely to be demolished when the fashion for golf wanes. Deer continue to multiply. How much longer will Foulness Island be protected by its military status? Hard-headed politicians talk again about the 'Thames corridor' as a place for further development of London: with reasonable luck, the geographical hazards of the area will not strike until they are out of office.

---

34 L. Sisitka, 'Pollarding experiences in Hatfield Forest, Essex', *Pollard and Veteran Tree Management*, ed. H. J. Read, Corporation of London, 1991, 19–21. P. Burman, 'Pollarding at Epping Forest', *ibid*, 42–43. J. White, 'Suggestions for re-pollarding oaks at Markshall, Essex', *ibid*, 46–47.

Mythmakers of the Landscape of Essex

BILL and SUE LIDDELL

*'No city or landscape is truly rich unless it
has been given the quality of myth by writer,
painter or association with great events.'*
                                        V. S. Naipaul

ESSEX IS A region which stimulated Sir William Addison, a
Northerner and proud of it, to become one of its most inspired
mythmakers. The county's distinction was noted by H. G.
Wells:

> 'there is a gap in the suburbs of London . . . Instead there
> is Essex. Essex is not a suburban county; it is a charac-
> teristic and individualised county which wins the
> heart.'
>   *(Mr. Britling Sees It Through)*

It certainly won Sir William. Yet he used his fine essayist's
pen to approach this land through description of its people, its
heroes, its literary connections; even where he most closely
approached the landscape, in *Essex Heyday* and *Epping Forest*
he rarely described the land. The landscape of Essex is a
compound of small hills, woods, and trees edging fields worked on
and lived in by small communities, bordered by marshland
invisibly moving into a sea from which rises an overarching,
immense and varying sky holding all together — a kalaeidoscopic,
indefinable region, embodied in myth, with at its centre a hidden
and secretive quality, parts of which are known only to its
people.

So Addison is correct; for 'myth' is 'a purely fictitious
narrative usually involving supernatural persons, actions or
events, and embodying some popular idea concerning natural or
historical phenomena' (O.E.D.), such as invasion and defence,
central to the Essex experience, that most Saxon and most
Norman of all English counties.

(Essex Record Office)

Figure 1. A winding lane near Halstead.

This understanding of the quality that is Essex has at least a thousand year history for the Battle of Maldon mythopoet used the genre to celebrate the popular historical idea of courage and bravery in defence of land and people:

> 'Pirates' messenger, deliver and say to your people the more hateful tale that here stands a famous earl with his forces, who will defend this land, the country of Ethelred, the people and the ground . . .'

> (Own translation)

And the land thus defended was part of the Essex 'landscape' — a word connected with pastoral, lyric, bucolic, idyllic genres of writing and with rustic, rural, agricultural, country ways of life carried on by the people of Essex who live and have lived here, like the people in the forest described by Edward Thomas:

> 'The green roads that end in the forest
>   Are strewn with white goose feathers this June,
>
> Like marks left behind by some one gone to the forest
>   To show his track.'

> (*The Green Roads*)

and those braving the bracing east winds of Long Crendon described by Norman Lewis:

> '. . . this part of Essex reminded me of the southern tip of South America, where the trees are deformed, a cold wind combs the grass and glum Indians, reserved and off-hand like the country people of Essex, are muffled in their clothes against the grey weather.'

> ('Essex' *Granta*, volume 23)

This collaborative relationship between man and landscape has been an abiding characteristic, and has coloured the choice and development of those events which define so much of Essex. Norman Lewis' first impression of Essex people was of a reserved and offhand race, but he came to be aware of their receptivity and adaptability to their most recent invader:

> 'Even in the recent past they had lived their private, separate lives behind tightly drawn curtains. Now they organised get-togethers in the American fashion.'

> (*Ibid*)

Figure 2.   Summer landscape near Langley, at Essex's highest point.

(Essex Record Office)

Fostered by this adaptable reserve is a spirit of personal initiative, enterprise and radicalism which still colours the events that control our understanding of the county's separateness (which other county has had so many rotten jokes told about its people!). Even before the Battle of Maldon, Essex tries to lay claim to the final battle of Boudicca against the Romans; the treachery and acquisitiveness of Odo, Bishop of Bayeux, as well as the duplicity of Richard II in visiting his uncle, the Duke of Gloucester at Pleshey, are seen as counterpoints to the honest individualism of the Essex peasant, echoed in Gloucester's account of his end:

> 'For lying at Pleshey my selfe to repose
> By reason of sickness which helde me full sore,
> The King espying mee apart from those
> With whom I confedered in hand before,
> Thought it not meete to tract the time more,
> But glad to take me at such a vauntage
> Came to salute mee with a friendly visage . . .
>
> Tooke time to accompliche his cruell intent;
> And in a small vessel downe by the streame
> Conveyed mee to alais, out of the realme,
> Where . . .
> Not nature, but murder, abridged my yeeres.'

(The Mirror of Magistrates, *1559*)

The Essex resistance to central authority and 'the establishment' is typified by the county's leadership in the Peasants' Revolt of 1381, and in John Ball's arguments for the freedom and equality of the natural, common man:

> 'What have we deserved or why should we be kept thus in servage? We be all come from one father and one mother, Adam and Eve: whereby can they say or shew that they be greater lords than we be, saving by that they cause us to win and labour for that they dispend? They are clothed in velvet and camlet furred with grise, and we be vestured with poor cloth; they have their wines, spices and good bread, and we have the drawing out of the chaff and drink water . . .'

But in the time of invasion by foreigners with the Spanish Armada, the Essex people were in a mood to support the monarch in her defiance of invasion and are pleased to be known as having the site from which Elizabeth spoke — in language similar to that

Figure 3. The Essex Marshes: Mystery of past and present.

(Essex Record Office)

of Byrthnoth at the Battle of Maldon and with bravery like
that of Boudicca:

> 'And therefore I am come amongst you at this time, not
> as for my recreation or sport, but being resolved in the
> midst and heat of the battle to live or die amongst you
> all; to lay down, for my God, and for my kingdom, and for
> my people, my honour and my blood, even in the dust. I
> know I have but the body of a weak and feeble woman,
> but I have the heart of a king, and of a king of
> England too.'

During the Civil War, the mood was variable, with the mythic
balance on the Parliamentarian, anti-Royalist and anti-clerical
side — thus beautiful Marabella, loyal Cavalier Simon Freeman
and saintly priest Jordan Ghyll, all are doomed to death and
failure in their attempts to save Lucas and Lisle at Colchester, as
told by Jesse Berridge in his novel, *The Stronghold*, written
between the two World Wars, in another period of uneasy
peace.

So these two strands in the myths built round the great
events of Essex history — the bravery and resilience in coping
with invasion and the fight for individual freedoms — continued to
be echoed and reinforced by more modern accounts. The King's
Head at Chigwell, described by Dickens as the Maypole in
Barnaby Rudge, has Royalist tendencies — with reservations:

> 'there was a legend, not only that Queen Elizabeth had
> slept there one night . . . but that next morning, while
> standing on a mounting block before the door, with one
> foot in the stirrup, the virgin monarch had then and
> there boxed and cuffed an unlucky page for some
> neglect of duty.'

while that independent spirit of energy and initiative is depicted
vividly in S. L. Bensusan's short story *Town v. Country*, when
Gammer Beagle and her grand-daughter turn the tables on the
hard-faced Mrs. Stride:

> ' "You thought Granny was a simpleton", interposed her
> grand-daughter. "We worked quite hard for you and you
> made over four pounds profit in some weeks. I didn't
> mind because I wanted to see how these things are done.
> You're not out of pocket, even allowing for the boards
> and the shed. Now Gran and I are going to see what we
> can do." '

Yet in an earlier strand of Essex mythmaking, Mrs. Stride would have been a wicked witch. In Essex, the central county of witchcraft, the supernatural is profound and widespread — we need only to think of the witches of Canewdon and the ghosts of Borley Rectory. Donald Maxwell's *Unknown Essex* makes much of

> 'Matthew Hopkins, the notorious seventeenth century 'witch-finder' (who) began his nefarious career by the discovery of "seven humble witches at Manningtree"... and was actually commissioned by Parliament in 1644 to seek out witches, and was paid a guinea for everyone he discovered . . . eventually (he) was burned alive, a fate which he thoroughly deserved!'

Such is legend, for Hopkins died in his bed, but the supernatural demands retribution. Even the mythic hero ('the first Essex man?') Dick Turpin, had to be hanged.

The whereabouts of the Essex Serpent, on the other hand, has remained mysterious. Sir William must have been delighted to find, as a true Northerner, that the Lambton Worm had crept down south to terrorise Henham-on-the-Mount, four miles from Saffron Walden:

> 'It was nine feet long and uncommonly strong,
> It had scales like a snake and teeth like a rake,
> And great rolling eyes very much wide awake
> It had wings like a bird, and the noise it would make
> Was enough to cause even the boldest to shake.'
>
>   (Charles E. Benham, *Essex Ballards*)

The eerie, frightening, supernatural and fantastic myths continued in such works of horrific genius as W. W. Jacobs' *The Monkey's Paw*, written, we think, whilst he lived in Essex, near the Forest, at Loughton.

These myths of the people and events of Essex are rooted in the greatest myth of all — that of Essex as an eternal green and pleasant land. Drayton in *Poly-Albion*, 1580:

> 'Essex is our dower, which greatly doth abound
> With every simple good that in the isle is found.'

and D. W. Coller in *The People's History of Essex*, 1861:

> 'It is, however, chiefly upon its Agriculture that the importance and reputation of the county depend.'

both highlight the fertile, rural myth of Essex with its picturesque unspoilt quality; ignoring bread riots, rural deprivation and continued social unrest. This quality is linked to art and nostalgia:

> ' "soft" pastoral (which) is a romance, a dream of celebration, carnival, song and love' which must be balanced with 'The other kind of pastoral (which) admits that rural life is "hard"; it is a realist narrative of labour and endurance.'
>
> (Hermione Lee, *Willa Cather: A Life Saved Up*)

Essex is fortunate in that those who have commented on its landscape have rather combined these two aspects in each single narrative, except for the poets who have illustrated the soft and nostalgic.

Isaac Mead in *The Life Story of an Essex Lad* provides details of farming methods, hard, tough and protracted:

> 'I was doing root-ditching, that is digging a trench two feet deep along the side of a field, cutting all roots from the hedges or trees that were robbing the soil, emptying ditches and taking off banks, and then digging clay out of the ditch to make a new bank. Then to lay a fence along the top of it . . .'

but cannot resist the picture of the warm, friendly, co-operative spirit:

> 'It used to be a pretty sight to see 8, 10, 14 or 16 men in different fields all whistling and merrily swinging their scythes, cutting the grain in beautiful swathes, right across a 20-acre field. No grumbling or grousing, but as happy as the day was long.'

David Smith in *No Rain in Those Clouds* seems more concerned with the practicalities of domestic life — and provisions:

> 'At the bottom of the passage a door on the right led down some steep stone steps to the cellar. It was always beautifully cool and kept the beer and butter in wonderful condition. In my grandfather's time there were two casks that held eight hogsheads and two casks that held five.'

Figure 4. The Forest near High Beach.

(Essex Record Office)

and the contribution women had to make to the family finances:

> 'Pea-picking was one thing the women looked forward
> to. It meant a bit of a change and some company for a
> few days, and, more important, it meant a bit of extra
> money; enough to pay for the children's boots for the
> winter, and perhaps a bit besides.'

Spike Mays in *Reuben's Corner* pinpoints the differences between the 'soft' and the 'hard':

> 'During the open season when the gentlemen came to
> shoot game there would be the greatest walk — or so it
> was regarded — because old and young of both sexes
> would turn out in droves to beat game to the guns . . .
> This was regarded as pleasant walking, though tiring,
> because it was communal . . . But many more miles a day
> would be covered in sullen dreary solitude; in the daily
> grind of following the plough, harrow, shim and roll . . .
> Evidence of these walks was to be found in the gaits of
> the older men. Their legs were often distorted, their
> perambulations extraordinary . . . from great distances
> one could identify the walkers, by the sound of their feet
> on the hard highway.'

To the poet, however, the landscape was art — an art of mixed woodland, hills and fields. Edward Thomas and John Clare represent the poet resident in Essex responding to the rural Paradise as escape.

> 'If I should ever by chance grow rich
> I'll buy Codham, Cockridden, and Childerditch,
> Roses, Pyrgo, and Lapwater,
> And let them all to my elder daughter.
> The rent I shall ask of her will be only
> Each year's first violets, white and lonely,
> The first primroses and orchises —
> She must find them before I do, that is.
> But if she finds a blossom on furze
> Without rent they shall all for ever be hers,
> Codham, Cockridden, and Childerditch,
> Roses, Pyrgo, and Lapwater —
> I shall give them all to my elder daughter.'
>
> (Edward Thomas)

'The brakes, like young stag's horns, come up in
Spring,
And hide the rabbit holes and fox's den;
They crowd about the forest everywhere;
The ling and holly-bush, and woods of beach,
With room enough to walk and search for flowers;
Then look away and see the Kentish heights.
Nature is lofty in her better mood,
She leaves the world and greatness all behind;
Thus London, like a shrub among the hills,
Lies hid and lower than the bushes here.
I could not bear to see the tearing plough
Root up and steal the Forest from the poor,
But leave to Freedom all she loves, untamed,
The Forest walk enjoyed and loved by all!'

(John Clare)

The novelist and descriptive writer on the other hand,
emphasises the uncomfortable, menacing, unhealthy world,
usually set in marsh and by the sea. Dickens in *Great Expectations*, and *Bleak House*, for example, shows a world where the
weird and uncanny haunt the mist:

'Fog everywhere. Fog up the river, where it flows among
green aits and meadows; fog down the river, where it
rolls defiled among the tiers of shipping, and the water-
side pollutions of a great (and dirty) city. Fog on the
Essex marshes . . .'

(*Bleak House*)

'. . . and slimy stakes stuck out of the mud, and slimy
stones stuck out of the mud, and red landmarks and
tidemarks stuck out of the mud, and an old landing
stage and an old roofless building slipped into the mud,
all about us was stagnation and mud.'

(*Great Expectations*)

while Defoe points out the transitoriness of life for the
newcomer:

'I have one remark more, before I leave this damp part
of the world, and which I cannot omit on the womens
account; namely, that I took notice of a strange decay of
the sex here; insomuch, that all along this county it was
very frequent to meet with men that had had from five
or six, to fourteen to fifteen wives . . . That when they

took the young lasses out of the wholesome and fresh
air, they were healthy, fresh and clear, and well; but
when they came out of their native air into the marshes
among the fogs and damps there they presently chang'd
their complexion, got an ague or two, and seldom held it
above half a year, or a year at most.'

(Tour of England and Wales)

Essex has no large towns — even Southend cannot be said to
be big in the northern industrial sense; everywhere seems to be
Georgian rather than Victorian in scale, apart from what Dickens
called 'London over the border'. This world is still invested with
myth and nostalgia — still a world which hides its secrets, yet
allows them to be glimpsed in fleeting moments as the light and
shade play upon one's imagination:

A Map of the Western Part of the County of Essex in England

Something forgotten twenty years: though my fathers
and mothers came from Cordova and Vitepsk and
    Caernarvon,
and though I am a citizen of the United States and
    less a
stranger here than anywhere else, perhaps,
I am Essex-born:
Cranbrook Wash called me into its dark tunnel,
the little streams of Valentines heard my resolves,
Roding held my head above water when I thought
    it was
drowning me; in Hainault only a haze of thin trees
stood between the red doubledecker buses and the
    boar-hunt,
the spirit of merciful *Phillippa* glimmered there.
Pergo Park knew me, and Clavering, and Havering-
    atte-Bower,
Stanford Rivers lost me in osier-beds, Stapleford
    Abbots
sent me safe home on the dark road after Simeon-
    quiet evensong,
Wanstead drew me over and over into its basic
    poetry,
in its serpentine lake I saw bass-viols among the
    golden dead leaves,

through its trees the ghost of a great house. In
Ilford High Road I saw the multitudes passing pale
    under the
light of flaring sundown, seven kings
in sombre starry robes gathered at Seven Kings
the place of law
where my birth and marriage are recorded
and the death of my father. Woodford Wells
where an old house was named The Naked Beauty
    (a white
statue forlorn in its garden)
saw the meeting and parting of two sisters
(forgotten? and further away
the hill before Thaxted? where peace befell us? not
    once
but many times?)
All the Ivans dreaming of their villages
all the Marias dreaming of their walled cities,
picking up fragments of New World slowly
not knowing how to put them together nor how to
    join
image with image, now I know how it was with you,
    an old map
made long before I was born shows ancient
rights of way where I walked when I was ten burning
    with desire
for the world's great splendours, a child who traced
    voyages
indelibly all over the atlas, who now in a far country
remembers the first river, the first
field, bricks, and lumber dumped in it ready for
    building,
that new smell, and remembers
the walls of the garden, the first light.

                         (Denise Levertov)

(With acknowledgements to Denise Levertov, Selected Poems, Bloodaxe Books Ltd.)

Despite the developers and the planners, the secret of Essex is still safely hidden with the mythmakers.

The Dunmow Progressives

An Edwardian vignette

VICTOR GRAY

'We shall be a little group of the Salt of the Earth in the Dunmow District soon!'
Frances Evelyn, Countess of Warwick[1]

THE LONG, HOT summer of 1914 has burned its way into the imagination of every following generation, a season heavy with irony, a sepia snapshot of trim lawns where white-dressed ladies refuse to hear our cries of 'Look behind you!'.

On 4 August, Bank Holiday Monday, the Countess of Warwick walked out onto the lawns of Easton Lodge to preside, as she did every year, at the Annual Flower Show. The sun shone, there were record entries for flowers and vegetables and the gardens were crowded. There were sports, a balloon race and a tennis tournament. The Essex Yeomanry Band played. In the evening there were fireworks.

At 11 p.m., with the memory of the last firework barely fading, Britain declared war on Germany.

Two years later, H. G. Wells breathed life into the memory of that day under the wafer-thin disguise of the Matching Easy Flower Show at Lady Homartyn's Clavering Park described in fond detail in his novel, *Mr. Britling sees it through*. 'The day was to live in Mr. Britling's memory with a harsh brightness like the brightness of that sunshine one sees at times at the edge of a thunderstorm.' A penumbra had been formed.

The words and images of *Mr. Britling sees it through* served, perhaps more than any other of the time, to provide the iconography of the days leading up to the War and of the changing mood of a people at war. Published in 1916, it had already, by the end of that year, run to thirteen editions. The Little Easton Flower Show had been transmuted into a national archetype — the last

1 Letter to R. D. Blumenfeld, 9 September, 1911. House of Lords Record Office, Beaverbrook Papers, Blumenfeld MSS, Warw. 16.

hot, lazy day of an era which, when Peace returned, had been changed beyond repair.

If the Matching Easy Flower Show is a convenient image for us of Edwardian langour, we might, with a little more persistence, unearth in this same area of west Essex, events and activities in that last pre-War summer which, though never caught so blindingly in the headlights of history, were in many ways more accurate reflections of the timbre and aspirations of an age which stopped, like a clock, at 11 p.m. on 4 August.

On a Wednesday afternoon in June of that year, for example, a large audience crowded into a barn in Little Easton to see the first performance of a new play by a local playwright. By the time the play — *The Furriner* by S. L. Bensusan — had finished its run of four performances, it had been reviewed in a clutch of national newspapers and had been described by the *Daily Express* as 'a new triumph for the newest movement in drama, the Essex school of folk-plays'.[2]

In itself the play was a slight enough piece, but in its theme and style and above all in the course of events which led to its production, we may see, faintly registered still, the imprint of ambitions which were characteristic of a generation whose social thinking and reforming enthusiasm have been largely overshadowed by the image of Matching Easy.

Prime mover behind the production was a journalist who had forsaken Fleet Street for west Essex a dozen years before. When John William Robertson Scott settled on Great Canfield as a rural retreat at the turn of the century, he fashioned a home for what was to become one of the best known *noms de plume* in Edwardian magazine journalism, 'Home Counties'. Under this name, he poured forth a constant stream of articles interpreting for townsmen the well-springs and economics of contemporary rural life. Much of his inspiration was to come from the fields and villages around him and, with the eye of a practised journalist, he made himself familiar with the local scene and local characters.[3]

In 1909, in what he described as a 'minor act of local patriotism' Robertson Scott had written and published locally a small

2 *Daily Express*, 18 June, 1914.

3 For Robertson Scott see John Cripps, 'J. W. Robertson Scott, C.H.', *The Countryman*, vol. 60, no. 1, Spring 1963. Robertson Scott's own reminiscences are widely scattered in his own works. His Great Canfield years are recalled in 'My wife and "The Countryman" ', *The Countryman*, vol. 53, no. 4, Winter 1956; *We and me: memories of four editors and of my own*

book on *The Strange Story of the Dunmow Flitch*. Three years later, in February 1912, with the support of the Dunmow Flitch Bacon Company, which had established itself as a co-operative in the town in 1909 and recognised, no doubt, what would today be described as 'a good sponsorship opportunity', a public meeting was held at which a motion was proposed for the revival of the Flitch ceremony which had last been performed in 1906.

Robertson Scott, in seconding the motion, went further and called for a 'pageant, procession, tableaux or old time sports' to enhance the occasion. His role in the proceedings, which took place on August Bank Holiday, was far from limited to playing the part of the Last Prior of Little Dunmow who, in the 200-strong pageant procession, moved through the streets of Dunmow, eyes no doubt lifted heavenward, preceded incongruously by a troupe of sixteen English maidens and the Revd. Conrad Noel leading his band of Morris dancers. He and his wife had, from the beginning, been members of the organising Committee and he had served on what must have been one of the most prestigious P.R. teams ever assembled to support a local event, a 'Press Committee' comprising alongside Robertson Scott; H. A. Gwynne, editor of the *Morning Post*; R. D. Blumenfeld, editor of the *Daily Express*; S. L. Bensusan, then making his name as a dialect writer; A. J. Dawson, editor of *The Standard of Empire*; and H. G. Wells. The direction of the pageant had been placed in the hands of Hugh Cranmer-Byng who was becoming known locally as a writer of pageants. His Saffron Walden pageant, with lyrics by his brother, Lancelot, had been a popular triumph in May 1910. His Flitch Pageant was no less successful. The *Essex Weekly News* reported a crowd of thousands, many of them from London and beyond.[4]

But important as the public reaction to the 1909 pageant had been, its influence was to reach further. It had given a local reality to ideas which had been forming in Robertson Scott's mind during his years as 'Home Counties'. His decision in 1899 to remove himself from London journalism and to steep himself in the life of the country — not an idealised, romantic country, but a countryside still blighted by agricultural depression — set him on a road which

editorships, 1956, and the Prologue to his *The story of the Women's Institute Movement*, 1925. His writings of this time are to be found in many journals, notably *The World's Work*, *The Country Gentleman* and *The Quarterly Review*.

4 *Essex Weekly News*, 9 August, 1912.

Figure 1. Launcelot Cranmer-Byng,
as drawn for Essex Leaders, Social and Political, 1906.

(Essex Record Office)

was to lead him ultimately, in 1927, to found *The Countryman*, a journal which he edited for twenty-five years. His years in Great Canfield were fired with a desire to bring to the problems of the English rural scene the campaigning vigour and the belief in Progress which he had learnt and practised in the 1880s as a journalist on W. T. Stead's *Pall Mall Gazette*.[5] The Flitch Pageant had shown him how the creative and organisational skills of the educated outsider could be used to galvanise a local community into action. The impetus must not be lost.

The result, which took shape in his mind as the Dunmow and District Progressive Club, was announced in November, less than three months after the Pageant. The heart of the Club and that which was to set it apart from the common run of village clubs and societies were in its objects. Improvement and progress were its goals; 'intelligent recreation and education in citizenship' were the banner under which it was to march; 'non-party' and 'non-denomination' were its watchwords. 'Things would surely be better in many country places if people, while holding fast to their political and denominational associations, realised that there is a wide field for non-party and non-denominational work, and that a better understanding would be brought about by all sorts and conditions of people rubbing shoulders and exchanging ideas with one another', wrote Robertson Scott in an article at the time. 'The Club is run by a large committee on which Church and Chapel people, Liberals, Conservatives and Socialists, Roman Catholics, Jews and Theosophists are represented.'[6]

The experience of producing the Pageant and the connections he had forged in his years at Great Canfield were now brought to bear to assemble a formidable supporting cast in the venture. The Earl of Warwick as Lord Lieutenant and leading local landowner could not be bettered as President though one suspects that, the rigours of precedence having been satified, it was the Vice-Presidency of Lady Warwick which was more vital to Robertson Scott. If he did not share her Socialist politics (he was a Liberal) they at least had in common a social idealism which must have infused the Robertson Scotts' visits to Easton Lodge which had begun soon after the couple's arrival in the area. Lady Warwick was to be the figure-head for the Club, almost its personification in the wild contradictions which sent her off to

5 For Robertson Scott's *Pall Mall* years see his *We and me*, 1956, and *The story of the Pall Mall Gazette*, 1950.

6 'A rural experiment', *Essex Review*, vol. 22, 1913, 137.

address Socialist meetings in the East End in chauffeur-driven elegance. She was ready to lend time, enthusiasm, backing and local weight to the Club.[7]

But it was to the talents of the area which Robertson Scott turned for its life-blood. By November 1912 the local press (no doubt encouraged by him) had begun to speak of a 'literary colony around Dunmow'. Scott himself had brought in as tenant, in an adjoining cottage, Harold Monro who, in the very same month as the Progressive Club was born, had parted company with the Poetry Society as editor of *The Poetry Review* and would, within four months have opened the influential Poetry Bookshop in London and founded the progressive flagship journal of the younger Georgian poets *Poetry and Drama.*[8]

Samuel ('Ben') Bensusan, another enthusiastic recruit, had moved in 1908 to Brick House on Duton Hill in Great Easton.[9] A journalist and music critic, he had taken to an Essex retreat at Asheldham in 1897 and had begun to write countryside sketches in 1907. But it was, ironically, through another interest, in theosophy, that he came to west Essex, having, in 1904, met the orientalist Lancelot Cranmer-Byng, co-editor of the *Wisdom of the East* series and descendant of a celebrated Essex family. Through visits to Cranmer-Byng, who was then living at Horham Hall, Thaxted, Bensusan came to know and love the area. His move to Brick House was the spur for a new journalistic venture when, in 1908, he began a series for the *Standard* under the title *From a small-holding.* This brought him into association with the editor, H. A. 'Taffy' Gwynne, who was later himself to move to Little Easton, taking up residence in Mawbyns where, with a break in the post-War years, he remained till his death in 1950.

It was another Conservative newspaper editor, R. D. Blumenfeld (known universally as 'R.D.B.'), who, in 1909, gave Bensusan his next chance with the *Nature Notes* column in the *Daily Express.* Blumenfeld had shot with both 'Lancie' and Bensusan since at least 1906 and probably moved into Hill Farm,

7 For Lady Warwick, see principally Margaret Blunden, *The Countess of Warwick*, 1967.

8 For Monro, see Joy Grant, *Harold Monro and the Poetry Bookshop*, 1967.

9 Bensusan's diaries and his unpublished autobiography, *Myself when young* are housed in the Albert Sloman Library, University of Essex. For a brief biography of Bensusan, see Laurence Peters, 'The skilful wordsmith', *Essex Countryside*, vol. 37, no. 387, March 1989. Mr. Peters is currently preparing a full biography.

Great Easton, at about the same time.[10] Given his strongly Conservative views — he was the founder of the Anti-Socialist League — it is astonishing that Blumenfeld's acquaintance with Lady Warwick blossomed as it did in the following years, but those who came into contact with each of them bore witness to the charm and charisma which each displayed and which transcended party politics in a way Robertson Scott no doubt admired and from which he perhaps took encouragement, if not even inspiration.

To complete the political boxing-ring and to add the jewel to the crown of this 'literary colony', there came into the life of the area in 1912 the towering reputation of the most celebrated writer and thinker of the day, H. G. Wells. *The history of Mr. Polly* had been published in 1910 to, by now, routine popular acclaim and *The new Machiavelli* (1911) was creating controversy with its discussion of freer love. He had broken with The Fabian Society following his clash with Bernard Shaw and the Webbs in 1908 but was still ardently attached to Socialist ideals.[11] For 'R.D.B.' to have invited Wells for a weekend at Hill Farm in the company of 'Taffy' Gwynne who was by then editing that most steadfast organ of the Conservative Party, the Morning Post and William Ashley, a Conservative Whip and chairman of the Anti-Socialist Union was, at best whimsical and at worst akin to bull-baiting. That it led to Well's moving into the former rectory at Little Easton (re-christened by him Easton Glebe) and taking Gwynne as his nearest neighbour was an outcome no one could have predicted.[12]

The Eastons were thus set in 1912 to become the setting for a weekly assembly which in its range and interests was the equal of anything to be found outside London. From Monday to Friday, Little Easton, with its population of 274 in 1911, might be as set in its slow agricultural rhythm as any other English village. But with Friday the trains from Liverpool Street would bring to the little Easton Lodge Halt, built for the Maynard family's convenience, a

10 R. D. Blumenfeld's recollections are scattered throughout a number of volumes. Most relevant are *R.D.B.'s diary, 1887–1914*, 1930, and *All in a lifetime*, 1931. A series of letters from the Countess of Warwick to R.D.B. survive in the House of Lords Record Office as part of the Beaverbrook collection (ref. Beaverbrook Papers, Blumenfeld MSS, Warw. 1–25).

11 The canon of Wellsiana is too large to list in detail. Most recently, see W. J. Mackenzie, *The life of H. G. Wells*, 1987.

12 Accounts of the weekend visit to R.D.B. are to be found in Mackenzie, *op. cit.*, 273 and in R. D. Blumenfeld, *All in a lifetime*, 1931, 175 *et seq.*

mixture of writers and personalities with their wits sharpened for the Wells' celebrated weekend parties of lofty progressive talk and their teeth clenched for the regular Sunday afternoon hockey matches or the Schoolroom floor skirmishes with toy soldiers and cannon. Meanwhile, at Easton Lodge, Lord and Lady Warwick would be entertaining their heady mixture of guests from the worlds of Society and politics and at Hill Farm, R.D.B.'s Fleet Street friends might have gathered. There would be frequent traffic between them.

The chemistry was at times explosive, but never boring. By Robertson Scott's standards it was also remarkably Progressive. Its presence in the area may have been fortuitous but it was also extremely fortunate. Not to press it into the service of his ideals in the particular shape they were forming at that time would have been remiss.

The precedent of the Flitch Pageant 'Press Committee' had demonstrated the value of contracting national names to an essentially local venture. The Progressive Club needed and must have the support of these, the makers of progress. With a deft stride they were netted. Eligibility for the Club's Council was set by Robertson Scott as local residence combined with the authorship of a book. Bensusan, the Cranmer-Byng brothers, Blumenfeld, Gwynne, and Monro found themselves inescapably swept up in the net, along with Sir Walter Gilbey of Elsenham Hall, writer of a number of agricultural works and the Irish novelist Henry de Vere Stacpoole who lived nearby in Stebbing and who was at the time squarely in the public eye for his latest work, *The Street of the Flute Player*.[13] Others who might prove useful were swallowed into honorary membership: Sir J. M. Barrie, who waived his performance royalty of five guineas for *The Twelve Pound Look* played at Little Easton in 1912; George Bernard Shaw, who offered free performance of one of his plays; Cecil Sharp, who came to lecture; and Arnold Bennett, a frequent visitor to Easton Glebe.

A programme quickly emerged. In November, a hastily assembled evening of lightning sketches and music was held in the New Street Schoolroom in Dunmow, the highspot being a series of impersonations by Mrs. Robertson Scott, whose acting abilities were admired by all who saw her and who, less than a month later, was to appear in the male role of Thersites opposite Edith Evans'

13 De Vere Stacpoole is barely remembered now, though his *Blue Lagoon* enjoyed a lasting success as a book, a play and a film. See *D.N.B.*, 1951–60.

leading lady in William Poel's quirky but important production of *Troilus and Cressida* at the King's Hall, Covent Garden.[14] Even in these light pieces, the Club insisted on serious 'modern' themes. Women's suffrage and the 'Back to the Land' movement both appeared as motifs.

In the same month, a series of fortnightly talks for Club members began, Robertson Scott himself opening the programme with a discussion of the decay of rural industries and painting the prospect of a rescuscitation made possible by the use of machinery and enlightened by adequate sanitary by-laws to ensure good working conditions. Bensusan followed with an illustrated lecture on his travel experiences in North Africa (his book *Morocco* had been published in 1904).

Meanwhile the programme of public entertainments was developing. In January, the Barn at Little Easton was pressed into service for a performance by members of the English Folk Dance Society under the direction of Cecil Sharp himself, who had founded the Society just thirteen months before. Lady Warwick's vote of thanks summed up the spirit of the Progressive revival of interest in the traditions of the past. 'She had a vision that evening of a very different countryside from what we had now — a village with amusements native to the soil and full of joy instead of the reflections of the cinema and music hall that were now too common. She expected to see bands of merry dancers on the village greens and the people of Easton dancing to meet the people of Dunmow.'[15] This was indeed Rural Progress by Merrie England out of Sweetness and Light, with Socialism as Midwife. The picture is balanced by Conrad Noel's more jaundiced reflection on the occasion as related in his autobiography: 'I had told her that the dances were for peasants and other working people, and although the team contained wonderful performers ... [they] were certainly not of the soil, and unkind critics might have said it smacked of Bloomsbury'.[16]

But, tradition aside, the members of the Progressive Club were not to escape exposure to the best of modern thought and word. In February came Harold Monro from his new Poetry Bookshop, in the middle of proof-reading the first issue of his new

14 There are several testimonies to Mrs. Robertson Scott's (née Elspet Keith) dramatic talents. See J. W. Robertson Scott, 'My wife and "The Countryman" ', *The Countryman*, vol. 53, no. 4, Winter 1956.

15 *Essex Weekly News*, 17 January, 1913.

16 Sidney Dark, ed., *Conrad Noel: an autobiography*, 1945, 106.

vehicle for the poetic avant-garde, *Poetry and Drama*. His
reading at Dunmow of Masefield's *The Everlasting Mercy*, which
had won the Royal Society for Literature's 1912 award as 'the
greatest poetry of the year', was seen by him as the opening salvo
in a national campaign by the young circle of poets, of which he
was the centre, to encourage the public reading of poetry.[17] It was
met with 'applause of an exceptionally hearty kind'. There
followed, in March, readings from W. S. Gilbert and W. W.
Jacobs.

The best of modern plays were also brought to the area for
'the representation of the best drama' was clearly stated as one of
the Progressive Club's principal aims. In May, the Barn Theatre at
Little Easton had been the venue for a double production by the
Dunmow Players (who operated as a wing of the Club) of Synge's
The Tinker's Wedding and J. M. Barrie's *The Twelve Pound
Look* with interlude sketches of topical and local interest. It was an
adventurous programme. The Synge play had received its first
performance at His Majesty's Theatre in 1909, after the author's
death. Barrie's piece had had an unsuccessful season, as part of a
triple bill at the Duke of York's in 1910. But it appeared to go down
well. The *Essex Weekly News* hoped that, after this promising
opening, the club would 'continue its efforts to present drama of a
class which cannot ordinarily be seen out of London' and reported
that the village folk 'are said to be displaying a greater interest in
general subjects and cultivating tastes superior to those which
contented them not so very long ago'.[18]

By the end of 1913, the Council of the Club were able to point
to an impressive list of achievements. A club-room had been
secured in Dunmow for billiards and other games. A reading room
with lending library and newspapers had been added. A programme of national speakers had been provided, membership had
been steadily rising, gymnastics classes and ladies' evenings had
been introduced and larger premises at St. Mary's Room pressed
into service to accommodate the fortnightly meetings. A new local
theatre had been fitted out to allow modern drama of London
standards to be staged and leading dramatists had offered their
work for production.

It was in this mood that Sam Bensusan accepted the
challenge to write for the Club the Essex dialect drama which was

17 Monro's campaign for poetry-reading is described in Joy Grant's *Harold
    Monro and the Poetry Bookshop*, 1967, though the Dunmow meeting and its
    significant timing is not recorded.

18 *Essex Weekly News*, 23 and 30 May, 1913.

to emerge as *The Furriner* and to achieve a brief *succes d'estime* in June 1914.

Bensusan's affection for the county had grown firmer over the fifteen years he had lived there, strengthened no doubt by the close study of the landscape and life required for his country columns in the national press but fuelled perhaps above all by the happiness of his life at Duton Hill, particularly after his marriage in 1909 to Marian Pritchard, a Henham girl whom he had met at an Easton Lodge garden party in 1905.

The writing and playing of a dialect drama were, without question, in part at least, an attempt to celebrate the county and its people. Bensusan was later to meet Thomas Hardy several times and was regarded by him as 'a friend, and not as a journalist'.[19] In his unpublished autobiography, Bensusan wrote of the effect of Hardy's novels on the public perception of Dorset and it is difficult not to believe that he himself hoped, in some measure, to do for Essex what Hardy had achieved for his native county.

Already he had published two collections of stories of Essex life, *A Countryside Chronicle*, published in 1907 and *Father William* which had appeared five years later and captured the critics' attention for its faithful rendering of the Essex dialect and its light humour. It was a formula which was to serve Bensusan well, carrying him through half a century and numerous collections of stories until his death in 1958.

The Furriner was Bensusan's first foray into stage-writing, except for a pantomime on which he had worked six years before with his friend, Hugh Cranmer-Byng and which may or may not have seen the light of day before disappearing without trace.[20]

The story is so skimpy as barely to survive summary. A mysterious 'furriner' arrives in Maychester and is suspected by the villagers — and in particular by the central character, Father William — of being an uncaptured London murderer of whom they have read in the papers. Far from being the murderer, he is in fact discovered in the last scene to be a famous detective living in retirement. Slight enough as plots go! True, there are woven around this core a series of comic interplays between the characters, in particular between the cantankerous Father William and his deaf, light-fingered housekeeper, Mrs. Silver, and between William and his son, the 'local boy made good', now a London

19 S. L. Bensusan, *Myself when young*, 250.

20 Bensusan's diary, October–November 1908, Albert Sloman Library, University of Essex.

*Figure 2. Members of the cast of Synge's 'Tinker's Wedding' outside the Barn Theatre, 1913.
(Left to right: Elspet Keith (Mrs. Robertson-Scott), Tom Gibbons, Elizabeth Keith, Hugh Cranmer-Byng.)*

(Essex Record Office)

policeman and given to airs. The characters, some of them already
veterans of Bensusan's stories, are the real matter and strength of
the play. The dialect and phrases are also played for laughs. But in
the end, the plot is simply not engaging enough; the débacle
falls flat.

Players, venue and audience, it has to be conceded, were as
much responsible for the London reviews as the play itself. The
cast included, in the dialect rôles, the senior partner of the local
brewery and a Poor Law Guardian,[21] a leading scholar of oriental
literature[22] and the ten-year-old daughter of the Countess of
Warwick. Among the audience were Lady Warwick, still —
perhaps increasingly — a controversial society talking-point,
H. G. Wells, the most prominent writer of the day and a coven of
local and national journalists. Lady Warwick's Barn Theatre,
originally converted as a recreation room for the Essex
Yeomanry's annual camp and then used for private entertainments, had undergone major refurbishment at her expense in
1913. Double-doors and a vestibule had been added, the roof had
been lined with asbestos and plastered, stoves had been
introduced and acetylene lighting for the stage had been found by
stripping the brass lamps from her ladyship's car.[23] It had opened
in May 1913 with the double bill of Synge and Barrie. Now it was
time to show it off to the world, with a local play by a local writer
played by local people in a local theatre — all of them capable of
meeting London standards.

If the acclaim with which *The Furriner* was greeted was to
fade more quickly than most, it was perhaps not to do with the play
itself but with the wider drama which was about to unfold.
Scarcely had the applause faded than the peace died, and with it
the Progressive Club. Robertson Scott, above military age and
despondent of preaching rural progress in a time of war, sold up
and left for Japan where he studied the rural scene. Following his

21 Tom Gibbons, senior partner in the Crown Brewery, Dunmow, combined
   numerous public functions in the area with the role of conductor of the
   Dunmow Musical Society and an apparently insatiable appetite for amateur
   dramatics. He was for many years 'Counsel for the Bacon' in the Flitch
   trials.

22 'Lancie' Cranmer-Byng.

23 *Essex Weekly News*, 17 January and 23 May, 1913; J. W. Robertson Scott,
   The life and death of a newspaper, 1952, 195. A fuller account of the Barn
   Theatre's history is to be found in Felice Spurrier, *The Maynards of Little
   Easton*, 1987 and *Lady Warwick's Barn Theatre*, 1988.

return, he moved in 1923 to the Cotswolds and never lived again in Essex.

For the others, the preoccupations of war soon absorbed the energy they had formerly put into the Club. Bensusan was put in charge of a Food Production Committee for the neighbouring villages and Lady Warwick, supporting the food drive and in a typical gesture of aristocratic socialism, slaughtered the deer in Little Easton Park to feed the area. For Blumenfeld and Gwynne, the editorship of newspapers in a time of war allowed no space for local idealism, though R.D.B., on his weekend excursions to a landscape unchanged physically but strangely altered in spirit, reflected on a countryside 'skinned of its young men'. Thinking back to the Progressive Club lectures, he reflected:

> 'They came and listened, and some of them understood and some did not, but generally they felt that the call of the land for their sons was more insistent than the call of Mars. They were so detached from the outer world that, though they loved their hearths and homes and families, and would fight like tigers for their particular part of Essex, they felt no rising lump in their throats in response to the appeal that the Empire was in danger. What was the Empire? They didn't know. How could they when for a thousand years and more they had looked upon people ten miles away as "furriners"? So our lectures were well attended but not over effective in rousing the latent patriotism of the slow-thinking peasantry. Then one dark moonless night a clanking, whirring, rattling Zeppelin blundered along over our heads and dropped some bombs in a field not far away. That settled it. The boys flocked to the recruiting office.'[24]

When the War ended, the pieces had been scattered. Robertson Scott was in Japan. Bensusan, offered a post as Head of the Press Department at the Board of Agriculture, gave up Duton Hill and moved first to Bishops Hill near Theydon Bois, then to Epping Upland. The Blumenfelds moved away (temporarily) to Kent. Wells remained until 1923, when he set up home in Provence with his new mistress, Odette Keun. He returned less and less to Easton Glebe and after his wife's death in 1927 gave up the house. He had long since fallen out with his neighbour 'Taffy' Gwynne who, in 1915, had published in a leader on Pacifism and Civilism reference to Wells' views which was interpreted by him,

24 R. D. Blumenfeld, *All in a lifetime*, 70.

in an ever more vituperative correspondence, as an accusation of 'shirking and cowardice'.[25]

But if the Progressive Club had not, in its eighteen or so brief months of life, taken deep enough root to survive the departure of its prime movers, its existence was not without effect. The idealistic spirit which Robertson Scott had brought to its inception followed him to Oxfordshire where, on a less ambitious scale, he recreated the Club in the weekly 'Village Neighbours' sessions he instituted at Idbury. On a wider front, in 1927, he brought to fruition, in the form of *The Countryman*, an idea for a 'modern presentation of rural life, rural industries and the best of rural thinking' which he had first discussed with Alfred Harmsworth while living at Great Canfield.[26]

But, in another sense, it remained in the soil of west Essex, watered by the continuing educational enthusiasm of Lady Warwick and H. G. Wells. In 1921, in an attempt to draw good teachers away from the town and into the rural areas which were so often seen as the last refuge of second-raters, Lady Warwick inaugurated the Dunmow and District Educational Fellowship, a project to bring teachers out into the country to courses at Easton Lodge, which survived until 1972.[27] In this she was able to count on the vital support of another member of the Progressive Club, 'Lancie' Cranmer-Byng, by then a County Councillor who would later become Chairman of the Essex County Elementary Education Committee. 'Lancie's' role in support of Essex and of the education of Essex people continued throughout his life and included the founding chairmanship both of the Library Committee and of the Records Sub-Committee of the County Council, which in 1938 brought into being the Essex Record Office.[28]

The Barn Theatre survived the demise of the Progressive Club and remains to this day a venue for local productions. The Dunmow Players likewise lived on under the leadership of Tom Gibbons who from the beginning had been Robertson Scott's leading man on stage and staunch supporter off.

The ideal of a dialect drama for Essex lingered on in the

25 The letters are to be found in the Gwynne MSS at the Bodleian Library, Oxford (MS Gwynne dep. 22).

26 The birth in Essex of this idea is described in Robertson Scott, *We and me*, 185 *et seq*.

27 See the accounts of the Fellowship in Felice Spurrier, *Beyond the forest: the Countess of Warwick and some of her côterie*, 1986.

28 A useful summary of some at least of 'Lancie's' activities as 'The late Captain L. A. Cranmer-Byng' in the *Journal of the South-West Technical College and School of Art*, vol. 2, no. 1, December 1945.

Figure 3. Members of the Warwick Circle at Easton Lodge, c.1910.
They include, extreme left, Mrs. Marian Bensusan; second from left, H. G. Wells; rear, Mrs. Jane Wells; centre, the Countess of Warwick; first from right, Hugh Cranmer-Byng; right, Sam Bensusan. The children are, left to right, Frank Wells, Lady Mercy Greville, George Wells.

(J. Bensusan-Butt)

minds of many of the Progressive Club Council, finally to resurface in the shape of the Essex Play Society, the brainchild of Hugh Cranmer-Byng, brother of 'Lancie' and veteran of the Saffron Walden pageant of 1910. The goals were set out in the preface to the first volume issued by the Society in 1933 which contained both the text of *The Furriner* (published for the first time) and of a more recent play by Hugh, *The Diddicoy*, produced in November 1931 at the Barn Theatre.[29] They were 'to provide a suitable setting and medium for the actors and actresses of the immediate district', 'to assist in preserving something of the dialect and indigenous humour peculiar to the Essex folk' and 'to create and foster an indigenous school of local play writers and actors'.

The printed list of members and guarantors included Lady Warwick, Bensusan, Blumenfeld, the Cranmer-Byngs, de Vere Stacpoole, Tom Gibbons and C. S. L. Sutthery from the days of the Progressive Club, alongside 'Rab' Butler, Dr. Mahon who had written the music for the 1910 Saffron Walden pageant, Lady Byng of Thorpe-le-Soken, herself a novelist and Gurney Benham who owned the press which produced the little half-crown volume.

A second volume appeared later in 1933, this time with Hugh's *Old Cottage Tales*, which had been produced at the Barn Theatre in 1929 with a cast of eighty to play the six scenes from Essex history — from the Roman occupation to the Dunmow Flitch — which were 'dreamed by John Shakeshaft and John Fuel in an old Essex cottage'. It was close to the pageant format with which Hugh had begun and which was enjoying a revival throughout the country. *The Wise Woman*, a one-act dialect play by Bensusan, about an Essex 'cunning woman' and her clients, formed the complement. A third volume with two plays by Hugh, *The Queen's Ring* and *Annie the Come b'Chance* came in 1936. Then all was silence.

*   *   *   *   *

Whether the Progressive Club would itself have survived had the War not cut it short can only be a matter of speculation. There can be no doubting the strength of the social ideals which lay behind its establishment, but whether those for whom it was principally designed, the man on the Dunmow omnibus and the toiler in the fields of Little Easton, really took it to their hearts we are no

29 Published as *Essex plays produced at the Barn Theatre, Little Easton,* Essex Play Society, 1933.

longer in a position to say. As the light of national publicity faded
— as inevitably it would have — would the attention of the more
prominent of its members have wandered? Can the Progressive
resist the urge to lift his eyes to the next horizon as one ideal turns
to reality?

Perhaps *The Furriner* itself, with its theme of native
suspicion of the 'townie' in-comer, provides us with a metaphor for
a further problem inherent in the circumstances surrounding the
Club's birth. In May 1914 the *Essex County Chronicle* published
an editorial which, while looking forward to the play's production,
was shot through with a darker, more questioning streak. 'There is
no gainsaying the fact that among the agricultural community the
makers of books and papers have long been regarded with a
feeling closely approaching a native suspicion.' It went on to
address one very practical aspect of this immigration: the
increasing adaptation of country cottages. 'At this moment, much
of the adaptation is being done in the Canfields, and it quickly
alters what was a farm labourer's house letting at £5 a year into a
country visitor's "little place" which will readily let at £20 a year.
Thus it will be seen that the "furriner", as the Essex countryman
calls him, is becoming a very real factor in these rural parts.'[30]

In the end perhaps no amount of Progressive camaraderie
could have pasted over the cracks that were inevitable as the
social fabric of the countryside changed. At the very moment *The
Furriner* was receiving its first performance, the Association of
District Councils were hearing at their annual conference in the
Guildhall how labourers were being ousted from their cottages by
weekenders. Bensusan had hit upon a theme closer to the hearts
of his audience than perhaps he realised.

And yet, there were embodied in the Progressive Club much
of the best of radical Edwardian thinking: a determined refusal to
recognise boundaries of party, sex or class, a fascination with the
reawakening of traditions and customs, a belief in the curative
power of the Modern. It was undeniably localised and short-lived
and ultimately proved to have been totally dependent on a
momentary confluence of personalities and ideas yet the brief,
heady experience of an ideal being played out in one small rural
community left its mark on the minds and future activities of most
if not all its leading players. Its aspirations were to blossom again
as soon as they were transplanted into a post-War soil. The
Matching Easy Flower Show, on the other hand, was never again
to be quite the same.

30 *Essex County Chronicle*, 8 May, 1914.

'The Merit of Conspicuous Bravery'
Essex-born Victoria Cross Winners 1856–1914

IAN ROBERTSON

OF PERENNIAL INTEREST to the local historian is the problem of how to treat people who, although originating from a particular county, have achieved fame, and sometimes fortune, far from their place of birth; politicians, inventors and soldiers are three broad groups coming readily to mind. To describe their lives in detail would be out of place in a localised study, but to ignore their achievements of national importance altogether would be to deny any influence resulting from circumstances of birth or early environment. To take the case of soldiers, common knowledge alone would suggest that during the two centuries of an imperial interventionist policy overseas by various British Governments, soldiers originating from Essex are likely to have distinguished themselves many thousands of miles away from home. Surely mere distance is not a sufficient reason to prevent those interested in the history of Essex from recognising the activities of those soldiers born in the County?[1]

It has never been necessary to have been a student of military history to appreciate the qualities of supreme courage and exceptional bravery needed to win the Victoria Cross with its simple inscription: 'For Valour'. Instituted by Royal Warrant, dated 29 January, 1856, the latter document in its sixth rule set out those requirements for the award which have most engaged the attention of subsequent generations, namely:

> 'It is ordained with a view to place all persons on a perfectly equal footing in relation to eligibility for the Decoration that neither rank nor long service nor wounds nor any other circumstance or condition what-

1 Ashley Cooper, *The Khyber Connection: The Furrow and The Raj*, 1985, is one of the few modern works to treat of the imperial connection from the point of view of local studies, specifically in this case between British India and the Suffolk–Essex border.

soever save the merit of conspicuous bravery should be held to establish a sufficient claim to the honour.'[2]

It might be thought that given the high prestige of the Victoria Cross the names of those winners who were born in the County of Essex would be generally known; not only is this not so, but their personal details are not easily ascertainable. For if one turns to the magisterial six-volume work by John Burrows entitled *Essex Units in the Great War*,[3] which includes the history of the antecedents of those County Regiments fighting in the 1914–18 War, one will indeed find much of interest on the 44th and 56th Foot, which were combined in 1881 to form the 1st and 2nd Battalions of the Essex Regiment, but not one of the winners of the Victoria Cross mentioned therein was born in Essex. Sergeant William McWheeney (Crimea, 1854), Lieutenant Robert Montresor Rogers (China, 1860) and Private John McDougall (China, 1860), all of the 44th Foot were born in, respectively, Bangor (County Down), Maidenhead (Berkshire), Old Town (Edinburgh), while Lieutenant Francis Newton Parsons (South Africa, 1900) of 1st Battalion the Essex Regiment was born in Dover (Kent).

The problem is simply the situation before the 1881 reorganisation (part of the series of Army Reforms previously initiated by Edward Cardwell), which instituted the system of linked infantry battalions (one at home, one overseas) and confirmed to each Regiment a county affiliation; although the 44th and 56th had associations with the County of Essex those links were much weaker than in the post-1881 period. Although Burrows in his historical writings is keen to give the Essex Units of the Great War an appropriate pedigree and indeed justify the contribution made by the Territorial Force and Kitchener's Army in that struggle, it must not be forgotten that men joining the Regular Army were under no compulsion ever to enter their own county-associated regiment; there was considerable freedom of choice in peace time, but sometimes little, if any, in war; the determinants of choice could range from family association or a

2   Quoted in M. J. Crook, *The Evolution of the Victoria Cross*, 1975, 280 from P.R.O. W098/1. Michael Crook's book is a comprehensive account of the history of the Victoria Cross, as opposed to a review of the exploits of the winners. J. W. Bancroft, *The Victoria Cross Roll of Honour*, 1989, is a helpful list organised by Regiment with an index arranged by War. The chapter in P. E. Abbott and J. M. A. Tamplin, *British Gallantry Awards*, 1971, is a concise and most useful introduction to the subject of the Victoria Cross.

3   Southend-on-Sea, 1923; scond edition, 1931.

wish not to serve in the infantry through to the presence of a recruiting party from a particular regiment in the vicinity of home. From this it follows that many Essex-born soldiers could and did serve in the period 1856 and 1914 in units other than the 44th, 56th and Essex Regiments. There was indeed the possibility that there might be Victoria Cross winners amongst them, but the problem was to find out who they were.

The solution was found in *The Register of the Victoria Cross*[4] which lists all V.C. winners and which is well indexed so that by searching for Essex locations it is possible to isolate those soldiers who were born in the County. To this information may be added that gleaned from the files of Canon Lummis now in the National Army Museum, Chelsea.[5] The Canon was a doyen of Victoria Cross students having spent many years in tracking down records relating to all the winners of the V.C.[6] From these two sources, it is possible to offer for the first time a list of Essex-born Victoria Cross winners during the period 1856–1914. It is appropriate to close the discussion with the beginning of the Great War because, taking into account all the recipients, 'in just over four years from 1914 to 1918 more Victoria Crosses (582) were awarded than in the whole of the previous fifty-eight years of the Cross's existence (522)'.[7] The addition of the Great War awards to those described in this paper would require more space than is available here for a proper consideration.

4 Compiled and researched by Nora Buzzell, second edition, 1988.

5 The Lummis V.C. Files are maintained at the National Army Museum by the Military Historical Society and they are a vital source for researchers. To save tedious repetition it may be assumed that *all* references in this paper, otherwise unattributed, are from the relevant Lummis V.C. Files. From the latter D. Pillinger and A. Staunton produced *The Victoria Cross Locator*, 1991, which provides precisely the most useful service indicated in its title.

6 William Murrell Lummis was born in 1885 and enlisted as a trooper in the 11th Hussars in 1904, subsequently being promoted R.Q.M.S. in 1913 and serving on the Western Front, 1914–19. After being commissioned into the 2nd Battalion The Suffolk Regiment in 1916 Lummis served in India during the 1920s and was promoted Captain in 1928, retiring in 1930, in which year he was ordained. Having served as a curate in Ipswich, Lummis became Vicar of Kesgrave (1933–41) and then Vicar of Holy Trinity, Bungay, Suffolk (1941–58); a Canon Emeritus of St. Edmundsbury, he died at Hindhead in 1985. His publications include, as co-author, *Honour the Light Brigade*, but it may well be that his series of files on the winners of the Victoria Cross and the original work contained therein will stand as a major memorial.

7 For the numbers of V.C.s, see Crook, *op. cit.*, 170.

Figure 1.   Private Frederick Corbett, V.C./David Embleton, K.R.R.C., 1883.
(National Army Museum)

Five soldiers have been thus identified and the scenes of their engagements are quite different (except in one case) from those of their fellow V.C. winners in the County-associated Regiment with no awards in the Crimea nor China. Instead we have: John Watson (India, 1857), Davis Hawkes (India, 1858), Evelyn Wood (India, 1858), Frederick Corbett/David Embleton (Egypt, 1882), and Isaac Lodge (South Africa, 1900). As it is not the purpose here to recount the chronological history of the campaigns,[8] and to help with future reference, as well as to respect the irrelevance of rank in the making of this award, the five Essex-born V.C. winners will be described in alphabetical order as follows:

1. *Frederick Corbett/David Embleton (1853–1912)*

The *London Gazette* for 16 February, 1883, carried the notice of the award of the Victoria Cross to Frederick Corbett; the details of the action were as follows:

> 'Frederick Corbett, Private, 3rd Battn. The King's Royal Rifle Corps. During the reconnaissance upon Kafra Dowar on the 5th Aug. 1882, the Mounted Infantry, with which Private Corbett was serving, came under a hot fire from the enemy, and suffered some loss, including Lieut. Howard Vyse, mortally wounded. This officer fell in the open, and there being then no time to move him, Private Corbett asked and obtained permission to remain by him, and though under a constant fire, he sat down and endeavoured to stop the bleeding of this officer's wounds, until the Mounted Infantry rceived orders to retire, when he rendered valuable assistance in carrying him off the field.'[9]

Corbett had a chequered military history which was summarised in an account (apparently used by later commentators) in the *Daily Graphic* of 14 September, 1904, which runs as follows:

> 'At Bow Street Police-court yesterday, Frederick Corbett, aged forty-eight, formerly a private in the

8 To set the campaigns mentioned in this paper in their broad context see M. Barthorp, *The Armies of Britain 1485–1980*, National Army Museum.

9 For this campaign see also I. L. Mortenson, 'The K.R.R.C. Mounted Infantry in Eygpt and Lieutenant Henry Granville Lindsay Howard-Vyse, 3804 Private Frederick Corbett, V.C., 1588 Private Solomon Howes', *The Journal of the Orders and Medals Research Society (J.O.M.R.S.)*, Spring 1990, vol. 29, no. 1, 18–22.

King's Royal Rifles, was charged on remand, before Mr. Marsham, with wilfully breaking a plate glass panel in a door at the War Office at noon on the 7th inst.

When arrested he said he had a grievance against the War Office, and wanted to call attention to it.

Police-Inspector Emerick now handed to the magistrate a communication which had been received from the War Office, stating that the prisoner was granted a Victoria Cross in February, 1883, for conspicuous bravery on August 5th, 1882, in the Egyptian war. He was discharged from the King's Royal Rifle Corps on June 18th, 1883. After his discharge, and before his re-enlistment, he sold his Victoria Cross. On December 15th, 1883, he joined the Royal Artillery, and in the following July he was convicted of stealing goods and embezzling money belonging to an officer, for which he was sentenced to twenty-eight days' hard labour. In consequence of that conviction his name was erased by an Especial Warrant from the Victoria Cross Register, and he was deprived of the V.C. pension. He was convicted again on February 28th, 1887, by district court-martial of losing by neglect his equipment, clothing, etc., and stealing the property of a comrade, and sentenced to eighty-four days' hard labour. On September 17th, 1889, he was again convicted by court-martial of striking a superior officer, and sentenced to eighty-four days' hard labour. He was discharged from the army without pension on January 16th, 1891, having been found to be medically unfit for further service. There were nine entries against him in the Regimental Defaulter Book, and seventeen in the Battery Defaulter Book. On December 10th, 1897, he was granted £2 from the Cambridge Fund, as he was destitute.

The prisoner said that before he lost his V.C. there was not a mark against him. He afterwards served five years in India, and strove hard to re-gain it, but he was always a marked man, and could never do anything right. He had put up with all that it was possible for a man to put up with, and at the end of it all he was sent away an invalid, without the slightest reward. After serving his country for so many years he thought that the army authorities ought to have done something for him, even if it was ever so little.

> *The Magistrate:* You kept on stealing while you were
> in the army, and could not expect to be treated in the
> same way as a man with a good character.
>
> It was stated that the prisoner's "discharge" papers
> were marked, "Conduct latterly good for one year".
> He was sentenced to one month's hard labour.'

Given that Frederick Corbett was allegedly born in Camber-
well, none of the above would be of interest to historians of Essex
were it not for the fact that Corbett's other, and apparently real,
name was David Embleton and that he came from Essex.
Although the fact that Corbett had an alias has long been known, it
is only with the personal details from family sources published[10] in
1991 by David Embleton's great nephew, P. A. G. Embleton, that
the latter is able to assert that Frederick Corbett 'was born David
Embleton in Maldon, Essex on 17 September, 1853, the son of
William (a baker) and Jane. He died in the Maldon workhouse on
25 September, 1912'.[11] According to family information also,
'Corbett lived for the army and fell into bad company after his
medical discharge'.[12] Certainly his keenness for military life is
attested by his re-enlistment into the Royal Horse Artillery after a
medical discharge from the King's Royal Rifle Corps, as well as by
the fact 'of his service with the Essex Rifle Volunteers of which he
was a popular member', according to the *Maldon Express* of 24
Febuary, 1883, which gazetted his award under his real name.[13]

Canon Lummis in a letter of 17 November, 1956, to Captain
A. G. Rumbelow took the view that 'Frederick Corbett (*alias*
David Embleton) was a real "bad hat", and it is a pity that he was
ever awarded the Victoria Cross'. However, Corbett/Embleton
was awarded the V.C. and despite all the inconsistencies, as yet
unresolved, his career is of especial interest for at least three
reasons: first, because the substitution of a V.C. for the original
award of a Distinguished Conduct Medal and the subsequent
forfeiture of the former, demonstrate the technical aspects of the
working of the Royal Warrant; secondly, by reason of his sale of his
V.C. after his first discharge from the Army, the possible existence

10 P. A. G. Embleton, 'Private Frederick Corbett, V.C.', *J. O. M. R. S.*, Summer
    1991, vol. 30, no. 2, 141–43.

11 *Ibid*, 141.

12 *Ibid*, 141.

13 *Ibid*, 142.

of one or two other replica V.C.s attributed to him[14] (one of which is held in the Royal Green Jackets Museum in Winchester), pose particular problems to researchers into the history of medals; and, thirdly, as a man marked by a sense of grievance and a difficult past, David Embleton is of great interest to family and local historians in his native Essex.

2. *David Hawkes (1822–1858)*

The *London Gazette* for 24 December, 1858, carried the notice of the award of the Victoria Cross to David Hawkes; the circumstances were as follows:

> 'Henry Wilmot, Capt. 2nd Battn. The Rifle Brigade; W. Nash, Corpl., and David Hawkes, Private. Date of Act of Bravery: 11 March, 1858. For conspicuous gallantry at Lucknow on the 11th March, 1858. Capt. Wilmot's company was engaged with a large body of the enemy near the Iron Bridge. That officer found himself at the end of a street with only four of his men, opposed to a considerable body. One of the four was shot through both legs and became utterly helpless; the two men lifted him up, and although Private Hawkes was severely wounded, he carried him for a considerable distance, exposed to the fire of the enemy, Capt. Wilmot firing with the men's rifles, and covering the retreat of the party.'

As a result of his wounds David Hawkes died on 14 August, 1858. Very little is known about him and it would seem that no photographs survive; the only clue is provided by a letter dated 10 February, 1859, to his next-of-kin, William Hawkes of Chipping Hall (*sic*), Witham, Essex, written on behalf of the Secretary of State for War which runs as follows:

> 'I am directed by the Secretary of State for War to transmit to you the decoration of the Victoria Cross which should have been conferred in accordance with Her Majesty's intention on your late son, David Hawkes, a Private in the 2nd Bn. Rifle Brigade, had he survived to receive it.
>
> This Cross is sent to you by The Queen as a memorial of your late son's gallant conduct in India as set forth in

---

14 E. J. Martin, 'Private Frederick Corbett's Victoria Cross', *The Bulletin of the Military Historical Society*, 1951, vol. 1, no. 4, 44–45.

the accompanying extract from the London Gazette of
24th December last . . .'

The transcript of this letter allows us to trace in the Baptismal Registers of the Parish of Witham[15] the entry for 23 June,
1822, in the name of David, son of William Hawkes and Sarah; with
the abode given as Witham and the occupation of the father as
'labourer'.

The last time David Hawkes's Victoria Cross was seen
publicly was when it was sold at Messrs. Glendining, London on 25
November, 1919, for £78. Above is set out the sum total of easily
ascertainable information about this brave soldier mortally
wounded rescuing a comrade-in-arms, less than for any other
Essex-born V.C. holder.

3.   *Isaac Lodge (1866–1923)*

This soldier's award of the Victoria Cross was unusual in that
Isaac Lodge was selected by ballot under Rule 13 of the Royal
Warrant which provided for collective acts of bravery when all of
those present had so distinguished themselves that it was impossible to select one person in preference to the remainder other than
by voting. Therefore there is no separate citation for Isaac Lodge
and to arrive at a description of the engagement it is necessary to
consult the details of the award to Major Phipps-Hornby,
announced in the *London Gazette* of 26 June, 1900. The circumstances were:

'Edmund John Phipps-Hornby, Major, Q Battery,
Royal Horse Artillery. Date of Act of Bravery: 31 March,
1900. On the occasion of the action at Korn Spruit on the
31st March, 1900, a British force, including two bat-
teries of the Royal Horse Artillery, was retiring from
Thabanchu, towards Bloemfontein. The enemy had
formed an ambush at Korn Spruit, and, before their
presence was discovered by the main body, had captured the greater portion of the baggage column and five
out of the six guns of the leading battery. When the
alarm was given, 'Q' Battery, Royal Horse Artillery, was
within three hundred yards of the spruit. Major Phipps-
Hornby, who commanded it, at once wheeled about and
moved off at a gallop under a very heavy fire. One gun
was upset when the wheel horse was shot, and had to be

15 E.R.O., D/P227/1/5, Baptisms 1813–91, no. 587.

Figure 2.   Gunner Isaac Lodge, V.C., R.H.A.

(National Army Museum)

abandoned with another waggon, the horses of which
were killed. The remainder of the battery reached a
position close to some unfinished railway buildings, and
came into action 1,150 yards from the spruit, remaining
in action until ordered to retire. When the order to retire
was received, Major Phipps-Hornby ordered the guns
and their limbers to be run back by hand to where the
teams of uninjured horses stood behind the unfinished
buildings. The few remaining gunners, assisted by a
number of officers and men of a party of mounted
infantry, and directed by Major Phipps-Hornby and
Capt. Humphreys, the only remaining officers of the
battery, succeeded in running back four of the guns
under shelter. One or two of the limbers were similarly
withdrawn by hand, but the work was most severe and
the distance considerable. In consequence, all concerned were so exhausted that they were unable to drag
in the remaining limbers of the fifth gun. It now became
necessary to risk the horses, and volunteers were called
for from among the drivers, who readily responded.
Several horses were killed and men wounded, but at
length only one gun and one limber were left exposed.
Four separate attempts were made to rescue these, but
when no more horses were available the attempt had to
be given up and the gun and limber were abandoned.
Meanwhile the other guns had been sent on one at a
time, and after passing within seven or eight hundred
yards of the enemy, in rounding the head of a donga and
crossing two spruits, they eventually reached a place of
safety, where the battery was reformed. After full consideration of the circumstances of the case, the Field-
Marshal Commanding-in-Chief in South Africa formed
the opinion that the conduct of all ranks of 'Q' Battery,
Royal Horse Artillery, was conspicuously gallant and
daring, but that all were equally brave and devoted in
their behaviour. He therefore decided to treat the case
of the battery as one of collective gallantry, under Rule
13 of the Victoria Cross Warrant, and directed that one
officer should be selected for the decoration of the
Victoria Cross by the officers, one non-commissioned
officer by the non-commissioned officers, and two
gunners or drivers by the gunners and drivers. A
difficulty arose with regard to the officer, owing to the

fact that there were only two officers — Major Phipps-Hornby and Capt. Humphreys — available for the work of saving the guns, and both of these had been conspicuous by their gallantry and by the fearless manner in which they exposed themselves, and each of them nominated the other for the decoration. It was ultimately decided in favour of Major Phipps-Hornby, as having been the senior concerned. Charles Parker, Sergt., was elected by the non-commissioned officers, as described above. Isaac Lodge, Gunner, and Horace Harry Glasock, Driver, were elected by the gunners and drivers as described above.'

As our particular concern is with the Essex connections of the V.C. winners, it is especially worthy of note that Isaac Lodge prepared his own account for publication and begins helpfully with some interesting background information:

'We most of us seem to have been named out of the Bible; my father's name was Elijah Lodge, my mother's was Rhoda. She was the daughter of William Ward, who lived at the farm down by the gates of Easton Park, where Lord Warwick lives. I was born at Great Canfield, near Dunmow, in Essex, and went to Great Canfield School. When I was eleven years old I was out at work; first on a farm, doing milking, and then I did various other things, tanning the barks of trees, and later on I was a gamekeeper, and my employer gave me two woods. It was a good job, but I *had* to be a soldier. Nothing put it into my head; it was there. And if had my time over again I should be a soldier again. If I weren't so deaf I should be in it now. I enlisted in with the Royal Garrison Artillery on the 29th Dec. 1888, at Warley Barracks; that was the way you got into the Royal Horse Artillery in those days; and after a few weeks was transferred to the R.H.A., and came to St. John's Wood into a service battery, and then went to India with B Battery. We were in Meerut in Mount Rocket lines, and then marched up to Rawalpindi, and were there two years. I was transferred from B Battery to Q Battery. General Brunker that is now, made Q Battery efficient. He worked very hard at it; not a pin could be out of place nor a round of ammunition, and every man had to know where everything was and how much there was of everything. The horses were trained over jumps, singly and in pairs. If he ordered a parade at ten o'clock he was there to the second, and he expected everyone else to be there too. General Fanshawe was just the same . . .'

There then follows an account of Isaac Lodge's subsequent service and his view of the particular engagement at Korn Spruit; this so caught the attention of the late Sir O'Moore Creagh, one of the editors of *The V.C. and D.S.O.*, that in the Preface it is recalled by his co-editor that 'Sir O'Moore said the best thing in the book was Gunner Lodge's description of the adventures of his battery in the South African War'.[16]

Isaac Lodge is a particularly well documented soldier as in addition to the account mentioned above, his record of service survives in the Public Record Office.[17] From the latter it is clear that he served in the 3rd Battalion, the Essex Regiment, from which he 'purchased discharge'; this Battalion was formerly (1853–81) the Essex Rifles, and before being so designated was the East Essex Militia, one of the two Militia units in the County.[18] Lodge attested at Warley Barracks, having answered the questions put to him by Colour Sergeant S. Bloomfield of the Essex Regiment, on 29 December, 1888, and joined the Royal Artillery at Great Yarmouth on the 31st of the same month. In addition to giving fuller details of Isaac Lodge's 21 years' military service (Home, India, Home, South Africa, Home'), his record of service also throws further light on his Essex connections. Perhaps the most surprising point is that his place of birth is shown as 'Great Cranham', when all the evidence is that Great Canfield was the location in question, although it must be said that a cursory glance at the Parish Registers for that area do not show him born there at the appropriate time.

From his record of service it is clear that he married Minnie Elizabeth Francis at Great Canfield on 23 July, 1903, and when his wife became his next-of-kin it is noted that his father and mother, Elijah and Rhoda, were then living at High Roothing. Lodge also indicated that his intended place of residence on discharge was to

16 The late Sir O'Moore Creagh, V.C. and E. M. Humphris, *The V.C. and D.S.O.*, London, n.d., c. 1920s. This is a most important source and the basic entries in the Lummis V.C. Files seem to be copies from pages of this book, e.g. Phipps-Hornby and Lodge as quoted above are on pages 113–15.

17 P.R.O., W097/5356 — Isaac Lodge's Record of Service.

18 Burrows, *op. cit.*, vol. 4, 161, 164–65.

be Great Canfield, although in fact be became a park keeper in Hyde Park, ultimately dying after an operation for a throat infection and being buried at Hendon, Middlesex.

At the time of his discharge on 28 December, 1909, at Aldershot at the end of his twenty-one years' service, Isaac Lodge is described as being forty-four years old, 5ft. 8ins. in height with a fresh complexion, blue eyes and dark brown hair, bearing a scar on his forehead and a small scar in front of his right ear. As he intended returning to his original occupation on enlistment of labourer it would no doubt be helpful to have his conduct described as 'Exemplary. No offence during last 17 years 7 months service'. Equally helpful would be the entry under 'Special qualifications for employment in civil life', in which it has been written 'obtained Victoria Cross at action of Sanna's Post, S. Africa 1900 — Has knowledge of game-keeping — is very active — smart appearance — is trustworthy — hardworking — has good manners and is always genial and obliging'.

The only additional piece of family information that may be gleaned from the records available is that Isaac Lodge had an older sister, Emma Mead, last known to be living in Dunmow on or before 1 January, 1889. That information comes from a partly damaged pay book which was given to the National Army Museum by Mrs. Mabel Parker, the daughter of Isaac Lodge, on the occasion when she presented his Victoria Cross to the National Army Museum on 16 September, 1983, together with his other medals and documents.[19]

19 Mrs. M. Parker's generous donation to the National Army Museum comprised: Isaac Lodge's medals – V.C. 1900; Queen's South Africa Medal 1899–1902; George V Coronation Medal 1911, awarded to Keepers of the Royal Parks; Long Service and Good Conduct Medal, Army, 1907; Ribbons of the above (N.A.M., 8309-68); Paybook 1889–1904 (N.A.M., 8310-13-1); Parchment Certificate of Discharge (A.F. D.426), 28 December, 1909 (N.A.M., 8310-13-2); Instructions (N.A.M., 8310-13-30 and a list of those attending (N.A.M., 8310-13-4); Garden Party for V.C. recipients, Buckingham Palace, 26 June, 1920, invitation to Home, R.A. Mess, Woolwich, 26 November, 1920 (N.A.M., 8310-13-5); press notices of his death in June 1923 (N.A.M., 8310-13-6 and 7); cigarette card featuring Lodge (N.A.M., 8310-13-8); book of 'Signatories to Presentation to Gunner Lodge, V.C.' (N.A.M., 8310-13-9); his copy of For Valour by Kate Stanway, 1905 (N.A.M., 8310-13-10); devotional book The Manual, given 18 March, 1884 (N.A.M., 8310-13-11); Book of Common Prayer, dated 1900 (N.A.M., 8310-13-12); Soldier's New Testament, South Africa, 1900 (N.A.M., 8310-13-13); photocopy of his daughter's Baptismal Certificate, May 1906 (N.A.M., 8310-13-14).

4. *John Watson (1829–1919)*

The particular incident for which John Watson received the Victoria Cross, announced in the *London Gazette* of 18 June, 1858, was described as follows:

'John Watson, Lieutenant, 1st Punjab Cavalry. Date of Act of Bravery, 14 Nov. 1857. Lieut. Watson, on 14 Nov., with his own squadron, and that under Captain, then Lieut. Probyn, came upon a body of the rebel cavalry. The Ressaldar in command of them — a fine specimen of the Hindustani Mussalman — and backed up by some half-dozen equally brave men, rode out to the front. Lieut. Watson singled out this fine-looking fellow and attacked him. The Ressaldar presented his pistol at Lieut. Watson's breast at a yard's distance and fired, but most providentially without effect; the ball must have by accident previously fallen out. Lieut. Watson ran the man through with his sword and dismounted him; but the native officer, nothing daunted, drew his tulwar, and with his sowars renewed his attack upon Lieut. Watson, who bravely defended himself until his own men joined in the melée, and utterly routed the party. In the *rencontre* Lieut. Watson received a blow on the head from a tulwar, another on the left arm, which severed his chain gauntlet glove, a tulwar cut on his right arm, which fortunately only divided the sleeve of his jacket, but disabled the arm for some time; a bullet also passed through his coat, and he received a blow on his leg which lamed him for some days afterwards.'

John Watson, having entered the Bombay Army in 1848, followed a distinguished career in India serving in the Punjab (1848–49), at the Siege of Mooltan, the Battle of Goojerat, the Indian Mutiny (1857–59), the Umbeyla Campaigns, and in commanding the Kuran Field Force in the Afghan War (1879–80); knighted in 1886 and promoted General in 1891, General Sir John Watson, V.C., G.C.B. died at Finchampstead, Berkshire, on 23 January, 1919.[20]

20 Major Vernon Charles Paget Hodson (1883–1963), the great nephew of William Stephen Raikes Hodson who raised Hodson's Horse, originally compiled a Card Index of officers of the Bengal Army 1758–1834; this was subsequently enlarged and bequeathed to the National Army Museum, where it is maintained and updated. He served in the 10th Duke of Cambridge's Own Lancers (Hodson's Horse). This Card Index is a major source of information on Indian Army officers, such as John Watson.

Interest in John Watson's life for historians of Essex begins with the fact that he was the son of William George Watson and Harriet, his wife, who lived in Chigwell Row, William being a merchant of 133 Fenchurch Street, London. Their son John was born on 6 September, 1829,[21] and baptised at Chigwell on 31 October the same year.[22] In the Baptismal Register the abode of the family is given as Chigwell and the status of the father as 'Esquire'. As John Watson grew up and joined the Honourable East India Company's Bombay Army, he did not sever his links with the area of his birth, because on 10 January, 1860, he married Eliza Jesser Davis (died 1892) at Ilford. In the Marriage Registers[23] John Watson is described as a Lieutenant and resident of Chigwell Row, while Eliza is termed a resident of Great Ilford. This marriage meant that John Watson of Chigwell was joining an influential West Essex family as can be demonstrated by the fact that Eliza's brother was John Coope Davis of Cranbrooke Park, Ilford, Essex. The entry for his family in *Burke's Landed Gentry*[24] encompassed not only East Horndon and Little Warley, and Leytonstone as well as Ilford, but virtually all the professions including the Royal Navy, the British Army, the Indian Army, the Church and the Law! The full text of that particularly interesting entry is as follows:

'DAVIS, JOHN COOPE, Esq. of Cranbrooke Park, Essex, *b.* 31 March, 1832: *m.* 6 Sept. 1866, Fanny Kate, elder dau. of the Rev. John Pearson, Rector of East Horndon and Little Warley, Essex. Mr. Davis, a Magistrate and Deputy Lieut. for the co., and Col. of the 3rd Battalion of the Essex Rifle Volunteers, is 2nd son of the late John Davis, Esq. of Cranbrooke Park, J.P., D.L. (who *d.* 1864), by Elizabeth Jesser his wife, dau. of John Coope, Esq., and is grandson of William Davis, Esq. of Leytonstone, Essex, and Wellclose, co. Gloucester, by Dorothy his wife. He has the following brothers and sisters; William (elder brother), of Wellclose, co. Gloucester, *m.* Adelaide, dau. of Miles Stringer, Esq.,

21 Hodson's Index Card for John Watson; *The Dictionary of Indian Biography*, 442; *Who Was Who, 1916–28*, 1100.

22 Hodson's Index Card confirmed by E.R.O., D/P166/1/7, Chigwell Baptismal Registers, 1813–50, no. 676.

23 E.R.O., St. Mary's, Great Ilford, Marriage Registers, no. 493.

24 *Burke's Landed Gentry*, 6th edition, 1879, under 'Davis of Cranbrooke Park'.

and has issue five children; Hugh, Commander R.N.;
Howell, Major 29th regt.; Arthur Harvey, Lieut.-Col.
Indian Army; Edward Gabriel, B.A. Trin. Coll.
Cambridge, Chaplain in India; Anna Maria, *m.* Rev.
Frederick French, Rector of Worlingworth, Suffolk;
Adelaide, *m.* William Cotesworth, Esq. of Cowden
Knowes, Melrose, N.B.; Eliza Jesser, *m.* Col. John
Watson, V.C., C.B.; Emilia, *m.* H. R. Mansel Jones,
Esq., Barrister-at-Law; and Mary.

Seat — Cranbrooke Park, Ilford, Essex.'

Further, the Davis family had been influential in promoting
the cause of Ilford as a separate unit of administration from the
medieval parish of Barking of which it formed a part until 1830 for
ecclesiastical and 1888 for civil purposes. St. Mary's Church in the
High Road, Great Ilford where John and Eliza were married had
been built in 1829–31 and the tower added in 1866 as a memorial to
John and Elizabeth Davis of Cranbrooke.[25]

Speculation is always dangerous for the historian, but it is
interesting to reflect that it is most unlikely that when John
Weston married in St. Mary's Church, Great Ilford, in 1860 (when
the Crown had just assumed responsibility for the East India
Company's Army and before Queen Victoria had been proclaimed
Empress of India), he would have foreseen that he would die at the
age of ninety within twenty-eight years of the end of British India
in 1947. Equally, one wonders how many at that wedding in 1860
foresaw that John Coope Davis, Eliza Jesser's brother, would in
due time sell the Cranbrooke Estate and that by 1901 the house
would be demolished with the lands divided up for suburban
building.[26]

5. *Henry Evelyn Wood (1838–1919)*

The action, for which the award of the Victoria Cross to Evelyn
Wood was announced in *The London Gazette* of 4 September,
1860, was described in the following terms:

'Henry Evelyn Wood, Lieut., 17 Lancers. For having, on
the 19th Oct. 1858, during an action at Sindwaho, when
in command of a troop of the 3rd Light Cavalry,
attacked with much gallantry, almost single-handed, a
body of rebels who had made a stand, whom he routed;

25 V.C.H., Essex, vol. v, 1966, 184, 198, 257.

26 *Ibid*, 198.

Figure 3.   Colonel Sir Evelyn Wood, V.C., 90th Light Infantry, c.1879.

(National Army Museum)

also for having subsequently, near Sindhora, gallantly advanced with a Duffadar and Sowar of Beatson's Horse, and rescued from a band of robbers, a Potail, Chemmum Singh, whom they had captured and carried off to the jungles, where they intended to hang him.'

Evelyn Wood enjoyed a long and distinguished military career, having first entered the Royal Navy in 1852, been wounded in the assault on the Redan in the Crimean War and joined the Army as a cornet in the 13th Light Dragoons. Having transferred to the 17th Lancers, Evelyn Wood went to India in 1857 and participated in the suppression of the Indian Mutiny in central India during which time he won his Victoria Cross. A transfer to the 73rd Foot in 1862 was followed by Staff College in 1864 and 'In 1871 Wood purchased a majority in the 90th Light Infantry, being one of the last officers to obtain promotion in this way'.[27]

Service followed in the Ashanti War of 1873–74, in South Africa in 1878–79, and again in that same location in 1881 where Wood was involved in the implementation of politically contro-versial policies. Successful campaigning in Egypt in 1882 was followed by Wood reorganising the Egyptian Army and in 1884 he commanded the line of communications when Lord Wolseley attempted to relieve General Gordon in Khartoum. Wood's next appointment was very much closer to home. 'From 1886 to 1889 he was at Colchester as head of the Eastern Command. Here he wrought many reforms and changes — in the canteen system, investigating causes of delinquency, practising infantry night marches,and considering the defences of the eastward approaches to London.'[28]

In 1893 Evelyn Wood became Quartermaster-General and reorganised the system of transporting troops, as well as negotiat-ing concessions with railway companies for officers and men going on leave. Appointed Adjutant-General in 1897 he was tasked with the mobilisation arrangements for the South African War (1899–1901). Appointed to command the Second Army Corps in 1901, his last active command, he was created Field Marshal in 1903.

By virtue of his distinguished military career, Field Marshal Sir Evelyn Wood, V.C., G.C.B., is undoubtedly the best remem-bered of the five Essex-born V.C. winners who together form the subject of this paper; indeed he is the only one of that group who

27 D.N.B., 1912–21, 591; this entry forms the basis for the biographical sketch in this paper, unless the source is otherwise acknowledged.

28 *Essex Review*, vol. XXIX, 1920, Obituary, 54.

merits a mention in Sir William Addison's *Essex Worthies*.[29]
Wood's connection with Essex begins with his birth at Cressing on
9 Febuary, 1838, by virtue of the fact that his mother, Emma
Caroline, was married to the Reverend Sir John Page Wood, rector
of St. Peter's, Cornhill, and vicar of Cressing. He maintained a
residential connection with the County having lived at Upminster
and particularly at Millhurst in Harlow where he died on 28
October, 1919. There was a further connection with the County
in that his sister Emma married in 1853 Sir Thomas Barrett
Lennard, Bt., of Belhus, where Evelyn Wood's mother, Emma
Caroline, Lady Wood, died on 15 December, 1879.

In the *Essex Weekly News*[30] it is noticed that the Field
Marshal had expressed a wish before his death on 2 December,
1919, to be buried next to his wife in Aldershot and 'As the hearse
moved through Harlow blinds were drawn at the houses and
shops'. Amongst the 7,000 troops who took part in the funeral
ceremony on 6 December there were officers of the 5th Battalion
Essex (Territorial) Regiment of which Sir Evelyn had been
honorary Colonel. As the funeral was taking place in Aldershot
there was a memorial service being held at Chelmsford Cathedral
during which the Bishop remarked:

> 'that they were met not merely to honour the memory
> of a great man, but to try to catch something of the
> inspiration that might be gathered from his life and
> deeds. Evelyn Wood was essentially an Essex man; he
> was born of parents associated with religious life in the
> county. His father was vicar of Cressing, not very far
> away. Not only was Sir Evelyn Wood born in Essex, but
> he was connected with the county, and especially with
> Chelmsford. It might be in the memory of some present
> that in 1879 a sword of honour was presented to him in
> that town; and some 15 years ago he was made the first
> honorary freeman of the borough.'

29 W. Addison, *Essex Worthies*, 1973, 205. It is worth remarking that there is no
    modern biography of Wood and the fact that his papers have been divided
    and dispersed will not make the task any easier. The two largest
    accumulations are in South Africa, twenty-eight volumes of 1873-1913 are
    held at the Natal Archives Depot, Pietermaritzburg, while approximately
    1,200 items of 1852-1919 are in the Killie Campbell Africana Library,
    Durban. 232 items of correspondence received by Wood during the period
    1848-1919 are in the William R. Perkins Library, Duke University, Durham,
    North Carolina, while the National Army Museum, London, has a volume of
    letters addressed to him by Kitchener from the years 1897-98.

30 *Essex Weekly News*, 12 December, 1919.

Recalling Sir Evelyn's last words, the Bishop said:

> 'he strove not only to live as a soldier, but for his God,
> his King, and his country. That was the real inspiration
> of his life. His life was straight, thorough, and true; he
> served his God and his generation and he had fallen on
> sleep. If we got real men of this type in every walk of life
> then he had no fear for the future of England.'

A memorial service was also held at St. Mary's Church, Harlow, on
Sunday afternoon, 7 December, 1919, and it is reported that:

> 'It was arranged for that day at the express desire of the
> late Sir Evelyn Wood, in order that his farming friends
> and hunting people might have an opportunity of
> attending without interference with the ordinary course
> of work or sport . . .'

The Bishop of Chelmsford, in an address, said:

> 'the late Field Marshal was truly a distinguished soldier,
> but much more than that. He was a man of prayer and a
> God-fearing man. This country had produced many
> men of that type from Oliver Cromwell down to Admiral
> Jellicoe and Field Marshal Haig. Their late friend, too,
> was an Essex man, and the county were proud of that
> fact. Like Nelson, he was the son of a country vicar. His
> exploits as a leader of men had gone far to make the
> history of the latter half of the last century. It was given
> to few men to achieve so much, or to receive so many
> honours. But apart from all that he was a man — a good
> citizen, a patriot, and a Christian. Addressing the Boy
> Scouts present, the Bishop held the late Field Marshal
> up as a pattern for them to live up to, and urged them
> ever to remember his great example of duty well done
> and life well lived.'[31]

Evelyn Wood's obituarist in the *Essex Review*[32] covers much
of the same ground, stressing his passion for hunting and his
writing to the press as well as penning his reminiscences and other
works. He states also what he thinks the Field Marshal's position
was so far as the British Army was concerned by writing: 'A
remarkable Essex man and a great soldier has been removed from
our midst. With him the last of the brilliant band of officers whose
names were associated with that of Lord Wolseley in the great

31 *Ibid.*

32 *Essex Review, op. cit.*, 53–55.

reconstruction schemes which made the British Army what it is, has passed away.'

In conclusion we may note from our consideration of these five heroes that the award of the Victoria Cross in the nineteenth century was indeed indiscriminate in so far as social class was concerned. It is also worth remarking that with the exception of Evelyn Wood, who was only twenty at the time of the incident that led to his award, all the others fell within a seven year span, with ages ranging from twenty-eight (Watson), twenty-nine (Embleton), thirty-four (Lodge), and thirty-six (Hawkes). Their keenness for Army life is self-evident in the case of the two officers, Watson and Wood, and explicitly stated in respect of Embleton and Lodge; further it is known that both the latter two, Embleton and Lodge, served in the non-regular forces before embarking upon a career in the Regular Army.

Isaac Lodge also stressed the importance of training in the Royal Horse Artillery in his personal account and it is interesting that the other two soldiers both belonged to rifle regiments which enjoyed a reputation for sound training. The overall impression is one of enthusiasm, discipline and training (and Embleton is included in this category despite his later difficult history), these qualities providing support to that indefinable quality of courage, which is required to overcome fear and thus to carry out feats of great bravery.

The final observation must be to remark upon the associations which the five maintained with their native County: all kept their family link, most married locally and two of the five resided in the County at the time of their respective deaths. Perhaps these five, linked together by 'the merit of conspicuous bravery', deserve better of Essex than the obscurity into which all but one have apparently passed.

Acknowledgements

This paper was prompted by knowledge of the resources available in the National Army Museum, especially the Lummis V.C. Files and the Hodson Index. A debt of gratitude is owed to the National Army Museum's curatorial staff, especially Peter Boyden and Lesley Smurthwaite, who produced material and answered questions. Bernadette Gillow, formerly of Harlow Museum, shared her familiarity with relevant archives and her knowledge of Sir Evelyn Wood's local connections. A final word of thanks is due to Elizabeth Carpenter and June Hicks of the National Army Museum, who produced this text in publishable form.

Essex: Some thoughts on the Heritage

'the stream flows silently on'

KENNETH NEALE

Introducing the Heritage

In this tribute to William Addison the essays have been presented by scholars and authors who, as friends and colleagues in their lives and work, have shared with him a love and interest in the heritage of Essex. It is a rich and rewarding arena. Each of the contributors has researched and refined discrete aspects of the unique pageant of Essex history, the intriguing complexities of genealogy, the architectural inheritance or the county's varied natural environment. The book does not purport to portray the Essex heritage in comprehensive perspectives. It has been entitled *Essex Heritage* to reflect the essential focus of the essays and to acknowledge William Addison's close involvement with the subject. A book on the Essex heritage in general, as yet unwritten, remains a tempting challenge to aspiring authors. There is, nevertheless, a pleasant if difficult editorial duty to offer, within the constraining compass of this essay, at least an overview of the heritage and the unifying strands in the compilation as a whole. This concluding chapter thus seeks to define the principal dimensions of the Essex heritage, to expose its unique qualities and further encourage the commitment to which the Lord Lieutenant refers in his Foreword.

The most conspicuous themes in the heritage are those that flow from the legacy of Essex history or are manifest in the landscape and the county's literary inventory. But there is also the endowment of a rich complex of related topics. These embrace the basic factors in county life that are the product of events, economic circumstances and technical innovation as well as the dynamic impact of significant individuals and influential social groups. They include also the surviving range of wildlife to be found in the fields, hedgerows, woodlands and waterways of the county. Important to the heritage in all these aspects of it are the archival treasures in the Essex Record Office and in smaller local repositories. These precious records, documentary, pictorial and cartographical illuminate the past with those flavours of authentic intimacy that only contemporary accounts can convey. All of these themes, the tangible, the conceptual, even the ephemeral demonstrate that the heritage is not an immutable paradigm of extant knowledge and experience. Every moment in time, every life, the consequences of human activity, each evolving nuance of the county scene in town and country modify the heritage in a fascinating, incremental progression. Historical events, in the terms in which they are understood, or understandable, endure in the record but they happen only once even in an evolutionary process. The visual heritage is permanent only in the sense that it is never absent. But its mobility is evident in the seasonal and climatic moods of the landscape and in the restless nature of human endeavour that thrives on intervention and change. It is, therefore, readily definable in general terms yet elusive and complex in detail. On that somewhat philosophical note we shall contemplate the heritage of Essex.

In an agreeable book[1] published in 1909 the author referred to Essex in words that, happily, remain valid today. It is, he wrote, 'a land of homely pleasantness, of unobtrusive charms . . .'. This certainly is an image readily assimilable in those areas of the county north of the urban conglomerations of the London periphery and Thames-side. The broad, open farmlands of the Essex arable, crowned with golden corn-laden fields in summer and relieved by the patchwork colouring of the other seed crops, define the scene. Among them huddle multi-textured villages of pleasant aspect, cosily small and comfortable in their rural settings. Isolated farmsteads and tiny pretty hamlets proliferate along winding lanes fringed with sturdy hedgerows, modest mixed woodlands and vestigial copses. In these areas, their shapes fashioned by ancient field patterns and the contrived geometry of early clearance and enclosure, agriculture is predominant as it always has been. Essex farmers are thus the custodians of much of the most precious of the landscape heritage. These environmentally sensitive areas impose a responsibility that must co-exist with the demands for food production stimulated now by international as well as domestic pressures. It is a difficult balance to achieve especially under the compelling disciplines of economic adversity. Happily, there is much that is positive and that encourages the belief that the challenge will be successfully met.

1 A. R. Hope-Moncrieff, *Essex*, 1909.

Sea-wards, along the Essex coast where the North Sea tides roll in upon the beaches, onto the mud, over the saltings and into the creeks there is still to be found a unique aspect of the Essex heritage. Characterised by a profound serenity it is an apparently inviolable natural habitat for a unique range of sea-coast plants and some of the largest resident and migrant bird populations to be found in Europe. The obverse is the impact on the Essex landscape of the development of the seaside resorts in the nineteenth century and, pre-eminently, of London. Whether viewed in the context of history or of the environment, Essex cannot be understood in isolation from the affairs of the capital. Throughout most of recorded history the political, economic and social interfaces between the county and London have been close and continuous. The development and prosperity of Essex have depended on this association. The dramatic disfigurement of riverside Essex caused by the eastwards intrusion of the suburbs and industry across the Lea and into the marshlands along the Thames was one consequence. The population overflow into the new towns like Basildon, Harlow and the once 'Arcadian' plotlands on the Langdon Hills and some of the sea-side settlements such as Canvey Island and Jaywick was another. Essex has been a pleasure ground for generations of Londoners. For them the county has meant trips in the 'Eagle' paddle-steamers to Clacton, train rides on the pier at Southend-on-Sea, cockles at Leigh, tea and cakes at the Epping Forest 'retreats'. These, and the important traditional function of Essex as a supplier to the capital of the products of its agriculture and husbandry, meat, eggs, cheese, butter, soft fruit, vegetables and cereals illustrate the complementary roles that have confirmed that relationship. Aesthetically, the beauty of Epping Forest, now in the care of the Corporation of the City of London, and the remaining examples of the fine country mansions sited in Essex by the wealthy courtiers and merchants of London symbolise the enduring links.

The vicissitudes of Essex history, its proximity to the European mainland and the maritime heritage have involved the county frequently with continental affairs and in the founding of the colonies in North America. These broad events have endowed the story of Essex with the strongest international emphasis among the English counties. Yet, perhaps surprisingly in view of the pressures of the association with London and the powerful influences of its overseas involvement, the county has retained its identity as our contemporary view of the heritage insists. Londoners in search of social betterment, Huguenots and other refugees from the Low Countries who established themselves in the developing textile industries in the Colchester–Braintree and Witham areas and the Scottish farmers who took on the marginal farmlands during the agricultural depressions were among the notable groups who made their mark on the Essex scene. Enterprising individuals, some of whom figure in these essays, have also left the imprint of their lives on the story of Essex. Inshore fishermen and deep-sea sailors are part of the tapestry of Essex maritime life which, the emphasis shifting towards modern container traffic and leisure boating, is nevertheless still true to its inheritance.

Language is one of the most significant legacies of the past. Modern English has its origins largely in the common roots of a range of Indo-European languages and dialects. It continues to grow and change as part of the evolving heritage as modern idioms and foreign and technical expresions are absorbed into the vocabulary of everyday speech. The spoken language in Essex, a vital ingredient in any regional pedigree, hardly lingering now in a greatly diluted dialect and modified pronunciation heavily overlaid by London influences is, however, still to be heard in the villages of the cornlands. Eventually it will go, perhaps soon, and later generations will no longer hear the long vowels, dropped syllables and the idiosyncratic idioms that decorated the Essex dialect. Perhaps, most of all, the authentic linguistic heritage is present in the place-names of the county where we find the Old English compounds are dominant as in Hedingham, Ashingdon and Wakering. Delightfully conjoined with the Norman patronymics the early Saxon place-names have embellished the county's nomenclature with such handsome names as Stansted Mountfitchet, Helions Bumpstead and Stondon Massey. Rare, but historically significant and enjoyable, are the earliest British survivals that are sometimes attached to topographical features such as the river names in Essex like Pant, Stour and Lea. The Danish intruders left a minor imprint in such as Thorrington, Kirby-le-Soken and Thorpe-le-Soken.

Naturally, the accelerating social changes that have been a feature of the twentieth century have improved and transformed the quality of life in the county. Over the centuries, below the level of the nobility, land-owning families and professional people, rural life was hard. William Cobbett, for all his uncompromising polemic, was not far wrong when he averred that the more corn that was grown the more miserable were the lives of the labouring poor. George Crabbe, whose incisive pen has left us with a brilliant and stylish vignette of rural life in East Anglia, reminds his readers in *The Village*[2] that:

> 'Where plenty smiles, alas,
> She smiles for few.'

When, as this essay will, we trace those strands of the heritage that reside in historic events, the lives of important people, the living landscape or our literary treasures that underlying dimension should not be forgotten. Things are different now but the heritage is also burdened by that which is ugly or disagreeable as well as being enriched by what is beautiful and enjoyable. That needs to be understood if the splendours of the heritage are to be appreciated in an appropriate perspective. Anyone who has researched the history of a rural community or listened to poignant voices from the past in the sound archives knows this. They know too of the kindly benevolence of humane squires, parsons, farmers and their caring wives who did what they could to ameliorate the worst asperities of life in households impoverished by circumstances largely beyond anyone's control. The prim and lovely cottages in our most attractive Essex villages today were often no more than hovels in the past. Today's tidy verges, hedgerows and the well maintained farmsteads were once overgrown and derelict during the hard times. It is all that which underlines the case for preserving the heritage and promoting what is best in our county's life and tradition.

The Historical Themes

Every community, whether that of a village, a town, a county or a nation derives its identity and status from its history. That is the major factor in the heritage. All claim their worthies. A few may take pride in personalities of heroic stature. The events that surround these people establish the experience and chronology which enable us to organise our knowledge and ideas about the nature of that heritage. It is, as I have implied, often transient in detail, generally permanent or slow to change in its intrinsic qualities. In one way or another everyone in all ages is touched by and leaves a mark on the history of their time. In that sense the historical heritage is paramount.

Who are the people of Essex who have created and now cherish the county heritage? Throughout the prehistoric periods people, continental in origin, migrated into the area. They have

2 G. Crabbe, 'The Village', *Poems*, 1807.

left the silent attributes of their presence on archaeological sites like Springfield Lyons which was inhabited from Neolithic times into the Saxon period. The later Belgic tribal groupings, identifiable by archaeologists, were those whom the Romans encounted, an event that brought them within the scope of history. The Romans were followed by Saxon, Danish and Norman invaders all of whom have left tangible evidence of their presence in the heritage. Later there were the flows of refugees from religious and political persecution. The infusions of alien cultures were compounded by the population transfers of the nineteenth and twentieth centuries between the urban and rural areas and the influx of people from the Commonwealth. The result of this is Essex life as we see it today and the human amalgam we now refer to as Essex people. They were the people who, under the pressure of events and circumstances, fashioned the mould within which the county heritage was cast.

Much of the county story, the migrations, the invasions, the coming of Christianity, economic development and social change is part of British history. However, the incidence of these nodal events in Essex has, naturally, a uniqueness that defines the heritage. The Romans bequeathed the county its finest town, Colchester, on the site of the tribal capital of the Trinovantes and their usurpers the Catuvellauni. They elevated the network of prehistoric trackways to the status of a cross-country road system that established the pattern of county communications and the siting of our major towns. Other such trackways, viable in Roman times, have declined into green, shrubby, banked and ditched paths like Sparepenny Lane at Great Sampford. The Saxon legacy includes the nomenclature of most of the towns and villages as well as such precious survivals as St. Peter ad Murum at Bradwell and St. Andrew's at Greensted-juxta-Ongar. The Norman era is represented by the splendour of the abbey at Waltham, the rugged mound, ramparts and the baileys that still define the village at Pleshey and the great brooding keep at Hedingham. The county Domesday,[3] that wonderful Norman archive, is a good example of the way in which a national episode may be localised in specific terms. Apart from the essential uniqueness of its contents the Essex and East Anglian Domesday survey, the 'Little Domesday', is a document distinct and different from the less detailed surveys that covered most of the rest of England.

It is implicit in what I have written that, for Essex as a

---

3 'The Domesday Survey (Essex)', *Victoria County History*, vol. I, 1903 and R. W. Powell, *Essex in Domesday Book*, 1990.

maritime county, the sea is an essential dimension of its heritage. The symbols of the decisive influence of the sea on the county's life and history are still to be seen on the bleak wind-swept coasts of the North Sea, in the holiday resorts and along the riverside reaches of the Thames. Coastal defence in Essex has been vital not only to repel invaders but to confront the aggression of the sea itself. The long, dangerous and arduous struggle against erosion and inundation is one of the most dramatic of the Essex story. The dykes and sea-walls have had to be continuously maintained to resist the inexorable assaults of tide, wind and wave. The now dormant relics of the military defences, along the coast from the Roman fort of Othona to the twentieth century, evoke minatory images of the recurring threat from continental invaders. Tilbury Fort was built to defend the approaches to London and dates from the late seventeenth century. It replaced an earlier, smaller fortification of the reign of Henry VIII. At Harwich, a destroyer base in the last two European wars at which I recollect the gallant old 'V and Ws', can be found the Redoubt, a moated circular fort of 1808. Also remaining to stimulate interest in the maritime heritage of Essex are the Coalhouse Fort by the Thames, the Purfleet Magazine, the Martello Towers and 'pill-boxes' of last war vintage. Barking, now a London borough, recalls the mid-nineteenth century heyday of fishing when the Hewett's Short Blue Fleet, famous for its well-ships, was a major enterprise among hundreds of Essex sea-going fishing vessels. Along with the harvest of the North Sea fishing grounds there are the inshore industries that have thrived on the epicurean taste for oysters and a more proletarian fancy for the other molluscs. There was boat and ship building too; the first iron-clad warship, the *Warrior*, was built and launched at Bow Creek in 1859. Colchester, Wivenhoe, Maldon, Manningtree and Mistley all have a maritime heritage of interest and importance. More nefarious activities, like smuggling, have a place in the story. The sea, just like the land, has defined the heritage. It is impossible to interpret Essex history without reference to its maritime traditions.

Writing, as I do, in the year of the Maldon Millenium I am constrained to mention first among our county's heroes the valiant leader of the Saxons, Byrhtnoth the Ealdorman of Essex, who confronted the Danish invaders with honour at the causeway on the Pant in August 991 A.D. His name and the memory of the gallant comrades who died with him is now enshrined in the most famous of the old English epic poems[4] as representative of the

4 E. V. Gordon, ed., *The Battle of Maldon*, 1937.

Figure 1. Sir Thomas Smith
Secretary of State to Queen Elizabeth,
from a print by Houbraken.

ideals and ethical standards of their race. But his is not the first name on the roll-call of Essex history. Preceeding him were the Belgic tribal leaders like Cunobelin — Shakespeare's Cymbeline — and the Roman legionaries, the centurion Favonius Facilis and Longinus, men whose names are known to archaeologists only from the lapidary inscriptions on their tombstones. Of profound and dramatic interest are the names of the early Christian leaders, Cedd at Bradwell and Erkenwald at Barking. King Alfred, perhaps England's most honoured king, the imperious Elizabeth I, and the queenly Victoria have a special place in the heritage of Essex.

The seemingly inexhaustible roll of prominent people of the Essex heritage allows me the opportunity to mention but a few others of special interest or importance. Among the Elizabethans we may surely include Sir Thomas Smith of Saffron Walden whose intellectual stature and mercurial temperament mark this Essex notable as a man of his time. In the field of science there were John Ray of Black Notley, one of Europe's greatest naturalists and Joseph Lister of West Ham whose enunciation of the principles of antisepsis and development of new techniques laid the foundations of modern surgical practice to the immense benefit of mankind. It is people such as these, Smith, Ray and Lister whose intellect enriched our society and raised the standards to which it aspires.

A part of the Essex heritage, in all its dimensions, is to be found in the United States. In New England, the familiar place-names of Essex itself and of Braintree, Wethersfield, Chelmsford and Harwich among others recall the Essex origins of many of the settlers who braved the stormy Atlantic crossing in the seventeenth century. Christopher Martin, who sailed in the *Mayflower* in 1620 with his wife Marie (Prower) and others from Billericay was a miller and victualled the expedition. He died shortly after the arrival of the Pilgrims at New Plymouth but the name Billerica found its way onto the map of Massachusetts. Laurence Washington, a paternal ancestor of the first American President, was the rector of Purleigh and was buried at Maldon. The trans-Atlantic links are strong and numerous. In our own time American servicemen and their families have reinforced them making the return journey to Essex in defence of the ideals of justice and freedom that are inherent in the philosophical aspects of the heritage. The historical themes, and the people who inspire them, nourish the heritage in a continuum within which all else exists.

The Natural Aspect

It is perhaps true that people today are more sensitive to the
environmental aspects of the heritage than to any other. To most
that means scenery but it is much more than that. The concept of
scenery should include the nature, extent and integrity of those
habitats that encourage and conserve the flora, fauna and
avifauna, not to mention the lesser orders like lepidoptera that are
an aesthetic delight and ecologically important to the survival of
our natural environment. The Essex Wildlife Trust and the Essex
Bird Watching Society are centres of expertise and the driving
forces in this area of the Essex heritage. In reality it is the concern
of all Essex people however marginal their scientific interest. No
study or proposal concerning the protection of the Essex heritage
should neglect this aspect.

How fortunate we are that, despite the pressure of modern
life and the impact of technology, Essex is still rich in wildlife and
graced by scenic vistas of charm and variety. Much, however, has
gone. I have already made reference to the environmental consequences of industrial development and urban sprawl. That beautiful animal the otter has disappeared from our rivers. Badgers are
much diminished in numbers by the loss of their natural habitats,
road casualties and illegal digging but their setts survive in
surprising locations. 'Aunt Sally', the Essex hare and 'Charlie', the
Essex fox still surprise and excite our enjoyment of the countryside as they bound unexpectedly across the fields and pathways.
One of the many delights of moon-lit nights is the graceful passage
of small parties of deer that make their gentle way across the
countryside. Nowadays we rarely see the sparrowhawk arrowing
towards its prey and the ghostly barn owl is in decline. We may
nevertheless enjoy Britain's most beautiful bird, the brilliant, shy
kingfisher on our winding Essex rivers and the scuttering
nuthatch, a favourite among the woodland birds. Among the
butterflies Essex has lost all eight of its fritillaries and others,
regarded as very common species are sadly diminished. Yet we
may still expect to see twenty or more varieties, including the
lovely tortoiseshells, brimstones, peacocks, red admirals and
holly blues, as well as numerous and often equally attractive
moths. Colourful, trembling dragonflies too, hawkers and darters,
charm as they hover by the waterways.

The orchids, twayblade, bee and early spotted are not lost
although others are. Despite intensive spraying and hedge-cutting
common flowers like yellow archangel, goatsbeard, agrimony,

centaury and fumitory persist although much reduced in their extent. Special among the Essex plants and confined to limited areas in the north-west of the county and towards Cambridge is the bardfield oxlip (Primula elatior) which is not to be confused with the cowslip which it tends to resemble at a glance. It was identified as a separate species in 1842 by Henry Doubleday of Epping who, although more celebrated as an entomologist was a botanist of high repute.[5] This is an Essex treasure indeed and, like the kingfisher, is deservedly symbolic of the county's natural heritage. The bold umbellifers that flank the roadsides with their lacy presence — there are more varieties than most people think — seem to withstand the regular 'tidying-up' of the verges as, happily, do the 'paigles' (cowslips) on the chalk which, along with primroses, violets and daisies are surely the joy of our lanes and hedgerows.

The elms which once enhanced the roadside canopy are virtually gone through disease and, despite some evidence of re-generation are not likely to recover in any permanent sense. But fine oaks, handsome beech, elegant birch, stately limes and others such as ash, alder, hornbeam and sweet chestnut still embellish the Essex scene. Devotees of Epping Forest will vouch for that. Trees, indeed, are environmentally significant in providing struc-ture, habitat and shelter for scenery, wildlife and shade-loving plants. Their loss is the most readily noticed and the 'wealth' they represent, perhaps, epitomises the issue of the county's natural heritage as no other living thing does. In this superficial reference the image is of the heritage in balance. Broadly speaking it is; though in some aspects it is precarious. However, there is much to be grateful for and some optimism, but not complacency, is justified. The Essex Wildlife Trust's slogan 'Watch over Essex' sums it all up rather well.

The Cultural Inheritance

The cultural inheritance of Essex is so extensive that, in a few paragraphs, I can hope only to indicate its scale and quality by reference to a few of its outstanding features and major con-tributors. I shall not even attempt to define the parameters of the cultural legacy but no-one, I imagine, will wish to quarrel with the inclusion of architecture, the visual arts, music and literature within its scope.

5 K. Neale, 'The Bardfield Oxlip', *Sampfords Society Village Notes*, 2, 1985.

Figure 2. Chipping Hill, Witham, 1832.

In Essex we are fortunate in the range and merit of individual buildings and, in the vernacular idiom, of village precincts — all 'cobbled pathways . . . cottage doors and hollyhocks'[6] — farm complexes and town housing. Conspicuous in the general perception of this inheritance are the fine medieval gildhall which is the centre-piece of Thaxted, the Norman keep of Colchester castle splendid in its setting at the heart of the old Roman Colonia, the formal grace of what remains of Audley End, the commanding presence of Waltham Abbey in the Lea valley and the de Vere's castle home at Hedingham. Ubiquitous and important in the context is the wonderful range of medieval and later churches of Essex in varying style and texture. Beautiful, interesting and evocative are those like Thaxted, the finest of Essex churches, Dedham for its handsome elegance, Blackmore and Navestock for their magnificent timbered towers, Greensted of Saxon provenance, the apsidal sanctuary at Copford for its Norman wall-paintings, Lawford for the glorious chancel and the stylish Georgian fane at Lambourne. In detail we may enjoy the stone screens at Stebbing and Great Bardfield, the stained glass at Rivenhall, the carvings on the bench ends at Danbury, the superb fifteenth century double-hammer beam roof structure at Great Bromley, the thirteenth century Madonna at Great Canfield and the consecration crosses in a remarkable series at Great Sampford. There are also, the triangular tower at All Saints in Maldon, the thirteenth century painted chest at Newport and the exuberant Art Nouveau masterpiece at Great Warley. Often these churches are sited in delightful surroundings that associate them with the historical development of the locality, the best of the Essex countryside or, comfortably, among the attractive period buildings of Essex towns and villages whose textures of plaster, flint, brick, thatch or tile beautify the vicinity. Little Bardfield, Little Sampford, Tillingham and Witham close by the ramparts of the Saxon burgh at Chipping Hill are good examples that satisfy those criteria.

Often the countryside is enhanced by handsome country houses of various periods[7] as at Ingatestone, Langleys, Horham, Faulkbourne, Spains Hall or the charming, though smaller, Southfields at Dedham. Fine town houses like the clothier John

---

6 *John Betjeman*, 1954; J. Adlard, comp., 'Essex', *Poet's England*, 6, 1984.

7 For a selective list of fine Georgian houses in Essex and a biography of the county's most distinguished Georgian architect see: Nancy Briggs, *Georgian Essex*, 1989 and *John Johnson, 1732–1814*, 1991.

Figure 3. The Courtyard, Southfields, Dedham.

Paycocke's at Coggeshall and the Georgian gem of Clarance House at Thaxted are to be found throughout the county. Minor buildings of immense interest and attraction like windmills; Upminster and Stammer's mill at Finchingfield are such. Dovecotes too, a delightful example being that tucked away at Pimp Hall Farm, Chingford and ancient barns in which the county abounds are numerous. Symbolic for the heritage are the incomparable medieval wheat and barley barns at Cressing Temple now acquired for the county as a happy result of an inspired initiative by the Essex County Council. The discerning devotee of the heritage may seek out the decorative folk-art of pargetting in the north-west where there are many fine examples of this patterned plasterwork, the magnificent brickwork of the late-medieval newel staircase in the Moot Hall at Maldon at the crest of that delightful riverside town, or the strapwork panelling in the Rose and Crown inn at Ashdon.

Cottage gardens are a feature of the Essex countryside and give much pleasure to those who cultivate them as well as to passing visitors. On another level the show-piece gardens of the county, many of them open for charitable purposes throughout the seasons, are of much charm and interest. Most of the greater country houses were improved in context and their social status raised by the art of the landscape gardeners. Prominent among them was Humphry Repton who worked from his home at Hare Street, Romford and achieved a reputation comparable with that of his contempory 'Capability' Brown. The Reptons originally intended to stay at Romford only temporarily but eventually remained until Humphry's death not from 'necessity, but because they came to love the place'.[8] In Essex he worked notably at Hill Hall, Claybury Hall and Rivenhall Place.

On that note we have come to the visual arts. Dedham reminds us of its close associations with England's greatest landscape artist, John Constable. Suffolk born, at East Bergholt just over the Essex border, his work is replete with Essex and Stour valley scenes daringly painted and evocative in his sensitive depiction of the landscapes and skies that he loved. Increasingly our generation recognises the fine and original work of the Bardfield 'School' which counted among its coterie the well-known artists Eric Ravilious, Edward Bawden, Michael Rothenstein and John Aldridge. Among other Essex artists the names of Brangwyn, Munnings and Bamford come readily to mind. It was,

8 E. Hyam, *Capability Brown and Humphry Repton*, 1971.

Figure 4.   Hill Hall, Theydon Mount, 1824.

however, William Morris of Walthamstow whose creative imagination and refined craftmanship had a profound influence on the
taste and quality of modern life-style. The products of his hand
and mind now decorate much of the furnishings and artifacts we
use in our Essex homes and across the world. His re-
interpretation of medieval imagery and design induced a whole
new approach that was followed by many others working in the
field of art and craft.

The literary range of the heritage is even more formidable in
its dimensions. The county has, naturally, had its links with the
greatest of English authors by residence or in the context of their
work. In that sense Dickens, Clare, Tennyson and others of similar
stature figure in the galaxy of literary talent with Essex
associations. It can claim too its place in the works of the doyens of
travel and topographical description, Camdèn, Drayton and
Holinshed. Of significance to Essex in this field is the work of
William Harrison, Rector of Radwinter (1558–93) and Vicar of
Wimbish (1570–81). An intellectual steeped in Protestant
disciplines, he wrote the *Description of Britain* that was
appended to Holinshed's *Chronicles* as well as a history of the
world the manuscript of which is at Trinity College, Dublin. Here I
intend only to focus on those writers whose work is characterised
by the flavour of Essex. So we find ourselves in the company of the
enigmatic S. L. Bensusan whose 'marshland' books have a
unique quality and portray a discreet area of Essex life in
atmospheric terms that no-one else has quite achieved. Or C. H.
Warren, who lived at Duck End, Finchingfield and wrote percep-
tively and with real affection about the county and its rural life and
personalities. Sabine Baring-Gould, the enigmatic 'squarson' and
folklorist Rector of East Mersea, author of the haunting Essex
marshland tale *Mehala*, the county shares with Devonshire his
family homeland. In contemporary Essex literature among the
pre-eminent names are those of William Addison to whom this
book is dedicated and Derick Emmison. Both have endowed the
county with works of importance and interest to Essex history and
the county heritage. It would, in this context, be unforgiveable not
to mention Philip Morant[9] the curate of Great Waltham whose
history of Essex has remained the jewel of Essex historiography
and informed its practitioners for more than two centuries. Only
the impeccable scholarship of the Victoria County History can
rival this work in importance and influence.

Despite the disciplines of space I must find room to refer to

9 P. Morant, *The History and Antiquities of the County of Essex*, 1768.

the specialist art and science of cartography in which the Essex archives are so rich.[10] There is the fine and definitive work of John Chapman and Peter André whose Essex map of 1777 has been indispensable to local historians. Perhaps, above all, we admire and value the cartographical skills of the Walkers of Hanningfield. Their beautiful and informative coloured maps of the sixteenth century were 'rescued' by Dr. Emmison, then the County Archivist and, more recently, described and analysed in depth in a magnificent book[11] definitively researched by A. C. Edwards and K. C. Newton. And now Dr. Stuart Mason has given another dimension to the study of Essex cartography in his brilliant book[12] on the eighteenth century land surveyors of Essex.

Maps are manifestly important to historians; they are important in other ways to travellers. In his engagingly robust account[13] of his travels in the remote areas of Scotland and the islands in 1773, Samuel Johnson remarks 'I was never in any house of the islands, where I did not find books ... except one from which the family was removed'; no doubt with their books! I am not sure how far that would be true of Essex today. But, we must surely value, as part of the heritage, that which is best in the county book collections of our public libraries, the Essex Record Office, the University of Essex and the Essex Society for Archaeology and History at Hollytrees House in Colchester. And, of course, the special collection that is housed in the charming and unique library bequeathed in 1704 by Dr. Thomas Plume to his native town of Maldon.[14] The Town Library at Saffron Walden, founded in 1834, is another important Essex treasury of fine and rare books.

Music is, I suppose, a largely abstract art form, but its place in the heritage must be represented by its people, instruments and manuscripts which are no less tangible than those associated with the other arts. In Essex there have been valued, if minimal, associations with several great English composers and musicians among them William Byrd, Vaughan Williams and John Ireland. More intimately connected have been others like Thomas Tallis,

10 Reference is invited to the catalogues of maps published by the Essex Records Office, ed., F. G. Emmison.

11 A. C. Edwards and K. C. Newton, *The Walkers of Hanningfield*, 1985.

12 A. Stuart Mason, *Essex on the Map*, 1990.

13 S. Johnson, *A Journey to the Western Islands of Scotland*, Folio Society edition, 1990.

14 For a fascinating account of this see W. J. Petchey, *The Intentions of Dr. Plume*, 1985.

the sixteenth century organist at Waltham Abbey, who was one of the most accomplished music masters of his time. Nearer in our recollection is the work of Gustav Holst, who despite a faltering start in making his home in Thaxted, stayed there to compose *The Planets* and eventually played a notable part in the revival of folksong and music in the town. Most recently the composer Alan Rawsthorne lived and worked for many years at Little Sampford in a cottage on the Stambourne Road.

Concluding Thoughts

In 1893 the Revd. John Vaughan, Vicar of Finchingfield, whose sister, Eliza, wrote several delightful and informative books[15] about the village and that of Rayne, wrote in Longman's Magazine[16] of life in Finchingfield in his time:

'Everything has changed. The old hedgerows, glorious in early summertime with honey-suckle and wild roses, have been stubbed up, and almost every tree has been cut down. Not a bank is left for the violets and the primroses and the lesser celandine. A dreary expanse of arable land, unbroken by even a solitary elm or holly-bush, is a sight common enough now. The wide stretches of waste land, besides the country lanes, where in autumn flocks of goldfinches might be seen feeding on the thistle-seed, are mostly enclosed and cultivated; and the birds are few in the district. The woods are strictly preserved, and all kinds of hawks and owls are indiscriminately destroyed. The kite, or *puttock*, as it was locally called, not uncommon in the middle of the century, is now unknown; and but rarely a buzzard is seen. Even sparrow-hawks and kestrels are becoming rare. Now and then an otter finds its way up the stream, but only to be hunted down and killed. A polecat has not been seen for years; and the last badger is dead. Some of the rarer wild flowers, too, are no longer to be found. Modern cultivation and scientific farming which demolishes the hedgerows and stubbs up the copses, and takes in every square yard of common land, is fatal to the flora as well as the fauna of a neighbourhood. The beautiful fritillary once blossomed

15 Eliza Vaughan, *Sketches of Village Life in Days gone by*, 1926 and *The Essex Village in Days gone by*, 1928.

16 J. Vaughan, 'Twenty-five Years of Village Life', *Longman's Magazine*, January 1893.

abundantly in a damp meadow near the trout stream; you can hardly find a leaf now. The rare martagon lily formerly flourished by the side of a green lane bordered by a thick lofty hedge; the hedge has been levelled and the plant is gone . . . Every summer the swifts shriek about the church tower, and the swallows build in the chimneys of the ancient almshouse. The cuckoo's voice will be heard in May, and the red-backed shrike will nest in the vicarage garden. The ring-doves will coo in the yew trees, and a pair of moor-hens may frequent the pond. And yet everything seems changed. The old families are gone. New names fill the parish register. The black oak furniture — chests carved with beautiful designs, and chairs, and cabinets with many a secret drawer — once common in the farmhouses, has all gone to the hammer. Boards are nailed over the windows of the empty cottages on the green. Poverty is stamped on the face of the village. Change and decay is everywhere apparent. Only the church bells ring merrily from the Norman tower, and the stream flows silently on.'

Here we have some poignant echoes of the anxieties and beliefs of a kindly and diligent observer who has also provided my sub-title. The same environmental issues that exercised his mind persist a century later; but the image of his village has changed almost beyond recognition. In much of what John Vaughan wrote about the village, its people and its natural aspect in the article, we have the substance and the philosophy of the Essex heritage. Nothing is excluded from it. There is much to be cherished and preserved for our posterity which will in turn create the heritage of the future.

In this concluding essay I have tried to introduce the heritage in a broader concept than that which has so far been expressed. The heritage of Essex seems to me to extend well beyond the generally accepted dimensions of landscape, buildings, history and archives. For me it also engages those aspects of life which have a cultural or literary basis. Naturally, all are entwined; there are no clear boundaries between history and literature, buildings and art. The definition I prefer includes all that is past, people, events, the products of mind and hand, yet remain in tangible form or continue to influence the quality of our lives and inform our knowledge and experience. Therein lies the richness of the heritage. The essays in this book have, I trust, etched a little more into our understanding and appreciation of the heritage of Essex.

INDEX